Extreme Metaphors

Also by J.G. Ballard

Extreme Metaphors

Selected Interviews with J.G. Ballard, 1967–2008

Edited by Simon Sellars and Dan O'Hara

FOURTH ESTATE • *London*

First published in Great Britain by
Fourth Estate
An imprint of HarperCollins*Publishers*
77–85 Fulham Palace Road
London W6 8JB

A catalogue record for this book is available from the British Library

ISBN 978-0-00-745485-3

Typeset by Palimpsest Book Production Limited
Falkirk, Stirlingshire
Printed in Great Britain by
Clays Ltd, St Ives plc

MIX
Paper from
responsible sources

FSC
www.fsc.org   FSC™ C007454

FSC™ is a non-profit international organisation established to promote the responsible management of the world's forests. Products carrying the FSC label are independently certified to assure consumers that they come from forests that are managed to meet the social, economic and ecological needs of present and future generations, and other controlled sources.

Find out more about HarperCollins and the environment at
www.harpercollins.co.uk/green

Extreme Metaphors

Contents

Contents

Contents

Introduction: A Launchpad for Other Explorations

Simon Sellars

I

The conditions of J.G. Ballard's childhood in wartime Shanghai are well known, exposed by the success of his semi-autobiographical novel *Empire of the Sun* (1984), and Steven Spielberg's film version of that compulsive self-mythology. Yet pre-*Empire*, Shanghai was admitted only in metaphor to Ballard's writing, and the war mentioned *en passant* in the ubiquitous mini-biographies adorning the front-papers of his novels. A typical example might have read: 'He was born in Shanghai in 1930 to English parents. The Japanese interned him for almost three years in a civilian war camp. He came to England when he was sixteen. He studied medicine at King's College, Cambridge. He worked as a copywriter, then as a Covent Garden porter, then as an editor on a scientific journal. He trained to become an RAF pilot. His first professionally published short story was "Prima Belladonna" in 1956. He was a leading light in the so-called "New Wave" of science fiction. He lives in Shepperton, England. *Crash* is his most notorious novel . . .' Occasionally, there would be self-reflexive variations, statements so intense they were surely the handiwork not of bored copywriters but of Ballard himself: 'He believes that science fiction is the authentic literature of the twentieth century' (or that 'science fiction is the apocalyptic language of the twentieth century'). 'He also believes that inner space, not outer, is the real subject of science fiction.'

Today, given Ballard's post-*Empire* canonisation, it's easy to forget he began as a writer of science fiction, although in the 1960s he established his name with a quartet of end-of-the-world disaster novels that keenly anticipated current conditions surrounding climate change: *The Wind from Nowhere* (1961), *The Drowned World* (1962), *The Drought* (1964) and *The Crystal World* (1966). In that decade, he also produced a number of short stories that inverted science fiction via one of its most cherished tropes, time travel, using the premise to formulate the fabled theory of inner space informing those early bios. Anticipating Marshall McLuhan and Jean Baudrillard, Ballard demonstrated how encroaching advertising and mass consumer culture played on submerged desire, implanting new, artificial subjectivities to create a schizophrenic underclass. In response to such conditions, his characters retreated into the private imagination – 'inner space' – cordoning it off as a virtual 'nature reserve', preserving its sovereignty by any means possible. A recurring theme was the idea of escaping or cheating time, precipitated by a period of psychic turmoil. Recording the Dalí-esque motif of stopped or 'melting' time, Ballard uses the symbolism of time (that is, the unit of measurement; clock time) as an arbitrary, man-made construct imposing order and control on the free reign and chaos of the unconcious. Faced with the reality of life in that tumultuous decade, inner space for Ballard was a far more strange and compelling setting for science fiction than its traditional environs in *outer* space.

Coining the slogan 'Earth is the only alien planet', Ballard joined forces with Michael Moorcock to lead the British New Wave, producing an extended, linked sequence of fragmentary, non-linear short stories that continued to address the psychosocial effects of the media landscape. These were mainly published in Moorcock's revolutionary *New Worlds* magazine, the mouthpiece for the New Wave, and later collected as *The Atrocity Exhibition* (1969), which, billed as an 'experimental novel', cemented his reputation as a dark magus, a writer able to face the most extreme aspects of our culture and divine a secret logic from the chaos.

In the mid-seventies, Ballard mostly abandoned formal experimentation in favour of a more traditional narrative technique, although the subject matter was just as confrontational, perhaps even more shocking for the neutral style encasing it. The novels of this period include *Crash* (1973), about a cult of bored, middle-class professionals who feel alive only after modifying their bodies via staged car crashes; *Concrete Island* (1974), about a man who crashes into a patch of wasteland beneath a motorway, subconsciously 'marooning' himself in the city; and *High-Rise* (1975), in which a high-tech apartment block descends into tribal warfare. These seductive, disturbing narratives seek out the edgelands of cities, making strange the familiar landscapes of suburbia, and have proved enormously influential for their clinical portrayal of the new roles we assume from the technological landscape. They have inspired not only writers but also musicians, artists and film-makers, who respond to Ballard's highly imagistic style (itself influenced by surrealism), and even architects and urbanists, drawn to his penetrating critique of the contemporary urban condition.

Then came a brace of unclassifiable novels: *The Unlimited Dream Company* (1979), *Hello America* (1981), *The Day of Creation* (1987) and *Rushing to Paradise* (1994). If an overarching theme could be detected, it's perhaps that each presented a lysergic vision of mythical lands (sometimes right before our eyes, as in suburbia) undermining and degrading the structural integrity of the urban West. In between were *Empire* and its sequel *The Kindness of Women* (1991), both playing surrealistic games with Ballard's life story.

In his later career, there was a final incarnation: Ballard, the writer of subversive crime fictions such as *Running Wild* (1988), *Cocaine Nights* (1996), *Super-Cannes* (2000), *Millennium People* (2003) and *Kingdom Come* (2006). Indeed, crime was the perfect genre for the age of conspiracy theory and inscrutable global power structures that would come to define the new millennium, and which Ballard's work had always foretold. Of course, he continued to write brilliant short stories throughout, as well as the novella 'Low-Flying Aircraft' (1976), about a near future in which humans are dying out, and regarded as among his finest work.

Actually, what this potted history suggests is that Ballard's career is almost impossible to summarise. Reading the blurbs of his later novels, therefore, with their Shanghai-*Empire* focus, feels like submitting to a ritual incantation designed to fix a public mask for this most elusive of writers. In reality, if your first introduction to Ballard is by way of, say, his short story 'The Drowned Giant' (1964), then you might think you have stumbled on to a master magical realist in the Swiftian tradition. If *Crash* is the initiation, then you might think twice before proceeding further, unless your palate is already sufficiently developed with a taste for the blackest intellectual meat. And what if your introduction is via one of the many interviews he gave across the arc of his career?

Ballard published approximately 1,100,000 words in novels, 500,000 in short stories and at least 300,000 in non-fiction. The combined word count of all the interviews he gave is around 650,000. In the Ballardian galaxy that's a second sun, an enormous parallel body of speculation, philosophy, critical inquiry and imaginative flights of fancy that comments critically on his writing, often explains it and, sometimes, extends or even goes beyond it. Ballard enjoyed talking about his work, in marked contrast to the contemporary literary landscape where authors see interviews as a tiresome duty, or as a PR exercise, a chance to push product, or even as a chance to vent spleen on real and imagined enemies. As Iain Sinclair said of him: 'He doesn't speak badly of anybody, any named individual. It's almost a superstition, no gossip.' In interviews, it was common for him to ignore any mention of literature and fellow writers altogether. Questions as to his literary influences were often deflected or summed up with a short list of his childhood reading.

Ballard was never comfortable defining his place within the canon, and had little time for contemporary literature, which he saw as stuck in the mode of the nineteenth-century 'social novel', unwilling or unable to confront the fragmented subjectivities induced by the new media landscape. In contrast, his stories and novels present psychosociological case studies, based on highly skilled readings of real-world trends in culture, consumerism, technology and media. Frequently, this predictive charge was fomented in the interview situation, a kind of philosophical 'laboratory' where he could test ideas, opinions and observations, and later smuggle them into the airlocked worlds of his fiction. The opportunity to review his interviews is therefore an important one, and, in the twilight zone of critical opinion that invariably follows an important writer's death, to be taken seriously. With the benefit of hindsight, and Ballard's complete body of work before us stretching back fifty-five years, not only are we able to unearth the philosophical and imaginative seeds that would spawn his most significant writing, but we are also able to experience a kind of extended remix of the themes woven throughout his work.

II

Arguably, Ballard's most striking interview is the one he gave to Carol Orr in 1974, soon after the publication of *Crash*, when his notoriety was riding high. Four years earlier, the entire run of the American edition of *The Atrocity Exhibition*, to be published by Doubleday, had been pulped after a Doubleday executive became apoplectic at some of the more controversial material within (principally the story 'Why I Want to Fuck Ronald Reagan'). Then, *Crash* was initially turned down by a publisher's reader with the infamous words: 'This author is beyond psychiatric help. Do not publish.' Ballard was probably about as 'cult' as a writer could be at the time, and although still regarded as primarily a writer of science fiction, was distancing himself farther and farther from the genre. As a writer of SF, his ostensible line of work was to collate the future, yet he undermines that job description by telling Orr that there is no future, that 'the present is throwing up so many options, so many alternatives, that it contains the possibilities of any future right now. You can have tomorrow today. And the notion of the future as a sort of programmatic device . . . a compass bearing . . . a destination that we are moving towards psychologically and physically . . . is rather outdated.' It is for this reason, he has claimed elsewhere, that science fiction is dead, its predictive capacity castrated by the ever-changing, real-world present. The prophetic nature of that observation can be gauged by the fact that William Gibson, among the most intelligent and successful of contemporary science fiction writers, has said in recent interviews that he has given up on writing SF for similar reasons – almost three decades *after* Ballard.

Orr asks Ballard about the likelihood of nuclear holocaust, and his response both predicts and undermines the nuclear hysteria and paranoia that would peak in the 1980s. Warning that networked technology and identity theft will become greater threats, he argues that we must be prepared for a coming age 'where bank balances will be constantly monitored and at almost any given time all the information that exists about ourselves will be on file somewhere . . . where all sorts of agencies, commercial, political and governmental, will have access to that information'. (This can be tested empirically: who among us has been the victim of online identity theft, and who of a nuclear holocaust?)

Compare with Alvin Toffler's bestselling non-fiction book *Future Shock*, published three years earlier but in 1974 still considered a frightening, all-too-real vision of the future. Toffler warned of 'massive adaptational breakdown' unless 'man quickly learns to control the rate of change in his personal affairs as well as in society at large'. He predicted turmoil on an epic scale, with most of the population struggling to cope with the psychological shock of a mass-mediated life. While Ballard is concerned about the effects of new technologies, he discerns a rather different outcome, rooted in his belief in the affirmative possibilities of technological advance. He tells Orr that modern urban dwellers are psychologically tougher than ever before, 'strong enough to begin to play all kinds of deviant games, and I'm sure that this is to some extent taking place'. He explains how the isolation that results from immersion in technological systems will invariably play into our latent fantasies: 'We tend to assume that people want to be together in a kind of renaissance city if you like, imaginatively speaking, strolling in the evening across a crowded piazza ... [But people] want to be alone. They want to be alone and watch television.' Orr is unsure, her voice trailing as she struggles to articulate: 'No, I can't agree with you there. I think it is not a question of a conscious decision ...'

Patiently, Ballard clarifies the true 'togetherness' of the technological age: people pressed together in traffic jams, aeroplanes, elevators, hemmed in by technology, an artificial connectedness. Protesting, Orr says she doesn't want to be in a traffic jam, but neither does she want 'to be alone on a dune, either'. Ballard counters: 'being alone on a dune is probably a better description of how you actually lead your life than you realise ... The city or the town or the suburb or the street – these are places of considerable isolation. People like it that way, too. They don't want to know all their neighbours. This is just a small example where the conventional appeal of the good life needs to be looked at again.' The exchange is significant because, with hindsight, we can determine Ballard testing the hypothesis behind *Concrete Island*, the follow-up to *Crash*, and a concentrated study in willed social isolation (marooning himself under a motorway overpass, and deciding to stay there indefinitely, *Concrete Island*'s protagonist finds new reserves of psychological strength in the process). Here, his interview-art is in full effect: running the test, storing the results, turning the tables on his interrogator.

In later interviews, Ballard would refine his views on affirmative social isolation, enthusing about the possibilities of private media and suggesting that the average home would soon acquire the processing power of a small TV studio, enabling us to broadcast our intimate fantasies to one another. In 1982 he told V. Vale that 'Everybody will be doing it, everybody will be living inside a TV studio. That's what the domestic home aspires to these days ... We're all going to be starring in our own sit-coms, and they'll be very strange sit-coms, too, like the inside of our heads. That's going to come, I'm absolutely sure of that, and it'll really shake up everything.' It is this vision, not Toffler's, that continues to resonate.

Yet for Ballard there was always a dark side. Today, online persona factories frame a fluid performativity enabled by the irresistible connective tissue of social media. What is YouTube – now inevitably banal, smoothly integrated into the fabric of everyday life – if not the medium for each of us to design and star in 'our own sit-coms'? Anyone familiar with Ballard's brutal short story 'The Intensive Care Unit' (1977) will surely recognise the dark shadow of those 'very strange' productions (indeed, of what we now recognise as social media), with its disturbing warning about the dangers that await when we have the capacity to broadcast 'the inside of our heads'. Ballard's futurism, always potent, extremely well reasoned and argued – frequently alarming – was, above all, uncannily accurate. He did not flinch, and he expected us not to, either.

III

From the moment I first read a Ballard interview (before any of his fiction, in fact), his slyly subversive conversational style colonised my thoughts and I became obsessed with tracking down every interview he ever did (my search continues; this collection merely scratches the surface). Back then, naive and inexperienced, I convinced myself that Ballard's interviews were superior to his novels. Sacrilege today, of course, but there was a case to be made, for I deeply admired how he worked the interview format with a neurosurgeon's skill, finessing philosophical positions and aesthetic strategies that would later find purchase in his work, triaging real-world scenarios into the dark revelations of his fictional mirror worlds. I would find a new fix in obscure zines. I would painstakingly transcribe his radio and TV appearances. I would badger my elder Ballard-watching associates for access to their magnificent collections, but I had a lot of catching up to do. Henry James gave just three interviews in his life; there are at least two hundred published Ballard conversations. Before he'd even uttered a word, Don DeLillo once presented an interviewer with a card that warned: 'I don't want to talk about it'; Ballard, in his heyday, could talk for hours, plying his interrogators with Scotch to keep things on an even keel.

He was courteous, approachable and generous with his time, and patient in explaining the terms and conditions of his work, although he once told an interviewer that 'the ideal interview is one where I remain silent and you just ask a stream of hundreds of questions. Or – the interviewer hasn't read the books he's asking questions about, and the author can't remember them!' (He came close to achieving this goal in one of the more unusual interviews in this collection, the series of yes/no answers he gave to Sam Scoggins in 1983, an exercise in stylised repetition that, like a tape loop of music, grows in the imagination the more it is repeated.) Of course, he was being flippant. His real interest in making that remark was probably psychoanalytical, wanting to uncover the hidden intentions behind a particular line of questioning, or to turn the process into an autodidactic, quasi-surrealistic game in which the outcome for both parties is dependent on each person's capacity to learn, the same result as in his fiction.

He championed the independent press, often granting interviews to obscure photocopied fanzines and other small publications. A review of the publication history of his interviews reveals titles like *Speculation*, *Corridor*, *Cypher*, *Vector*, *Search & Destroy*, *Aether SF*, *Etoile Mecanique*, *Hard Copy*, *The Hardcore*, *Hard Mag*, *Albedo One*. These are labours of love on the parts of their publishers, mimeographed enthusiasm, largely forgotten, even in the all-seeing digital age. After *Empire of the Sun*, of course, mainstream newspapers and magazines clamoured to speak to him, but still he held court with the underground. In the early days, it was the SF zines that came knocking on his door, but after RE/Search, specialists in 'industrial' culture, published Vale's remarkable 30,000-word interview with him in 1984, punk and music periodicals picked up the pace. Ballard welcomed them, for he did not think his art was 'pure' and could speak for itself, nor did he appear to think it was degrading to explain his work, or that he had a certain type of audience, high or low.

In a 2010 article on 'why novelists hate being interviewed', Tom LeClair notes a recent trend: novels that portray interviewers as 'irresponsible or unworthy of respect'. According to this 'genre', interviewers are hapless lackeys of the evil media machine, pilloried by long-suffering novelists because they haven't read the books they're supposed to be asking about, or they put words into the novelist's mouth, or they want to talk about gossip and nothing else, or the novelist is forced to do the interview out of contractual obligation to the publisher. Finally, LeClair wonders 'if the novelists' animus against interviewers might be displaced animus against passionately curious readers, those who want to learn about authors to better comprehend their books. It appears that some novelists want to be understood, but not too thoroughly understood. [Philip Roth] suggests a darker, Oedipal motive for the animus: "Old men hate young men". Such charges cannot be levelled at Ballard, who talked to almost anyone willing to make the trip down the motorway to his home in Shepperton or to ring the phone number he nonchalantly allowed to be listed in public phone directories right up until his death.

Of course, earlier in his career, he had little time for 'fandom' as at least one interview in this collection attests, but he was always prepared to converse with those genuinely interested in the mysterious forces propelling his work, which he catalogued in his prose poem 'What I Believe' (1984). There, we find an index of his obsessions, including the 'power of the imagination'; motorways; birds (indeed, flight of all kinds, powered and unpowered); the 'confidences of madmen'; 'the beauty of the car crash'; abandoned hotels; forgotten runways; Pacific islands; 'all women'; supermarkets; the 'genital organs of great men and women'; the death of the Space Age; Ernst, Delvaux, Dali and Chirico; and 'all the invisible artists within the psychiatric institutions of the planet'. In fact, that small list could be a mini-index to this present volume, in which all its elements are present and correct, and which in turn function as launchpads for other explorations, other themes: psychological, ontological, metaphysical, sociological, political, satirical, comical.

As evidenced by the reference to 'Ernst, Delvaux, Dali and Chirico', visual art was a touchstone for Ballard, and he often said he wished he'd been an artist rather than a writer. Perhaps it is within that discipline, rather than the navel-gazing, venom-inked pens of literature, that we might find the light that can illuminate Ballard's inimitable strengths as an interviewee. Daniel Miller, in an essay on the function of interviews in the art world, wrote of the interview itself 'as art form'. This is meant both literally and figuratively, the former in that the conversation piece becomes a thing of crafted beauty, and the latter in that it becomes an appendage of the visual artist, albeit one with a mutually beneficial, symbiotic function: 'the principal vehicle of public relations and vital theoretical supplement to artistic practice'. Miller identifies interviewer and interviewee as switches in a circuit, an 'actor network' (after Bruno Latour) that also includes inanimate and virtual objects. Because visual artists, perhaps more than any other creative discipline, are constantly in negotiation with institutional and bureaucratic politics in order to find funding – 'negotiation, exploration and strategy' – they are also constantly in negotiation with their ideas and their work, and the best ways to present them in order to ride the dynamism and flow of the network they are enmeshed within. In this respect, Miller explains, 'the interview serves both as a clinic in which abiding patterns are seen to and as a laboratory in which new connections are forged'.

In the same way, Ballard sought to make new connections in the interview setting, to use the occasion as a workshop for experimentation, a test bed for later integration into his art. Nonetheless, these are experiments based on familiar patterns, for repetition is vitally important to his work (both in the fiction and in the interviews, and in the body of both combined), as a kind of linguistic hypertext that endlessly turns in on itself, erases itself and erects itself anew, providing no discernible start or end point – evading linear time once again, even in death – yet still providing familiar markers with which to orient oneself. It is not for nothing that interviewers came to refer to Ballard as the 'Seer from Shepperton', for the insights he offered so casually were always infused with that deep intelligence, itself informed by a vast cosmology of inner space. All who interviewed him knew it well. We were struck by it, lost deep in thought, sometimes confused or disconcerted, after it came to us as part of that disarming mix of full-frontal future shock and old-world, erudite charm, delivered like a child's spoonful of medicine that turns out to be surprisingly pleasant to the taste.

Doubtless you, too, will become enamoured of the taste as you make your way through the chronology we have assembled, spiralling down through wormholes to the far side of his fiction, and a parallel universe familiar but strange, where Ballardian pronouncements reveal their covert meaning, as he pulls all the outer limits and farthest reaches of his career into sharper focus.

Simon Sellars, Melbourne, Australia, March 2012

Acknowledgements

This collection would not have been possible without the network provided by David Pringle, Mike Holliday, Rick McGrath and Mike Bonsall. Their tireless efforts in bringing to light the more obscure corners of Ballard's career, and in providing new perspectives on the more familiar elements, laid the foundation for this project and their ongoing support allowed it to be completed. We also gratefully acknowledge the valuable support of the Estate of J.G. Ballard: Fay Ballard and Bea Ballard; the Wylie Agency, especially Sarah Chalfant, Emma Paterson and Amy Rutherford; Clare Reihill and Olly Rowse at Fourth Estate; and Claire Walsh. Of course, we are indebted to the contributors, agents and publishers that have allowed their interviews with Ballard to be reproduced here. In particular, we wish to thank Langdon Jones, Janet McKenzie Spens, Michael Spens, Miguel Benavides, Michael Butterworth, Carolyn McCarthy, Andy Sawyer, Peter Nicholls, Philippe R. Hupp, David Pringle, Rein A. Zondergeld, Jon Savage, Joachim Körber, Sam Scoggins, V. Vale, Nicole Rudick, Peter Rønnov-Jessen, Tony Cartano, Maxim Jakubowski, James Verniere, Rosetts Brooks, Joan Bakewell, Lukas Barr, Ashley Crawford, Claire Weatherhead, Damian Love, Peter Fydler, Mark Dery, Richard Kadrey, Suzanne Stefanac, Zinovy Zinik, Iain Sinclair, John Gray, Hans-Ulrich Obrist, Chris Hall, Jeanette Baxter, Toby Litt, David Kerekes, Jonathan Weiss, Hari Kunzru and Vicky Mitchell.

From Simon
Thank you to Sarah Tayton for love and understanding while I nurtured my obsessions, and for not divorcing me after I 'insisted' she read *Crash*. And thank you in advance to our new baby, whom we have not yet met, but who will be born by the time this volume is published. Ballard once

Acknowledgements

said, 'for the real novelist the pram in the hall is the greatest ally – it brings you up sharp and you realise what reality is all about'. Although I'm not a 'real novelist', merely a writer/editor for hire, I know I'll be 'brought up sharp', too.

Finally, thank you to Dan O'Hara for shepherding the book home with me. Thank you also to the readers of ballardian.com and its contributors for maintaining a groundswell of support that has allowed me to continue my investigation into Ballard's work, of which this book is a culmination of sorts.

From Dan
Thank you to Franziska Raabe for her ongoing contribution to the future of Anglo-German relations; and thank you to Simon Sellars, for the tireless commitment and energy that have maintained ballardian.com for the last seven years.

Biographies

Simon Sellars lives in Melbourne, Australia. He is the editor of the magazine *Architectural Review Asia Pacific* and the publisher of ballardian. com. His writing on architecture, urbanism, film, travel and Ballard has been published widely.

Dan O'Hara is a philosopher of technology and a literary historian. He lives in Rio de Janeiro, Brazil.

1967: George MacBeth. The New Science Fiction

Originally published in Langdon Jones (ed.), *The New S.F.*, London: Hutchinson, 1969

Technically, Ballard's first published interview was in 1951, when he won the Crime Story Competition held by *Varsity*, the Cambridge University newspaper. *Varsity* published his winning entry 'The Violent Noon' alongside this brief snippet of conversation: '[Ballard] admitted to our reporter yesterday that he had in fact entered the competition more for the prize than anything else, although he had been encouraged to go on writing because of his success. The idea for his short story, which deals with the problem of Malayan terrorism, he informs us, he had been thinking over for some time before hearing of the competition. He has, in addition to writing short stories, also planned "mammoth novels" which "never get beyond the first page".'

However, his first full-length interview did not appear until 1967, when novelist and poet George MacBeth interviewed him for BBC Radio's Third Programme. The transcript was later published in *The New S.F.*, edited by Langdon Jones, and in the infamous Doubleday edition of *The Atrocity Exhibition*, pulped on the orders of a shocked Doubleday executive. MacBeth, a perceptive interviewer, captures Ballard at the start of that long interregnum from 1966 to 1973, when he took a break from writing novels to focus exclusively on short stories (and a few multimedia experiments), including the strange, elliptical narratives that would make up *Atrocity*.

After it was published Ballard always referred to *Atrocity* as a 'novel', but as this fascinating insight into his method demonstrates, the idea

1

of a sustained narrative binding the chapters was but a glimmer in his eye at this time, albeit a persistent one. Elsewhere, there are penetrating remarks about the 'non-linear' nature of 1960s life and ideas that point towards *Crash*'s artistic breakthrough, such as when he declares that 'the fictional elements [of today] have overwhelmed reality', an observation paraphrased in *Crash*'s introduction. [SS]

MACBETH: You have been writing science fiction short stories and novels for several years now, but your story 'You and Me and the Continuum' is one of a recent group which, I think, in structure are really quite different from your earlier ones. Perhaps the most striking feature to someone reading 'You and Me and the Continuum', for example, for the first time, is that it is constructed not in continuous narrative, but in a sequence of short paragraphs, each of which has a heading – in fact, they're arranged in alphabetical order. But the key point, I think, is that they are broken up. Why did you move on to using this technique of construction?

BALLARD: I was dissatisfied with what I felt were linear systems of narrative. I had been using in my novels and in most of my short stories a conventional linear narrative, but I found that the action and events – of the novels in particular – were breaking down as I wrote them. The characterisation and the sequences of events were beginning to crystallise into a series of shorter and shorter images and situations. This ties in very much with what I feel about the whole role of science fiction as a speculative form of fiction. For me, science fiction is above all a prospective form of narrative fiction; it is concerned with seeing the present in terms of the immediate future rather than the past.

MACBETH: Could I break in there? Would you contrast that with what the traditional novel does in the sense it's concerned with perhaps the history of a family or a person?

BALLARD: Exactly. The great bulk of fiction still being written is retrospective in character. It's concerned with the origins of experience, behaviour, development of character over a great span of years. It interprets the present in terms of the past, and it uses a narrative technique, by and large the linear narrative, in which events are shown in more-or-less chronological sequence, which is suited to it. But when one turns to the present – and what I feel I've done in these pieces of mine is to rediscover the present for myself – I feel that one needs a non-linear technique, simply because our lives today are not conducted in linear terms. They are much more quantified; a stream of random events is taking place.

MACBETH: I'd like to ask you a question here about the characters in these stories. Of course, you've written as well as 'You and Me and the Continuum' three or four others which have already been published in *New Worlds*, *Impulse* and *Encounter*, and one feature of them is that certain characters seem to recur from story to story. When I call them 'characters', they are not always perhaps, to the reader, immediately recognisable as characters so much as named areas of consciousness.

BALLARD: Yes, I don't see them as 'characters' in the conventional sense of the term; they are aspects of certain character situations. They haven't got the same name, but they have variations of the same name.

MACBETH: I remember a case of this myself. There's a character called Tallis in one story and a character called Traven in another, and they seem to have something in common.

BALLARD: In effect they're the same character, but their role in the stories is not to be *characters* in the sense that Scobie, let's say, in [Graham Greene's] *The Heart of the Matter*, or any other *characte*r in the retrospective novel is a character, an identifiable human being rather like those we recognise among our friends, acquaintances and so on.

MACBETH: Could we take a specific case from 'You and Me and the Continuum' here – Dr Nathan, who seems to be, as far as the reader or listener can put a label to him, a psychiatrist? Could you elaborate on what his function is in the story?

BALLARD: He serves the role of analysing the events of the narrative from the point of view of the clinical implications. He represents the voice of reason, whatever the limitations of that term might be.

MACBETH: The central 'consciousness' or area of character in the story is sometimes a composite one in some ways; somebody who has gone through an extreme situation or a psychological crisis or a public crisis; somebody in a mental hospital who might also be the pilot of a crashed

3

bomber; and so on. What are you trying to do with this sort of merged consciousness?

BALLARD: All these characters exist on a number of levels. I feel that the fictional elements in experience are now multiplying to such a point that it is almost impossible to distinguish between the real and the false, that one has many layers, many levels of experience going on at the same time. On one level one might have the world of public events, Cape Kennedy, Vietnam, political life; on another level the immediate personal environment, the rooms we occupy, the postures we assume. On a third level the inner world of the mind. All these levels are, as far as I can see them, equally fictional, and it is where these levels interact that one gets the only kind of valid reality that exists nowadays. The characters in these stories occupy positions on these various levels. On the one hand, a character is displayed on an enormous billboard as a figment in a Cinemascope epic; on another level he's an ordinary human being moving through the ordinary to-and-fro of everyday life; on a third level he's a figment in his own fantasies. These various aspects of the character interact and produce the main reality of the fiction.

MACBETH: Yes, I think this element of layers also comes out in the density of some of the stories – the way you seem to link together references from a wide variety of fields. I quote if I may, as an interesting example, one passage from 'You and Me and the Continuum', which is the kind of passage that recurs in a number of these stories:

> Kodachrome. Captain Kirby, MI5, studied the prints. They showed: (1) a thick-set man in an Air Force jacket, unshaven face half-hidden by the dented hat-peak; (2) a transverse section through the spinal level T-12; (3) a crayon self-portrait by David Feary, 7-year-old schizophrenic at the Belmont Asylum, Sutton; (4) radio-spectra from the quasar CTA 102; (5) an antero-posterior radiograph of a skull, estimated capacity 1500 cc.; (6) spectro-heliogram of the sun taken with the K line of calcium; (7) left and right handprints showing massive scarring between second and third metacarpal bones. To Dr Nathan he said: 'And all these make up one picture?'

BALLARD: Exactly. They make up a composite portrait of this man's identity. In this story I was examining the particular role that a twentieth-century messiah might take, in the context of mid-twentieth-century life.

I feel that he would reappear in a whole series of aspects and relationships, touching an enormous range of events; that he wouldn't have a single identity, in the sense that Jesus had – he would have a whole multiplex of contacts with various points.

MACBETH: I see this, but why do certain particular kinds of imagery recur? You may claim that these are the appropriate and inevitable ones, but you do seem as a writer to have a sort of 'thing' about certain kinds of imagery; for example, certain kinds of landscape – landscapes which involve sand keep recurring. Can you give any further explication of why these come in?

BALLARD: I think that landscape is a formalisation of space and time, and the external landscapes directly reflect interior states of mind. In fact, the only external landscapes which have any meaning are those which are reflected, in the central nervous system, if you like, by their direct analogues. Dali said somewhere that mind is a state of landscape, and I think this is completely true.

MACBETH: You do literally, in many of these stories, draw connections between pictures of parts of the human body and certain landscapes, don't you?

BALLARD: Yes. In the story 'You: Coma: Marilyn Monroe' I directly equate the physical aspect of Marilyn Monroe's body with the landscape of dunes around her. The hero attempts to make sense of this particular equation, and he realises that the suicide of Marilyn Monroe is, in fact, a disaster in space-time, like the explosion of a satellite in orbit. It is not so much a personal disaster, though of course Marilyn Monroe committed suicide as an individual woman, but a disaster of a whole complex of relationships involving this screen actress who is presented to us in an endless series of advertisements, on a thousand magazine covers and so on, whose body becomes part of the external landscape of our environment. The immense terraced figure of Marilyn Monroe stretched across a cinema hoarding is as real a portion of our external landscape as any system of mountains or lakes.

MACBETH: Are you aware of deliberately using surrealism as references in these stories? Quite often you refer to Dali in particular and some-times Ernst, and sometimes to real pictures by them. How far is there

5

a direct connection with those pictures and the events or descriptions in the stories?

BALLARD: The connection is deliberate, because I feel that the surrealists have created a series of valid external landscapes which have their direct correspondences within our own minds. I use the phrase 'spinal landscape' fairly often. In these spinal landscapes, which I feel that painters such as Ernst and Dali are producing, one finds a middle ground (an area which I've described as 'inner space') between the outer world of reality on the one hand, and the inner world of the psyche on the other. Freud pointed out that one has to distinguish between the manifest content of the inner world of the psyche and its latent content. I think in exactly the same way today, when the fictional elements have overwhelmed reality, one has to distinguish between the manifest content of reality and its latent content. In fact the main task of the arts seems to be more and more to isolate the real elements in this goulash of fictions from the unreal ones, and the terrain 'inner space' roughly describes it.

MACBETH: Yes, one often has the sense that certain of the events in these stories, insofar as they are 'events', might be taking place within, particularly, a Dali painting. I also have the sense in reading these stories that there's a kind of hallucinatory vividness and clarity about the descriptions which remind me of certain techniques used by the cinema in the 1960s. Are you aware of being influenced by films at all?

BALLARD: Some films. *The Savage Eye* had a tremendous impact on me because it presented a completely fragmented and quantified narrative through which the heroine evolved her own identity. Most films, though, are still made in linear terms, and I find that painters, perhaps because a painting is a single image, are much more stimulating; they corroborate my own preoccupations much more.

MACBETH: Yes, indeed; it seems very much that your central preoccupation is, in the very loosest sense, with time and the absence of time, with a massive kind of stasis that embodies a sense of time moving. However, there are a number of difficulties here. I think that particularly this seems to lead you towards the special kind of density I've mentioned, and that, in a way, leads to the stories working perhaps rather more like poetry than like prose; they have overtones, associations and resonances. And I think most readers are likely to find them literally very difficult.

BALLARD: I think that's simply the inertia of convention. If you could scrap all retrospective fiction and its immense body of conventions, most people who, for example, find William Burroughs' narrative techniques almost impossible to recognise – in exactly the same way that some aboriginal tribesmen are supposed to be unable to recognise their own photographs – would realise that Burroughs' narrative techniques, or my own in their way, would be an immediately recognisable reflection of the way life is actually experienced. We live in quantified non-linear terms – we switch on television sets, switch them off half an hour later, speak on the telephone, read magazines, dream and so forth. We don't live our lives in linear terms in the sense that the Victorians did.

MACBETH: I can understand that, but I think it's slightly more complicated than that, in that the reader has to move at quite a different speed through these stories; he has to pause, he has to reread, he perhaps even doesn't have to start at the beginning and go to the end, he may want to shift about to get a bigger concentration on certain key sections; he also, almost certainly I think, has to work with a number of reference books available, because there are in all of these later stories words that certainly I didn't know the meaning of at first and I would want to look up. At the same time, interestingly enough, you are publishing in science fiction magazines, which contain material that in terms of structure and content are obviously much simpler. I wonder really how far the audience you're getting is naturally equipped to treat these stories in the right way. Does this worry you?

BALLARD: No, I think the science fiction readership, if there is such a readership, is much more sophisticated than one might imagine, far more sophisticated probably than the general readership of conventional fiction. These devices which I use are not as outrageous as they seem; they don't in fact dislocate the elements of the narrative to anything like the extent they appear to do at first glance at the page.

MACBETH: Yes, I can see that, and historically speaking I can also see that your earlier stories do seem to be preoccupied with certain similar themes, though in a much less dense and exciting way. This theme of time emerges in a number of much more straightforward stories; the story of yours called 'The Time Tombs', for example, which does again have this thing about sand in it. Now the turning point, it seemed to me, was a story of yours called 'The Terminal Beach', which seemed to be midway between your older stories and your new ones.

BALLARD: Yes, there I made my first attempt at a narrative in which the events of the story were quantified in the sense that they were isolated from the remainder of the narrative and then examined from a number of angles.

MACBETH: The stories you've written which we've been talking about are those such as 'You and Me and the Continuum', *The Atrocity Exhibition*, 'You: Coma: Marilyn Monroe' and 'The Assassination Weapon'. In fact, it sometimes seems, as I've read these, that one could almost translate bits of one into bits of the other. They seem, in a certain sense, not four independent stories, but four fragments of a kind of sequence. Are you aware of them relating, and do you have in your mind further ones which you will write, such that, taken as a group, they will shed extra light on each other?

BALLARD: I think they're all chapters in a much longer narrative that is evolving at its pace. I don't think it's evolving in a sequential sense, in the sense that the events of, say, *Moby-Dick* evolve one after another; they're evolving in an apparently random sense, but all the images relate to one another, and I hope when more stories have been written they will reinforce one another and produce something larger than the sum of their parts.

MACBETH: Despite what you said about the science fiction audience, I suppose you wouldn't think of yourself as a writer of science fiction; you'd think of yourself as just a writer, presumably.

BALLARD: I don't regard myself as a writer of what most people would call modern science fiction, which is predominantly American, even though much of it has been written by English writers. Modern American science fiction grew out of magazines such as the *Popular Mechanics* of the thirties; it's an extrovert, optimistic literature of technology. I think the new science fiction, which other people apart from myself are now beginning to write, is introverted, possibly pessimistic rather than optimistic, much less certain of its own territory. There's a tremendous confidence that radiates through all modern American science fiction of the period 1930 to 1960; the certainty that science and technology can solve all problems. This is not the dominant form of science fiction now. I think science fiction is becoming something much more speculative, much less convinced about the magic of science and the moral authority of science. There's far more caution on the part of the new writers than there was.

1968: Uncredited. Munich Round Up – Interview with J.G. Ballard

Originally published in German as 'Interview mit J.G. Ballard' (uncredited), *Munich Round Up* 100, 1968. Translated by Dan O'Hara

Early in 1968, Bavarian TV ran a four-part educational series on science fiction, the third episode of which featured excerpts from an interview with Ballard. The footage of this episode is no longer available, and is presumably now lost. Like so much valuable TV footage of that era, it was probably shot on tape which, owing to its expense, was reused, thereby erasing the interview. Later that year the director of the series, Brian Wood, published a translation of a full transcript of the interview in a German-language science fiction fanzine called *Munich Round Up*. The 'zine also contained 'Notiz aus dem Nirgendwo', a German translation of Ballard's 1966 piece 'Notes from Nowhere'.

Although I have retranslated this interview into English, inevitably such a process is unsatisfactory – after all, one must read Ballard's words through the lens of another language. Yet it is striking just how difficult it is to strip Ballard's words of their distinctive character, and very little of his meaning is lost in translation. It seems likely that this 1968 interview is in fact a transcript of the German subtitles used in the TV programme, as the interview here contains no questions. I have therefore chosen to translate back into English as literally as possible, preserving some of the odder and more interesting artefacts produced by the original translator, Gary Klüpfel. One of the most obvious of these is Ballard's assertion that he uses the diamond ('Diamant') as a symbol of timeless structure in *The Crystal World*.

Clearly the original translator decided that Ballard intended a more conventional symbol of eternity. [DOH]

On the early works

BALLARD: I believe that SF is important because it is the sole form of literature we have today that looks forward. All forms of literature other than science fiction are oriented towards the past. Their character is backwards-looking, whereas SF concerns itself with the future and interprets the present day in terms of the future, rather than of the past. It uses a vocabulary that is on the whole exclusively oriented towards the world of tomorrow, with all its science, its technology, and with all its developments in politics, sociology, advertising and so forth.

I have written three novels – *The Drowned World*, *The Drought* and *The Crystal World* – which form a trilogy dealing with the topic of time. In *The Drowned World* I deal with the past, and employ water as the central metaphor. In *The Drought* I deal with the future, taking sand as the central image. In *The Crystal World* I am concerned with the present, the symbol of which is the diamond or the precious stone which – so I believe – possesses a timeless structure.

In *The Drowned World* I describe the return of the entire planet to the era of the great Triassic forests, which covered the earth some 200 million years ago. I tell how human beings likewise regress into the past. In a certain sense, they climb down their own spinal column. They traverse down the thoracic vertebrae, from the point at which they are air-breathing mammals, to the lumbar region, to the point at which they are amphibious reptiles. Finally they reach the absolute past, which on one hand represents the birth of life itself in the hot womb of the primeval jungle, and which in another sense represents their own origins and birthplace in the mother's womb. I show humanity face to face with the difficulty of making sense of this decline in their status to non-entities.

I use this portrait of the spinal column as a vessel containing a reflection of the memory of the past, and the details of the entire evolutionary development of the human race, as a literary device, as I was dissatisfied with the traditional forms used by SF writers to realise time travel. It seems to me that the method of investigating the imaginative capacities of the central nervous system gives a more reliable and more precise account of how the human race has evolved in time, and of how we as individuals have evolved in our own time, than Wells' time machine.

In my novel *The Drought*, I see the future as a world dominated by sand. It is the end of the planet, and the few people who survive on the planet are governed by perfectly abstract relations, through an entire geometry of space-time, of emotion and action. It is a completely abstract world, as abstract as the most abstract of painters or sculptors one can imagine.

On SF

I believe that SF will become more and more an aspect of daily reality. It has migrated from the bookshelf to daily life. One sees the landscapes and imagery of SF, one sees their contents playing a part in the world of pop music, of film, even that of psychedelic experiences. The reason being, that SF was always concerned with psychological perceptions, and the world of pop music, film and psychedelic experience is now greatly concerned with the senses, with perspectives of our own psychological space-time, and has not so much to do with questions of individual histories, the past and so forth, as were the prejudices of the literature and cinema of the past.

I believe that in the last ten years the entire basis of SF has changed rapidly. Modern SF began at the end of the 1920s and the beginning of the thirties, and was at that time an authentically vernacular vision of the future, a future seen through the lens of science and technology and, above all, in the light of outer space, so I believe. Now in the last ten years SF as I see it has turned full circle. The physical sciences now play less of a major role than do the biological, inner space, the world of the mind – which once more reflects the altered attitudes of people towards science in general. After Hiroshima, the whole magic and authority of science was called into question. Now, I don't think that the authority of biologists was attacked to such an extent, and to a considerable degree the biologist and the psychologist took over something of the functions of a lay church, in exploring man's place in the universe.

On inner space

I define inner space as an imaginary realm in which on the one hand the outer world of reality, and on the other the inner world of the mind, meet and merge. Now, in the landscapes of the surrealist painters, for example, one sees the regions of inner space; and increasingly I believe that we will encounter in film and literature scenes which are neither solely realistic nor fantastic. In a sense, it will be a movement in the interzone between both spheres.

1968: Jannick Storm. An Interview with J.G. Ballard

Originally published in *Speculation* 21, 1969

Jannick Storm, a Danish publisher and writer, visited London in the late 1960s and became involved with the key players in the British New Wave of science fiction. He had a short story published in Michael Moorcock's *New Worlds* and in 1970 founded Denmark's first fanzine, *Limbo*, inspired by *New Worlds*. Storm was close to New Wave figurehead Brian Aldiss, who dedicated his book *Billion Year Spree* to him, and to Ballard. Throughout the sixties, Storm translated many of the individual *Atrocity Exhibition* pieces for Danish publications almost as soon as Ballard had written them. Subsequently, he was responsible for the world first edition of *The Atrocity Exhibition*, convincing Rhodos of Copenhagen to publish *Grusomhedsudstillingen* (1969), *Atrocity* in Danish, with Storm's translations.

The following interview was conducted at Shepperton on 5 July 1968. It was originally recorded for a Danish radio programme on science fiction, and the transcript appeared in Peter Weston's fanzine *Speculation* in 1969. It covers Ballard's thoughts on the New Wave, his experiments in graphic design, his admiration for the work of William Burroughs, the media landscape of the sixties and, as a controversial parting shot, his withering views on science fiction fandom. The latter got Ballard into hot water with *Speculation* readers who took umbrage in hostile letters to the editor, in turn provoking Ballard to tell Weston he no longer wished to receive further copies of the 'zine. Weston lamented this in a later editorial, although Moorcock leapt to Ballard's defence in *Speculation* 25: 'I sympathise with Jimmy Ballard's remarks, and, at times, find myself close to agreeing with them.' [SS]

STORM: How did you start writing?

BALLARD: I was studying medicine at Cambridge University. I was very interested in medicine, everything I learned there I put to very good use. All the anatomy and physiology and so on. It seemed an enormous fiction. They have an annual short story competition at the University, and I wrote a story for that and won the competition that year. I suppose that was a green light, so I gave up medicine, and after a few years I had my first story published. I'd tried originally to write stories for English literary magazines like *Horizon* and that sort of thing. Just general fiction of an experimental character. And then I thought that science fiction, which in those days was all Asimov and Heinlein and Clarke – this was in the middle fifties – I thought, those writers were not really making the most of what science fiction could be. I felt that a new kind of science fiction should be written.

STORM: Your kind of science fiction, you say, is different from the old science fiction. In what way?

BALLARD: Modern American science fiction of the 1940s and 1950s is a popular literature of technology. Anybody who can remember reading magazines in the thirties, or looking at books published in the thirties, will know what I mean – they are full of marvels, the biggest bridge in the world, the fastest this or the longest that – full of marvels of science and technology.

The science fiction written in those days came out of all this optimism that science was going to remake the world. Then came Hiroshima and Auschwitz, and the image of science completely changed. People became very suspicious of science, but SF didn't change. You still found this optimistic literature, the Heinlein–Asimov–Clarke type of attitude towards the possibilities of science, which was completely false.

In the 1950s during the testing of the H-bomb you could see that science was getting to be something much closer to magic. Also, science fiction was then identified with the idea of outer space. By and large, that was the image most people had of science fiction. The spaceship, the alien planet. And this didn't make any sense to me. It seemed to me that they were ignoring what I felt was the most important area, what

I called – and I used the term for the first time seven years ago – 'inner space', which was the meeting ground between the inner world of the mind and the outer world of reality. Inner space you see in the paintings of the surrealists, Max Ernst, Dali, Tanguy, Chirico.

They're painters of inner space, and I felt that science fiction should explore that area, the area where the mind impinges on the outside world, and not just deal in fantasy. This was the trouble with SF in the early fifties. It was becoming fantasy. It wasn't a serious realistic fiction any more. So I started writing. I've written three novels and something like seventy short stories over the last ten years – I think that perhaps in only one story there's a spaceship. It's just mentioned in passing. All my fiction is set in the present day or close to the present day.

STORM: Well, this is why your landscapes are not real, I suppose. They are sort of symbolic?

BALLARD: Well, they are not real in the sense that I don't write naturalistically about the present day. Though, in the latest group of stories I've started to write, these stories written in paragraph form, which I call 'condensed novels', there I'm using the landscape of the present day. The chief characters in these stories are people like Elizabeth Taylor, Marilyn Monroe, Jacqueline Kennedy and so on. There I'm using present-day landscapes. Obviously if you're going to set most of your fiction several years ahead of the present, you're going to have to use an invented landscape to some extent, because you can't write naturalistically about London or New York twenty years from now. It must be an invented landscape to a certain extent.

STORM: You seem to be quite hostile towards science, like Ray Bradbury, for instance, but not in the same way, I suppose?

BALLARD: I'm not hostile to science itself. I think that scientific activity is about the only mature activity there is. What I'm hostile to is the image of science that people have. It becomes a magic wand in people's minds, that will conjure up marvels, a kind of Aladdin's lantern. It oversimplifies things, much too conveniently. Science now, in fact, is the largest producer of fiction. A hundred years ago, or even fifty years ago, even, science took its raw material from nature. A scientist worked out the boiling point of a gas or the distance a star is away from the Earth, whereas nowadays, particularly in the social, psychological sciences, the raw material of science is a fiction invented by the scientists. You know, they work out why people chew gum or something of this kind . . . so the psychological and social sciences are spewing out an enormous amount of fiction. They're the major producers of fiction. It's not the writers any more.

STORM: What do you think of the so-called New Wave, as it manifests itself in *New Worlds*, for instance?

BALLARD: I am the New Wave! Well, the New Wave . . . I think it's only at the beginning. Having knocked my own head against a brick wall for ten years . . . you know, it's only now that people begin to accept that I'm not a deliberate fool, which a lot of people thought I was when I first started writing. It's taken so long that I don't expect any miracles to happen overnight, but already you see a group of younger writers coming along. People like Tom Disch, John Sladek, Michael Butterworth, Pam Zoline, the young American painter over here. They're starting to write a different kind of science fiction, but whether they will stay within science fiction long enough to consolidate the so-called New Wave or whether – as I think will happen – they'll just move out of science fiction altogether and begin writing a speculative fiction that doesn't owe anything to science fiction, I don't know.

STORM: Well, the same applies to you. You don't consider yourself a science fiction writer?

BALLARD: I don't consider myself a science fiction writer in the same sense that Isaac Asimov or Arthur C. Clarke are science fiction writers. Strictly speaking I regard myself as an SF writer in the way that surrealism is also a scientific art. In a sense Asimov, Heinlein and the masters of American SF are not really writing of science at all. They're writing about a set of imaginary ideas which are conveniently labelled 'science'. They're writing about the future, they're writing a kind of fantasy-fiction about the future, closer to the western and the thriller, but it has nothing really to do with science. I studied medicine, chemistry, physiology, physics, and I worked for about five years on a scientific journal.

The idea that a magazine like *Astounding*, or *Analog* as it's now called, has anything to do with the sciences is ludicrous. It has nothing to do with science. You have only to pick up a journal like *Nature*, say, or any scientific journal, and you can see that science belongs in a completely different world. Freud pointed out that you have to distinguish between analytic activity, which by and large is what the sciences are, and synthetic activities, which are what the arts are. The trouble with the Heinlein–Asimov type of science fiction is that it's completely synthetic. Freud also said that synthetic activities are a sign of immaturity, and I think that's where classical SF falls down.

STORM: You've been running some advertisements in *New Worlds*. What do you think of them, what is the meaning of them?

BALLARD: It occurred to me about a year ago that advertising was an unknown continent as far as the writer was concerned, a kind of virgin America of images and ideas, and that the writer ought to move into any area which is lively and full of potential. It occurred to me I had a number of ideas which I could fit into my short stories, my fiction general, but they would be better presented directly. Instead of advertising a product I would advertise an idea. I've done three advertisements now, and I hope to carry on. I'm advertising extremely abstract ideas in these advertisements, and this is a very effective way of putting them over. If these ideas were in the middle of a short story people could ignore them. They could just say, 'It's Ballard again, let's get on with the story'. But if they're presented in the form of an advertisement, like one in *Vogue* magazine, or *Life* magazine, people have to look at them, they have to think about them. I hope I can go on, the only problem being the expense. I hope eventually the magazines will pay me to put advertisements in their pages.

STORM: In *Ambit* – where you're prose editor – you've had a competition for things written under the influence of drugs, but as you admitted yourself in *Ambit*, the things which came out of it were pretty close to the things that you normally produce in *Ambit*. Would you comment on this?

BALLARD: Literary competitions never produce anything all that outstanding. Newspapers and magazines for years have been running competitions for the best short story and the best travel story and so on, and the stuff that is sent in is never all that original, or all that exciting. I think the entries we received were interesting, but probably not so much for literary reasons as for biographical reasons, the circumstances in which people write stories, write poetry. This was interesting, and I think it was worth doing. Also, there was a lot of talk at the time about psychedelia, a kind of psychedelic revolution, that a whole lot of new arts were going to be produced, based on or inspired by drugs. And it was interesting to see as a result of the competition that in fact drugs didn't have all that big an effect, that they're very much a short cut and a short circuit.

STORM: Well, you're a well-known admirer of William Burroughs. Would you say that his style has influenced yours?

BALLARD: No, I wish it had. Burroughs and I are completely different writers. I admire him as a writer who in his way has created the landscape of the twentieth century completely as new. He's produced a kind of apocalyptical landscape, he's close to Hieronymus Bosch and Bruegel. He's not a pastoral writer by any means. He's a writer of the nightmare. I only started reading Burroughs about four years ago, and it may be that he will influence me, I can't say. But certainly he hasn't influenced me now, though some people say he has. They're completely wrong.

STORM: Actually there's been quite a development in your style of writing. You started out with some quite ordinary stories, and now you have got these 'condensed novels', as you call them.

BALLARD: It has been a process of evolution rather than revolution. I wrote a novel called *The Drought*, after *The Drowned World*. That was a novel about desert areas. I noticed while I was writing it that I was beginning to explore the geometry of a very abstract kind of landscape and very abstract relationships between the characters. I went on from there to write a short story, 'The Terminal Beach', set on Eniwetok, the island in the Pacific where the H-bomb was tested. There again I was starting to look at the characters, and the events of the story, in a very abstract, almost cubist way. I was isolating aspects of character, isolating aspects of the narrative, rather like a scientific investigator taking apart a strange machine to see how it works. My new stories, which I call 'condensed novels', stem from 'The Terminal Beach'. They're developments of that, but I don't think there's been a revolution in what I've done. There's just been a steady change over the years.

STORM: In your new stories you are using actual persons like John F. Kennedy and Elizabeth Taylor and so on. Why?

BALLARD: I feel that the 1960s represent a marked turning point. For the first time, with the end of the Cold War, I suppose, for the first time the outside world, so-called reality, is now almost completely a fiction. It's a media landscape, if you like. It's almost completely dominated by advertising, TV, mass-merchandising, politics conducted as advertising. People's lives, even their individual private lives, are getting more and more controlled by what I call fiction. By fiction I mean anything invented for imaginative purposes. For example, you don't buy an airline ticket, you don't just buy transportation, let's say, to the south of France or Spain. What you buy is the image of a particular airline, the kind of miniskirts the hostesses are wearing on that airline. In fact, airlines in America are selling themselves on this sort of thing.

Also the sort of homes people buy for themselves, the way they furnish their houses, even the way they talk, the friends they have, everything is becoming fictionalised. Therefore, given that reality is now a fiction, it's not necessary for the writer to invent the fiction. The writer's relationship with reality is completely the other way around. It's the writer's job to find the reality, to invent the reality, not to invent the fiction. The fiction is already there. The greatest fictional characters of the twentieth century are people like the Kennedys. They're a twentieth-century House of Atreus.

These figures that I use, I don't use them as individual characters. As I said in one of my stories, the body of a screen actress like Elizabeth Taylor, which one sees on thousands of cinema hoardings, thousands of advertisements every day, and on the movie screen itself, her body is a real landscape. It is as much a real landscape of our lives as any system of mountains or lakes or hills or anything else. So therefore I sought to use this material, this is the fictional material of the 1960s.

STORM: In *SF Horizons*, Brian Aldiss wrote that 'Ballard is seldom discussed in fanzines'. Time has certainly proved him wrong, and now you are one of the most discussed people in fandom. What do you think of fandom itself?

BALLARD: I didn't know that was the case, because I never see any fanzines. I don't have any contact with fans. My one and only contact with fandom was when I'd just started writing, twelve years ago, when the World Science Fiction Convention was being held in London, in 1957, and I went along to that as a young new writer hoping to meet people who were interested in the serious aims of science fiction and all its possibilities. In fact there was just a collection of very unintelligent people, who were almost illiterate, who had no interest whatever in the serious and interesting possibilities of science fiction. In fact I was so taken aback by that convention that I more or less stopped writing for a couple of years. Since then I've had absolutely nothing to do with fans, and I think they're a great handicap to science fiction and always have been.

1970: Lynn Barber. Sci-fi Seer

Originally published in *Penthouse* 5:5, 1970

From 1967 to 1974 journalist Lynn Barber worked for *Penthouse*, becoming the magazine's literary editor in the late 1960s, when she discovered *New Worlds* and the New Wave. This interview was the first of three she would conduct with Ballard over the course of his career, conversations that betrayed their familiarity with each other. In their 1987 interview, she berated Ballard for the unkempt nature of his Shepperton abode, the most prominent in a long line of interviewers baffled by his modest living arrangements. In their 1991 encounter, she provided background to their relationship: 'When I first knew him in the sixties, he was a familiar, but jolly peculiar, figure on the *New Worlds* or Arts Lab scene. He was older than most – thirty-something rather than twenty-something – rather obviously public-schooly and ex-RAF, whereas the other sci-fi writers were all beard-and-sandals brigade. He drank whisky while everyone else smoked pot, and often turned up with startlingly famous friends, such as Lucien Freud and Francis Bacon and Eduardo Paolozzi.' It was in this interview that Barber claimed Ballard liked to show photographs of his girlfriend's car-crash injuries to party guests, although Ballard later denied this.

By the time of this first interview, Ballard had published *The Atrocity Exhibition*, which was gathering a good deal of notoriety owing principally to the pulping of the US edition. While it would be three years before his next novel, *Crash*, he kept himself busy with an array of extra-curricular activities: full page, sexually charged ads in magazines; acting in a surreal short film with Gabrielle Drake, based on *Atrocity* fragments; attempting a multimedia play based around the car crash; and staging his notorious exhibition of crashed cars, which managed to enrage its audience of drunken guests.

The original *Penthouse* introduction provides a perfect summation of the early Ballardian manifesto: 'He talks to Lynn Barber about the space programme, the outlook for science, car crashes, violence and his vision of a deviant sexual future'. [SS]

BARBER: Your books and your pronouncements about science fiction ('the apocalyptic literature of the twentieth century' and 'Outer space is the symbol of inner space') are miles away from conventional science fiction. Do you consider yourself a sci-fi writer?

BALLARD: Not in the tradition of Isaac Asimov, Ray Bradbury or even H.G. Wells. But I believe that science fiction is far more than the kind of popular space fiction that had its heyday between 1930 and 1960 and is now pretty well dead. American magazine sci-fi – Arthur C. Clarke and Heinlein and so on – that's finished. Dammit, we're living in the year 1970, the science fiction is *out there*, one doesn't have to write it any more. One's *living* science fiction. All our lives are being invaded by science, technology and their applications. So I believe the only important fiction being written now is science fiction. This is *the* literature of the twentieth century. I am convinced that in, say, fifty years' time, literary historians looking back – if they bother, which they may not – will say: 'You can forget about the social novel, you can forget about everything except sci-fi.' Even bad sci-fi is better than the best conventional fiction. A ton of Proust isn't worth an ounce of Ray Bradbury. It's one hundred years since Verne wrote his *Voyage to the Moon*. I think it was published in 1870 or thereabouts and they landed on the moon almost one hundred years later to the day, and this is the only literature that matters a damn. Everybody should be forced to read it all the time. It's true.

BARBER: Did the moon landing mean such a lot to you?

BALLARD: Of course it did. It's probably the only important thing that has happened in the twentieth century. I had this feeling after they landed on the moon that in a way it gave me the moral right to do anything I wanted, because it didn't matter what I did. I felt we were like a lot of animals in an abandoned zoo, and that the only important thing that was going to happen in our lifetime had happened. But the spin-off from the space programme – which should have had enormous effects on everybody's lives, from the way we drive our cars to the way we light our cigarettes – and the effect on people's imaginations, was absolutely nil. In fact when you think of the hundreds of millions of pounds that the Russians and Americans have invested in the space programme, the real effects of the moon landing could only be described as a gigantic flop, the worst first night in history. I noticed this after the first orbital flights a few years ago: within a day people had totally lost interest in them. How many people, if you asked them, could tell you the names of the men who first orbited the moon, the Christmas of – when was it? – 1968? How many people could tell you the names of those men who recited the extract from the Book of Genesis? Yet it was a fantastic voyage, a triumph of technology, courage, science, organisation, everything.

BARBER: If you think the moon the only important thing likely to happen in your lifetime you presumably have no great expectations of 2001?

BALLARD: We're ahead of the clock, that's the whole point. It's like Buckminster Fuller, you know, saying that World War III is already over and we lost. People aren't interested in the future any more. The greatest casualty of World War II, I think, was that the past ceased to have moral authority for people, the authority of precedent, tradition, one's father, social background, everything. That ended with World War II, and thank God. But what has happened in the twenty-five years since then is that the future has become a casualty too. One could say that the moon landing was the death knell of the future as a moral authority. No one thinks that the future is going to be a better place – most people think it's going to be a worse place. The moral authority of science was colossal in the 1930s. I can remember myself that children's encyclopedias were loaded with scientific marvels – the greatest bridge in the world, the longest tunnel, the biggest ship, Professor Picard in his stratosphere balloon. But the idea that science was building a bigger and better world ended with Hiroshima and Eniwetok. Now people feel that science may not bring a better world, but a nightmare. Dr Barnard may really be Dr Moreau. Now people are frightened of science and they're frightened of the future. They no longer feel that because something's going to happen tomorrow it's going to be better than today.

So the idea of America is dead, I think, because America was built on the assumption that tomorrow was a better day. The American Dream is the American Nightmare now. I think that's why American sci-fi of the forties and fifties has come to a full stop. Nobody is writing it any more, no new writers have come into the field, because people don't accept the authority of the future any more. God knows, the present is infinitely more varied and bizarre and fantastic. People have annexed the future into the present, just as they've annexed the past into the present. Now we have the future and the past all rolled into the present – one day you're wearing Edwardian clothes, the next you're dressed like an eighteenth-century samurai. One can visualise by, say, the end of the century calendars no longer existing. They won't be necessary, there'll be no dates, there won't be a year 2000, because no one will be interested. And if the proverbial visitor from outer space lands here in the year 2000 (by his calendar, because we won't have them) he might find himself in anything from Elizabethan England to ancient Rome to Nazi Germany to a *Barbarella* fantasy of the year 1,000,000 AD.

BARBER: Now you're making a prediction about the future yourself.

BALLARD: Yes, because we're still in the dying twilight of tomorrow, we can still see the idea of the future. But my children, or today's teenagers, they're not interested in the future. All the possibilities of their lives are contained within a different set of perspectives, an inner life. If you look back over the past ten years you can see a continuous retreat inwards. I coined the expression 'inner space' about ten years ago and usually sci-fi writers' predictions are proven wrong with 100 per cent consistency, but in this one instance I was certainly right: that what you see is the death of outer space, the failure of the moon landing to excite anyone's imagination on a real level, and the discovery of inner space in terms of sex, drugs, meditation, mysticism. Just look at the career of the Beatles and you see this retreat from the exterior by steady stages, through drugs, then meditation, to a more or less complete involvement with their own bodies. Lennon and Yoko seem to be rediscovering the tactile existence, the organic reality of their own embraces, and it's very beautiful, I think.

BARBER: If what you say is true, why is there so much science journalism around? Why so many articles on the future of genetic engineering, or heart transplants, or the population explosion?

BALLARD: Most science journalism is really fiction masquerading as fact. Almost anything you care to name nowadays is really fiction, serving someone's imaginative end, whether it's a politician's, or a TV executive's, or a scientist's. So-called hard science is now the new show business. Take someone like Desmond Morris, a so-called scientist who is really one of the leading pop entertainers. He's as much a showbiz performer as John Lennon.

BARBER: What about Barnard?

BALLARD: I think he became show business afterwards. That was where science created its first superstar, the moment Washkansky had his new heart, the first one, that was something unique. I'm sure that most scientific developments in the future are going to be made in the Barnard way. There'll be no more of the absent-minded professor in his laboratory stumbling on penicillin and taking five years to develop it. No, he'll be a pushy, ambitious, publicity-oriented scientist who will launch himself not just into the new discovery, but into show business at the same time.

BARBER: Do you also dismiss the sort of science journalism that deals with serious extrapolations of the future, the population explosion, pollution, demographic factors?

BALLARD: This is the Herman Kahn school of distant extrapolation, which I find absolutely meaningless. They say something about the present and they say something about the mind of Herman Kahn, but they don't say anything about the world fifty years from now, because one simply can't anticipate. The world rate [sic] changes so fast you don't need to be much of a mathematician to work out that things will be so different even in ten years' time that one won't be able to say anything about them now. It's like women's fashion – one can't even guess what it'll be like this time next year.

BARBER: Most of your novels and stories seem to be set in the future, and give the impression of a future after the holocaust, after some terrible catastrophe has changed the world.

BALLARD: Well, the facts of time and space are a tremendous catastrophe, aren't they? Each day millions of cells die in our bodies, others are born. Every time we open a door, every time we look out across a landscape – I'm deliberately trying to exaggerate this – millions of minute displacements of time and space are occurring. One's living in a continuous cataclysm anyway – our whole existence takes place in the eye of a hurricane.

BARBER: But those changes aren't a sudden worldwide disaster which would change the character of life on this planet.

BALLARD: Well, look at the events of the last thirty years, the slaughter of human life alone, anything from thirty to fifty million people dead in World War II. World War III, still a possibility, would multiply that figure by ten presumably. That's one cataclysm that's already occurred and another that's possible, of the order of anything invented by science fiction.

BARBER: Are you a pessimist?

BALLARD: I don't know. Perhaps I'm just being honest. What I'm trying to do is to look at the present and to get away from the notion of yesterday, today, tomorrow.

BARBER: Your latest book, *The Atrocity Exhibition*, seems to use more personal or autobiographical material than before.

BALLARD: A little more, yes. I mean when I say I want to write fiction for the present, I'm clearly not trying to pretend that I'm not influenced by the past, because we all are to a tremendous degree. Besides, enough time has now elapsed for me to be able to look back. In fact, the setting of *The Drowned World*, the apartment blocks rising out of the swamp, is like the landscape of immediate post-war China where I was brought up. I was interned during the war in a camp a few miles from Shanghai and I used to look out through the barbed wire across these deserted paddy fields where one saw big abandoned apartment houses of the French Concession surrounded by unbroken areas of water in the sun, especially in the flooding periods. There was a big Japanese airfield adjacent to the camp and it was under attack by the Americans throughout the last year of the war. I'm sure now that was the landscape I used in *The Drowned World*, though I thought I'd invented it when I was writing the book.

BARBER: As doctors and hospitals figure prominently in your recent stories, perhaps this is a reflection of your early medical training?

BALLARD: Maybe it is. Doing anatomy was an eye-opener: one had built one's whole life on an illusion about the integrity of one's body, this 'solid flesh'. One mythologises one's own familiar bits of flesh and tendon. Then to see a cadaver on a dissecting table and begin to dissect it myself and to find at the end of term that there was nothing left except a sort of heap of gristle and a clutch of bones with a label bearing some dead doctor's name – that was a tremendous experience of the lack of integrity of the flesh, and of the integrity of this dead doctor's spirit. Most cadavers, you know, are donated by doctors; and the doctors can visualise what's going to happen to their bodies after death, because they've done dissection themselves.

BARBER: What happened to your medical training – did you complete it?

BALLARD: No, I didn't. I guess I learnt enough medicine to cure myself of wanting to be a doctor. That sounds pat but I wanted to be a doctor for neurotic reasons and once I'd got over the neurosis, solved whatever problems I'd had, I found that medicine was a sort of fiction – all that anatomy and physiology. *Gray's Anatomy* is the greatest novel of the twentieth century. By comparison with our ordinary experience of our bodies, to read *Gray's Anatomy* is to be presented with what appears to be a fantastic fiction, an epic vastly beyond *War and Peace* and about as difficult to read. This is serious.

BARBER: Does early science training help in writing sci-fi, and must a sci-fi writer get the 'sci' part right?

BALLARD: No, one's not dealing with facts like the boiling point of lead or the density of neon or the precise formula of DDT. The science one's writing about is the science that comes out of one's TV tube, the mass magazines, the labels on oral contraceptive wallets, whatever. Just as the novelist, when he's writing about other people's emotions, doesn't have to know the blood pressure of the young woman who's getting excited by her lover.

BARBER: Actually, you tend to put that sort of fact into your stories.

BALLARD: Because I'm interested in that sort of thing. What I'm talking about, though, is the *kind* of scientific information that one is accurate about. It's the technology of everyday life, if you like, and how you use particular kinds of soup mix, what proof a certain brand of whisky is, how much you dilute your car antifreeze.

BARBER: Rather like Len Deighton?

BALLARD: Exactly. I think Deighton is marvellous. His narration is absolutely packed with fact material, and it's the right fact material. His eye is looking at the right things. I think Fleming did the same before he lapsed into fantasy. He knew exactly what make of camera a Japanese secret agent would carry in Europe, and this is important, because when you go on holiday in Venice or somewhere and you see Japanese wandering round they're always carrying a particular brand of camera. People's behaviour all over the world, whatever they're doing, reflects this kind of technology of everyday life. Mass magazines are based on this kind of expertise – from clothes to furnishings to food to sex to holidays. That's why the old-fashioned kind of novel is so boring, because it doesn't relate to all this.

BARBER: Haven't you said somewhere that the writer is obsolete?

BALLARD: Yes, obsolete in the traditional sense of storyteller. I think most of the people who move across the media landscape – presidents and presidents' widows, great surgeons, film stars, whatever you like to name – are generating fictions far beyond anything the writer can produce, and they're more interesting and real because they're earned out of actual experience.

BARBER: You don't think, like McLuhan, the writer's becoming obsolete because people won't read any more?

BALLARD: They probably won't read in the future. At the moment they are reading, but they're reading different things. They're reading pornographic magazines, a huge range of magazines and periodicals which offer them an instant replay and comment on their own lives. Not books – the technology of the book publisher is so out of date, he hardly has a technology. You think of the idea you want to write about, you take perhaps a year before the book is finished, you then send it through your agent to a publisher and a certain amount of wheeling and dealing goes on. Perhaps a year later – that's two years after you thought of it

29

– the book is finally published in hardcover. Two years after that it goes into paperback. So it's *four years* before a large (so-called large) audience reads the book. Well, that's the time it takes for a signal to come from the nearest *star*! So most of my writing is done for magazines because there the feedback of response from editor and readership is much quicker. Also you appear sandwiched between advertisements for motor cars and brassieres and this context is much more exciting than marbled endpapers.

BARBER: This interest in advertising, brand names, etc., seems to echo the pop painters.

BALLARD: Absolutely. I feel a tremendous rapport with pop artists and in a lot of my fiction I've tried to produce something akin to pop art. For instance, I've just published a piece in *New Worlds* called 'Princess Margaret's Facelift', in which I've taken the text of a classic description of a plastic surgery operation, a facelift, and where the original says 'the patient', I've inserted 'Princess Margaret'. So I've done precisely what the pop painters did, using images from everyday life – Coca-Cola bottles, Marilyn Monroe – and manipulated them. The great thing about pop painters is their honesty. They've turned their backs on the traditional subject matter of the fine arts – which had hardly changed since the Renaissance – and looked at their own environment and decided: yes, the shine on domestic hardware, like the refrigerator or the washing machine, the particular gleam on the mouldings of a cabinet, the moulding of door handles, are of importance to people, because these are the visual landscapes of people's lives, and if we're going to be honest we're going to use reality material instead of fiction. I want to do the same.

BARBER: Have you ever been involved in a car crash – you seem preoccupied with car crashes recently.

BALLARD: No, I've never been in one. Serious car crashes take a very long time to recover from, and if I'd been in one I'd probably have a different view of them. But the car crash is probably the most dramatic, perhaps the only dramatic, event in most people's lives apart from their own death, and in many cases the two will coincide. It's true people are dying in Vietnam and people are being involved in all kinds of other violence, but in America something like 35,000 people die in car crashes every year, and about 7,000 over here, and about 12,000 in Germany. And the totals are rising. It's a tremendous dramatic event, fascinating and even exciting. That's why all safety campaigns which aren't backed up by penal legislation are doomed to failure.

A car crash harnesses elements of eroticism, aggression, desire, speed, drama, kinaesthetic factors, the stylising of motion, consumer goods, status – all these in one event. I myself see the car crash as a tremendous sexual event really, a liberation of human and machine libido (if there is such a thing). That's why the death in a crash of a famous person is a unique event – whether it's Jayne Mansfield or James Dean – it takes place within this most potent of all consumer durables. Aircraft crashes don't carry any of these elements whatever – they're totally tragic and totally meaningless. We don't have any individual rapport because we're not moving through an elaborately signalled landscape when we go aboard an aircraft: it's only the pilot who's moving through that. It's like people who are good chess players watching top chess players play chess. When one player defeats another, the good chess player understands what has happened, whereas you and I wouldn't have a clue.

Really, it's not the car that's important: it's *driving*. One spends a substantial part of one's life in the motor car and the experience of driving condenses many of the experiences of being a human being in 1970, the marriage of physical aspects of ourselves with the imaginative and technological aspects of our lives. I think the twentieth century reaches just about its highest expression on the highway. Everything is there, the speed and violence of our age, its love of stylisation, fashion, the organisational side of things – what I call the elaborately signalled landscape.

BARBER: Surely the twentieth-century image ought to be something like a computer?

BALLARD: I don't see that. Computers may take over that role in fifty years' time, but they certainly don't play it now. Most people have no first-hand contact with computers yet. My bank balance may be added and subtracted by a computer but I'm not aware of it.

BARBER: How do people respond to your car crash theory? How did they react to your exhibition of crashed cars at the New Arts Lab this spring?

BALLARD: People used words like 'cynical' or 'perverse' or 'sick'. There's a whole series of subjects people are not really honest about. Violence is another one. Most people take the view – I would myself – that violence is wholly bad whatever form it takes, whether it's the huge violence of Vietnam or the violence of, say, police brutality. But the point is that we're also *excited* by violence, and if we are attracted to it, it may be for good reasons. If we were honest about the Vietnams of the world, the real appeal of these events, we'd see them in a totally new light and they might never happen again.

Honesty always enriches our lives, just as it has in the area of sex. I think it's good to explore it, to find out why *Mondo Cane* movies are such tremendous successes, why the newsstands of Japan and America are loaded with sadistic literature. Obviously this serves some sort of role. Conrad said: 'Immerse yourself in the most destructive element' – if you can swim, fine. I just want to know why people need violence and how can one come to terms with this thing. The Vietnam War clearly fulfils certain needs and one must be honest and work out what they are. We've all taken part in this war, given the tremendous TV coverage; we're all combatants.

BARBER: Surely the point is that we're not being shot, we're just enjoying the show.

BALLARD: Absolutely right. The important thing is that it *is* a show. All of us have made the world in which we live – we're not *forced* to watch the newsreels on television, we don't *have* to look at the pictures in illustrated magazines. This war, if it is a show, is a show at which we are the paying audience, let's remember that. All I'm saying is that one ought to be honest about one's responses. People didn't in fact feel the kind of automatic revulsion to the Biafra war that they were told they should feel. They were stirred, excited, involved. It may be that one needs a certain sort of salt in one's emotional diet.

BARBER: Perhaps these overexcited responses come from leading sheltered lives?

BALLARD: Everybody has a sheltered life. Life in northern Europe is particularly sheltered. What's the old quotation by Villiers de L'Isle-Adam: 'As for living, our servants can do that for us'. Living is one of the most boring things one can do. The really exciting things, the most interesting experiences, go on inside one's head, within those areas covered by the intelligence and imagination. It's not particularly interesting to go to the supermarket and buy six TV dinners, or have your car filled up with petrol, or shuffle up an airline escalator queue. It's much more interesting, let's say, to *think* about those things.

BARBER: That could apply to sex as well.

BALLARD: Right. I believe that organic sex, body against body, skin area against skin area, is becoming no longer possible simply because if anything is to have any meaning for us it must take place in terms of the values and experiences of the media landscape, the violent landscape – this sort of Dionysiac landscape of the 1970s. That is why I bring in things like the car crash. A whole new kind of psychopathology, the book of a new Krafft-Ebing, is being written by such things as car crashes, televised violence, the new awareness of our own bodies transmitted by magazine accounts of popular medicine, by reports of the Barnard heart transplants, and so on.

There's a new textbook of psychopathology being written, and the old perversions are dead. They relate to a bygone age. A fantasy like a man dressing his wife in a gymslip and beating her belongs to the past. What we're getting is a whole new order of sexual fantasies, involving a different order of experiences, like car crashes, like travelling in jet aircraft, the whole overlay of new technologies, architecture, interior design, communications, transport, merchandising. These things are beginning to reach into our lives and change the interior design of our sexual fantasies. We've got to recognise that what one sees through the window of the TV screen is as important as what one sees through a window on the street. But I don't mean exclusively television when I talk about the communications landscape: I mean every facet of one's experience through newspapers, magazines, television. If you take something like travelling by aircraft to Paris, it's a very fictional experience. One's actual physical experience of going from London to Paris by air is completely overlaid by advertising and commercial and fashion concepts.

BARBER: Who or what controls this sort of experience?

BALLARD: Well, it's a democratic world. It's controlled by the people who design the handrails of airport stairways, who design hostesses' dresses – the smiles the hostesses give you are themselves a kind of fictionalised smile based on an image of the sort of smile they should give us. Nothing is spontaneous, everything is stylised, including human behaviour. And once you move into this area where everything is stylised, including sexuality, you're leaving behind any kind of moral or *functional* relevance. I mean, this is the thing about the pill – not that it gives women freedom, because it doesn't – but it removes the orientation provided by the reproductive impulse so that, let's say, there's no longer any reason why intercourse per vagina should be any more satisfying or any more desirable or any more right, morally or organically, than say intercourse per anus, per navel or armpit or anywhere else you care to dream up. This is serious. In fact, women may not be necessary anyway, just as men may not be necessary to women. With various electronic aids – closed-circuit TV, videotape feedback and so on – one can see sexuality extended into a whole series of new perversions, new unions.

When people travel, have more experiences and meet more people, they tend to have more sexual experience – as they would have more meals. I feel that so-called normal sexuality (if there ever was such a thing), i.e. heterosexual relationships oriented around genital sex of a reproductive character, which sustained people through most of their adult lives in the past, will probably in future be exhausted within a few years. People may well go through a phase of their young lives, say their late teens and early twenties, when their sex lives take place in genital terms and they have children, but that will be the adolescent stage. One's real puberty will be reached when one moves into the area of, let's say, conceptualised sex, when sex is between you and a machine, or between you and an idea.

BARBER: When sex becomes so totally detached from any genital procedure, it surely ceases to be sex and just means pleasure. In those terms, food is sex.

BALLARD: Exactly. The analogy *is* with food. Apart from economic and minor religious obstacles, there's been unlimited freedom to explore every avenue and byway imaginable, and some of the greatest delicacies world cuisine can offer couldn't be farther removed from the basic nutritional requirements of the human body. I'm talking about frogs' legs, bird's nest soup, etc. Eventually, conventional sex is the first of the new perversions. Just as you would think it odd to meet an intelligent adult who ate tapioca three times a day, though nutritionally it's perfectly sound (and it's the staple diet of the Polynesians), so I think in future we'll regard people who only have conventional sex as odd. People will begin to explore all the side streets of sexual experience, but they will do it *intellectually* – there won't be any kind of compulsion to become, let's say, a high-heel fetishist – which is a monomaniac impulse. Just as recipes are now given on TV for making a veal escalope, so in twenty years' time TV will offer nightly new sexual experiments and deviations, and we'll put them into practice. Sex won't take place in the bed, necessarily – it'll take place in the head. And in a sense the head is a much richer place than the bed. Well, it is!

1971: Frank Whitford. Speculative Illustrations: Eduardo Paolozzi in Conversation with J.G. Ballard

Originally published in *Studio International*, 182: 937, October 1971

Ballard enjoyed a lifelong friendship with artist Eduardo Paolozzi, stimulating some of his most memorable writing. Like many foundation stones in his career, the connection stemmed from *New Worlds*. Just after Moorcock had taken charge of the magazine, positioning Ballard as his star writer, he wanted to broaden the scope by including articles about visual arts. Ballard knew that Paolozzi was interested in science fiction, got in touch and visited his studio with Moorcock. Paolozzi then became a contributor to *New Worlds*. Later, when Ballard became prose editor of Martin Bax's *Ambit* magazine, he and Bax recruited Paolozzi into the fold.

Ballard had long admired Paolozzi's work. In 1956, the year he published his first professional short story, 'Prima Belladonna', he attended the ground-breaking *This is Tomorrow* exhibition at the Whitechapel Art Gallery, an event widely seen as the birth of pop art. The show featured teams of architects, painters and sculptors building 'environments' around their ideas of what the future might hold, and Paolozzi was in a team with artist Nigel Henderson and architects Peter and Alison Smithson. Ballard was struck by the exhibition's focus on the consumer landscape and the surface texture of supermarkets and advertising, which he saw as the kind of everyday material that science fiction should be concerned with. Paolozzi's work left a lasting impression on him, and he rhapsodised about 'Paolozzi's great early sculptures . . . and his brilliantly original screen-prints'. Ballard sensed a kindred spirit in the artist, who would wander around scrapyards looking for industrial detritus to use in his work, reassembling it into what Ballard called 'these Easter Island totems made of machine parts . . . somewhere between circuitry and organics, a hybrid'.

Ballard and Paolozzi share certain obsessions: the mystery and symbolism of technology, and its almost sentient nature; surrealism and the nature of reality; violence as catharsis. In this fascinating conversation, chaired by art critic Frank Whitford, they touch upon these subjects, and express respect for each other's work. The original interview started with Whitford explaining that he 'began by putting it to Ballard that both he and Paolozzi are working within a surrealist tradition, a tradition which, especially in [England], has never been taken very seriously'. [SS]

BALLARD: There's something about surrealism which touched the whole Puritan conscience. It's a variety of symbolism, I suppose, a twentieth-century variety using psychoanalysis as its main language. And if you accept as a definition of a symbol that it represents something which the mind tries to shield itself from you can understand why people in puritanical northern Europe and North America have always been uneasy in the face, not just of surrealism, but of symbolism as a whole. What sort of incursion into the imaginative life of all the arts in England and North America have the symbolist poets made – Rimbaud, Baudelaire, Jarry and so on. Almost none. And the surrealists get the same treatment. But I don't see myself working in a surrealist tradition at all because surrealism was like Hollywood in a sense, was a one-generation movement. You can refer to the surrealists in connection with my own fiction, but I certainly don't use the basic techniques of surrealism, automatic writing, for instance.

PAOLOZZI: I wouldn't quarrel with the use of the word surrealism in my case because, after all, it's the reason I went to Paris, to see the surrealists. Any book on surrealism excites me still. I don't mind trying to extend the tradition. It's easier for me to identify with that tradition than to allow myself to be described by some term, invented by others, called 'pop', which immediately means that you dive into a barrel of Coca-Cola bottles. What I like to think I'm doing is an extension of radical surrealism.

BALLARD: Surrealism took one of its main inspirations from psycho-analysis, accepted the distinction between the inner world of the mind and the outer world of reality. But one, the world of the mind, is largely ruled by the laws of fictions, by one's dreams, visions, impressions and so on, and the whole idea of the unconscious as a narrative stage. Surrealism moulds the two worlds together, remakes the external world of reality in terms of the internal world of fantasy and fictions. Now what has happened, and one reason why there are really no surrealist painters in the true sense of the term today, is that this position has been reversed. It's the external world which is now the realm, the paramount realm, of fantasy. And it's the internal world of the mind which is the one node of reality that most of us have. The fiction is all out there. You can't overlay your own fiction on top of that. You've got to use, I think, a much more analytic technique than the synthetic technique of the surrealists. Eduardo does this in his graphics. He's approaching the subject matter of the present day exactly like the scientist on safari, looking at the landscape, testing, putting sensors out, charting various parameters.

The environment is filled with more fiction and fantasy than any of us can singly isolate. It's no longer necessary for us individually to dream. This completely cuts the ground from under all the tenets of classical surrealism. Why I admire Eduardo is because he's making within the span of his own lifetime as an adult sculpture and graphic art which is a complete turnabout. I mean that he's accommodated himself to this change. From his early sculpture, where he was using the technique appropriate at the time of overlaying an external reality, the world of nuts-and-bolts technology, with his own fantasies, he's gone round now to the opposite position. He is now analysing external fictions.

WHITFORD: And yet, Eduardo, you think that although it's all out there in the external world it takes a creative leap in order to recognise what's out there, and that the majority of people don't recognise, or are incapable of recognising, precisely what is there to be seen unless it's presented to them in a fine art context. You once pointed out to me the irony of the situation when we were in an apartment in New York full of pop art when all the real art, the truly significant material, was just outside the window.

PAOLOZZI: Yes, I keep thinking about that. But I'm also thinking about the way in which reality surpasses the fictions of even the wildest imagination. Like the machine for milking a rat. Incredible, yet it actually exists.

WHITFORD: But people are curiously unable, aren't they, to get outside the categories which have been imposed on them from the outside. They approach art with a very different kind of mental set from that with which they approach reality. And somehow the two worlds don't touch. Would you therefore think your role to be to take something of significance from out there and to put it in a context in which it can be appreciated with that kind of mental set?

PAOLOZZI: Well, that may be too simple. If you look at the series of etchings, the Olivetti project, the basic image remains to all intents and purposes unchanged. But the very fact of presenting it as an etching means that you have to look at this image in a much more serious way than you would if you just found it in the pages of *Time* or *Newsweek*. But it has to be a particular image; one chooses one from three thousand which one has collected over twenty years. That's what I call normal. I try to reject the ordinary ways of making the art image. But just as, possibly, for want of a better parallel, a classical artist might have done 500 drawings based on a friend, one's looking at 500 images involved with a kind of global situation and one's choosing an image which acts as a metaphor for one's particular feeling. But unless one emphasises and arranges the images into patterns of irony the point will be lost.

WHITFORD: Both of you often choose images which have to do with crashes, violence of all kinds, but particularly with car crashes. For which particular ideas or feelings does the car crash act as a metaphor?

BALLARD: Well, I don't altogether know, and I'm glad I don't know. I follow my hunches and obsessions and I agree with something Eduardo said the other day. That violence is probably going to play the same role in the seventies and eighties that sex played in the fifties and sixties. There's what I call in my book *The Atrocity Exhibition* the death of feeling, that one's more and more alienated form any kind of direct response to experience.

Although our central nervous systems have been handed to us on a plate by millions of years of evolution, have been trained to respond to violence at the level of fingertip and nerve ending, in fact now our only experience of violence is in the head, in terms of our imagination, the last place where we were designed to deal with violence. We have absolutely no biological training to deal with violence in imaginative terms. And our whole inherited expertise for dealing with violence, our central nervous systems, our musculature, our senses, our ability to run fast or to react quickly, our reflexes, all that inherited expertise is never used. We sit passively in cinemas watching movies like *The Wild Bunch* where violence is just a style.

Just over a year ago I put on an exhibition of crashed cars, what I called new sculpture, at the New Arts Lab. And I had three cars brought to the gallery. It was very easy to mount the show because the technology of moving cars around is highly developed. A crashed Mini, an A40 and a Pontiac which had been in a massive front-end collision, a Pontiac from that last grand period of American automobile styling, around the mid-fifties. Huge flared tail-fins and a maximum of iconographic display. And I had an opening party at the gallery. I'd never seen 100 people get drunk so quickly. Now this has something to do with the cars on display. I also had a topless girl interviewing people on closed-circuit TV so that people could see themselves being interviewed around the crashed cars by this topless girl. This was clearly too much. I was the only sober person there. Wine was poured over the crashed cars, glasses were broken, the topless girl was nearly raped in the back seat of the Pontiac by some self-aggrandising character. The show went on for a month. In that time they came up against massive hostility of every kind. The cars were attacked, widows ripped off. Those windows that weren't broken already were smashed. One of the cars was upended, another splashed with white paint.

Now the whole thing was a speculative illustration of a scene in *The Atrocity Exhibition*. I had speculated in my book about how the people might behave. And in the real show the guests at the party and the visitors later behaved in pretty much the way I had anticipated. It was not so much an exhibition of sculpture as almost of experimental psychology, using the medium of the fine art show. People were unnerved, you see. There was enormous hostility.

PAOLOZZI: But you didn't predict the acts of aggression against the crashed cars.

BALLARD: That's true. I didn't predict the acts of aggression against the crashed cars. That's the one thing I didn't imagine.

WHITFORD: Eduardo's exhibition is going to be organised, we hope, around four or five pieces of most recent sculpture, you know, the hopper, the bombs and so on. I think this is going to be tough, to make it heavy going for a lot of people. And it's right too that artists should make it difficult for us.

BALLARD: The man in the street might not know the difference between Duchamp and anyone else but his sophistication, his appreciation of colour, forms and so on, is enormously subtle and one can almost visualise a time when the sort of separate role of the painter or sculptor is no longer necessary, when the engineer of a Boeing designs a new airliner and the shape he chooses for an engine may itself contain all the ironic and imaginative comments on itself that the specialised imagination of people like Eduardo now provides. Eduardo can now look at some technological object and in his sculpture give it that ironic and imaginative replay in which other people recognise their first perception of that object, that first blunted perception heightened and illuminated. But the day may come when his role is no longer necessary. But at present he is necessary and his graphics are concerned with the nature of the environment on a compacted and subtle level. How new techniques in microscopy or a whole range of scientific techniques are providing access for the imagination to reach into the world of modern technology and illuminate it for the imagination of other people. I mean, he is looking at very complex worlds where you need a lot of training before the doors can even be opened.

PAOLOZZI: The public's dilemma comes from the fact that they're still looking for objects, you see, objects in the fine-art tradition, and it's this kind of object the public usually gets. Most of the American pop painters fit absolutely into the tradition of, say, post-Corot painting. A Liechtenstein is no more radical really than, say, a Manet. I mean, Manet completely revolutionised painting. If I can cast myself back to 1850, or whenever it was, I can see that Manet delivered a body blow to the safe and comfortable posture of the intelligent eye. How can any pop painter be said to have had that kind of impact, to have advanced beyond that?

As far as I'm concerned there's a slight note of disillusionment with America now; the American Dream is over. I like to think that the Olivetti things take a cool look at a special kind of pornography, the pornography of human values. And in a way forcing people to look at a state they accept, like having monkeys working with computers, and also perhaps suggesting the kind of corporate image, the faceless man. That whole world of *Fortune* magazine, the whole business language of the American stock exchange, the faceless white-collar worker turning into a mechanical man. It's not just technology, it's looking with as fresh an eye as possible at the whole realm of human experience.

WHITFORD: Jim, you were suggesting earlier that the average person now is highly sophisticated when it comes to fine art, and to grasping points made visually, and I don't think it's true in many cases. For example, there is still very little acceptance of the ideas to which Eduardo gave general currency during Independent Group meetings all those years ago, when was it, in 1952. He still puts on slide shows of images culled from all kinds of sources similar to the ones which took up the first part of the first meeting of the IG and there's still incomprehension, isn't there? Things like the source material for the Olivetti project and *BUNK!*, which is, in fact, a series of graphics reproducing many of the images first shown at that IG meeting. There is hostility even in art schools when Eduardo gives such slide shows.

PAOLOZZI: Art schools are in a desperate situation. The students are all hooked up on concept art and sub-Christo, can one say sub-Barry Flanagan? Is such a thing possible? And they see it all the time in the pages of *Studio International*. I think that kind of thing needs to be said. They're all hooked on ironic statements now. You know, someone fills a room with mud, so now we've got to fill a room with mud that's been chromium plated.

WHITFORD: Jim, were you aware of the Independent Group while it was going on?

BALLARD: I remember going to the *This is Tomorrow* exhibition in 1956, a long, long time ago. But if that show were to be mounted now I think it would be as fresh and as revolutionary in many ways. I think you have to give pop painters every credit for what they did. They liberated the external environment, perceived it at first glance. But now I think we need to look at the external environment at second glance and look beyond the worlds of consumer goods and mass iconography. You'd agree with that, wouldn't you?

PAOLOZZI: Well, you know the bombs at the Tate are my answer to the Brillo boxes.

BALLARD: To go to the Whitechapel in 1956 and to see my experience of the real world being commented upon, played back to me with all kinds of ironic gestures, that was tremendously exciting. I could really recreate the future, that was the future, not the past. And abstract expressionism struck me as being about yesterday, was profoundly retrospective, profoundly passive, and it wasn't serious. Why I became a science fiction writer – of marginal interest – was because the future was clearly better and the past was clearly worse. Abstract expressionism didn't share the overlapping, jostling vocabularies of science, technology, advertising the new realms of communication. *This is Tomorrow* came on a year before the flight of the first Sputnik, but the technologies that launched the Space Age were already underpinning the consumer-goods society in those days. How much of this did abstract expressionism represent? If an art doesn't embrace the whole terrain, all four horizons, it's worth nothing.

WHITFORD: The other day I inferred from something you said that, in your view, visual artists now more often produce relevant statements than writers do, that the fine arts today seem curiously more able to find metaphors for contemporary life than poets or novelists. Is this fair enough?

BALLARD: In the fine arts there was a major revolution somewhere about 1860 and in the field of literature that revolution hasn't yet taken place. There's a consciousness in English life that we also lack, a missing revolution here, too, which would have redefined the landscape. The fact is that the main tradition in the fine arts for the last fifty years at least has been the tradition of the new. The main pressure on the sculptor or painter is the pressure of the new. The new to the new. But in literature the main tradition is the tradition of the old. Where Eduardo and his fellow painters and sculptors are expected to find something new to say, my fellow writers and myself are expected to find something old, and to go on saying it. And nothing alerts, will strike terror into the ear of a publisher, so much as the word 'experimental'. And the next most alarming word is 'new'.

You see, the novel, despite what appears to be the technical advance of Joyce or William Burroughs, the novel is basically an early nineteenth-century structure. The writer still sees himself in the role of an Academy painter producing historical paintings. The sort of revolution achieved by the Impressionists, limited simply to its effect on the choice of subject matter, has not yet been achieved in literature. I mean, no one is yet writing like Corot painted, if you see the connection. Most writers see themselves in the same role as Homer. They're telling the story of how it happened.

PAOLOZZI: I think Ballard's subject matter and mine touch at certain points. We're both involved with the encounter with machines, and we're both involved with forcing people to look and with preventing them from escaping from certain facts. I don't want to make prints that will help people to escape from the terrible world. I want to remind them.

WHITFORD: The imaginations of you both are obviously stimulated, excited to an unusual degree, by all aspects of technology, and yet, it seems to me, the vast majority of us haven't the imagination to cope with the enormous riches which technology has conferred on us. For example, when a satellite was first used to beam TV from one continent to another for the general public someone somewhere had a brainwave. Let's use this previously undreamed-of facility to create a truly wonderful programme. But was the imagination up to it? Not at all. In the face of all that awe-inspiring technology, the switches, batteries, angles, circuits all working like magic, all they could think up was to show the first tram leaving Sydney depot at 4.30 in the morning, a baseball match from San Francisco and the Beatles in the studio in London singing a song they'd composed specially for the occasion. It was all live, of course, but it might just as well have been on film. They could have saved themselves all the trouble. Here is a classic example of how the imagination has failed to keep pace with the possibilities afforded by technology of all kinds.

PAOLOZZI: This is quite true. I'm prepared to spend the rest of my life on that premise. A lot of people who are actually manipulating the mass media are curiously undereducated. And the media are such tremendously well-made machines, like warfare, which also has a tremendous amount of money spent on it, and the machinery protects the inefficient, the amateurish, because there are so many compensatory devices. So that the bad photographer will be rescued by the art editor, the incompetent interviewer rescued by the man on the cutting-room floor.

BALLARD: Another example: I believe the space programme, both Russian and American, has failed to excite the public imagination in real terms, and I think this may also have something to do with missed opportunities by the mass media. To have been alive, to have watched Armstrong as his foot landed on the surface of the moon . . . yet the effect on people's imaginations was nil. Now why? I think you're getting a sort of radical social classification into two groups of people: those who work within modern science and technology and modern communications, who actually appreciate what's going on, and those who are outside it. And we are just members of the studio audience. We are watching the acrobats but have absolutely no understanding. We are like a charabanc party that's arrived by mistake at Sadler's Wells and are watching a ballet we don't understand. But I think it's the role of the artist to connect the two. His subject matter is no longer the world of manner and the world of ordinary appearances. He has to illuminate the real world for the ordinary person, the new world which technology and communications have created.

WHITFORD: But what is this reality? Our experience of the world is now so often at second hand, has been processed and reprocessed by many kinds of high- and-low definition reproduction methods, so that what we often take to be the reality is simply the distorted reflection of it. What I'm trying to say is something like this: a hi-fi enthusiast who knows his Beethoven only from records is likely to be disappointed when he finally hears Beethoven live. The pianist makes mistakes, the audience coughs, he gets all kinds of things not on recordings which turns the whole thing into a totally different kind of experience. Or when people see a Van Eyck in a high-quality reproduction and then see the original they can quite easily prefer the photograph. And I think that Eduardo is especially strong in exporting the subtle changes that occur, almost accidentally, from one translation into another medium. So that in the Olivetti etchings you get the original, which is a photograph reproduced in a newspaper, which is then blown up in a new photograph, retouched, and then etched, and there is a dialogue at the time between the image and the medium into which it's being transferred.

PAOLOZZI: It's got to the point where I would rather have a carpet made to look like the Mona Lisa than the real thing. It's got to that. But a multitude of experiences, of simultaneous happenings often of very disparate kinds, is a very twentieth-century thing. You watch Apollo taking off on a TV in a bar in San Francisco then go round the corner to have your shoes shined by a topless shoeshine girl. These kinds of ironical juxtapositions happen in life all the time. But what we do know is that – and there are many good funny films about this – the mass media demolish experience, negate real experience. You know, in the crowded underground train everyone's reading the *Standard* with headlines like '20,000 dead'. Any of these large human disasters, Pakistan, Ireland, but Dad, Dad still comes home and Mum's still fussing because he's fifteen minutes late. And that's what I mean by the insulating against experience.

BALLARD: But technology in terms of videotape machines and so on may make it possible to have a continuous alternative to direct experience, and I mean any alternative. You can have this played back in a slow motion, or do you want it in infrared, or do you want it this or that. Take your pick, like a jukebox. Technology may make it possible to have a continuous feedback to ourselves of information. But at the moment I think we are starved of information. I think that the biggest need of the painter or writer today is information. I'd love to have a tickertape machine in my study constantly churning out material: abstracts from scientific journals, the latest Hollywood gossip, the passenger list of a 707 that crashed in the Andes, the colour mixes of a new automobile varnish.

In fact, Eduardo and I in our different ways are already gathering this kind of information, but we are using the clumsiest possible tool to do it: our own hands and eyes. The technology of the information-retrieval system that we employ is incredibly primitive. We fumble around in bookshops, we buy magazines or subscribe to them. But I regard myself as starved of information. I am getting a throughput of information in my imaginative life of one hundredth of what I could use. I think there's an information starvation at present and technology will create the possibility of knowing everything about everything.

When Apollo 99 blasts off to Alpha Centauri we will know everything about the crew all of the time. It's always struck me that Eduardo's studio is lavishly equipped with photographic and recording equipment of various kinds. He spends a large part of his time on information collection and sorting, and an equal amount of time ensuring that he has a ready access to all the material he has around him. It's a far cry from the nearest thing I can visualise which is books on shelves in a library where one has a kind of notional access to the material but no real access because it's not all scanning in front of your mind.

And it struck me that the information system Eduardo has designed for himself comes very close to the sort of information-retrieval systems that a scientist has. For instance, Dr Christopher Evans at the National Physical Laboratories uses very similar devices and has a similar internal scanning system to make sure that he keeps up to date with whatever touches his imagination. I know no writer, other than Len Deighton, who maintains this sort of system. Most do not even grasp the fact that they need information to keep their imagination up to par. Deighton used to have, perhaps still does have, a computer, a telex and an electric typewriter plugged into the system.

PAOLOZZI: Just think that only two people in Bucharest are going to read this.

1973: Peter Linnett. J.G. Ballard

Originally published in *Corridor* 5, 1973

This interview appeared in *Corridor*, a fanzine that, as critic Phil Stephenson-Payne wrote, was 'a cheaper, thinner, *New Worlds* and featured many of the same authors'. *Corridor* was the first partnership of Michael Butterworth and David Britton, who went on to build the controversial Savoy Books empire. Britton later wrote the notorious *Lord Horror*, which led to his imprisonment in England, while Butterworth was already a published writer, having had short stories published in *New Worlds* between 1966 and 1970. Ballard, an inspiration to both Butterworth and Britton, edited some of these.

The interview took place in February 1973, with *Crash* about to be published and *Concrete Island* recently written. Ballard talks to Peter Linnett about his rejection of 'hard science fiction', about the genesis of *The Atrocity Exhibition* and about his later switch from experimental fiction to a more conventional narrative style. Ballard also tests soon-to-be familiar riffs, including what is surely the first airing of his famous equation: 'sex times technology equals the future'. [SS]

LINNETT: How did you come to be a writer?

BALLARD: This goes back to when I was a child. In fact the first book I ever produced was when I was about twelve years old, on how to play contract bridge. But my real start, oddly enough, came at school. The whole form was given, for some reason, ten pages of lines to copy out. The masters didn't give a damn what we wrote out – all they wanted to see was all this paper covered. I was copying lines out of a thriller, and I found that it was easier if I didn't bother to transcribe, but just made up the story myself. That was the first time I realised it was exciting to invent things. That set me off. I was writing all through school. Then when I went to Cambridge there was an annual short story competition in *Varsity* – I entered it, and won it. By that time I was about twenty, and pretty well convinced I wanted to be a writer.

LINNETT: How about science fiction, was that what you were starting out to do?

BALLARD: At that stage no. When I came out of the air force at the age of twenty-four I'd written a lot of short stories of a general kind, and was vaguely writing a novel, but there was something missing from all of this, as well as from most of the fiction being published then. It didn't seem to me interesting enough or about the real world. I saw the middle fifties as being more and more dominated by science and technology; and the only fiction that was about life then was science fiction. If the whole of previous fiction had not existed, if you started out from scratch in 1956, to write about the world in which you lived, you would write something pretty close to SF. You had to write it, to write about your own world.

It's a paradox – people thought of SF as something fantastic and remote from ordinary experience. But I felt that was a wrong impression; in fact here was a marvellous area, a tremendously exciting area, that ought to be explored. I wasn't interested in interplanetary travel and time travel and so on – this was the other thing, I felt SF hadn't really tapped its own possibilities. This was what I set out to do.

LINNETT: I think your first published story was 'Prima Belladonna', in *Science Fantasy* in 1956. I don't suppose the SF markets were very lucrative at this time?

BALLARD: No, the payments were extremely small – a flat rate of two pounds per one thousand words. But over the years a lot of the short stories have made a good deal of money for me, through being reprinted so many times. Some I've made a total of 1,000 pounds from – each. And many have been anthologised thirty times. The point about writing for the SF magazines was, the demand was unlimited. You were under pressure by the editor, if you had any talent at all, to go on writing. You could have a short story in every issue of a magazine, for a whole year. Which was quite unlike any of the general fiction magazines like *Argosy*, or the literary magazines – they would take a story from you but they wouldn't want another one for a long while. That's still true today. So there was this great pressure to produce material; and it was a tremendous test of one's talent and imagination.

LINNETT: Your first published novel was *The Wind from Nowhere*, in 1962, which seems rather different from the rest of your work.

BALLARD: That was really done as a kind of joke. At the time I wrote it, in 1961, my wife and I were extremely short of money. The one thing I wanted to do was to be able to give up my job as an editor of a scientific magazine so that I could write a decent novel, to think about where I was going as a writer. We'd moved to Shepperton in 1960, and I had this tremendously long railway journey in the evenings, coming home from work; there were all these small children running around, I was absolutely exhausted. The future looked extremely dismal, professionally speaking; I'd been writing short stories since 1956 but I felt I was getting nowhere. I needed a break. I didn't want to begin lowering my sights and begin churning out novels that were partly serious – you know, money-spinners. I had two weeks' holiday – I think my wife suggested it: why don't you, just for the hell of it, write a novel in two weeks? I'd always been intrigued by the idea of writing a novel very quickly and I still am. I'd like to be able to write a novel in three days. So I sat down and wrote *The Wind from Nowhere*, in literally I think ten working days. I set myself a target of something like 6,000 words a day, which I kept up for ten days. I didn't make very much money from it, but I made enough, straight away, to be able to give up my job. Soon after I wrote my first serious novel, *The Drowned World*.

LINNETT: Why did you use the form of the disaster story in your three subsequent novels?

BALLARD: I wanted to deal with a large canvas. I was interested in events, if you like; systems, of a very large area. The entire biological kingdom viewed as a single organism, as a single continuing vast memory. In fact I've never thought of them as being disaster stories, because I don't see them as having unhappy endings. The hero follows the logic of his own mind; and I feel that anyone who does this is, in a sense, fulfilling himself. I regard all those novels as stories of psychic fulfilment.

LINNETT: The apocalyptic scene is really just the means of sending the hero on this journey?

BALLARD: Right. Also I was dealing with states of tremendous psychological crisis and transformation. Possibly because of my own background in the Far East during the war, and so on, I've always felt that there are situations such as great natural disasters, or wars – huge transformations of ordinary life where the barriers between the external world and internal world of the mind begin to break down, and you get a kind of overlap. All this seemed to me a very potent, very powerful area – for my imagination anyway.

LINNETT: That's inner space? Did you coin that term?

BALLARD: I don't know whether I was the first person to use it; when I first used it I was using it in conversation, in the late fifties. When I began writing I used it specifically within the context of SF, as a counterstroke against the phrase 'outer space', which roughly speaking summed up the whole of SF. I wanted inner space, psychological space.

LINNETT: Do you prefer using a specific locale in your work? In *The Crystal World*, for instance, you set the scene in Central Africa.

BALLARD: I use the locales that seem suitable to the subject at hand. I'm drawn to certain kinds of landscape: deserts, jungles, deltas, certain kinds of urban landscape. I suppose I like very formalised landscapes, like great dunes or sandbars. I'm drawn to freeways, concrete flyovers, the metallised landscapes of giant airports. As far as naming a particular place goes – well, take something like *Atrocity Exhibition*. It's not really set anywhere. It probably is England, in fact, but it could equally be elsewhere. A lot of Americans think it's the United States. It's not specifically the US but it could be. It's really a landscape we see in our minds, which we carry around with us, which we might see as we dream.

LINNETT: Why did you start writing the so-called condensed novels?

BALLARD: I wanted to write directly about the present day, and the peculiar psychological climate that existed in the middle sixties, when I started writing them. I think the key to that book was Kennedy's assassination in Dallas, which I saw – and still do see – as the most important event of the whole of the 1960s. It seemed to me that to write about this, and about similar events that were taking place, like the suicide of Marilyn Monroe, and the emergence of political figures like Ronald Reagan, and the whole tremendous explosion of the mass media, the way politicians and advertising corporations were using them – well, it was to try to come to terms with all this. It seemed to me it was creating a landscape around us that was almost like a gigantic novel; we were living more and more inside a strange, enormous work of fiction.

LINNETT: Reality and fiction were crossing each other.

BALLARD: Yes, they'd begun to reverse – the only point of reality was our own minds. It seemed to me that the only way to write about all this was to meet the landscape on its own terms. Useless to try to impose the conventions of the nineteenth-century realistic novel on this incredible five-dimensional fiction moving around us all the time at high speed. And I tried to develop – and I think successfully – a technique of mine, the so-called condensed novels, where I was able to cross all these events, at right angles if you like. Like cutting through the stem of a plant to expose the cross-section of its main vessels. So this technique was devised to deal with this fragmentation and overlay of reality, through the fragmentation of narrative. Although the plot lines are very strong in those stories.

And they're all variants. Each of the main stories in that collection describes the same man in the same state of mental crisis, but they treat him, as it were, at different points along a spectrum – as you might compile a scientific dossier about someone, explore various aspects of his make-up. On the one hand a story like 'The Summer Cannibals', where a man and a woman have turned up at a kind of superheated resort. This is a completely naturalistic account of two people on the level of their sweat glands. In fact they don't have names, because their names are not important. Right through to the other extreme, where the character is seen as a kind of cosmic hero, a second coming of Christ, in 'You and Me and the Continuum'. The same character appears in a whole series of different roles. Any of us could be fragmented in the same way, we are all to some extent.

LINNETT: The three heroes of your earlier novels seem to be variations of the same character. Do you worry very much about character – getting across a person's character?

BALLARD: This one figure is a dominant character of mine; I suppose he's a version of myself. It's a journey towards myself – I suppose all writing is. On the whole, SF is not that interested in characterisation; it's interested in psychological roles which operate on a slightly different level.

LINNETT: *Atrocity* wasn't liked very much by critics.

BALLARD: It had very bad reviews over here, on the whole. But in Europe, oddly enough, the response was completely different. Denmark, Germany, Holland – it had a terrific reception, absolutely stupendous. What impressed me about the reviews was not that they were flattering, but that they grasped straight away what the book was about. Most of the English reviewers seemed to resent not just the technique, the style in which the book was written, but also the subject matter, that I should want to talk about such things.

In America the entire Doubleday edition was destroyed, on the orders of an executive, for similar reasons. The book has just been published in America under a different title [*Love and Napalm: Export USA*], by Grove Press. As far as response to the stories on the US SF scene goes, you've got to bear in mind that there I was seen as the originator of the so called New Wave – terrible phrase – and I was absolutely loathed by most of the American SF establishment. The old guard – Isaac Asimov and company – would almost go red in the face with anger. But that particular storm, New Wave versus Old Wave, has died down; it was just a sort of last spasm of the old guard, I think.

The so-called New Wave began long before it was seized on by the old-guard SF fans. When Ted Carnell was still editing the magazine, in the late fifties, he was already publishing the sort of material by me that was going to outrage American fans. He published 'The Terminal Beach', a story which actually started me off on the series that led to *The Atrocity Exhibition*, in 1963. Some of my early stories were already arousing tremendous hostility on the part of the British fans. They were writing to Ted and telling him, stop publishing this nonsense. So the trouble was brewing a long, long while ago.

LINNETT: *The Atrocity Exhibition* was published in 1970 – could you say anything about what you've done since?

BALLARD: Well, my last novel [*Concrete Island*] I finished three weeks ago. I'd rather not give the story away as it won't be published here for a year. But a previous novel, *Crash*, will be published in June by Cape. I spent about two years writing that. As the title implies it's about the motor car, and its whole role in our lives. It's a cautionary tale in a sense, how I see the future. Sex times technology equals the future. In the novel I take the motor car as most clearly representing technology in our lives.

LINNETT: Taking off from *The Atrocity Exhibition*?

BALLARD: In a sense it's a follow-on, but it's written in completely conventional narrative. I felt that was the best technique to use.

LINNETT: So you still feel it's OK to use conventional structures?

BALLARD: I think one has to adjust the style to the subject matter. People have accused me of being an experimental writer, but I've written ninety short stories and six novels, of which eighty short stories and six novels are completely conventional, in technique and form. I think the subject matter comes first. The style and technique serve the subject matter, and I still think there's a place for conventional narrative. It's the idea that needs to be needled. My real criticism of most of the fiction written today is that the content is so banal, so second rate, so imitative of itself. It's a fiction based on fiction, other people's fiction, rather than based on experience and ordinary life.

LINNETT: Finally, have you any advice to offer to budding writers?

BALLARD: Yes, I'd warn anyone beginning his career that the days when a writer could think of having a career, writing fiction as a main life's activity, are probably over. I think it's going to be more and more difficult for the novelist and short story writer to make a living of any kind over the next twenty years. All the signs are that fiction sales are sliding downwards, continuously. Don't regard yourself as being anyone special, as having any right to even a modest financial success, because you're a writer. So be very wary about committing yourself entirely to being a writer. I think the writer's role is very much in decline, at least for the time being.

As for SF, it's one of the healthiest fields in fiction – sales of SF books all over the world are going up, one's stuff is endlessly reprinted. I would say that SF is one of the few areas where you could actually be successful, if you have the flair. There's no problem within SF; it's outside the field that the problems lie, for the writer there.

1974: Carol Orr. How to Face Doomsday without Really Trying

Previously unpublished

This is the edited transcript of an interview conducted by Carol Orr for the Canadian Broadcasting Corporation. It was included in the series 'How to Face Doomsday without Really Trying', broadcast on the CBC radio show *Ideas* in March 1974 and produced by Judith Merril, the influential SF critic once described by Ballard as the 'strongest woman in a genre for the most part created by timid and weak men'. The series featured science fiction writers discussing doomsday scenarios, and, besides Ballard, guests included Frederik Pohl, Isaac Asimov, John Brunner, Samuel Delaney and Arthur Gibson.

The interview is remarkable for its range. Ballard discusses the perceived threat of nuclear war, backlashes against technology, the peculiar atemporality of Western societies (where any and every lifestyle choice seems immediately available), the 'greatness' of modernist architect Le Corbusier and the aesthetic qualities of concrete overpasses. The latter tangent produces some memorable quotes. When Ballard declares that he feels 'there's a certain beauty in looking at a lake that has a bright metallic scum floating on top of it', there is a sense that he is provoking Orr, and yet he is also making a serious point when he aligns the metaphoric impact of that observation with the oft-maligned freeway system of Los Angeles. For Ballard, urban infrastructure is often constructed with great skill and intelligence (a 'motion sculpture . . . of great beauty') and needs to be appreciated on its own terms, rather than automatically dismissed as a blight on the landscape. In this light, his 'urban disaster' triptych (*Crash, Concrete Island* and *High-Rise*, which take place almost wholly within a landscape of motorways, overpasses and apartment blocks, and are invariably characterised as 'dystopian' by critics) demands to be reassessed.

The interview, conducted just before the publication of *Concrete Island*, demonstrates Ballard's predictive power. In the earlier Lynn Barber conversation, he suggested that in the twentieth century the computer was unlikely to play a major role in most people's lives. Here he revises that statement, asserting that the average person has more to fear from identify theft via computer than a nuclear conflict (the 'doomsday' scenario most in vogue at the time). Elsewhere, Ballard elaborates on the ideas essayed in his introduction to *Crash*, particularly the distinction between inner space and the outer world of fictionalised reality. [SS]

BALLARD: It is quite obvious today that people are tremendously concerned with a huge range of problems that in previous generations tended to be handled by professionals, by politicians, theologians, philosophers and the like. Now we find the situation where everybody is concerned about the world in which they live, and to a large extent people have the vocabulary to talk about these critical matters. The last ten or fifteen years have shown that communities and individuals, small groups, can take actions on matters of immediate interest to them and their personal environment. They can get bus routes altered, they can have bridges built for children going to school, they can have lakes cleaned up if effluents pour into them. I'm all for people being engaged.

But at the same time there is a sort of neurotic or overemotional backlash against technology as a whole. There's been a tremendous reaction against technology in the last ten or fifteen years. I would suppose it is one of the consequences of World War II, the A-bomb, the H-bomb. In world affairs in the fifties, the whole threat of nuclear, technological warfare turned people against science and against technology, and we're seeing some of the fruits of that now. I think that's a shame because whatever we may think, science and technology are going to continue to transform our world. You know, it's the old game, if you can't beat 'em, join 'em, and we might as well join science and technology. They're going to dominate the future far more than they've dominated the present.

ORR: You don't see nuclear holocaust as a plausible doomsday?

BALLARD: I don't think that's likely in any way whatsoever. I wouldn't have thought if there were any danger to life on this planet it would come from the possibility of nuclear warfare. Far more from the misuse of, say, antibiotics, the misuse of computers or of overpopulation as a product of better health, better nutrition and the like, and a general lack of control. What I'm concerned with is that people, by reacting against technology, by taking a very Arcadian view of what life on this planet should be, may no longer be able to deal with the *real* threats when they begin to come from technology, which they probably will.

Threats to the quality of life that everyone is so concerned about will come much more, say, from the widespread application of computers to every aspect of our lives where all sorts of science fiction fantasies will come true, where bank balances will be constantly monitored and at almost any given time all the information that exists about ourselves will be on file somewhere – where all sorts of agencies, commercial, political and governmental, will have access to that information.

By turning our backs against technology, I think to some extent we are going to prevent ourselves from learning how to cope with it. Because this is something that's got to be done: it's like refusing to learn to drive a motor car.

ORR: Do you agree with Alvin Toffler that we should be adapting ourselves to the inevitable technological change?

BALLARD: We've got to, as far as possible, control the growth of technology, to steer it in the right direction. We've got to make extremely important judgements about our lives and not let technology force its judgements on us. I think we have to look very hard at the extent to which, for example, one is going to allow the widespread use of computers, of data-processing and storage devices, by commercial and governmental agencies. This is a judgement one has to make.

We might reach a point where, say, massive fingerprint files held by agencies like the FBI and Scotland Yard would have to be destroyed after a certain period. One would have, say, an automatic destruction after five years of all information about ourselves. There might be a legal requirement that all sorts of information would have a finite life, and we couldn't go on accumulating, stockpiling information about people. That's just a minor example, but I think there are huge ranges of examples that one could pick.

But I'm more interested, actually, in looking farther ahead towards the future of technology, and I can see us making a much more intimate marriage of ourselves and technology. I mean, if I were to trot out a very simple equation, I would say 'the future equals sex times technology'. And by sex I mean the whole organic expression of our personalities in terms of our bodies and our responses to life. I think all kinds of intimate junctions are going to be made between sex and technology, between *life* and technology, that will reverse the sort of logics that we accept today. One is moving almost towards a realm of morally justified psychopathology.

This is a frightening realm, but it's the sort of logic that works, for example, when you go to any motor car race. The fact that people are mangled to death in these huge machines spinning around at 150 miles an hour is something that is accepted. We accept the thrills and spills of the speedway track. Now we accept all kinds of violence. For example: for ten years Vietnam was just a TV war; it was just wallpaper, mental wallpaper. I think one learnt to enjoy – it's a terrible thing to say – but one learnt to enjoy some of the apparently insane marriages between violence and technology that took place.

ORR: Do you have some kind of faith in the future?

BALLARD: I think there are going to be enormous changes. The rate of change over the next fifty years is going to be greater. I think sometimes that more events took place in the last ten years than happened in the whole of previous history. The rate of change is just *extraordinary*. Where we are, in the early seventies, is in a sense a doldrums period. So much happened in the sixties that people were exhausted by the change – people can only take so much change. Once you could see the enormous changes that took place all over the world during the sixties, you knew it was pretty obvious that this couldn't go on for ever and it became obvious that everyone needed a period of consolidation. This is taking place now. But I think the process of radical change is going to begin again.

Now the materials are at hand thanks to advances in transplant surgery, of developments like the extra-uterine foetus, above all the application of the computer and its various spin-off devices to every aspect of domestic life as well as commercial and political life. Computers above all are leading us into a realm of really stupendous change where we'll have to look twice to even identify ourselves. I think they're going to offer us in the next twenty to thirty years a realm of bizarre possibilities that will far transcend anything that's happened so far.

ORR: Insofar as we are able to grasp the opportunities more correctly than perhaps we have in the past?

BALLARD: Yes, but we're moving into a realm where it is getting increasingly difficult to make moral judgements, to know what is right. I can only speak chiefly of England, but for example, popular views on capital punishment, on drugs, on pornography, on sexual freedom – these have changed enormously over the last ten to fifteen years. Even though there's a certain backlash against permissiveness, we're still enjoying a range of freedoms in those fields which were *unthinkable*, say, twenty years ago.

This process will continue, but we're moving into a realm where it's going to become even *more* difficult to make a judgement about whether such and such an activity is morally reprehensible or not. Whether it's of moral value to institutionalise, say, homosexual marriages between consenting adults, men or women, and the whole view of the sanctity of the family as the basic social unit on which society rests – whether that is going to be jettisoned simply because the range of experiences available to somebody in the future will preclude the establishment of very durable personal relationships of the kind that are necessary to bring up children, and the like.

Again, one sees this in the overlay of an enormous range of changes where it is difficult to make out what is right and what is wrong. The old yardsticks don't really help. One can visualise all kinds of social behaviour which run quite contrary to the sort of social and moral principles which we have been brought up on – sex, drugs, etc. These are all topics which are crying out at us from the headlines. But it is very difficult to apply the old moral yardstick to the new situations. This is why, by retreating from technology, as I think a lot of people are, we are in danger of losing our grip on the changing situation.

ORR: What is your reaction to Frederik Pohl, who said that science fiction ought to be propaganda? Did Wells and Huxley and Swift write propaganda?

BALLARD: Well, *yes*. I think science fiction has always had a sort of a cautionary role – of warning people. Warning its readers against the possibilities of the future. But I also see science fiction having a propaganda role. I see the SF writer looking into the future and saying: 'Well, twenty years from now black may be white, morally and every other way'. Think about a world in which this or that social relationship is something that may appal us. Now this might very well be the norm – it might be a social crime to think about having a child.

The whole tradition of valuing people who bring up large families, by giving them every conceivable welfare benefit and the like, tax advantages and so forth – that may be turned on its head. I mean, to think in terms of monogamous sexual relationships oriented around the idea of reproduction, of having children, may become morally offensive, it may be a crime on all levels to do this. One's got to bear in mind that a complete reversal of that kind may take place. This sort of casualness in promiscuity may become much admired: they may be necessary virtues which society as a whole will encourage.

ORR: Except that there's a difference we ought to draw here between propaganda and warnings. In order to write propaganda you must necessarily take a moral stance, mustn't you?

BALLARD: Yes, I suppose that's true but it's a science fiction writer's job, to some extent, to live on a sort of boom, on the bowsprit in front of the boat. I mean, he's got to live at least a few minutes ahead of everybody else, if not a few years. He's got to anticipate the sort of world which may exist and offer either encouragement or warning. And I think a lot of encouragement is needed. We must *urge* people to face the future, for I think that people turn their backs on the future. In a sense, our whole notion of past, present and future has become a little worn out.

One of the biggest casualties of World War II, for example, certainly as far as Europe was concerned, was that the past ceased to exist. The whole social order, based on an intimate, continuing understanding of the past and all its forms going back for many generations, underpinning the present in every conceivable way – *that* ended. I mean, you now meet people who have no idea who their *grand*parents were, which in this country, in England, was unthinkable twenty years ago.

But I think another casualty, in a sense, is the future. The present is throwing up so many options, so many alternatives, that it contains the possibilities of *any* future right now. You can have tomorrow today. And the notion of the future as a sort of programmatic device – a direction, a compass bearing that we can look forward to, a destination that we are moving towards psychologically and physically – I think that possibility is rather outdated.

We're living in a kind of continuum of past, present and future, where anything is possible. The whole distinction between fiction and reality is turned on its head. The external environment now is the greatest provider of *fiction*. We are living inside an enormous novel, written by the external world, by the worlds of advertising, mass-merchandising, politics conducted as a branch of advertising, and so on and so forth. The one node of reality left to us is inside our own heads.

ORR: This is the 'inner space' you were talking about?

BALLARD: In a sense. I suppose we are moving into a realm where inner space is no longer just inside our skulls but is in the terrain we see around us in everyday life. We are moving into a world where the elements of fiction are that world – and by fiction I mean anything invented to serve imaginative ends, whether it is invented by an advertising agency, a politician, an airline or what have you. These elements have now crowded out the old-fashioned elements of reality.

ORR: But surely that's always been a part of any consumer society? That's not something peculiar to the twentieth century.

BALLARD: It's a matter of degree. Twenty or thirty years ago the elements of fiction, that is politics within the consumer society or within one's private life, occupied a much smaller space. I can't quantify this exactly but it was sort of fifty-fifty. But now I don't think this is the case. I think we have seen the invasion of almost every aspect of our lives by fictions of one kind or another. We see this in people's homes – the way they furnish their houses and apartments. Even the sort of friends they have seem to be dictated by fictions, fantasies, by standards invented by other people to serve various ends, not necessarily commercial. But we're living more and more in a hot mix of fictions of every kind.

Now I think the writer no longer needs to invent the fiction. The fiction is already there. His job is to put in the reality. The writer's task now is to become much more analytic, especially the science fiction writer. He has to approach the subject matter of ordinary lives the way a scientist approaches nature, his subject matter. You know, one devises some sort of hypothesis and then applies it to one's material, to one's subject matter, and tests it to see whether the hypothesis is correct.

In *Crash*, I took an apparently absurd – well, terrifyingly absurd – idea, that car crashes might conceivably have a beneficial role, and tested that against the reality that people were actually experiencing. It seems to me that it may well be the case, in some strange way, that my hypothesis is correct. It fits the facts. The writer's role now is much more investigative.

ORR: I wonder if we could discuss one of the points Judith Merril was discussing with Frederik Pohl and Arthur Gibson: in planning for the future, which things do you go about altering? They were discussing reality in terms of altering human psychology, saying that you have to somehow inspire in people a desire to do what is either (a) of personal benefit, or (b) of social benefit. Now it seems to me that those two are contradictory.

BALLARD: I think it's very difficult to stand outside one's own time and take a completely dispassionate view of what's happening. I think a kind of relativity applies that makes it extremely difficult to know who we are, where we are, and where we are going at any given time. So I'd be very wary of deciding what our destination should be and suggesting that people should change or conform to it.

ORR: For people living in the thirteenth century, the sixteenth century was just as far off as we are now from the eighteenth.

BALLARD: We are living now in a radically different environment. We share our environment with the manifold products of science and technology. I mean, you can't say that a man driving a motor car is alone if he hasn't any passengers – he's sharing reality with the motor car and the highway. He's not alone in any sense whatever. I don't think people are getting weak minded, I think quite the contrary – they are getting very much more tough minded than ever before. I think they need to be.

We take in our stride a high degree of ruthlessness in ourselves, in our private lives. We take for granted a wide range of options that we exercise without any second thoughts, without any self-doubts. It's only at the fringes of our lives that we question this or that. I think quite the contrary, that people are getting very tough minded. I think that is why the future is going to be a very electric and aggressive place.

ORR: Do you agree with Pohl that we need that kind of small apocalypse to force a change?

BALLARD: Well, I think all the disasters have taken place, haven't they? I don't think there's any need for another Hiroshima or another World War II – I don't think we need another involved preview of Armageddon. These changes are taking place all the time. I welcome them: the more information flowing, the better. I mean, I prefer high-density information to low-density. I'm all for more and more experience of a more and more random kind: I think it makes for a richer and more exciting life. I think one should embrace all kinds of possibilities, no matter how bizarre, or perverse, or morally reprehensible they may seem. Change is almost good in itself.

ORR: Couldn't Hiroshima be used as an argument that mankind is bent on a kind of suicidal path?

BALLARD: No. I think nuclear weapons and the limited amount of nuclear warfare that has actually taken place shows that people are fully able to master these weapons in a way that campaigners for nuclear disarmament twenty years ago certainly wouldn't have accepted. I think mankind as a whole – the small number of men who control the use of these weapons – have made intelligent and sensible decisions, and the proof is in the pudding. We haven't had any nuclear war and I don't think we're likely to.

ORR: Surely the intelligent decision is not to have them.

BALLARD: I don't think that's the intelligent decision at all. The object of having these weapons is to preserve peace and national security and they've achieved that. No major power is likely to renounce them, so any argument about them is academic.

ORR: What about other forms of doomsday – ecology and pollution?

BALLARD: Personally, I'm not that opposed to pollution. I think the transformation of the old landscape by concrete fields and all that isn't necessarily bad by definition. I feel there's a certain beauty in looking at a lake that has a bright metallic scum floating on top of it. A certain geometric beauty in a cone of china clay, say, four hundred yards high, suddenly placed in the middle of the rural landscape. It's all a matter of a certain aesthetic response. Some people find highways, cloverleaf junctions, overpasses and multi-storey car parks to be ugly, chiefly because they are made of concrete. But they are not. Most are structures of great beauty.

When Los Angeles is forgotten, probably what will remain will be the huge freeway system. I'm certain people in the future – long after the automobile has been forgotten – will regard them as enigmatic and mysterious monuments which attested to the high aesthetic standards of the people that built them, in the same way that we look back on the pyramids or the mausoleums in a huge Egyptian necropolis as things of great beauty – we've forgotten their original function. It's all a matter of aesthetics. I think that highways for the most part are beautiful. I prefer concrete to meadow.

ORR: Why? I can see liking one or the other. I don't understand preferring something . . .

BALLARD: I feel that a modern high-rise building, or a concrete seven-storey car park, or a cloverleaf roadway junction, reflects and embraces within itself all the aesthetic laws of good design that we apply to the sorts of things we regard as beautiful in our lives, like well-designed cutlery and kitchen equipment. They embrace all the aesthetic standards of modern sculpture.

The last 100 years have consistently led us towards industrial design and the set of standards and aesthetic yardsticks which we apply in our everyday lives – to our judgement of which washing machine we buy, which motor car we prefer, which coffee percolator we like. But we must apply these yardsticks right across the board. They're the same yardsticks, the same criteria that you see in the design of motorway junctions. They are motion sculptures of great beauty. Now, to say because it's a road, it must therefore be automatically ugly is illogical. I simply accept the logic of the world in which I live.

There was a tremendous outcry over here about a year ago, when a section of motorway was built in central London, called the Westway, a six-lane concrete highway built on pillars which ran through what had been one of the most shabby areas of London around Harrow Road. People living in terrible conditions in these old Victorian, or pre-Victorian, houses – slums for the most part – raised this enormous outcry about the ugliness of this huge structure that swept through their neighbourhood. The irony is that if you drove along the highway it was actually a thing of great beauty. It's a motion sculpture beautifully constructed and designed. The ugliness resides in the landscape it is supposed to be desecrating, in these ancient, tilting, collapsing Victorian houses, which are a blot on the landscape, socially, aesthetically and in every conceivable way. That's an example of the sort of absurd and paradoxical logic that people apply.

ORR: Well, that's part of clinging to the past.

BALLARD: I think it is. But I think it's clinging to a whole set of conventional ideas that need revisiting every so often, simply because they're no longer relevant to the situation. We see the sort of general reaction against technology that is taking place, the conventional response that anything made of concrete is ugly. Quite the contrary. Le Corbusier, the great French [sic] architect, fifty years ago was claiming the great beauty of concrete, building in concrete. Architects all over the world followed him. Concrete is a beautiful material – handled intelligently it's much more a twentieth-century material than, say, wood or brick. I think we ought to look very hard at many aspects of our lives, where we take for granted that such-and-such a thing is wrong or bad. If we look at that situation, we will find that we are being illogical.

ORR: You were talking about the role of the science fiction writer – how does that affect your style? You write in a style that is very difficult, I would say. For instance, the Kennedy piece ['Plan for the Assassination of Jacqueline Kennedy'] from *The Atrocity Exhibition*.

BALLARD: Some of my experimental speculative writing is at first glance difficult, but in fact it's merely unfamiliar. One could find analogies all over the place – in the visual arts, say, when a new school of painting appeared on the scene. When the cubists first arrived, everyone was appalled. What were they doing? Why didn't they paint like the Impressionists? (Who, in their turn, in the late 1870s, horrified everybody who looked at their paintings.)

Look at every new school of painting in the same way as aboriginal peoples look at photographs and are unable to identify what's in them because the visual conventions are so strong. Our whole perception of the visual world around us is based on a whole system of conventions that help us distinguish a door or a window, or a flat tyre, or what have you. Once you begin to provide a new set of conventions, a new set of objects, everybody is thrown into confusion.

ORR: Are you writing strictly in that style now, or in the style of *The Crystal World*?

BALLARD: My last two books have been written in a completely straight-forward style. When I was writing about the Kennedys I was writing about the world of the 1960s, a world of multiplying confusions of every conceivable kind, and I used an episodic and, if you like, non-linear technique appropriate to the sort of television landscapes that we were living in then. Now, in *Crash*, my book about the motor car – and my next book, *Concrete Island*, about a man who's marooned on a traffic island in a rather large city – I'm using what I think is the appropriate technique, straightforward narration, simply because the ideas them-selves, particularly in *Crash*, are so unexpected, and incomprehensible to some people – challenging, if you like. The best way of expressing them is in a straightforward way.

ORR: You talked about whether or not there was a positive aspect to the automobile crash. Is man by nature a killer? Does he in fact want to improve his future?

BALLARD: That's a very good question. I myself think that man, if you like, is a naturally perverse animal, that the elements of psychopathology or perversity or moral deviancy are a very large part of his character. I don't think that can be changed. I think attempts in the past to provide a very rigid moral framework succeeded to some extent. I think they're going to break down now, simply because the opportunities for limitless freedom are so great.

One is moving into a realm where one will be able to practise all kinds of perversions, perform all sorts of psychopathological acts without any feeling of corruption, or without any kind of sense of moral failure. One will be genuinely free to perform, to behave in ways that now seem perverse, just as we ourselves now in the mid-seventies have a degree of freedom, feel entitled to behave in ways that, say, our parents would be deeply shocked by.

I think we're moving into a realm where moral yardsticks won't apply anyway. These words, 'psychopathology', 'moral perversity' and the like, are so heavily loaded in their own disfavour, as it were, that it's very difficult to use them. There simply isn't any other vocabulary. But I think one's got to face an event like the car crash – it does obviously satisfy people in ways they aren't prepared to recognise. There might be something about violence that provides a necessary salt in our psychic diet. And this is the sort of thing people find very difficult to accept.

ORR: Well, whether you're right or wrong it certainly means that you must ask the question if you are prescribing for the future. Does collective humanity want to improve its lot? In reading your novel *The Drought*, it seems to me that the character Ransom expresses that kind of ambiguity.

BALLARD: Right. I think we are on the threshold of a total moral ambiguity where it will be impossible to make a value judgement – yes or no, bad or good – in large areas of behaviour, because those areas aren't going to be amenable to the conventional wisdom and morality of the past. Most of our behaviour now takes place in the realm of our own completely private worlds, where our imaginations can have full play, where there are no yardsticks to apply – one can behave in any way one wishes. I think this is the big change that is coming, made largely possible by our increased wealth. I mean, we all spend less and less of our lives actually supplying the basic necessities of food and shelter – most of our spending is discretionary, more and more in the field of what one could call entertainment, or of intelligent pleasure. This is indeed a realm where anything is possible.

ORR: In classic political theory, you could attribute it to the rise of the middle class.

BALLARD: Maybe. I think you are probably right. In Europe we have seen the decline of the so-called 'working class'. In many countries of western Europe – Germany, Switzerland, Scandinavian countries – one has the impression that there is no working class, or there's a very small manual or labouring class. Most people are middle-class. I think the same is sort of true of North America. But I think we're moving into a realm where the middle class will be the next to go. To use a class terminology, everybody will be upper-class, everybody will be rich. We're moving into a realm where it will be like, say, California.

It sort of ties in with the doomsday idea. People have had this obsession at various periods that the world was coming to an end, and in the last ten years the backlash against technology and all the anxieties about pollution and the energy crisis and so on tend to feed this doomsday obsession. I find highly unlikely the notion that Western civilisation as we know it is going to be over in ten years time, as various people – what I call 'airport thinkers' – pronounce it. No, man is much too aggressive and self-seeking and determined a character to go down that easily. I mean, if you ask me if there's going to be a doomsday at all I will say 'no'. I don't think there's going to be a doomsday.

If we could see the future fifty years from now, I think we'd all be absolutely shocked. We might regard it as absolute Babylon, in the same way that, let's say, an Anglican clergyman of fifty years ago would regard life in England as being very close to that of Babylon – fifteen-year-old girls in miniskirts having their second abortions, that sort of thing. The whole freedom of the so-called permissive society would appal such a man, would have appalled my grandparents. Would have appalled my parents when they were my age.

I think we'd be shocked by the future, but I don't think people living in the future – and this is the real criterion you must apply – in the time of this emotional doomsday would regard it as such. I think they'll probably regard that doomsday in the same way the inhabitants of Las Vegas regard their city. And I think the future is going to be like Las Vegas, one enormous jukebox playing some very strange tunes. But it won't be doomsday to the people living there then.

ORR: I wonder about some of your characters. The 'Woman in White' keeps reappearing, of course, and in some of the stories I have read she always seems to be more a part of the landscape than her own self. Is that a sort of 'future' person?

BALLARD: I think so. If you ask me for a visual picture of the future, I think it'll be increasingly lunar. The psychological landscape is going to be somewhat like the physical landscape of the moon. It's going to be a matter of sharp edges, of a very sharp and angular geometry. Individual actions and individual pieces of behaviour and individual thoughts will sit in isolation, like pieces of sculpture embedded in a dune.

I think the future is going to be angular, rather hard geometrically, stripped of ornament. Unpredictable, with rapid temperature changes from black to white in the sun. I think the future will be very lunar, and people will behave in a very lunar way, very isolated from each other. Does that appeal to me? Yes it does, because I think people will have more freedom there. I mean, the freedom of isolation, the freedom of complete choice in one's behaviour. It's the difference between being in an empty city or being in a resort out of season or being on a crowded beach.

ORR: But surely there's something between that. That sounds absolutely horrifying to me.

BALLARD: I don't think there are going to be any more in-betweens. That's my latest prophecy! No, I think one's moving into a realm where everything will become increasingly stylised. It's quite obvious that nothing is going to exist at all that doesn't serve some sort of imaginative role in the future. It won't simply be because we won't notice its existence – just as we don't notice a piece of furniture unless it happens also to be an aesthetic object, if it conforms to various visual conventions of the day.

We tend to assume that people want to be together in a kind of renaissance city if you like, imaginatively speaking, strolling in the evening across a crowded piazza. I don't think people want to be together, I think they want to be alone. People are together in a traffic jam or in a crowded elevator in a department store, or on airlines. That's togetherness. People don't want to be together in a physical sense, in an actual running crowd on a pavement. People want to be alone. They want to be alone and watch television.

ORR: I don't.

BALLARD: Most people do, actually.

ORR: I don't want to be in a traffic jam, but I don't want to be alone on a dune, either.

BALLARD: No, I didn't suggest that you should be. But I'm saying that you probably have more privacy in your life than you realise. One lives in a world where, even if one's apartment or hotel room tends to be small, one tends to be the only occupant of it. One is not living in something like an eighteenth- or nineteenth-century city where it was, metaphorically speaking, like a crowded noisy tenement, where we knew every neighbour, where we were surrounded by relations of many generations, in an intimate sort of social context made up of hundreds of people. This isn't the case.

Most of us lead comparatively isolated lives. 'Being alone on a dune' is probably a better description of how you actually lead your life than you realise, compared with the life you would have lived fifty years ago, or 150 years ago, where you would have been surrounded in a large tenement or a large dwelling in an overcrowded city, say. If you think of a medieval town, well, probably every inhabitant knew every other inhabitant intimately, or at least knew something of them. One's not living in that world any more.

The city or the town or the suburb or the street – these are places of considerable isolation. People like it that way, too. They don't want to know all their neighbours. This is just a small example where the conventional appeal of the good life needs to be looked at again. I don't think people would want to have the sort of life that was lived 100 years ago or 200 years ago.

ORR: On that note we're going to have to close up shop . . .

1974: Robert Louit. Crash & Learn

Originally published in *Foundation, The Review of Science Fiction* 9, November 1975. Translated by Peter Nicholls

Like Jannick Storm, editor and translator Robert Louit played a critical role in promoting Ballard's work beyond the English-speaking world. Louit lived in London in the early 1970s and translated many of Ballard's novels into French (as well as some by Philip K. Dick), and, again like Storm, he was there at the birth of one of Ballard's most significant works. According to Ballard's then agent John Wolfers and Ballard archivist David Pringle, Louit played a major part in editing the original, extensive manuscript of *Crash* down to a publishable size.

This interview first appeared in April 1974 in *Magazine Littéraire*, with Louit translating Ballard's answers into French. The version here is a back-translation by science fiction critic Peter Nicholls, who, in an earlier review of *Crash*, wrote that Ballard was 'advocating a life style quite likely to involve the sudden death of yourself or those you love'. When Nicholls came to realise that Ballard's aims were less shock tactic and more social commentary, he decided as editor of *Foundation* to correct that earlier assessment by reprinting the *Magazine Littéraire* interview alongside Ballard's introduction to the French edition of *Crash* (again, back-translated by Nicholls from the Louit version). In his original introduction, Nicholls relates that Ballard had told him 'a number of interesting things ... about the reception of *Crash!* [sic]. He commented that it had been received less enthusiastically in the USA, and more enthusiastically in France, than he expected. He now believes this is because "there is a tradition of intellectual pornography in France, while in America pornography is still disreputable".'

The interview covers Ballard's views on science fiction, the experimental nature of *The Atrocity Exhibition*, the commodification of surrealism and the increasing dominance of television. At this stage, *Concrete Island* had been published but was yet to appear in France, so Louit made no mention of it. Note the exclamation mark in *Crash*'s title, consistent with the French publication. [SS]

LOUIT: What's your position today with respect to science fiction?

BALLARD: When I began writing, towards the end of the fifties, science fiction was the only branch of literature which permitted speculative writing making evaluations of human reaction to the various upheavals, scientific, technological, political, which were happening them. I turned naturally towards the genre. I'm tempted to say that half of my work preceding *The Atrocity Exhibition* was science fiction; the other half belongs to fantasy or to allegory pure and simple – for example, my short story 'The Drowned Giant'. I consider that I left the genre completely with *The Atrocity Exhibition*, but I don't have any substitute terminology to offer you for what I actually write. *Crash!* is not a science fiction novel, but could nevertheless be read as one, because it contains elements of political and 'sociological' thought which one finds in certain works of the genre. I wouldn't want a reader tackling *Crash!* to let himself be fenced in by the limitations (which don't, however, necessarily imply a pejorative judgement) that are habitually attributed to science fiction.

LOUIT: You once defined science fiction as 'the literature of techno-logical optimism, born in America in the twenties'. It seems to me that your work takes the exact opposite course to the one implied by this. Perhaps the subject matter remains to a certain extent technological, but you are less occupied in speculating on the future than on the present, whose strangeness and fascination you unveil. The result is not always optimistic.

BALLARD: Exactly. I don't see much I could add to that description. For some years I have been trying to show the present from an unusual angle.

LOUIT: This evolution of yours culminates in the 'fragmented' stories of *The Atrocity Exhibition*.

BALLARD: In effect. The determining factor for me was the assassination of John Kennedy in 1963: it is, among other things, the subject of *The Atrocity Exhibition*. I wrote a lot about the Kennedys at that time because they seemed to me a kind of twentieth-century House of Atreides. Their history illustrates particularly well the way in which, little by little, the fictional elements of everyday reality have ended up by completely masking the so-called 'real' elements. It's the same in politics: presidential elections in the USA are nothing less than the crashing together of two spheres of fiction, like the collision of two galaxies. As to private life, it too is obedient to the influence of images projected by newspapers, television, advertising posters, etc. These can be sensed in the way people decorate their homes, the way they dress, in the whole apparatus of their relation to others. To speak of this new world I was led, in *The Atrocity Exhibition*, to fragment contemporary reality so that I could reassemble its elements paragraph by paragraph and show its springs. This method allowed me to examine simultaneously the different strata that make up our own experience of the actual world: the level of public events such as war, the conquest of space or the story of Kennedy; the level of everyday life, of people who get into the car every morning, work at the office, convalesce in a hospital etc.; and the level of our fantasies. In *The Atrocity Exhibition*, then, I tried to blend these three levels just as we constantly do in life, every day. The conventions of the ordinary 'realistic' novel don't allow this approach. Linear narrative is like a railway running from one point to another from which one cannot deviate; it prevents simultaneous perceptions. Now, my aim is to show that these three levels, public, private and fantastic, cut backwards and forwards across one another: that points of intersection exist between them. In spite of the linear aspect of its narrative, *Crash!* relies equally on this technique, which you could compare to a kind of radar.

LOUIT: So the construction of your latest books exactly reflects our way of seeing the world every day.

BALLARD: Yes. It's a little as if I were leading the reader to a deserted laboratory, and that I put a collection of specimens and all the necessary equipment at his disposal. It's his job then to relate these elements together and create reactions from them. I believe that contemporary fiction has to direct itself more and more in this direction. The novelist must stop looking at things retrospectively, returning to past events which he lays out meticulously as if he were preparing a parcel which he will afterwards deliver to the reader, telling him: 'It was like that'. The essence of the traditional novel is in the formula 'that's what happened'. I believe that today it's necessary to write in a more speculative way, to write a kind of 'investigation novel' which corresponds to the formula 'this is what's happening' or 'this is going to happen'. In an enterprise of this kind, the author doesn't know in advance what he's going to produce. He loses his omniscience.

LOUIT: For the classical novel, which is an object enclosed and complete within the spirit of its author, you substitute an open narrative in which the act of reading itself becomes part of the creative process, or rather the process of investigation.

BALLARD: That's it. In *Crash!* I'm content to give the reader a spectrum of possibilities, but it's up to him to choose between them. In the classical novel, we can discover the moral, political and philosophical position of the author in every event described. In *Crash!* my position hasn't been clarified, since I'm content to supply a cluster of probabilities. It's the reader's reactions that assure the functioning of the book: in the course of the story, everyone has to reach a limiting position beyond which he is not able to accept what is proposed to him. I don't say that I expect the world to end in a sort of automotive apocalypse fed on sex and violence; I offer this vision as one extreme hypothesis because it seems to me inscribed in the present.

LOUIT: In *Crash!* you systematically establish correspondences between parts of the body, parts of the automobile, elements of the landscape, real people and the mythical images of the media.

BALLARD: I wouldn't want to give the impression of being excessively schematic, but I'm convinced that when an event takes place on one of the three levels of reality we spoke about earlier, it necessarily affects the other two in a more or less perceptible way. So, when I evoke the suicide of Marilyn Monroe in *The Atrocity Exhibition*, it's because it doesn't appear to me as simply the death of a woman, but as a kind of space-time disaster, a catastrophe which created a rupture in our perception of time and space, as if we saw the abrupt subsidence of an immovable object before our very eyes. In effect, Marilyn Monroe, the Kennedys, the astronauts, are part of our mental landscape with as much right as the streets and houses that we frequent.

LOUIT: I feel bound to repeat the celebrated epigram of Dali, made from the same perspective: 'The soul is a condition of landscape'.

BALLARD: That seems a very important point to me. I'm very interested in a certain period of surrealism, particularly among the painters, for it seems to me that I recover from them a demeanour of the spirit close to my own. Dali splits up the elements of reality and assembles them to constitute a kind of Freudian landscape. We entertain certitudes about the subject of reality which permit us to live: I'm sure that there is an elevator at the end of this corridor which will bring me to a level whose solidity is not in doubt. The work of Dali and other surrealist painters is to undermine these certitudes. There again, it's necessary to propose an extreme hypothesis.

LOUIT: This surrealist influence applies especially to your work before *The Atrocity Exhibition*.

BALLARD: But surrealism itself is behind us today; it is a finished period. For Dali to be able to paint soft watches, it was necessary that real watches be hard. Now today, if you ask someone the time in the street you might see the effigy of Mickey Mouse or Spiro Agnew on the dial. It is a typical and entirely commonplace invasion of reality by fiction. The roles have been reversed, and from now on literature must no so much invent an imaginary world as explore the fictions that surround us. I realise that I am hesitating more and more to invent things when I write. In *Crash!* I reduced the number of characters and situations to the minimum, because from now on it seems to me that the function of the writer is no longer the addition of fiction in the world, but rather to seek its abstraction, to direct an enquiry aimed at recovering elements of reality from this debauch of fiction.

LOUIT: The first part of your work seems directly inspired by painting, while your more recent books find their sources in photography, the cinema and television. This corresponds also to a change of construction material: you are moving from the beach sands of *Vermilion Sands* to the motorway concrete of *Crash!*

BALLARD: The reason for this change is that until *The Atrocity Exhibition* I was describing imaginary places. Afterwards, I turned to the landscape of technology and the communications industry. And it's photography and the cinema above all which provide us with reflections of this landscape. Television seems to me to play a particularly important role, in the continuous flood of images with which it inundates our brain: it perceives things on our behalf, and it's like a third eye grafted on to us.

LOUIT: You even integrate certain specifically cinematic techniques, such as slow motion, into your writing.

BALLARD: Slow motion introduces a different sense of time, a fresh perception of things – often associated today with acts of violence, or more or less physical excitements. It happens in the violent episodes in the films of someone like Sam Peckinpah, and in the sports programmes on television, where important incidents of a contest are shown a second time in slow motion only an instant after they have taken place. A moment of terrifying violence like the collision of two cars hurtling together at full speed can in this way be metamorphosed into a kind of slow and gracious ballet. What interests me in this technique is that while it suppresses the classical emphasis on character, it brings about a stylisation of events which confers on them a formidable weight.

1975: Philippe R. Hupp. Interview with J.G. Ballard

Originally published in French as 'Entretien avec J.G. Ballard', *Magazine Littéraire* 96, January 1975. Translated by Dan O'Hara

Ballard's novels have always been translated into French with alacrity. *Concrete Island* was already in translation in time for review in the January 1975 edition of *Magazine Littéraire*, and Antoine Griset's review was both penetrating and positive. Griset immediately connected the predicament of Ballard's protagonist, stranded on an urban desert island between motorway intersections, with the extremes of social inequality within our society. 'The image or the idea of a man dying of hunger only a step away from a haven of abundance is tragically familiar,' Griset writes, noting how absurd it is that such distress has become a banal commonplace. While admiring the 'immense talent' of Ballard in transforming a vague, banal terrain into a hallucinatory hell – a feat also achieved in *Crash* – Griset observes that although *Concrete Island* may be a continuation of the earlier novel, this time the automobile is a mere symbolic pretext for an examination of the flip-side of our ordered, automated, aseptic lifestyle.

Griset sees the real focus of *Concrete Island* as being on the flotsam of urban Man Fridays (or should that be 'Men Friday'?) living in the interstices of modern cities: the invisible masses we observe daily from behind the safety of the windscreen or the office window. In the novel Maitland, an affluent architect who crosses this invisible barrier, decides to remain on the concrete island, having triumphed over its obstinate vagrants. Yet Griset suggests that if the Maitland who first arrived on the island dies and is transformed into a new, stronger version of himself, he also remains afraid to recognise his own true nature. In a brilliant insight into Ballard's metafictional method, Griset implies that this transformation of the protagonist is intended to provoke a similar transformation in the reader. *Concrete Island* is less concerned with awakening a new moral knowledge than with demonstrating the ways in which the mirror-world of own native brutality is just on the other side of the windscreen.

The following brief interview was printed alongside Griset's review. Mostly concerned with the novel Ballard was then in the early stages of writing, *High-Rise* (which Hupp seems to believe would be called *The Towers*), it contains an intriguing reference to Ballard conducting research on the relation between criminal behaviour and the urban environment. It is an important nugget, because it seems to have started a line of enquiry that became a central topos of his writing, leading from *Concrete Island* through *High-Rise* to *Running Wild* and the loose tetralogy bookended by *Cocaine Nights* and *Kingdom Come*. [DOH]

HUPP: You're in the process of writing a new novel called *The Towers*.

BALLARD: In fact I still haven't found a title. It's a book about what in England and the USA are called 'high-rises', these residential towers which can have forty or fifty floors or more. I saw a film about Poland last week, in which one complex of apartments had twenty floors and was a kilometre in length! I've been interested for several years now in new lifestyles which permit modern technology; skyscrapers have always attracted me. The life led there seems to me very abstract, and that's an aspect of setting with which I'm concerned when I write – the technological landscape.

HUPP: Have you read *The World Inside* by Robert Silverberg? It's a novel in which people live in groups of 800,000 in vertical cities. And Silverberg, instead of simply planting the people of today in a futuristic setting, is concerned with showing how their mentality and their social life would be affected.

BALLARD: I haven't read that book, but what interests me is the present. I don't want to extrapolate too far – there's the risk of becoming detached from reality. Although I did write a story a few years ago, 'Build-Up', in which one city occupied the entire universe. It's a quite fascinating subject.

HUPP: You've already examined housing schemes?

BALLARD: I did research before sitting down to write. For example, in cities, the degree of criminality is affected by liberty of movement; it's higher in culs-de-sac. And high-rises are culs-de-sac: 2,000 people jammed together in the air . . .

HUPP: Entirely isolated.

BALLARD: Cut off from the rest of the world. In this kind of situation, all sorts can happen. Above all I'd like to examine the psychological modifications which occur without the knowledge of the inhabitants themselves, to see to what degree the mind of someone who drives a car or lives in a concrete high-rise has been altered. In the course of my investigations, I observed that there now exists a new race of people who are content in their little prisons, who tolerate a very high level of noise, but for whom the apartment is nothing more than a base allowing them to pass the night in comfort, as they're absent during the day.

HUPP: Will this new novel be as symbolic as *Crash* and *Concrete Island*?

BALLARD: I think it will be in the same vein, although this time I'm no longer concentrating on one single character.

HUPP: And after that, will you further continue your series on the 'technological landscape'?

BALLARD: No. I don't have an idea for a novel, but I'd very much like to write several stories that I haven't had the time to write these last few years. And it's been a long time since I've written anything in the way of imaginative narratives, romances . . .

1975: James Goddard and David Pringle. An Interview with J.G. Ballard

Excerpted from the original published in James Goddard and David Pringle (eds), *J.G. Ballard: The First Twenty Years*, Hayes: Bran's Head Books, 1976

Anyone studying Ballard's work owes a debt of gratitude to David Pringle. For over forty years, he has excavated almost everything there is to know about Ballard's career and the forces that shaped his writing. From 1975 to 1995, Pringle conducted seven interviews with him. With James Goddard, another respected SF editor and critic, who had previously interviewed Ballard in 1970 for his fanzine *Cypher*, he edited the first book-length publication on the author's work, *J.G. Ballard: the First Twenty Years* (1976). It included an expanded version of the interview excerpted here.

Pringle published two further books on Ballard, *Earth is the Alien Planet: J.G. Ballard's Four-Dimensional Nightmare* (1979) and the exhaustive *J.G. Ballard: A Primary and Secondary Bibliography* (1984), which contained another long interview. From 1981 to 1996, he produced twenty-five editions of *JGB News*, a Ballard newsletter with frequent input from Ballard himself. He compiled the material for Ballard's non-fiction collection, *A User's Guide to the Millennium* (1996), and produced special Ballard editions of the journal *Foundation* and the science fiction magazine *Interzone* (he was editor of both at different stages). In 1982, based on a conversation of several hours' duration, he pieced together Ballard's remembrances about Shanghai, the pressures of war and his first years in England, resulting in an oral biography, 'From Shanghai to Shepperton', published in *Foundation* 24. At the time, it was Ballard's longest meditation on his war years, a taste of what was to come in *Empire of the Sun*.

This interview, conducted at Ballard's Shepperton home on 4 January 1975, takes place just after Ballard had written *High-Rise* and covers much ground: the Shanghai years, the mystery of ruins and abandoned buildings, Ballard's aversion to being branded an 'experimental' writer, his tenure in the RAF, the leisure class of the future, the habits of French drivers and the death of the Space Age. [SS]

GODDARD: Do you think your period of internment under the Japanese has had any effect on the kind of fiction you produce?

BALLARD: I would guess it has. The whole landscape out there had a tremendously powerful influence on me, as did the whole war experience. All the abandoned cities and towns and beach resorts that I keep returning to in my fiction were there in that huge landscape, the area just around our camp, which was about seven or eight miles from Shanghai, out in the paddy fields in a former university. There was a period when we didn't know if the war had ended, when the Japanese had more or less abandoned the whole zone and the Americans had yet to come in. All of the images I keep using – the abandoned apartment houses and so forth – must have touched something in my mind. It was a very interesting zone psychologically, and it obviously had a big influence – as did the semi-tropical nature of the place: lush vegetation, a totally waterlogged world, huge rivers, canals, paddies, great sheets of water everywhere. It was a dramatised landscape thanks to the war and to the collapse of all the irrigation systems – a landscape dramatised in a way that it is difficult to find in, say, western Europe.

PRINGLE: Your Far Eastern childhood interests me. Did you live anywhere else apart from Shanghai?

BALLARD: No, but we travelled a fair amount in the Far East. We made a trip to America in 1939, just before the outbreak of the war, across the Pacific via Hawaii. By the time I came to England at the age of sixteen I'd seen a great variety of landscapes. I think the English landscape was the only landscape I'd come across which *didn't* mean anything, particularly the urban landscape. England seemed to be very dull, because I'd been brought up at a much lower latitude – the same latitude as the places which are my real spiritual home, as I sometimes think: Los Angeles and Casablanca. I'm sure this is something one perceives – I mean the angle of light, density of light. I'm always much happier in the south – Spain, Greece – than I am anywhere else. I think a lot of these landscapes meant a great deal. The English one, oddly enough, didn't mean anything. I didn't like it, it seemed odd.

England was a place that was totally exhausted. The war had drained everything. It seemed very small, and rather narrow mentally, and the physical landscape of England was so old. The centre of London now is a reasonably modern city – so much of it has been rebuilt. Then, of course, none of these high-rise office blocks existed, only the nineteenth-century city. The rural landscape of meadow didn't mean anything to me. I just couldn't latch on to that. That's why the SF of John Wyndham, [John] Christopher and so forth I can't take. Too many rolling English meadows. They don't seem landscapes that are psychologically significant, if that means anything.

PRINGLE: The visual values are a strong element in your writing. Is this just from growing up in a place like Shanghai, or did you have any artistic background?

BALLARD: Not particularly. I've always wanted really to be a painter. My interest in painting has been far more catholic than my interest in fiction. I'm interested in almost every period of painting, from Lascaux through the Renaissance onwards. Abstract expressionism is about the only kind of painting I haven't responded to. My daughter, about two years ago, bought me a paint set for my birthday. I'm still waiting to use it. When I start painting I shall stop writing!

I've said somewhere else that all my fiction consists of paintings. I think I always was a frustrated painter. They are all paintings, really, my novels and stories. The trouble is I haven't any talent – that's a bit of a handicap. I approach many of these stories of mine, like the *Vermilion Sands* stories – even the novels like *Crash* – as a sort of visual experience. I'm thinking particularly of painters like – I hate the phrase pop art because it has the wrong connotations – the British and American pop artists, or people close to them, like Hamilton and Paolozzi over here, and Wesselmann, Rosenquist. Warhol above all: a tremendous influence on me. I composed *Crash* to some extent as a visual experience, marrying elements in the book that make sense primarily as visual constructs.

PRINGLE: I recall in 'The Assassination Weapon' where you simply say: 'Guam in 1947', and this evoked for me the landscape of some American airbase littered with rusty wire, etc. Have you actually seen these things?

BALLARD: Yes, I have, absolutely. A lot of that post-technological landscape stuff that people talk about is a straight transcript. After World War II, the American war machine was so prolific – you got B-29s stacked six deep on the ends of airfields. The riches of this gigantic technological system were just *left*. Right from early on I was touched not just in an imaginative way – but as though some section of reality, of life, and movements of time, were influenced by the strange paradoxes that are implicit in, say, a field full of what seem to be reasonably workable cars, washing machines or whatever, which have just been junked there. The rules which govern the birth and life and decay of living systems don't apply in the realm of technology. A washing machine does not grow old gracefully. It still retains its youth, as it were, its bright chrome trim, when it's been junked. You see these technological artefacts lying round like old corpses – in fact, their chrome is still bright. All these inversions touch a response to the movements of time and our place in the universe. There's no doubt about this. I think perhaps my childhood was spent in a place where there was an excess of these inversions of various kinds.

I remember when the Japanese entered China after Pearl Harbor, in December 1941. I was going to do the scripture exam at the end-of-term examinations at the school I went to. Pearl Harbor had just taken place, the previous night, I suppose, and I heard *tanks* coming down the street. I looked out the window and there were Japanese tanks trundling around. It doesn't sound very much, but if tanks suddenly rolled down this street you'd have a surprise – Russian tanks, say. The Japanese took over the place, and they segmented Shanghai into various districts with barbed wire, so you couldn't move from Zone A to Zone B except at certain times. They'd block off everything for security reasons, and on certain days the only way of going to school was to go to the house of some friends of my parents who lived on one of these border zones, between I think the French Concession and the International Settlement. There was an abandoned nightclub, a gambling casino called the Del Monte – this is just a trivial example – a huge building in big grounds. We'd climb over the fence and go through, and go up the main driveway on the other side of the border zone, and go to school. This abandoned casino, a huge multi-storeyed building, was decorated in full-blown

Casino Versailles style, with figures holding up great prosceniums over bars and huge roulette tables. Everything was junked. I remember a roulette table on its side and the whole roulette wheel section had come out, exposing the machinery inside. There was all this junk lying around, chips and all sorts of stuff, as if in some sort of tableau, arranged, as I've said, by a demolition squad. It was very strange.

Now I was only about eleven when this was going on. Examples like this could be multiplied a hundred times. Our camp was a former university campus, occupying I suppose about one square mile. In fact, we occupied about two-thirds of the campus. There was a section of buildings which for some arbitrary reason – maybe the Japs were short of wire – they'd left out. Something like fifteen buildings were on the other side of the wire. You can imagine a little township of big, two- or three-storey buildings, the nearest of which was about twenty yards away. A complete silent world, which I looked out on every morning and all day from my block.

After about a year the Japs agreed to allow these buildings to be used as a school, so we used to enter this place every day, and walk through these abandoned rooms. Military equipment was lying around all over the place. I saw rifles being taken out of a well. All rifles were taken away, but spent ammunition, ammunition boxes and bayonets, all the debris of war, was lying around. We used to walk through this totally empty zone. It had been deserted for years. I'm sure that that again must have had a great impact on me. There were curious psychological overtones. One's the product of all these things.

PRINGLE: Do you regret the world of the past, the pre-war world, in any way? I'm thinking of your story, 'The Garden of Time', where one man appears to be trying to halt history.

BALLARD: No, I don't. I think some social changes that took place in this country in the mid-sixties are the best and greatest thing that ever happened here. It's slid back now, but for about five years this country entered the twentieth century, and a whole new generation of people emerged – the youth explosion. The class divisions began to break down, which was so marvellous. It all slammed into reverse a couple of years ago, which is a shame. But I certainly don't feel nostalgic, because I came from a background where there was no past. Everything was new – Shanghai was a new city. The department stores and the skyscrapers were about my age. I'm exaggerating a bit, but not much. The place didn't exist before the year 1900. It was just a lot of mosquito-ridden mudflats. I was brought up in a world which was new, so the past has never really meant anything to me. The use in that story of an old aristocrat, or whatever he was, was just a convention.

PRINGLE: You studied medicine at Cambridge. Many of the protagonists of your stories have in fact been doctors. Is there a rationale for this?

BALLARD: Well, I suppose if I hadn't become a writer I would have been a doctor. So in a sense the protagonists of these stories are myself. I couldn't make them writers – the obvious thing to do was to make them doctors. My training and mental inclination, my approach to everything, is much closer to that of a doctor than to that of a writer. I'm not a literary man. But I am interested in – admittedly popular – science. I approach things as a scientist would, I think. I've a scientific bent; it's obvious to me that these characters are what I would have been if I hadn't been a writer.

PRINGLE: Your National Service period in the RAF – did that influence you at all? Were you a bomber pilot?

BALLARD: No, I did a sort of basic training course but I left after a while. In fact, I didn't do National Service. I was exempt. I thought I'd like to try flying, to see what it was like. I thought I'd like to try service life, because it was at least sort of forward-looking and that helped. This was in 1954. I was in a bit of a dead end. I hadn't started reading SF. I wanted to be a writer. I was writing short stories, planning a novel like any novice, but I wasn't organised. It struck me – I was very interested in aviation – that it might be worth going into the service for a couple of years – one of those short service commissions they had then. You could go in for a very short space of time, just to see what it was like.

But in fact it wasn't anything. It was completely unlike anything I imagined. I didn't like service life at all. Also, I spent my entire period in Canada, out in the back of beyond. I was writing while I was there. The moment I got myself organised I wanted to get out of the RAF and get back to London, and start churning the stuff out. So I resigned my commission and came back to England. I had to get a job. Ted Carnell arranged for me to get a job with the parent company, on a technical journal. I moved from there to being assistant editor of a scientific journal. I stayed there until about 1961.

PRINGLE: You were actually writing before you'd read any SF?

BALLARD: Oh yes. I wasn't writing SF, though. It never occurred to me. I started writing SF partly because it seemed very exciting – and the sorts of things I wanted to do in SF had not been done by anybody else – also because there were so many magazines. You could write for so many. This was when I was a complete novice, hadn't published a single story. I could see at a glance. There were ten American magazines and about four English ones. So there was a market greater than the literary field then. There were very few literary journals of any kind, and they were very prestigious – you know, *Horizon*, etc. It was obvious you couldn't make a career out of writing short stories for *Horizon*. It wasn't a matter of making money, but of actually being able to write a good deal, to write with freedom too, which you could do in the SF magazines. You were free, within the rough conventions of the field. You don't have that sort of freedom in literary journals.

PRINGLE: The picture you draw of yourself as being interested in science, editor of a science journal and so on, makes me wonder for the first time why you wanted to be a writer at all.

BALLARD: If one's got an imagination, if the imagination's going over-time, you have to start writing it down. If you've got a talent for that sort of thing, you write it down without too much difficulty. As a child, I was good at essays, writing stories. Even at school, I was writing short stories. It was something that just grew out of childhood. I would have qualified as a doctor, without any doubt, but for the fact that the imaginative pressure to write was so strong. I was beginning to neglect medicine altogether. I was primarily interested in anatomy and physiology. These were the subjects that I did for two years. Once I had covered the basic course in those subjects, I found more advanced medicine so technical that it didn't relate to the system of metaphors that, say anatomy is so rich in, or physiology, or pathology. Once you've dissected the cadaver – thorax, abdomen, head and neck, etc. – you go on to more exhaustive anatomy, of, say, the inner ear, and the metaphors aren't so generously forthcoming.

So I'd had enough of it in two years. I could see it then became a very technical matter and also became applied. I'd go into hospital and actually be lancing boils and looking at people with skin diseases. I didn't want that. I was more interested in the general scientific underpinning of medicine. In some ways I wish I had become a doctor. Such a mind-blowing course. If you've known anybody that's gone through the medical degree course, they all say that you leave half your mind behind. The feats of memory required are really absolutely gigantic.

GODDARD: One of the most popular areas of your work is the series of *Vermilion Sands* stories. A critical reading of these shows that they are all, to some extent, variations on the same theme. Could you tell us something about why you wrote these stories?

BALLARD: I've never really analysed them myself. I suppose I was just interested in inventing an imaginary Palm Springs, a kind of world I imagined all suburbs of North America and northern Europe might be like in about two hundred years' time. Everyone will be permanently on vacation, or doing about one day's work a year. People will give in to any whim that occurs to them – like taking up cloud sculpture – leisure and work will mesh in.

I think everybody will be very relaxed, almost too relaxed. It will be a landscape of not so much suburbia but exurbia, a kind of country-club belt, which will be largely the product of advanced technologies of various kinds, for leisure and so forth. So you will get things like computers meshed into one's ordinary everyday life in a way that can be seen already. I'm just writing about one direction that the future is taking us. I think the future will be like *Vermilion Sands*, if I have to make a guess. It isn't going to be like *Brave New World* or *Nineteen Eighty-Four*: it's going to be like a country-club paradise.

PRINGLE: Is this a sort of literary conceit, or what you really think the future's going to be like?

BALLARD: I'm not a literary man at all. That's my guess at what the future will be like!

PRINGLE: It's not the impression of the future people would get from your books as a whole, where you tend to write about disaster and doom.

BALLARD: I think that's a false reading of my stuff. I don't see my fiction as being disaster-oriented, certainly not most of my SF – apart from *The Wind from Nowhere*, which is just a piece of hackwork. The others, which are reasonably serious, are not disaster stories. People seem to imply that these are books with unhappy endings, but the reverse is true: they're books with happy endings, stories of psychic fulfilment. The geophysical changes which take place in *The Drought*, *The Drowned World* and *The Crystal World* are all positive and good changes – they are what the books are about. The changes lead us to our real psychological goals, so they are not disaster stories at all.

I know that when *The Drowned World* was accepted by my American publisher about twelve years ago he said: 'Yes, it's great, but why don't we have a happy ending? Have the hero going north instead of south into the jungle and sun.' He thought I'd made a slight technical mistake by a slip of the pen, and had the hero going in the wrong direction. I said: 'No, God, this *is* a happy story.' I don't really understand the use of the word 'disaster'. I don't regard *Crash* as a disaster story. In a sense, all these are cataclysm stories. Really, I'm trying to show a new kind of logic emerging, and this is to be embraced, or at least held in regard. So I don't really see any distinction between any of my work – between *Vermilion Sands* on the one hand, and the rest on the other.

GODDARD: Why have you never produced a work with a sympathetic male/female relationship?

BALLARD: My fiction is all about one person, all about one man coming to terms with various forms of isolation – the total sense of isolation, that the hero of 'The Voices of Time' feels, various other kinds of isolation, psychological isolation of the kind the hero of 'The Terminal Beach' feels. The protagonists of most of my fiction feel tremendously isolated, and that seems to exclude the possibility of a warm fruitful relationship with anybody, let alone anyone as potentially close as a woman. I don't think this has anything to do with any quirks of my own. I've got three children with whom I'm extremely close, and yet I've never introduced a child into any of my stories.

PRINGLE: There have been one or two dead children.

BALLARD: Yes, that's true, but there are no living children in my fiction – yet all the people who know me closely know that I'm a very fond father and all the rest of it. It's just that children are not relevant to my work.

GODDARD: Could you tell us more about your four disaster novels, which you insist aren't disaster novels? *The Wind from Nowhere, The Drowned World, The Drought* and *The Crystal World* all have disaster in them, in the classic British SF form.

BALLARD: You're right when you say that it's a classic English SF form, but that's the reason why I used the formula of the disaster story. Usually these disaster stories are treated as though they *are* disasters, they're treated straight, and everyone's running for the hills or out of the hills or whatever. If it's going to be cold they're all pulling on overcoats. I use the form because I deliberately want to invert it – that's the whole point of the novels. The heroes, for psychological reasons of their own, embrace the particular transformation. These are stories of huge psychic transformations – I'm talking retrospectively now. And I use this external transformation of the landscape to reflect and marry with the internal transformation, the psychological transformation, of the characters. This is what the subject matter of these books is: they're transformation stories rather than disaster stories.

If you take that classic among English disaster stories, *The Day of the Triffids*, I think it's probably fair to say that there's absolutely no psychological depth. The characters react to the changes that are taking place, but they are not in any psychological way involved with the proliferating vegetation, or whatever else is going on. They cope with the situation in the same way as the inhabitants of this town might cope with, say, a reservoir bursting. In the classic English disaster story there's no involvement on a psychological level with whatever is taking place. My novels are completely different, and they only use the form superficially.

PRINGLE: On the question of space travel: you imply that it's an improper subject for SF writers, but of course increasingly it is taking place.

BALLARD: No, you're wrong. *Decreasingly* it's taking place. I wrote a review of some book in *New Society*, a mad book – *The Next Ten Thousand Years* – in which I said the Space Age lasted about ten years. It's true. That's the extraordinary paradox. At the time of Gagarin's first flight in 1961, everybody really thought that the Space Age would last for hundreds of years. One could say: 'Now the Space Age begins, and it's going on for ever.' In fact, it ended with the last Skylab mission.

PRINGLE: You really believe that?

BALLARD: Absolutely. It happened. I'm sure there will be a Space Age, but it won't be for fifty, 100, 200 years – presumably when they develop a new means of propulsion. It's just too expensive. You can't have a Space Age until you've got a lot of people in space. This is where I disagree, and I've often argued the point when I've met him, with Arthur C. Clarke. He believes that the future of fiction is in space, that this is the only subject. But I'm certain you can't have a serious fiction based on experience from which the vast body of readers and writers is excluded. It's absurd. In fact there are very few manned flights, if any, planned now. I think there are none.

PRINGLE: There's the Soviet–American link-up flight this year.

BALLARD: Sorry, yes – orbital flights, but not lunar flights. Public disinterest became evident in the seventies, really. People weren't even that touched by Armstrong landing on the moon. That was a stupendous event. I thought the psychological reverberations would be enormous, that they'd manifest themselves in every conceivable way – in department store window displays and styles of furnishing, etc. I really did believe that the spin-off from that event, both in obvious terms and in psychological terms, would be gigantic. In fact it was almost nil. It's quite amazing. Clearly, the Space Age is over. Also, I think it's rather difficult because, when SF writers have a monopoly of space travel they can define, they can invent the machinery literally, and they are the judges of their own authenticity.

This is one of my objections to SF, that the decks are all stacked, the reader doesn't have a chance. As I've said for years, the stuff isn't won from experience. It lacks that authority therefore. Now the SF writers are competing with the facts of real space flight. I haven't read any recent SF. Perhaps it's good, I don't know.

GODDARD: For a few years in the mid-sixties your work had a sort of Jekyll-and-Hyde nature about it. You were producing both linear SF stories and the so-called experimental stories. Were you testing the water before taking the plunge, gauging public reaction?

BALLARD: They weren't called experimental by me – I dislike that term. It implies a test procedure of uncertain outcome. The trouble with most British experimental writing is that it proves one thing, and that is that the experiment has not worked. I wasn't influenced by market considerations at all. In fact, all through the sixties I was writing conventional short stories at the same time – there weren't very many of them but I was still writing them. I've started writing some more now. In a review that Peter Linnett wrote, he said something about my giving up writing those *Atrocity Exhibition* pieces for financial reasons. I don't know where he got that idea from. The simple fact is that the ideas that went into that book, good or bad, took years to generate. I'd like to write a follow-up to it, but it will take me ten years, probably, to accumulate the material inside my own head. Also, the climate is wrong now.

PRINGLE: There may have been no financial reasons for you to stop writing them, but were you at all influenced by adverse criticism?

BALLARD: Criticism by whom? By the SF readership? The literary critics or reviewers? I don't know. Obviously a book like that is not going to be as popular as a conventionally written book, there's no doubt about that, just as a book like *Crash* is not going to be popular. I found those stories in *The Atrocity Exhibition* produced more response from people than anything else I've ever written; people whom I'd never had any contact with, from all over the world, took the trouble to get in touch with me, which is a sure test of something. I felt the response to that book was better and larger than anything else I've ever had. In fact, I was encouraged to go on, because as I wrote the stories over a period of four or five years the response grew.

PRINGLE: I'd like to ask about the change from the non-linear style of *The Atrocity Exhibition* to the more conventional style of the two recent novels. Does this reflect a change of mind on your part about the worth of such techniques?

BALLARD: No. Maybe, when I was writing the stories and people questioned me about why I broke everything up, I tended to exaggerate a bit in the hope of getting something through. I may have made overlarge claims for non-linear narrative or whatever you want to call it, but basically I still feel that the subject matter comes first and the technique you adopt comes second. It was the subject matter of those stories that defined the way in which they were written. At the same time it's true that once you develop an approach like that it, of itself, opens up so much more territory. I once said those condensed novels, as I called them, are like ordinary novels with the unimportant pieces left out. But it's more than that – when you get the important pieces together, really together, not separated by great masses of 'he said, she said' and opening and shutting of doors, 'following morning' and all this stuff – the great tide of forward conventional narration – it achieves critical mass, as it were, it begins to ignite and you get more things being generated. You're getting crossovers and linkages between unexpected and previously totally unrelated things, events, elements of the narration, ideas that in themselves begin to generate new matter.

I haven't read any of those stories for a long time, but I remember it comes out of them – the crossovers become very unusual. It was very exciting to do. But those stories were written very much about their period, which was the middle to late sixties. I know I shall write more stories in that style, but a) it takes a long time to generate material, and b) Mary McCarthy said somewhere that the novel should be news, and those things were news – they were like newsreels above all. There isn't any news in that sense, nothing is happening. It sounds silly, I suppose, but in a way the events in the external world are not equal to the requirements of that narrative approach. It would be very difficult to write stories of that kind about 1975. But I'm waiting for the subject matter to come along. Meanwhile, other ideas occur to me.

GODDARD: How do you view your books since *The Atrocity Exhibition* in the greater science fiction context, in which you maintain they still have a niche?

BALLARD: You're entirely right, and I've said so myself, they do still have a niche. I was tremendously exhilarated when I started reading American science fiction – the excitement, the enormous power of imagination, etc. But I felt they weren't really making the most of their own land-scapes and subject matter. Right from the start what I wanted to do was write a science fiction book that got away from spaceships, the far future, and all this stuff which I felt was basically rather juvenile, to writing a kind of adult science fiction based upon the present. Why couldn't one harness this freedom and vitality? SF is a form, above all else, that puts a tremendous premium upon the imagination, and that's something that seems to have left the English novel in the last 150 years. Imagination is enormously important, and I felt that if one could only harness this capacity to think imaginatively in an adult SF, one would have achieved something.

Right from the beginning I tried with varying success to write a science fiction about the present day, which is more difficult to do than one realises, because the natural tendency when writing in a basically allegorical mode is to set something at a distance because it makes the separateness of the allegory that much more obvious. I wanted to write about the present day, and I think *Crash, Concrete Island* and the book I've just finished, which are a kind of trilogy, represent the conclusion of the particular logic I've been trying to unfold ever since I began writing. Are they SF? I don't know – maybe the science fiction of the present day *will* be something like *Crash*. They come into the category of imaginative fiction, don't they? With a strong moralistic, cautionary and exploratory note. But I don't know whether they're SF or not.

PRINGLE: What do you mean by 'moralistic'?

BALLARD: Trying to say something about the quality of one's moral direction in the ordinary sense of the term.

PRINGLE: There's one thing that people who dislike your work often talk about, and that's a lack of moral standards, a lack of some sort of touchstone, where you stand. This disturbed a lot of people who reviewed *Crash*.

BALLARD: They were supposed to be disturbed. When I set out to write *Crash*, I wanted to write a book in which there was nowhere to hide. I wanted the reader, once I'd got him inside the book, never to lose sight of the subject matter. As long as he continued reading he was face to face with the subject matter. It would have been very easy to write a conventional book about car crashes in which it was quite clear that the author was on the side of sanity, justice and against injuring small children, deaths on the road, bad driving, etc. What could be easier? I chose to completely accept the demands of the subject matter, which were to provoke the reader by saying that these car crashes are good for you, you thoroughly enjoy them, they make your sex life richer, they represent part of the marriage between sex, the human organism and technology. I say all these things in order to provoke the reader and also to test him. There may be truth in some of these sentiments, disagreeable though they are to consider. Nobody likes that they'll think 'God, the man's mad', but any other way of writing that book would have been a cop-out, I think.

GODDARD: Why did you call the protagonist of *Crash* 'Ballard'?

BALLARD: Well, that was part of the whole business of being absolutely as honest as I could. I wanted a first-person narrator to stand between Vaughan and the reader – the honest thing to do was to give him my own name. Although the superficial landscapes of the book's 'Ballard' and my life are different, there are many correspondences. Also, I wanted to anchor the book more in reality; I had a named film star [Elizabeth Taylor], who never speaks, of course.

The constant striving of the writer over the last few years has been to lower the threshold of fiction in what he writes, to reduce the amount of fiction. One's seen this in the theatre over the last fifteen years, and in the visual arts it started a long, long time ago. The move is to reduce the fictional elements in whatever one is doing and get it to overlap reality as much as possible, rather than keep it separate from reality and ordinary experience.

GODDARD: How do you react to criticism of your books? I'm thinking particularly of inane criticisms. Going back to Martin Amis and his review of *Crash*, he said something like 'he uses the word penis 147 times'.

BALLARD: I didn't read that. I didn't read any of the reviews of *Crash* in this country. There didn't seem any point after the reviews of *The Atrocity Exhibition* – nobody read the book. Having been a reviewer myself, I can always tell when somebody has stopped reading the book he's reviewing. As for criticism in general, well, science fiction writers have always been handicapped by a lack of intelligent critical response. That's why it's so encouraging to find intelligent magazines like *Cypher* around now, and intelligent critics like David Pringle here – they didn't exist ten years ago.

On the other hand, in America particularly, the critical response to SF has got totally out of hand. Now and then someone shows me a copy of the *New York Review of Books*, and I recently saw an ad for some of the most extraordinary stuff, either a series of lectures someone was giving, or a series of publications – sort of Levi-Strauss and Heinlein's such and such – all of them sounding like self-parodies, the application of serious literary criticism to popular SF authors.

GODDARD: In *Billion Year Spree*, Brian Aldiss said of your early work that you had never resolved the problem of writing a narrative in which the central character pursues no purposeful course of action. That seemed rather harsh..

BALLARD: It ties in with what I was saying earlier. I think Brian is at heart an SF fan, and he approaches my stuff – about which he is very generous and always has been – like an SF fan. He judges what he sees. To him, these books have a sort of vacuum at their centre – the character's behaviour superficially seems to be either passive or meaningless in the context of the events. Why don't they just run for the hills? Why don't they head north? There won't be a problem – there won't be a novel either, of course. Therefore I think he fails to realise that, in a novel like *The Drowned World* – and this applies to all my fiction – the hero is the only one who is pursuing a meaningful course of action.

In *The Drowned World*, the hero, Kerans, is the only one to do anything meaningful. His decision to stay, to come to terms with the changes taking place within himself, to understand the logic of his relationship with the shifting biological kingdom, and his decision finally to go south and greet the sun, is a totally meaningful course of action. The behaviour of the other people, which superficially appears to be meaningful – getting the hell out, or draining the lagoons – is totally meaningless. The book is about the discovery by the hero of his true compass bearings, both mentally and literally. It's the same in the others: in *The Crystal World* the hero decides to go back and immolate himself in a timeless world. In 'The Terminal Beach' why does the man stagger ashore on an abandoned island, what is he doing there? I can well understand that to the SF fan his behaviour is meaningless or lacks purpose – this, I think, means that Brian may have read too much SF.

PRINGLE: Can you tell us about your physical methods of writing, and whether they've changed over the years?

BALLARD: They haven't changed. I don't find that I work late in the evening now unless I really have to. My eyes are tired. But basically I haven't changed my approach. I set myself a target, about a thousand words a day – unless I just stare out of the window, which I do a lot of anyway. I generally work from a synopsis, about a page when I'm writing a short story, longer for a novel. Unless for me the thing works as a story, unless it works on the anecdotal level, unless I feel it holds the attention of the reader, I don't bother with it. It's got to work on that level, as a pure piece of storytelling. If it does I begin writing.

I spend a tremendous amount of time, I won't say doing research, but just soaking myself in the mental landscapes, particularly of a novel. Most of the time I'm thinking about what I'm writing, or hope to write. Particularly with *Crash* and *The Atrocity Exhibition*. I was carrying these for something like six or seven years. I was totally immersed mentally in this very overcharged world. It was an exciting time, but very tiring.

PRINGLE: Did you actually visit motorways and inspect the landscape?

BALLARD: Oh yes, I did a lot of research of that kind. I photographed this, that and the other.

PRINGLE: Was the inspiration for *Concrete Island* an actual place?

BALLARD: No. I've always been interested, since it was built, by the Westway motorway near Shepherd's Bush, where I set the novel. It always struck me, driving around these complex interchanges, what would happen if someone stood by the wayside and tried to flag you down? Of course, nobody would stop. You can't stop – you'd just have a multiple pile-up. You'd be dead if you tried to stop. France is a much more technologically oriented country than England, with the big high-speed boulevards that circle Paris. You can drive on the motorway from the Channel – it's not the outskirts of Paris by any means, you can see the Eiffel Tower half a mile away – on their equivalent of our circular road. You can circle Paris if you want to, and you can pick up the motorway going south without stopping at a single traffic light. It's an enormous complex of interchanges and multilevel high-speed avenues, and the French seem to drive much more aggressively than people do over here.

It often struck me there, every summer if you were marooned up on one of those balustrade ramparts – it's not just a two-dimensional island, they've got three-dimensional islands up in the air – you'd never get off. The traffic seems to be flowing twenty-four hours a day. The French are ruthless, they don't stop for anybody. Jesus Christ himself could be crucified by the wayside and nobody would stop. It was an obvious sort of idea to have. What's so interesting about the technological landscape is the way it plays into people's hands, people's possibly worst motives. It's difficult to maroon yourself on the A1, but much easier to maroon yourself on Westway.

GODDARD: Would you care to tell us something about what your future plans are?

BALLARD: Well, I finished a novel about three weeks ago, and since then I've written a couple of short stories and am writing a third now, and just catching my breath a bit.

PRINGLE: What's the new novel called?

BALLARD: I call it *The High Life* provisionally [renamed *High-Rise*]. I may change it, I may stick to it. I don't know.

GODDARD: You've no plans for another trilogy of novels on the lines of the last three?

BALLARD: I just tend to write whatever comes mentally to hand, and what I find interesting at a particular time. These decisions as to what one's going to write tend to be made somewhere at the back of one's mind, so one can't consciously say 'that's what I'm going to write'. It doesn't work out like that!

1976: Jörg Krichbaum & Rein A. Zondergeld. 'It would be a mistake to write about the future'

Originally published in German as 'Es wäre ein Irrtum, über die Zukunft zu Schreiben: J. G. Ballard im Gespräch mit Jörg Krichbaum und Rein A. Zondergeld', Franz Rottensteiner (ed.), *Quarber Merkur: Aufsätze zur Science Fiction und Phantastichen Literatur*, Frankfurt am Main: Suhrkamp, 1979. Translated by Dan O'Hara

This interview, conducted at Shepperton on 1 March 1976, was first published in German in the science fiction magazine *Quarber Merkur*, and later republished in a paperback collection of articles from the magazine in 1979. In retranslating it into English, I've strayed from the rather formal style of the German version, trying to recover a little of the feel of Ballard's own intonations and rhythms. Naturally this involves some distortion of the literal meaning conveyed in the German, but by the same token, it also involves the elimination of some of the more prolix distortions of Ballard's original phrases.

Ballard's comments on Russian writers and his explanation of his own use of specific filmic techniques are perhaps quite novel. His concern here is to define the uniqueness of his own work, set against the kind of science fiction favoured in Germany at the time, such as that by Stanislaw Lem (in fact, many of the other articles in this collection are by or about Lem), and he does this by implicitly dismissing both utopian and dystopian modes, especially where they deal with the future. What he emphasises instead is how he takes the stuff of the contemporary world as his subject, repeatedly mentioning ways in which he derives his techniques, formal methods and diction from the present. [DOH]

KRICHBAUM/ZONDERGELD: Before we talk about SF in England and America, in eastern Europe there's also a great tradition of SF, Lem, for example, or the Strugatskis. What do you think of them?

BALLARD: To be honest, I find Lem rather hard going. His whole attitude towards the subject matter is entirely different from my own. He has something so demonstratively scientific and . . . messianic. In my work I proceed analytically, whereas he assembles vast systems synthetically. There's something reminiscent of *Star Trek* in his work, 'The Big Concept'. I don't like Russian SF, or at least not that which I've read. Previously I often wrote reviews for the newspapers here. And I would sometimes get a Russian anthology sent to me, but I found it lacking in imagination. I say it reluctantly, but it was as if the spark was missing. It was never exciting, all grey on grey.

KRICHBAUM/ZONDERGELD: This style of grey mediocrity, which is also the principal quality of official socialist-realist literature . . .

BALLARD: Right, that's exactly what I meant. You know, you always get these stories in which people are sitting around in tiny flats in Moscow. And then: 'Agricultural Controller Woroschilow said . . .' or some computer specialists bustle about the prose, you know. They rarely get off the ground, there's something dead in it, like the regime of Soviet style. SF needs these old-fashioned things: the consumer society. It needs the media, which trickles slowly down to us. In SF it's not a matter of science, but of pop science, and that's something entirely different. Pop science, in how it's transmitted for a mass audience through the media, TV and newspapers, through encyclopedias, which are published in a series of volumes. That's the wave that carries SF. If one doesn't have this whole mass media, then the material of SF is simply missing. It's a peculiar thing.

KRICHBAUM/ZONDERGELD: In your earlier books, an interesting thing there is the relation between painting and literature, especially the relation to surrealist painting. Could you perhaps briefly say something about the possibilities of one artistic discipline influencing another? In your case, this seems particularly clear.

BALLARD: Yes, that's true, actually. The surrealist painters have strongly influenced me. I don't believe I've been influenced in this way by other literature. It's been said that I was influenced by Joseph Conrad . . .

KRICHBAUM/ZONDERGELD: . . . why Conrad?

BALLARD: . . . but when the critics wrote that, I had still never read anything by Conrad. I first began with him a few years ago. But the surrealist painters were important. The essence of the surrealist imagination is its ability to translate the apparent forms of the world, the outer forms, into inner ones, into mental forms. The surrealist painter doesn't seek to interpret the outer world as the classic schools of painting did, the Impressionists or the cubists or what you will; these painters analyse the real world without violating its integrity, although the techniques can vary greatly. But the surrealists recreate the outer world, completely, in fact! And this was exactly the right method for SF, which needs something very similar. I used this concept of 'psychological space', and that again I found in surrealist paintings. I thought to myself, that's exactly what we need in science fiction.

KRICHBAUM/ZONDERGELD: The combining of elements which don't necessarily seem to be heard together.

BALLARD: Right. This traditional division between the inner and the outer world, between the mental, and the reality surrounding us, becomes fully abolished. There's no longer any dividing line, it's all a continuity. And this method is the most fertile for a writer, because the outer world nowadays so resembles a dream. We live as though in an immense novel and therefore can only approach things in this way.

KRICHBAUM/ZONDERGELD: Could you imagine that your work might have influenced painters in return?

BALLARD: Yes, that could happen. You know, surrealism is without a doubt the most important direction in painting before the war; cubism is all well and good, but we had that already during the First World War, after which surrealism was dominant for decades. But the next development, therefore after the Second World War, that was most especially important for writers was pop art. Many authors were influenced by that.

KRICHBAUM/ZONDERGELD: In your later books like *The Atrocity Exhibition*, but also already in *The Four-Dimensional Nightmare*, you seem at times to have adopted filmic structures. Could you say something about that?

BALLARD: There are many connections there. I've transferred what one in film calls the 'cut' into my literary work. I also use various other filmic methods: like the close-up, slow motion and similar. I wanted to apply equivalents of these methods in the novel. In the traditional novel the close-up means that one looks somebody in the eye and starts to study their mental state, their motives and so on, whereas in film a close-up doesn't have to mean anything that corresponds to this level of depth. It can be that one wants to show only the skin of the face, its condition. In spaghetti westerns, for example, you see a close-up of Charles Bronson waiting at a station, that is, you see only a shot of the back of his head, with a fly crawling around it. Such a kind of close-up isn't intended to explain anything about the man's personality, it shows only a detail. And in *The Atrocity Exhibition* I use close-ups that for example show only a girl's arm against the background of an automobile.

KRICHBAUM/ZONDERGELD: Therefore only as an object.

BALLARD: Only objects, exactly. Like in a Hitchcock film, where one catches sight of a close-up of some object on a table, of a fried egg on a plate or a pair of spectacles, for purely atmospheric reasons! That applies also to slow motion, which is very significant, as it sometimes transforms an intrinsically violent piece of action, for example the collision of two automobiles, into a ballet of great elegance and beauty.

KRICHBAUM/ZONDERGELD: A change of aesthetic dimension.

BALLARD: Right, but a complete change. These filmic techniques can be used by a writer; they powerfully extend the resources at his disposal.

KRICHBAUM/ZONDERGELD: Have you had no desire to make a film yourself?

BALLARD: Oh, quite, I'd like to very much. But I lack the technical essentials.

KRICHBAUM/ZONDERGELD: Is there not perhaps one director with whom you'd like to work?

BALLARD: Oh, there are many directors I admire. Kubrick, for example, he's a great director. And Godard, who's also very important, albeit in a different way.

KRICHBAUM/ZONDERGELD: Godard uses almost the same techniques as you.

BALLARD: That's true, yes. I also like Antonioni a great deal. But it's hard to give a plain answer. I've never really considered it.

KRICHBAUM/ZONDERGELD: Is there a film script written by you?

BALLARD: I wrote a script from my novel *Concrete Island*, that a French director wanted to film. That was last summer. I don't know if he'll actually make the film. And then I once also wrote a script from my early novel *The Drought*, which was bought up for TV by David Frost, but he's never used it. I am actually interested in film.

KRICHBAUM/ZONDERGELD: Up to now we still haven't mentioned your *Vermilion Sands* stories. It seems as if there the influence of decadent literature makes itself felt, of the *fin de siècle*.

BALLARD: You're thinking of Huysmans here? Yes. You know, *Vermilion Sands* corresponds to my vision of the future. It will not be like *Nineteen Eighty-Four*, but rather like *Vermilion Sands*. If one goes to the Mediterranean coast in the summer, one sees the future there already. Half of Europe finds itself in this linear city that runs from Gibraltar to Athens. A city that's three thousand miles long and a hundred metres wide. And that is, in my opinion, the future.

KRICHBAUM/ZONDERGELD: In your books there are many technical terms from the various scientific disciplines, from medicine, climatology, physics and geology, for example. Don't you think that this fact could complicate the reading process for many of your readers?

BALLARD: There's something in that. As it is, I try not to use so much of this kind of terminology. But on the other hand I think that people nowadays have such a level of general knowledge . . .

KRICHBAUM/ZONDERGELD: . . . a truly optimistic view!

BALLARD: You know, everyone has a little bit of knowledge about these fields. Doctors are always complaining about the fact that their patients read more medical journals and know more about medicine than they do themselves. All things considered, I don't think that my stuff is incomprehensible.

KRICHBAUM/ZONDERGELD: You don't therefore consciously write for a wholly special kind of reader, for a smaller public than most SF authors?

BALLARD: No, I write for all readers; at least, I try to.

KRICHBAUM/ZONDERGELD: Is there a book or a film which has made an especially strong impression on you or by which you've been particularly influenced?

BALLARD: Now, I admire William Burroughs, for example, and I greatly love Genet's book *Notre dame des fleurs*, and many older authors, Huysmans and his *À rebours*, to give just an example. I found Kubrick's film *Dr. Strangelove* outstanding, a masterpiece, absolutely overwhelming. Recently I saw Fellini's *Dolce Vita* again on the TV, and again this film made a great impression on me.

KRICHBAUM/ZONDERGELD: It's interesting that you mention Genet and Burroughs, because both those authors write books without conventional plots. There is no more plot, or not as one normally understands it. In your case, it's hardly conceivable, however, that you could abandon tight structuring and plot. Your books function too hermetically, they're too self-contained.

BALLARD: Right, I need a convincing plot to write in my way, a clear structure. Even in the latest books. Those are very highly developed stories. Sometimes I also try to conceal the story, but there has to be something like a bridge, otherwise everything falls apart.

KRICHBAUM/ZONDERGELD: One could imagine a hopefully purely hypothetical situation in which, if your development took yet another turn in an experimental direction, you might one day find yourself without publishers. Or do you not have this worry?

BALLARD: Up to now I've had a lot of luck with my publishers. Certainly the latest books weren't printed in Germany, but in England the latest books were also very successful. *Crash*, it's true, was no success in America, but it was an immediate bestseller in France, which was a considerable surprise to me as I'd expected quite the reverse.

KRICHBAUM/ZONDERGELD: If one takes into account the success or absence of real success, for example in West Germany, one must surely conclude that certain books are simply flops in certain countries.

BALLARD: That's surely not wrong. National psychology is a particularly difficult field.

KRICHBAUM/ZONDERGELD: Is there for you a special relationship to America?

BALLARD: Oh yes, I've always been greatly interested in America. There, I find the landscapes of my books, about which we already spoke earlier. But on the other hand I'm sure that in some twenty or thirty years a new renaissance will take place in Europe. Now that borders are gradually being abolished and we're getting away from the past, there will be quite a bit of change. The new developments, of this I'm sure, will come from Europe and not from America.

1978: Jon Savage. J.G. Ballard

Originally published in *Search & Destroy* 10, 1978

In 1978 journalist Jon Savage interviewed Ballard at Shepperton for *Search & Destroy*, a fanzine about the American punk scene. *Search & Destroy* was published by the enigmatic V. Vale, who would go on to achieve acclaim as the head of RE/Search Publications, publisher of subversive books about underground culture, including four volumes on Ballard. Savage brought a new sensibility to Ballard interviews. He was young, he didn't have a literary or science fiction background (although he was well read in the genre) and he wrote almost exclusively about music. However, he connected the dots between punk's self-conscious urban anomie – manifest in songs about bleak overpasses and run-down high-rise blocks – and similar imagery in *Crash* and *High-Rise*. In turn, Ballard betrays his own interest in the terms that propelled the punk scene to notoriety. Consequently, he spends more time discussing social conditions and the new consumerism than he does his actual books, although there is a fascinating glimpse into an incident he witnessed on holiday that would spark the creation of *High-Rise*.

Ballard is as perceptive as ever. He predicts the end of the novel – 'the form of the extended narrative' – in an age of short attention spans, the almost immediate recoupment of rebellion by consumerism, and perhaps most strikingly a near future in which every home would have a computer terminal, allowing us to record and broadcast intimate details of our lives, dismantling the power and authority of old media. There is also a perhaps surprising personal revelation, when he discloses that the reason he hadn't been to America for twenty-five years was the increasing violence he had heard was occurring there.

Savage would go on to write *England's Dreaming* (1991), the definitive analysis of the English punk scene, in which the tower blocks of *High-Rise* and the motorways of *Crash* would become touchstones in both his investigation and the recollections of the musicians he interviewed. [SS]

SAVAGE: I've just been reading *High-Rise*. What interested me was the idea of a modern sort of barbarism in the midst of technology, or the fact that technology is creating a situation *for* that. It seemed very much what's happening now, in microcosm, because coming on the way here on the M3 [motorway], I noticed it was all very beautiful, all these beautiful new gleaming buildings, despoiled by graffiti – very strange.

BALLARD: Yes, apparently the events I described in that novel have taken place. There's a cluster of blocks near Manchester which are scheduled for demolition because they're just not viable social structures. But I was trying to point out that people discover there's some dubious pleasures of life tapped by advanced technology. They canalise and tame and make tolerable perverse impulses that in previous societies would've been nipped in the bud. Modern technology makes possible the expression of guilt-free psychopathology – I really feel we're moving towards that. In *Crash*, I tried to show the first signs of a sort of institutionalised, morally free psychopathology emerging, in which people will be able to, almost *encouraged* by the nature of the societies in which they live, give vent to all sorts of perverse impulses which won't be socially damaging!

SAVAGE: An interesting thing I noticed in the book: it was much more of an American high-rise situation. In England the high-rises are usually council. I presumed that was a sort of vehicle, a way of doing it.

BALLARD: Funny enough, the idea of *High-Rise* came to me way back fifteen years ago. My parents had a flat in Red Lion Square, Victoria. There's a little complex of office blocks, and there's one block of flats – mostly rich business people live there, with Rolls-Royces and immodestly appointed flats, huge rents. The women (they were the ones at home) spent all their time bickering with one another, complaining about small things constantly: 'Who's going to pay for the maintenance of the potted plant display on the seventeenth-floor landing?' and 'So-and-so's curtains do not match'. The most incredible triviality.

Then, about five years ago, I was in Spain. I rented a flat for a month close to the Costa Brava; really it's a French resort, near Dali's place. Most of the people there were French middle-class professional people – they all had their bloody boats. And they spent an enormous amount of their time bickering about things. I remember one of the residents was standing with his back to the sea, looking up at this big block, about twelve storeys high, with a camera. I thought, 'What is this – this man's a peeping tom!', because my girlfriend was walking around in the nude. But there was an enormous amount of antagonism between the people in the lower floors and the people in the top. Because there was this constant onshore wind flow, cigarette ends in particular, flung down into the flats and also water – some child would kick over a bucket of water – the whole damn lot would come down over everyone else's balconies.

A notice went up saying, 'Residents are asked not to throw cigarette ends over their balconies'. This chap said in his notice, 'I am taking photographs of any offenders and these photographs will be pinned on this noticeboard'. I remember thinking, 'This is unbelievable, I think I'll keep this – who would believe it?' A *holiday* in this expensive block, and here's this guy so upset with the misbehaviour of those people on the twelfth floor that he stands with his back to the sea with his camera, waiting to catch somebody in the act. Some guy who's probably a dentist, so obsessed with the sort of hostilities that are easily provoked.

SAVAGE: You were talking earlier about this sort of new class.

BALLARD: A new professional class, right. If you take a thirty-five-year-old working-class dentist from Lyons – he has more in common with another thirty-five-year-old dentist of the whatever class than he has with someone who grew up in the same street. Members of a professional caste, or whatever you like to call them – social group – in an elaborately signalled landscape where they understand all the codes that govern, and once they've mastered the system of codes, they become sort of a separate social group. The old caste criteria don't apply.

Marxism is a social philosophy for the poor, whereas what we need nowadays is a social philosophy for the rich, which is what most people are. Having been brought up in the Far East, I know what *poverty*'s about.

SAVAGE: Another thing about *High-Rise* was a new tribalism, barbarism. The professional class got broken down to the actual floor [of the building], so it's right down to *territory* – basics. It all got basic and barbaric, but in a very perverse way. Do you see that happening now in England, generally?

BALLARD: Yeah, I think it is happening, rather less dramatically than it takes place in that book. The rate of change is so slow that it's imperceptible, but by God change is taking place.

SAVAGE: I think the media accelerate change, and a lot of people are beginning not to be able to cope with that and are actually going to go psychotic or catatonic.

BALLARD: Yeah. Every now and then people seem to wake up, look around them and decide they've had too much, more change than they can stand, so the pendulum appears to swing in the direction of conservatism. I mean, people like Mary Whitehouse do express the kind of half-conscious need by people to slam on the brakes. Most people can't take too much change; most people aren't happy with change, that's why science fiction isn't *that* popular. That's why it's most popular with the young, who embrace change, and need it and are eager for change.

SAVAGE: Also, science fiction's not particularly respectable.

BALLARD: It's less unrespectable than it used to be. It's changing, particularly in the States – you can bloody nearly take a degree in SF. It's cutting in slowly – you can probably find *Day of the Triffids* on some reading lists. I even find my own output being chased, particularly in France, also in Italy – people writing MA theses on my stuff, you know. *That* strikes me as hilariously funny. People are getting MAs on this sort of stuff – *that* side of it I don't like. I like fiction that is free, vulgar even, noisy, not worrying about dropping its aitches. *Vitality* is the most important thing where the imagination is concerned. I don't care about the rough edges.

SAVAGE: One of the things I like about science fiction is that, for me, it isn't future fiction, it's an alternative present.

BALLARD: Well, it's become that. When I started writing it was very much future-oriented, twenty years ago. It was very difficult then to write, really, science fiction set in the present. Editors, readers were very nervous.

SAVAGE: How did that break down?

BALLARD: By persistence, I may say, on my own part – a lot of rejection slips, slowly getting your message through. Also for internal reasons. SF, rather like Hollywood, was sort of a one-generation business. The modern cinema, let's say from 1935 to 1960, was one generation of cameramen, one generation of lighting men, writers, producers, directors, stars even. Once this generation grew old, there was no new generation to take its place. And this happened in SF too, once Asimov, Heinlein, Bradbury and company stopped writing. Once they had established conventions of a modern literature, there was nobody else to take its place, so it was decided to start establishing conventions of another, even more modern literature, and this has happened.

SAVAGE: It will be interesting to find out whether there'll be another generation.

BALLARD: I think there are the first signs of it taking place. What you're going to get is the first generation of writers to whom SF is part of the normal landscape, rather than something separate. Rather than an alternative to the present day, we are going to get a generation to whom SF *is* the present. Obviously William Burroughs is the most important writer to emerge since World War II. I first read, fifteen years ago, *Naked Lunch*, *The Ticket that Exploded* and *The Soft Machine*. I stood up and cheered because I thought 'God, this man's a genius, he's changed everything'. There are elements of SF in all Burroughs because they're part of the landscape, part of the air one breathes.

SAVAGE: Some of the things he said are very important, about technological control. And the pace of his books. I remember one day I was reading *Maldoror* and I was reading *Naked Lunch* and I couldn't read *Maldoror* – the pace was so slow.

BALLARD: Burroughs reads like Rimbaud, full of drive.

SAVAGE: These days, I think people's attention time spans are a bit less.

BALLARD: I think the *form* is part of the reason the novel has been losing ground for the last half-century. The form is wrong, the form of the extended narrative, the long story doesn't accord. It may accord with the way people lived, or thought they lived, in the nineteenth century, but it doesn't accord with the way people see themselves in the twentieth, certainly not the late twentieth, whereas Burroughs jettisons the long scale of narrative and action and drama and all the rest are sort of subsumed within each paragraph. Does it take a writer of genius to write like that? Maybe, because there have been so many bad imitations of Burroughs, the hazards of that sort of thing.

SAVAGE: Did you ever see *The Man Who Fell to Earth*?

BALLARD: Yes I did. I guess it was a brave failure, the accent on 'brave' and not the 'failure'. It needed a slightly stronger storyline. I know the screenwriter [Paul Mayersberg] because he actually has written a film script for *High-Rise*, and he has a tendency to sacrifice the overall storyline in order to follow up his own little obsessions, which is a shame. I mean, Nic Roeg is a good film-maker, but he too actually needs a stronger storyline.

SAVAGE: *Walkabout* . . .

BALLARD: An amazing film, lovely film. I loved the landscape too. Apparently a desert, but every twenty yards there's a wreck of an old car or something, like Shepperton.

SAVAGE: The landscapes around here *are* extraordinary.

BALLARD: But people aren't aware of it. You know, most people see the world though a very traditional focus, through a very traditional lens. Just as somebody reared on, say, Renaissance and post-Renaissance painting, with formal perspectives and all the rest of it, is absolutely unable to take, say, cubism or any form of non-representational painting. It's difficult now to realise just how, say, the Impressionists, who strike us as damn nearly chocolate in sweetness, how at the time, in the 1870s to 1880s, Impressionism was virtually described as a criminal conspiracy to destroy a civilisation.

SAVAGE: Which it was . . .

BALLARD: Well, it was *in a way*. It merely offered an alternative viewing hole. This is why people drive around, live in a landscape like this or around Heathrow without realising what is going on. What I'm interested in is – you see it coming in London – that type of inner-urban development which is not designed for pedestrians, certainly, but also not really designed for motor cars as well. You get it say in Paris around the Montparnasse Tower – you drive to a place like that, and you have to know your destination. You want to go to such-and-such a building, you go into the car park of *that* building and that's it, baby. You don't walk around. You don't drive around. You've got to have a *specific target*, like to the Festival Hall or the Shell complex. You don't have any options.

SAVAGE: That's another thing very noticeable in *High-Rise* and *Concrete Island* – that modern isolation. Because of all that, as in the case of the guy in *Concrete Island*, you can actually be on the road trying to hitch a ride but you might as well be light years away.

BALLARD: You can't stop here and you can't stop there. Well, even if you wanted to, if you were driving along say the Westway near Shepherd's Bush at sixty miles an hour, and you saw somebody, you saw somebody bleeding by the roadside. You try to stop, you'll be in a multi-car pile-up, you'd be dead – you'd be hit by about fifteen or twenty cars. And of course you don't want to stop – the whole system is engineered around the assumption that nobody is going to express any impulsive charity – or do anything impulsive, for that matter! You can no more express some original impulse than somebody riding a roller coaster who suddenly decided to get off – once the roller coaster begins you have to ride it through to the end!

Many of these modern roads are beautifully landscaped, actually. The old people who live around there are complaining like mad. They're not complaining about the noise, but the destruction of the visual amenities: 'We remember what the Harrow Road was like and look at it now!' But the motorway's the most elegant structure in that part of London – the houses are all decaying wrecks.

SAVAGE: A group called The Clash did a song called 'London's Burning' – the guy who wrote it lived in one of those flats by the Harrow Road with a view down the Westway. He was saying: 'What a lovely way to spend a night/It's so great/driving in the red and yellow lights (on the Westway).'

BALLARD: Someone told me that Hawkwind based a song on *High-Rise*, but I doubt that myself. [In fact, this did happen.]

SAVAGE: High-rise blocks are very compelling pieces of architecture, and when you look from Archway to Hampstead Heath, the City of London looks like a graveyard, the tall office buildings look like tomb-stones. Very frightening. An interesting thing: the top things you see are flat. It used to be the churches would rise, ever upward, and now you've got this 'flat' which keeps you down on the ground.

BALLARD: A couple of years ago, when I drove back from Sussex and I passed Croydon, about a mile away, suddenly I looked up to my right and there was a cluster of high-rise blocks like mini-Manhattan that had just sort of come up from nowhere. It was weird.

SAVAGE: Have you been to Manhattan?

BALLARD: No. I haven't been to the States in about twenty-five years. I must go again. Also, people who've been there tell me frightening stories about all the violence, which I'm afraid rather puts me off.

SAVAGE: I think London is pretty violent, some places.

BALLARD: The notion of a completely random event as the result of just some sort of meaningless attack lasting ten seconds – one may be not necessarily killed, but profoundly traumatised, even severely physi-cally disabled for years. I mean, I can walk around in parts of London that I visit, let's say – or I can walk around those parts of Paris I visit, or Rome – with complete confidence that a meaningless attack is not going to happen, any more than, say, an engine is going to fall off an aircraft and land on my head!

Well, you're getting a certain element of *political* violence now, aren't you? If one had scripted an episode five years ago, and had a scene where some passengers in an airline bus were machine-gunned as they got out of their hotel in Grosvenor Square in broad daylight by an Arab terrorist – I mean, it would be put down as a ludicrous fantasy, you know. One just wouldn't have believed something like that.

J.G. Ballard

SAVAGE: Do you watch much television?

BALLARD: All the time. I enjoy it. I think it's terribly important to watch TV. I think there's a sort of minimum number of hours of TV a day you ought to watch, and unless you watch three or four hours of TV a day, you're just closing your eyes to some of the most important sort of stream of consciousness that's going on! I mean, not watching TV is even worse than, say, never reading a book!

I think the biggest developments over the next twenty, thirty years are going to be through the introduction of VHS systems, and I don't just mean the cassette thing, playback gadgets – that in itself would be quite revolutionary – but when, say, every room in everybody's house or flat has got a camera recording what's going on – the transformation of the home into a TV studio is a creation of a new kind of reality. A reality that is electronic.

SAVAGE: But what's it going to do? Make people introverted or self-conscious?

BALLARD: I think only in the short term, in exactly the same way as when you at last get a camera, you spend your time photographing children playing in a paddling pool. But after a while, you get more ambitious and you start taking an interest in the world at large. I think the same thing will happen, beginning with people endlessly photographing themselves, shaving, having dinner together, having domestic rows. Of course, the bedroom applications are obvious. But I think they'll go beyond that, to the point where each of us will be at the centre of a sort of non-stop serial, with all kinds of possibilities let in. You may be able to splice in bits of *Key Largo* and *Casablanca* into the daily record of your life, to the point where you literally *do* become a character in a Bogey movie.

SAVAGE: They always say that people fantasise about making love with somebody else. Is this just a logical extension of that?

BALLARD: I can see that coming. But I can see a sort of huge extension of video. Live material which will be accessible at the press of a button, so that as now you can dial a poem or a record of the weather, you'll be able to dial a visual input of, say, all the newsreel material filmed yesterday in Los Angeles – I'm talking about somebody living in a London suburb.

SAVAGE: There was a story in *Low-Flying Aircraft* [Ballard's 1976 short-story collection] about recreating history on TV.

BALLARD: Oh yes, 'The Greatest TV Show on Earth'. But I can see that happening – one will have access to a vast amount of filmed information of every conceivable kind. One will be able to sort of merge one's own identity with a huge flux of images of various kinds being generated elsewhere.

SAVAGE: But how will that fit in socially? Will that mean people will spend less time working? I think the four-day work week is already around the corner.

BALLARD: Well, most people are already working a three-day week without realising it. They're going to work on a five-day-a-week basis, but they are probably *working* a three-day week. It's just a social convention to work Monday through Friday.

SAVAGE: By the way, I am very pessimistic about the likelihood of natural man-made catastrophes over the next twenty years.

BALLARD: I don't see western Europe or the United States, societies there, derailing themselves – quite practically, I don't think that's likely to happen. I think the reason why it won't happen is that the rate of change itself is going to be so great, positively exponential, particularly when there's a whole development at present of what I call an invisible technology: mostly computers, processing devices, etc., which is going on around us, which we don't know about. I mean, I think the rate of change is a sort of *pause suppressant* – twenty years from now, one will begin to realise the extent to which the applications of the computer, in a thousand and one ways, will really create a state of perpetual change which will be a tide that will just sweep everybody along without . . .

SAVAGE: . . . being able to do anything about it.

BALLARD: Right! They'll be happy to go along with the tide. I think you'll get an inflammation, a rate of information flow, and a rate of change, in the last two decades of this century and the first two of the next, equal to the enormous rate of visible, enormous rate of change that took place in the first thirty years of this century, let's say from 1880 to 1920. In everything! Autos are obvious things, I mean things you can see, like houses, electric lights, cars, radios, telephones, bridges, ships – everything! The creation of the twentieth century took place. What we may see, I think, in the years 1980 to 2020, will be the creation of the twenty-first century. It could be done in terms of information systems, TV, the whole video world.

SAVAGE: The whole thing now is access to information.

BALLARD: Yeah, but that'll end. Once everybody's got a computer terminal in their home, to satisfy all their needs, all the domestic needs, there'll be a dismantling of the present broadcasting structure, which is far too limited and limiting.

SAVAGE: Do you think there'll be enormous social changes that a lot of people will not be able to cope with?

BALLARD: I don't know about that – I think that people are far more flexible than they realise. Take somebody with a fairly sort of limited social background in this country today, without any advantages of birth, education, intelligence or special talent, let's say. Say some factory worker in the Midlands. He takes for granted a range of possibilities in his life – an average holiday in the Bahamas, or if not the Bahamas the Seychelles, a fairly high standard of medical care in absolute terms, etc., TV, records, a vast range of goods hygienically presented in supermarkets. His local high street offers a range of fabrics, styles, furnishings, you name it – a staggering diversity of possibilities, of a kind that, say, his father in the 1930s would have been amazed at.

But this is the average sort of working class taking it in his stride. I think this applies on all levels. My father took for granted things that would've amazed his father. I look at my own life or the lives of my friends, people in their forties – we make a whole huge list of assumptions about things, say, that my mother, if she were still alive, would really be rather shocked by. I mean, a kind of built-in tolerance, for example, of a huge range of what to my mother would have been regarded as rather *deviant* interests – like being interested in abstract painting. I think tolerances are something that's increasing.

SAVAGE: I hope so. I'm not quite as confident as you are. I see a lot of intolerance in lots of people, especially younger people, people younger than me, and I find that very frightening.

BALLARD: Yes. I think the main threat comes from the very young. My son did something that really surprised me – he was brought up in a, say, agnostic, humane, intelligent and loving home atmosphere. The first thing he did when he went to Warwick University three years ago was join a Christian Union – he became a sort of devout Christian. I don't think there's anything particularly unusual about this; somebody was telling me that he was at John's Chapel – some Sunday service or something – and was amazed to find half the place full of undergraduates!

And at Warwick, and at most universities these days, the largest student society now is the CU. Curiously enough, I noticed that my son, although he's a very engaging, pleasant character, has become surprisingly dogmatic and moralistic.

SAVAGE: It's the dogma that I worry about.

BALLARD: That's frightening! I sometimes worry because, he's now twenty-three, he may well make a rather repressive parent. It may be just a temporary phase.

SAVAGE: Well, even so, it's going to have its effect . . .

BALLARD: Actually, about the height of 'Swinging London', 1966/67, a long time ago, I thought to myself, 'Well, being young is synonymous with freedom, tolerance and all the rest of it.' And I thought to myself, 'I'm an SF writer,' and I tend to just play around with ideas and invert things deliberately. I visualised a society where the young all wore Mao uniforms and were extremely puritanical and moralistic. This was ten years ago. But you actually see this going on. One can see, actually, a whole range of new orthodoxies emerging: attitudes about 'race', about 'inherited intelligence', about 'women's lib', 'women's place in the world'. Attitudes about all sorts of things have sort of fossilised into a sort of fixed position, where if you in any way deviate, you're in trouble! You're attacked merely because you choose to express an original opinion on the subject, and don't subscribe to the established orthodoxy.

I mean, you see it in, say, *Time Out*. I like *Time Out* and have contributed to it myself – I think it's a great magazine – but you see a whole set of received opinions there going through its columns, both political and aesthetic. Aesthetic orthodoxies are paraded in that magazine, in every issue. I'm thirty years older than the oldest *Time Out* contributor, but it's not them that bothers me so much as the fact that I don't know quite what to expect.

SAVAGE: When an orthodoxy gets set up, I almost per se want to attack it.

BALLARD: Oh, right! Me too, rather wilfully.

SAVAGE: And make a nuisance of myself. I mean, you talked about the sixties, maybe you observed it. In what case did you think the generation failed or succeeded, if you can think of it in those terms.

BALLARD: Well, I certainly wasn't part of it. I was an outsider. I was thirty-five by the time 'Swinging London' got into its stride – 'never trust anyone over thirty'. I think the transformation of English life that took place between 1965 to 1970 is absolutely to be admired. The biggest shot in the arm this country ever has seen, marking the real revolution, social revolution, as big as the creation of the welfare state, and the social revolution that was part of it, that took place after '45. I thought it was a stupendous event: the young people of the sixties, who saved this country from Middle Ages oblivion.

SAVAGE: But I think now there's a new generation of people.

BALLARD: I think that's totally true. The trouble is, the sort of means of achieving one revolution become institutionalised. I mean, the formulas that are liberating become clichés and the Establishment of the next. So it seems to me that, if you take that social revolution which was achieved between '65 and '70, it was made of many, many things. Of course, among them were, say, pop music, a certain kind of fashion free of 'class' and all the rest of it, the drugs, psychedelics – they were all revolutionary in their different place. They've now become part of an established way of life. I mean, you now go to parties in this part of the world, say, and you find people with BMWs in their drives, smoking pot on immaculate lawns, and these people are thirty-five and absolutely in every sense pillars of the Establishment. I mean, they are young professionals who hold society together.

SAVAGE: Right, and a lot of them take cocaine.

BALLARD: So I think you're right, there is a new shot in the arm needed, it'll probably come.

SAVAGE: I think punk is making a start.

BALLARD: I think so, because from my point of view, what I'm interested in, thinking of *High-Rise*, is a new conceptualisation of psychopathology, where you're getting a real liberation of the apparently deviant, but merely an expression of certain sort of universal quirks.

SAVAGE: You get squeezed by society today in certain ways, and the squeeze is bound to produce the quirks.

BALLARD: Yeah, well, by 'quirk' I mean merely the particular shape that each of us takes in time and space. Normally the means of expressing we've got are very limited – each of us are allowed very little freedom to express our own identities; and we have a very impoverished – meagre – vocabulary for expressing our own identities. What is interesting about 'punk' is a fairly extensive, in its way, vocabulary for expressing certain parts of ourselves. It's come out! And I think that's great.

SAVAGE: I can see a lot of very interesting strands there. I can see a strand, as I was saying to you earlier – 'psychedelic without drugs' and an attitude of being social-realistic.

BALLARD: My impression is that the original punk groups were reacting in a very direct way against the establishment music scene. Someone like Mick Jagger, he's as much a part of the show business establishment as Frank Sinatra and Bing Crosby. And although he is regarded as of some importance to us as a 'great rebel', in fact he's a completely socially accepted and integrated performer. And I guess the original punk was reacting against that sort of thing. What is interesting now is that the time span between the rebel – the revolution – and total social accept- ance is getting shorter and shorter. It took Jagger about ten years.

SAVAGE: It took Johnny Rotten a year and a half!

BALLARD: In the future – this is part of the problem in the 'arts' as well – you will get some radical new idea, but within three minutes it's totally accepted, and it's coming out in your local supermarket.

SAVAGE: Andy Warhol has been so perceptive about this.

BALLARD: Absolutely, everything Warhol's said he is so right about. He's a genius.

SAVAGE: The group he worked with is probably one of the most influential groups ever: The Velvet Underground. Their ideas are so compressed, they're full of ideas, and people have made careers by just taking one strand of it. There's a very heavy Burroughs influence that's been coming into punk in the last year or so, very indirect, but there is a strand of groups now who are really attacking media and technological conditioning.

BALLARD: To be honest, I don't listen to music. It's just a blank spot.

1979: Christopher Evans. The Space Age Is Over

Originally published in *Penthouse* 14:1, 1979 (UK edition)

Ballard was famously fond of what he called 'invisible literature' – medical reports, technical manuals and market-research surveys – and maintained a repository of old medical and psychiatric journals. His friend Christopher Evans, a computer scientist and psychologist at the National Physical Laboratory, and the inspiration, in part, for the character of Vaughan in *Crash*, used to send him a regular parcel of the contents of his wastepaper basket, having noticed Ballard's interest in such things. The basket held out-of-date psychiatric journals, case studies, scientific bulletins and the like.

Ballard's huge confidence in his own prognostications in this interview stems from this close and productive relationship with Evans, who Ballard once described as his closest friend. Evans died of cancer later in 1979 at the age of forty-eight. [DOH]

EVANS: Science fiction is supposed to reflect the future. How well do you think it has done that over the years?

BALLARD: I think it's been amazingly accurate, not necessarily in terms of the technology itself, but in predicting society's response to technology. Jules Verne, over a hundred years ago, was the first writer of any kind to respond to the impending transformation of society by technology, and from his time onwards science fiction has picked out the main preoccupations and anxieties of the Industrial Age, identifying them way ahead of their appearance. Incidentally, it has also anticipated the present unease about science, which has recently become a public issue, but which was featured in SF as far back as the 1930s. I suspect it will also turn out to have been extremely accurate in the way in which it is now predicting or anticipating the peculiar affectless quality of life in the 1980s and nineties.

EVANS: What kind of things?

BALLARD: Well, for example, the way in which the traditional together-ness of the village is giving way to the inbuilt loneliness of the new high-rises, or the peculiar fact that people nowadays like to be together not in the old-fashioned way of, say, mingling on the piazza of an Italian Renaissance city, but, instead, huddled together in traffic jams, bus queues, on escalators and so on. It's a new kind of togetherness which may seem totally alien, but it's the togetherness of modern technology, and the science fiction writers of the forties, fifties and sixties picked it out unerringly as being a dominant feature of the future – often without realising what they were doing.

EVANS: Can you give an example?

BALLARD: You've only got to look at copies of *Galaxy Magazine* and *Astounding Science Fiction* of the early fifties to see the anxieties and wish-fulfilment fantasies of modern suburbia and city life – the escapist dreams of jetliners and airport lounges – all absolutely contained in the science fiction of the period. Take Pohl and Kornbluth's classic novel, *The Space Merchants*. Here the future is portrayed in terms of a world totally dominated by the advertising agencies. It's a world run not by the Pentagon and the Kremlin but by Madison Avenue, with giant rival advertising consortia fighting to control everything and everyone through the mechanism of the mass media. And indeed, we can look back now and realise that the logical evolution of Western society of the 1950s would have been a world in which the copywriter was king. It seems obvious in retrospect, but it took science fiction writers to spot it and write about it a quarter of a century ago.

EVANS: You evidently don't rate too highly science fiction's highly successful predictions about space travel?

BALLARD: Well, you can't underestimate that achievement, but in many ways space travel was the *least* adventurous of all SF concepts. It so happens that my first stories were being published at almost exactly the time that Sputnik One – in case you've forgotten, that's the first artificial satellite – was launched in 1957. At the time I remember a great mood of optimism in science fiction circles. It seemed that the Sputniks had ushered in the Space Age, and that everything that the science fiction writers had been predicting for 100 years was coming true. And with the Space Age, science fiction was set fair for a golden era. Now I remember paradoxically responding to this general euphoria by being intensely pessimistic rather than optimistic. Although I had no real evidence to support my hunch – quite the opposite, in fact – I felt very strongly that the age of space, as far as science fiction was concerned, was *ending* rather than beginning. And indeed the Space Age did *end* and far from lasting hundreds or even thousands of years, its total lifespan was hardly more than a decade.

One can date its end quite precisely. The Space Age clearly ended in 1974 when the last Skylab mission came to earth. This was the first splashdown *not* to be shown on TV – a highly significant decision on the part of the networks which signalled the fact that space simply wasn't interesting any more. As I said I had a strong hunch that this was the case, but didn't have any unequivocal evidence to back it up. But in the summer of '74 I remember standing out in my garden on a bright, clear night and watching a moving dot of light in the sky which I realised was Skylab. I remember thinking how fantastic it was that there were men up there, and I felt really quite moved as I watched it. Through my mind there even flashed a line from every Hollywood aviation movie of the forties, 'it takes guts to fly those machines'. But I meant it. Then my neighbour came out into his garden to get something and I said, 'Look, there's Skylab', and he looked up and said, '*Sky*-what?' And I realised that he didn't know about it, and he wasn't interested. No, from that moment there was no doubt in my mind that the Space Age was over.

EVANS: What is the explanation for this? Why are people so indifferent?

BALLARD: I think it's because we're at the climactic end of one huge age of technology which began with the Industrial Revolution and which lasted for about two hundred years. We're also at the beginning of a second, possibly even greater revolution, brought about by advances in computers and by the development of information-processing devices of incredible sophistication. It will be the era of artificial brains as opposed to artificial muscles, and right now we stand at the midpoint between these two huge epochs. Now it's my belief that people, unconsciously perhaps, recognise this and also recognise that the space programme and the conflict between NASA and the Soviet space effort belonged to the first of these systems of technological exploration, and was therefore tied to the past instead of the future. Don't misunderstand me – it was a magnificent achievement to put a man on the moon, but it was essentially nuts-and-bolts technology and therefore not qualitatively different from the kind of engineering that built the *Queen Mary* or wrapped railroads round the world in the nineteenth century. It was a technology that changed people's lives in all kinds of ways, and to a most dramatic extent, but the space programme represented its fast-guttering flicker.

EVANS: You were one of the leaders of the New Wave in science fiction. Could you say something about that? Was the New Wave a response to the shift from one technological epoch to another?

BALLARD: Yes, in a sense. You see, technology advances on a number of fronts and opens up a number of different doors. The transformation of London by its tube system in the nineteenth century, the spread of the telephone in the 1920s and thirties, the coming of radio and the dominance of TV in the fifties and sixties were all tied up with technology, but with communications and information transfer rather than with giant feats of Meccano engineering. I was born in 1930, and I am old enough to remember the popular encyclopedias of the day, the mass magazines like *Life* in which space exploration was seen as a natural extension of the development of aviation. It took fifty years from the Wright Brothers to the first faster-than-sound rocket planes in the fifties. It then seemed only natural that the next step was outer space and these were the sort of projections that 'Old Wave' science fiction made about the future. And while the logic of our past history seemed to be a continued expansion *outwards*, a persistent invasion of extraterrestrial territory, the growth of communications technology in the fifties and sixties was already suggesting that these huge spatial excursions were becoming not only less and less necessary, but also less and less *interesting*.

The world of 'outer space', which had hitherto been assumed to be limitless, was being revealed as essentially limited, a vast concourse of essentially similar stars and planets whose exploration was likely to be not only extremely difficult, but also perhaps intrinsically disappointing.

On the other hand, inside our heads, so to speak, lay a vast and genuinely infinite territory which, for the sake of contrast, I termed 'inner space'. The New Wave in science fiction – it's not a phrase I care for, actually – reflected this shift in priorities, from outer space to inner space, and in my own writing I set out quite deliberately to explore this terrain.

EVANS: Was your novel *Crash* an investigation of inner space?

BALLARD: Yes and no. *Crash* was really about the psychology of the motor car, or about people's attitudes to the motor car, and it tried to highlight the vast range of emotional ties that man has with this highly specialised piece of technology. It was a kind of science fiction of the present, if you like. I'm not interested in motor cars myself, by the way, but I *am* interested in what motor cars say about modern man, and about how they reflect man's needs and aspirations. Many people make the mistake of assuming that people buy motor cars because of great advertising and external social pressures. Nothing could be farther from the truth. Since the 1930s, when styling first began to be a big feature of design in the States, the automobile industry has emerged as a perfect example of a huge technological system meeting profound psychological needs.

The motor car represents, and has done for forty years, a very complex mesh of personal fulfilment of every conceivable kind. On a superficial level it fulfils the need for a glamorous package that is quite beautifully sculptured in steel and has all sorts of built-in conceptual motifs. At a deeper level it represents the dramatic role one can experience when in charge of a powerful machine driving across the landscape of the world we live in, a role one can share with the driver of an express train or the pilot of a 707.

The automobile also represents an extension of one's own personality in numerous ways, offering an outlet for repressed sexuality and aggression. Similarly it represents all kinds of positive freedoms – I don't just mean freedom to move around from place to place, but freedoms which we don't normally realise, or even accept we are interested in. The freedom to kill oneself, for example. When one is driving a car there exists, on a second-by-second basis, the absolute freedom to involve oneself in the most dramatic event of one's life, barring birth, which is one's death. One could go on indefinitely pointing out how the motor car is the one focus of so many currents of the era, and so many conscious and unconscious pressures. Indeed, if I had to pick a single image which best represented the middle and late twentieth century, it would be that of a man sitting in a car, driving down a superhighway. *Crash* was an attempt to explore this vast facet of human existence, and to that extent, I suppose, was part of the exploration of inner, as opposed to outer, space.

EVANS: What was the general response to this shift of direction in science fiction?

BALLARD: Although initially it seemed as though the various New Wave writers of the sixties were significantly off beam because of the apparent success of the space programme, I believe now that we were very much more in tune with the public mood than perhaps we realised. Don't forget that the sixties were the years of the resurgence in pop culture, and a turning away from the external material culture of the early twentieth century. People no longer saw their lives in terms of estab-lishing basic material securities – I must have a job, I must have an apartment, cars, washing machines. They all had jobs, apartments, cars and washing machines.

What people wanted to gratify were psychological rather than mate-rial needs. They wanted to get their sex lives right, their depressions sorted out, they wanted to come to terms with psychological weaknesses they had. And these were things that a materialistic society was unable to supply – it couldn't wrap them up and sell them for a pound down and ten pence a week. Now this rejection of external in favour of internal values was mirrored in the great popular movements of the time. Take the career of the Beatles, who began in the traditional materialistic mould of young rock 'n' roll stars – flashy cars, expensive clothes, big stadium concerts and all that – but turned in the end towards medita-tion, mysticism, the pseudo-philosophical drug culture of the psyche-delics, and so on. In other words there was a great current moving through western Europe and the USA in the sixties in a direction completely opposite to that emanating from the Kennedy Space Centre. The stars and the planets were *out*, the bloodstream and the central nervous system were in. It's no wonder that by the time Armstrong had put his foot on the moon, no one was really interested.

EVANS: Does that mean that the space programme has ended once and for all? Are you saying that we'll never go any farther?

BALLARD: Oh, no, there'll be a Space Age some day, perhaps thirty, forty or even fifty years from now, and when it comes it will be a real Space Age! But it will depend upon the development of some new form of propulsion. The main trouble with the present system – all these gigantic rockets sailing up off the launch pads consuming tons of fuel for every foot of altitude – is that it just hasn't got anything to do with space travel. The number of astronauts who have gone into orbit after the expenditure of this great ocean of rocket fuel is small to the point of being ludicrous. And that sums it all up. You can't have a real Space Age from which 99.999 per cent of the human race is excluded.

Far more real – and we don't have to wait fifty years for it – is the invisible Space Age, which exists already; the communications satellites, literally thousands of them, television relay systems, spy satellites, weather satellites. These are all changing our lives in a way that the average person doesn't yet comprehend. The ability to pass information around from one point in the globe to another in vast quantities and at stupendous speeds, the ability to process information by fantastically powerful computers, the intrusion of electronic data processing in whatever form into all our lives is far, far more significant than all the rocket launches, all the planetary probes, every footprint or tyre mark on the lunar surface.

EVANS: How do you see the future developing?

BALLARD: I see the future developing in just one way – towards the home. In fact I would say that if one had to categorise the future in one word, it would be that word 'home'. Just as the twentieth century has been the age of mobility, largely through the motor car, so the next era will be one in which instead of having to seek out one's adventures through travel, one creates them, in whatever form one chooses, in one's home. The average individual won't just have a tape recorder, a stereo hi-fi, or a TV set. He'll have all the resources of a modern TV studio at his fingertips, coupled with data processing devices of incredible sophistication and power. No longer will he have to accept the relatively small number of permutations of fantasy that the movie and TV companies serve up to him, but he will be able to generate whatever he pleases to suit his whim. In this way people will soon realise that they can maximise the future of their lives with new realms of social, sexual and personal relationships, all waiting to be experienced in terms of these electronic systems, and all this exploration will take place in their living rooms.

But there's more to it than that. For the first time it will become truly possible to explore extensively and in depth the psychopathology of one's own life without any fear of moral condemnation. Although we've seen a collapse of many taboos within the last decade or so, there are still aspects of existence which are not counted as being legitimate to explore or experience mainly because of their deleterious or irritating effects on other people. Now I'm not talking about criminally psychopathic acts, but what I would consider as the more traditional psychopathic deviancies. Many, perhaps most, of these need to be expressed in concrete forms, and their expression at present gets people into trouble. One can think of a million examples, but if your deviant impulses push you in the direction of molesting old ladies, or cutting girl's pigtails off in bus queues, then, quite rightly, you find yourself in the local magistrates' court if you succumb to them. And the reason for this is that you're intruding on other people's life space. But with the new multimedia potential of your own computerised TV studio, where limitless simulations can be played out in totally convincing style, one will be able to explore, in a wholly benign and harmless way, every type of impulse – impulses so deviant that they might have seemed, say to our parents, to be completely corrupt and degenerate.

EVANS: Can you be sure that their exploration, even if they don't involve other people in the 'real sense', will be purely benign?

BALLARD: Well, it seems to me that these kinds of explorations have been going on, if only in a limited sense, since time immemorial. Take the whole business of organised sports and games, which have been a major preoccupation of man for tens of thousands of years. Now there's no point in pretending that these games are played and watched solely because of the fact that they determine some trial of skill or bravery between opposing teams. The exhilaration of sport, from the pumping of one's lungs, the twisting of ankles, the bruising of the rugger field, the physical damage of the boxing match, and right at the other end of the scale the multiple deaths of a Formula Two pile-up, are all major components, and all might seem like totally deviant pleasures if they were not long-established components of participant and spectator sports.

Even today the idea that people watching a car race get some measure of excitement from being an observer of an accident which produces pain, mutilation and death is somehow slightly shocking, and yet it's clearly one of the reasons why people go to motor races. But I think we'll shortly be moving into a realm where we will be prepared to take for granted the existence of these seemingly deviant interests and through the limitless powers of our home computers and TV we will be granted universes of experience which today seem to belong to the dark side of so-called civilised behaviour. Of course, this doesn't apply solely to sport or to activities like the space programme; with the kind of simulations I'm envisaging it may never be necessary to go into space. One's own drawing room will be a thousand times more exciting and, in a peculiar way, more 'real'. No, there will be a huge range of activities, our sex lives included, in which we can explore endlessly the permutations of possible relationships with our friends, wives, lovers, husbands, in a completely uninhibited way, but also in a way which is neither physically hurtful nor psychologically or morally corrupting.

EVANS: Will people really respond to these creative possibilities themselves? Won't the creation of these scenarios always be handed over to the expert or professional?

BALLARD: I doubt it. The experts or professionals only handle these tools when they are too expensive or too complex for the average person to manage them. As soon as the technology becomes cheap and simple, ordinary people get to work with it. One's only got to think of people's human responses to a new device like the camera. If you go back thirty or forty years the Baby Brownie gave our parents a completely new window on the world. They could actually go into the garden and take a photograph of you tottering around on the lawn, take it down to the chemist's, and then actually see their small child falling into the garden pool whenever and as often as they wanted to. I well remember my own parents' excitement and satisfaction when looking at these blurry pictures, which represented only the simplest replay of the most totally commonplace. And indeed there's an interesting point here. Far from being applied to mammoth productions in the form of personal space adventures, or one's own participation in a death-defying race at Brands Hatch, it's my view that the incredibly sophisticated hook-ups of TV cameras and computers which we will all have at our fingertips tomorrow will most frequently be applied to the supremely ordinary, the absolutely commonplace.

I can visualise, for example, a world ten years from now where every activity of one's life will be constantly recorded by multiple computer-controlled TV cameras throughout the day so that when the evening comes, instead of having to watch the news as transmitted by the BBC or ITV – that irrelevant mixture of information about a largely fictional external world – one will be able to sit down, relax and watch the *real* news. And the real news of course will be a computer-selected and computer-edited version of the day's rushes. 'My God, there's Jenny having her first ice cream!' or 'There's Candy coming home from school with her new friend'. Now all that may seem madly mundane, but, as I said, it will be the *real* news of the day, as and how it affects every individual. Anyone in doubt about the compulsion of this kind of thing just has to think for a moment of how much is conveyed in a simple family snapshot, and of how rivetingly interesting – to oneself and family only, of course – are even the simplest of holiday home movies today.

Now extend your mind to the fantastic visual experience which tomorrow's camera and editing facilities will allow. And I am not just thinking about sex, although once the colour 3D cameras move into the bedroom the possibilities are limitless and open to anyone's imagination. But let's take another level, as yet more or less totally unexplored by cameras, still or movie, such as a parent's love for one's very young children. That wonderful intimacy that comes on every conceivable level – the warmth and rapport you have with a two-year-old infant, the close physical contact, his pleasure in fiddling with your tie, your curious satisfaction when he dribbles all over you, all these things which make up the indefinable joys of parenthood. Now imagine these being viewed and recorded by a very discriminating TV camera, programmed at the end of the day, or at the end of the year, or at the end of the decade, to make the optimum selection of images designed to give you a sense of the absolute and enduring reality of your own experience. With such technology interfaced with immensely intelligent computers I think we may genuinely be able to transcend time. One will be able to indulge oneself in a kind of continuing imagery which, for the first time, will allow us to dominate the awful finiteness of life. Great portions of our waking state will be spent in a constant mood of self-awareness and excitement, endlessly replaying the simplest basic life experiences.

EVANS: But isn't this tremendously passive?

BALLARD: Just the opposite. I would say we were moving towards an era where the brain with its tremendous sensory, aesthetic and emotional possibilities will be switched on, totally instead of partially, for the very first time. The enormously detailed, meticulously chosen reruns I have been talking about will give one a new awareness of the wonder and mystery of life, an awareness that most of us, for biologically important reasons, have been trained to exclude. Don't forget that man is, and has been for at least a million years, a hunting species surviving with difficulty in a terribly dangerous world. In order to survive, his brain has been trained to screen out anything but the most essential and the most critical. Watch that hill crest! Beware of that cave mouth! Kill that bird! Dodge that spear! And in doing so he has to screen out all the penumbral wonder of existence. But now the world is essentially far less dangerous, and the time has come where the brain can be allowed to experience the true excitement of the universe, and the infinite possibilities of consciousness that the basic needs of survival have previously screened away. After a million or so years, those screens are about to be removed, and once they have gone, then, for the first time, man will really know what it is to be alive.

1982: Werner Fuchs & Joachim Körber. An Interview with J.G. Ballard

Originally published in German as 'Ein Interview mit J. G. Ballard', Joachim Körber (ed.), *J.G. Ballard: Der Visionär des Phantastischen*, Meitingen: Corian-Verlag, 1985. Translated by Dan O'Hara

This interview was conducted in Shepperton at some point during autumn 1982, shortly before the publication of Ballard's short-story collection *Myths of the Near Future*. Ballard's next book would be *Empire of the Sun*, but his concerns here seem far from his own past. Although he ranges casually and knowledgeably through topics of concern to his interviewers – punk, pornography, LSD – he harnesses each of these contemporary phenomena to his own promulgation of the imagination as a true moral arbiter. An editorial note mentions that the interview took place 'at a time when youth unrest in Britain was hitting the headlines' – presumably in reference to the riots in Brixton, Toxteth and Handsworth the year before – but Ballard sees no prospect of class war coming to Britain, which he finds an 'expressly conservative country'. In this light, the violence-as-leisure motif of the later novels such as *Kingdom Come* might be seen as a logical extension of Ballard's version of British conservatism, wherein the middle classes merely react to any threat to their self-willed anaesthesia.

Much of the interview concerns influences, and Ballard is particularly strident in his rejection of the influence of Burroughs, whom he appears to see as a modernist after the fact. He stresses the distinction between the modernists' exploration of subjective consciousness and his own method, which affirms the outer world as a reality to be comprehended by consciousness, rather than created by it. Rarely has he stated his materialism so explicitly. In this context, his assertion that *The Atrocity Exhibition* is like a machine working to analyse the concrete relations of the outer world seems hardly a metaphor. [DOH]

FUCHS/KÖRBER: Even today quite a few critics are still of the opinion that science fiction concerns itself with the future. Yet you yourself have said repeatedly that it is with the present that SF must concern itself. The present in England is surely interesting enough to deal with. How do you see it and its possible consequences for the future?

BALLARD: Now, we have here at present a situation such as has never arisen before. We find ourselves in a process of drastic social transformation. I can't say what the world will look like if these upheavals take effect, but they will in any event be significant. Youth rebellion, violence in the street, such things have never yet occurred in Great Britain, and the middle classes and moneyed upper classes particularly are faced with a problem, as they lack any experience of it. Of course, there have been social revolutions that only took place through violence in all eras, for example in the twenties, when fascism was strong, but I scarcely believe that these developments can be compared to each other. Nowadays there are fewer poor, and the revolt issues less from need and much more from weariness.

Violence in the streets is something one knows rather better from continental Europe, but not in England, where such things are quite unheard of. I can't imagine a larger proportion of the working classes in this country being drawn towards the right wing, especially since it was precisely the Conservative administration which is at least in part responsible for the current state of affairs. But I also don't see any danger of class war coming here, that might change some aspect of the British system. England is an expressly conservative country, it was always so, and that's as true as ever today. The unrest is not as bad as the media and particularly television would have us believe. It is in fact true that many of the young are in revolt, skinheads, punks and so on, but their number is smaller than one would suspect – which naturally should not be taken to mean that their cause or their concerns are any less serious or important on that account.

FUCHS/KÖRBER: That you yourself have mentioned punk directly offers us an excellent opportunity to redirect things to another subject. The modern punk revolution, especially in music, seems to be comparable with the mood of literary upheaval in the sixties, which in the end led to SF's New Wave. This is also the view of Michael Moorcock, then the principal writer. What's your view of this?

BALLARD: Now, one can certainly draw some parallels. Punk is a movement of rebellion against outdated and overbearing values. But there, the parallels are in my view already exhausted, as the New Wave was a cultural affair in the first place, a quest for a literary breakaway, whereas punk goes much farther. Punks often aren't looking for any new direction, but only to denounce the old. And the New Wave oriented itself towards the future, whereas punk rock, as much as I pick up from listening to the radio, is really reliant on older musical traditions.

FUCHS/KÖRBER: Let's stick closer to literature. Even when you published your first stories there was, in certain ways, a dominant atmosphere of upheaval, even if it was entirely different. Or can one not see it that way?

BALLARD: Certainly one can! My first story appeared in 1957, and that was the year of Sputnik. I still remember it all exactly today: we sat in front of the radios and listened to the signals from this first artificial satellite – nothing more than *bleep, bleep, bleep*. And that really was a break such as one dramatically, emphatically cannot understand. This event seemed to change everything at a stroke. On the radio it was as if it was a celebration of the beginning of a new world, and it was also actually the beginning of the Space Age. It was unimaginable: one heard messages from other planets!

1957 was the real beginning of the space era, and it seemed to confirm everything that the old guard of SF authors had dreamed of and written together up to then. In those days it was like an intoxication; Campbell's prophecies seemed to be really becoming true. [Laughs.] And yet I was already back then of the view that outer space was not the right environment for science fiction. SF concerned itself with the gigantic proportions of outer space, and as a result the psychological component was forgotten completely – and naturally the literary aspect, too. I knew the way couldn't lead outwards, because the space programme had already taken off. There was nothing really interesting to explore. The way had to lead inwards, in my view. That was natural for me, as I'd always been greatly interested in psychology. For me, SF was and is the only legitimate literature of the Space Age, but back then it took a wrong turn in a direction which never interested me personally because it wasn't based on a psychological component, at least not in a clear and deliberate way. The fifties were an interesting time in various ways (as it seems the eighties will also be), and one didn't need a literature dealing with imaginary worlds when the most fascinating was the current-day on our own planet.

In my opinion, it's important for a science fiction author to pay attention to and describe the present, the modern landscape of communications, technological and scientific developments, and so forth. Even in the fifties so many changes had begun, the media landscape expanded, TV, high-circulation magazines, tourism gradually grew, pop music, all these developments had a direct influence upon human life, and in fact a much more direct influence than the space programme and the like – and no one dealt with it in a proper way. The first computers were developed, the automation of modern industry began, technology also gained an ever greater influence over the lives of people who had nothing at all to do with it directly. And then naturally there was always the nuclear threat in the background, which hadn't been there to such an extent before. And if one thinks of all these fascinating facts, it really is just too laughable that a literature such as science fiction, with such great opportunities, concerned itself with what was taking place on Proxima Centauri, or with invasions of giant dragons and such trivialities. The future began back then, in the present, and we were all witness to it!

FUCHS/KÖRBER: And your view found nothing to mirror it in American science fiction?

BALLARD: I believe a little of it rubbed off there, too; at least they still talk of a New Wave over there even now, in connection with authors like Harlan Ellison or Roger Zelazny. But I don't believe one can compare that with the actual New Wave in England. Authors like Zelazny or Harlan Ellison represent the world without reflecting on the times in which they live or write, they chiefly plunder ancient myths and dress them up in new clothes. That may be new and fascinating for American SF, but it isn't original. At present, the big market for science fiction in America is the cinema, with films like *Star Wars* and so on. And hence SF is reduced to the level of comic strips, and from that a view all too easily arises that the whole of science fiction is worthless rubbish.

Science fiction is very popular today, and it was in those days too, but what differs from then is that today, the whole machinery is more geared towards commercial exploitation. Back then there were magazines like *Galaxy*, *F&SF* and *New Worlds*, in which one could publish original and unusual material. I find it rather hard to believe that a magazine like for example the very popular *Omni* would today publish one of the really innovative and groundbreaking stories of the fifties, like something by Pohl and Kornbluth. Of course they'd be published there today, but only because they're now known.

We live today in an era in which the sci-fi game is becoming ever more popular, and naturally that's bad news for the serious science fiction writer. To outline things from my point of view: when I began SF had just had a terrifically big boom; in the USA there were thirty-five different magazines on the market, and even in this country there were six. That offered the serious interested writer a great opportunity to express himself. Writers like Philip K. Dick were popular back then.

FUCHS/KÖRBER: How did the New Wave proceed, anyway? In the sixties there existed a brigade of interesting authors who were relatively quiet in the seventies. And just now, at the beginning of the eighties, many are coming late to fame and honour. One could perhaps here mention John Sladek as one of the best examples. What was the matter with the New Wave in the seventies? And why have many authors become popular only now? Do you think that the time is ripe for the kind of literature which they wrote back then, and which largely disconcerted the readership?

BALLARD: Now first of all, the magazine *New Worlds* was suspended, which had been a common forum for many of us for a long time. That was a hard blow. Also many simply lost interest in SF, and went into other fields. Most simply didn't manage to break into the American market, since there were no more opportunities to publish in England, at least no magazines that were sold under the label 'science fiction'.

As far as I myself am concerned, I also distanced myself a little from SF at the beginning of the seventies. After the stories in *The Atrocity Exhibition* appeared in book form, I worked very intensively on the novel *Crash* . . . and that's how it went. I think I also somehow lost interest in the American magazine market. The USA was not nearly as interesting as in the fifties and sixties, and I think back then that applied to the whole of western Europe. The USA had lost its supremacy in every respect, nothing really original and new came out of it any more. Europe in the seventies was (and still is today) far more interesting. Nowhere in the world can one follow such a clash of opposing political ideologies as in western Europe. In this respect, there must surely also follow a cultural rapprochement with the Soviet Union at the least, in the long term the Soviet Union has to open itself to Europe – but Europe must also reciprocate. And the USA is an obstacle to this process.

I think that Europe is a far more fascinating place, because the United States has simply lost the flair it had in the fifties, it no longer has a monopoly on the future, the unlimited possibilities it once had. I said at the beginning that I expect interesting developments in this country. I think one can confidently extend that comment to the whole of Europe. Europe is a bubbling cauldron of constant psychological and political change, whereas in the USA there isn't anything at all like politics in our sense. In the USA we have something to do not with opposed political ideologies, but at best a power struggle between men neither of whom is any better than the other, who are at most perhaps more power-hungry. Look at how mediocre American politicians are! Or the trade unions – in the United States the unions are completely apolitical, something unthinkable in Europe. Men like Reagan, for example . . . or let's take Ted Kennedy, who is already regarded as a left-leaning liberal in his country. Here – I don't mean just in Germany – but here one would undoubtedly put him at best in the liberal wing of the Conservative Party.

Many writers here lost interest completely in the USA and instead concerned themselves more with Europe. I can say that for myself, at the least. At the beginning of the seventies I wrote *Crash*, *The Concrete Island* [sic] and *High-Rise*, and none of these books is strictly speaking science fiction – they are all concerned rather with certain social trends that were becoming apparent in Europe, and I tried to realise them novelistically. Accordingly these books did very poorly in the USA.

The same is true of Moorcock. In the fifties we all looked to the USA, because SF there produced original achievements in those days. But no longer, in the seventies. Take Moorcock's Jerry Cornelius novels – they're very typically European, inspired by London and the so-called pop culture of 'Swinging London', a radical departure from the American model.

For me the gap between European and American science fiction opened up in the sixties, because the public there simply couldn't understand the New Wave experiment – still less the editors and publishers.

And if for once one of the New Wave books did stray over to America, it was mostly by mistake, because publishers bought in an author without seeing the work. That happened to me with *The Atrocity Exhibition*, and I recall a very nice story about that, one which in many respects demonstrates the exact situation. *The Atrocity Exhibition* was bought by a US press, and shortly before the distribution of the book, this respectable publisher glanced over the contents and saw to his horror that it contained stories such as 'Why I Want to Fuck Ronald Reagan' and the like. Consequently he had the whole print run pulped, all but my author's specimen copies. Unbelievable! And afterwards I permitted myself the pleasure of sending a copy to Ronald Reagan, complaining about whichever respectable US publisher dared to publish this smut and filth. Of course I never got any reply, but it was worth it, for me.

Back to the topic. If a movement such as the New Wave forms, it always takes a while until new borderlines are defined and the whole thing takes shape. In the sixties there arrived many new authors who were published in the genre, and who afterwards seemingly abandoned it. The only reason for that is that the complete shape of the innovations of the New Wave still wasn't fully defined throughout. I myself never set out with the conscious intent: 'And now you write science fiction'. I always only wrote what was important to me at a particular moment, and then realised it was science fiction in retrospect. In the sixties the situation was different again. In those days I wrote much that wasn't strictly speaking science fiction, but that was published in related magazines and anthologies. The anthologies grew particularly in the seventies, when the great dying-off of the magazines began. For me that was a shame in all sorts of respects. I like anthologies, I like to read original anthologies, but still they lack the freshness of a monthly magazine. Anthologies get created in publishing house offices, and by and large they're conceived by the publishers as being in the same mould as a magazine. Also one can usually publish more quickly in magazines, get in touch with the public more quickly. Original anthologies are entirely different, there it can sometimes take years before something gets published, and that's no good because by the time of publication the writer may very well find himself in an entirely new phase of creativity.

Magazines are more flexible in this respect. All my early stories appeared in Carnell's magazine, I think I wrote something like fifty for him. Maybe more, but there were certainly fifty in the period from 1957 to 1964. And he never turned even a single one down. Everything I wrote got published, because he needed the material. He had a magazine to fill, some twelve issues a year appeared, and that's not uninteresting to an author in any case, if he has a stable and reliable market. I'm extremely sorry about the end of *New Worlds*, it was a shame the magazine had to be closed down.

It would be my greatest wish for a new magazine to come out right now, as these times resemble the fifties, and we could urgently do with one about them. I think that drastic changes in our lifestyle will come directly from new technologies. The video revolution, for example, will change everything. In the fifties TV came along, which changed everything, the whole world, and video will also change the world, lastingly, in fact. Everyone can experiment with video, everyone can be his own artist. It will have serious consequences, the extent of which is not yet at all quantifiable. We absolutely need a new magazine, the eighties deserve to be examined more closely. With these continuous upheavals, the eighties are really much more like the fifties than were the sixties or seventies. I would rather it were a small-format magazine like Carnell's *New Worlds*, as with a large illustrated magazine there's always the danger of it ending as so many such ventures do, that is, with the illustrations spreading and starting to displace the stories.

FUCHS/KÖRBER: And what do your plans for the eighties look like? How will J.G. Ballard deal with the dawning of this new era in his work?

BALLARD: I've already written some new short stories and novellas emerging from the end of the seventies and beginning of the eighties, and they will also appear shortly in a collection. In all sorts of ways they're a return to 'pure' science fiction, and a re-envisioning of what I wrote in the fifties.

FUCHS/KÖRBER: What are the actual influences forming you yourself, and your work? Several of the stories in the sixties were influenced by the new French literature, and if one takes a look around right here, one sees books about the surrealists everywhere. Have they had an influence upon your style of writing, and if so, which ones?

BALLARD: Yes, naturally, it's true that I'm a great admirer of all the surrealist painters. I can't say with such certitude what influenced my work in the fifties. My early books are stuffed full of allusions to the surrealists, that's also true, but that was more of an expression of the admiration I felt for them. I don't believe that the literature I've written would have developed differently had I never heard anything of the surrealists. I do want to say, not once have I consciously taken surrealist paintings as a model for my short stories or novels, even though naturally stories like 'The Voices of Time' or the *Vermilion Sands* stories do display certain parallels. It was more of a homage on my part, rather than a direct influence on their part. Moreover, in practice it's impossible to recast sculpture or painting in a narrative form because it's a question of fundamentally different forms of art. It is simply impossible to capture the mood expressed in a Dali painting in the right words.

If painters have influenced me at all, it was the pop art artists, initially much later, when I wrote the *Atrocity Exhibition* stories. Writing had already become an important business to me when I was at the beginning of my twenties, and in those days the great French symbolists of the nineteenth century may have exercised an unconscious influence upon me.

FUCHS/KÖRBER: Your influences lie in any case outside science fiction to a considerable extent?

BALLARD: Most certainly. I first came across SF when I was in Canada with the air force, it must have been 1953 or 1954. Before then I'd read no science fiction at all, but in the base there they kept SF magazines to sell in the canteen, everything possible from pulps to the better digest magazines. I realised that a lot of the magazines back then contained really interesting, colourful stories that in various respects were better suited to the times than so-called 'contemporary literature'. It's true that they were hideous in design, with these ghastly covers – one knows them quite well enough – but the content was sometimes genuinely interesting. Sheckley, Pohl, Kornbluth, Jack Vance – those were the authors I liked to read back then. Kornbluth was an intelligent author, and I thought to myself, my God, here are really vital and interesting stories! But they were nonetheless still stories that were published in popular and commercial magazines, and that meant that the authors were quite freely subject to certain laws of the mass market, and so furthermore, they only went just as far as they could and no farther. They employed no idea solely of their own accord. And suddenly it was all clear to me: here you have exactly the right environment for the kind of literature you really want to write, a literature of limitless possibilities. I had a head full of ideas and stories, and here was a medium that offered me the chance of expressing them adequately. I knew one could push open the window of commercial science fiction and let a little fresh air stream in. Outside there was a whole new world waiting for the literati to comment on it. And shortly after I'd got to know science fiction, I left off reading it again, because I made up my mind to write it myself.

FUCHS/KÖRBER: Let's stay with your career for a moment. You published as you said something like fifty stories in Carnell's magazine, some in the US also, and then came the point when time started to play an important role, when the stories became freer and more experimental. They lost the linear narrative of a story and brought in different events taking place simultaneously. That was the starting point for the later 'condensed novels'. For science fiction it was new and revolutionary.

BALLARD: That may be, but as with much that was 'new' in the New Wave, it was rather an aspect of that which was already recognised in literature generally. That goes for the New Wave in general, and for my collection *The Atrocity Exhibition* especially. That too was not new in modern literature. There were already experiments taking place even in very early modernist literature, for example in the novels of Virginia Woolf. The sole meaning of the more experimental literature of the late nineteenth and early twentieth centuries lay in an exploration of different subjective states of consciousness. The big difference in the New Wave and my own 'condensed novels' was that it wasn't exactly very important to me to investigate different subjective conditions of consciousness, at least not in the first place. What concerned me primarily was to take the traditional themes and view them through subjective eyes, through the eye of science and the changes introduced by it, if one will.

If one takes a look at *The Atrocity Exhibition* one will realise that, naturally, the book has a hero of a much more subjective type, who has possibly been driven from a nervous breakdown into madness, but actually he isn't the 'hero' of the book at all: that's much more the experimental landscape of the world in the sixties. That's the subject of the book: the communications landscape, the intersecting mirages of fiction and reality with which we all live, they're the real heroes. It's not important to me to investigate an internal sensibility, as the great modernist writers did. In this context I actually don't like hearing the phrase 'experimental literature', exactly, as when it's used here in this country, it appears mostly in a critical sense, because unfortunately 'experimental' literature is mostly really nothing more than the ego trips of different people into their own psyches, which hardly anyone can follow and which are ultimately only of interest to themselves. That's the case with much of what's generally considered 'High Literature'. Unfortunately.

With *The Atrocity Exhibition*, on the contrary, that's not the case. Here, the outer world is omnipresent, whereas in such books as those I've just mentioned, it has no relevance whatsoever. Consequently the book isn't just a daydream, but consists of concrete relations throughout.

FUCHS/KÖRBER: What actual influence did the works of William S. Burroughs have on *The Atrocity Exhibition*? Do you appreciate him only as an author, or has he also made a lasting impression upon you?

BALLARD: He's had no influence on me at all. I like several of his works. I often hear that Burroughs must have been a great influence on me and that it's particularly noticeable in *The Atrocity Exhibition*. But it's untrue. If one looks at Burroughs' books, one can see that they're entirely unstructured stylistically, that they consist almost completely of a 'stream of consciousness' in the Joycean sense, and are hence of a fully subjective world, and his works are improvised, frayed at every point, without a clear aim. His narrative structure is without architecture, written straight out of the feelings, without planning. And I've never used the so-called cut-up technique. I've been acquainted with Burroughs for several years, and he is quite of the opinion that his cut-up and fold-out techniques are very helpful in representing the world around us as it really is. He is of the opinion that the true nature of the world will be revealed by his random associations. My stories in *The Atrocity Exhibition* are entirely in opposition to that, they have a very precisely designed structure; the 'condensed novels' are like a machine working towards a clearly defined goal.

FUCHS/KÖRBER: On to the seventies. Your first novel to be published in this new decade was *Crash*.

BALLARD: Right. It developed directly out of *The Atrocity Exhibition*; there was even one of the 'condensed novels' with that title. The automobile accident has always interested me, and *Crash* is actually a model of the fictionalisation of reality in the sixties. In the 'condensed novels' there appears at one point a protagonist who puts together an exhibition of crashed cars, that was before I'd yet written *Crash*, the theme already held an extraordinary fascination for me. I wanted to have this exhibition as a sort of test for my theories, and I held this art exhibition as a psychological experiment as it were. What interested me particularly was how the visitors to this exhibition would react. So, we exhibited these automobiles that were heavily crash-damaged in a gallery in London, a gallery that was otherwise completely bare, only white walls, nothing else, no posters, no other exhibited items, just the junked cars. And naturally no explanation of what it was all supposed to mean, just the three cars displayed as sculpture. And then I had an internal monitor system, as well as a topless girl who went about interviewing the audience, and this would be recorded on the monitors.

When the exhibition opened, people would react with shock and nervous laughter. One of the cars was a Pontiac that had had a frontal collision. The cars were intact up to the forward part and the front seats, where the motor had been impressed into them, as it were; or better, the other way round. Especially these cars with their emblematic American appearance and the psychological contouring embodied in American cars, these cars had a very particular fascination for people. People were stunned. And the girl who conducted the interviews was actually supposed to do it entirely naked, but when she saw the cars she decided to refuse. And when she conducted the interviews and people saw themselves on the monitors being interviewed in the cars, they would shift into the back seats at the drop of a hat.

And also the cars got in worse condition the longer they were on display, the remaining windows smashed in with bottles and so on. The result of this test was in any case extraordinarily odd, and quite evidently I touched people's nerve, a psychological nerve. Many people came to the exhibition several times, just to attack the cars and destroy them further. Ultimately, this exhibition convinced me that I ought to write *Crash*. I'm still of the firm conviction that everything I wanted to express in *Crash* is true.

And something fascinated people, as the book went through two hardback editions here, which is unusual, and it was a big success, especially in France. It's a pity that it never appeared in Germany. Incidentally, the book was a flop in America, despite great expense on publicity. But that might be because Europeans are mostly faced with uncompromising subjects more frequently, particularly in France, where there's a very long literary tradition of pornographic texts. In France pornography was always recognised as a serious literary stylistic movement, their tradition stretches back as far as people like Sade. And also all the principals in the French Revolution wrote pornographic or erotic literature. In France it's recognised, whereas people in this country or in America maintain a very strict distinction between it and other literature, because it's only just started to be published during the last fifteen years, and most of that is of dubious character.

FUCHS/KÖRBER: After *Crash*, *Concrete Island* and *High-Rise*, the two other novels which both essentially take issue with modern technology, there was another short-story collection published, *Low-Flying Aircraft*, which when set against the stories from the sixties also contains new material that proceeds more from your earlier stories . . .

BALLARD: Oh, I've always only written basically a certain type of literature. People always think that in the middle of the sixties I only wrote *The Atrocity Exhibition*, but that's not the case. In actual fact I also wrote a great number of entirely conventional short stories during that time. People tend to think that I left off writing 'condensed novels' in 1970 because they weren't accepted by the public, just as they're of the opinion that I left off writing conventional stories after 1965, because they were no longer accepted. One also often reads that, but it's not true. In 1965 I wrote my fifty-fourth short story, and that was 'The Assassination of JFK', and story number fifty-five was 'You and Me and the Continuum'. Then in 1970 I wrote my eighty-sixth short story. Between 1965 and 1970, that's thirty-one stories all told, and of those, twenty were certainly entirely conventional stories. I've therefore never turned my back on them.

I admit that in a certain way 1975 was the end of a period. I'd written four books all tending in one particular direction, if one counts *The Atrocity Exhibition*, all dealing with the communications landscape and modern technology. Afterwards I'd simply had enough of it and I went off towards other themes. That will also be apparent in the new collection, which I've just finished. It will have the title *Myths of the Near Future*, and many of the stories it contains are pure imagination, so they range about in the zone of free, fantastic literature, like both of my last novels, *The Unlimited Dream Company* and *Hello America*.

FUCHS/KÖRBER: In the newer novels there's somewhat of an absence of the forceful hallucinatory images that your earlier books like *The Crystal World* contained. Did those descriptions back then have their origins in drugs, and have you yourself ever experimented with drugs or written under the influence of drugs, as many have supposed of *The Crystal World*?

BALLARD: Now, I wrote *The Crystal World* in 1964, and 'The Illuminated Man', the short story upon which the novel was based, must have come into being in about 1961. In those days LSD had certainly not yet become an issue, and I myself first tried it in 1967. Back then it was the great fashion, and everyone tried it once, psychedelic culture came directly out of it. Naturally there are states of affairs described in *The Crystal World* – the prismatic world, the static elements, the complete absence of time and so on, even experiences – that bear a marked resemblance to an LSD trip. Yet the novel didn't emerge from a drug experience, and that to me is further evidence that nothing comes even close to human imagination, it can do it all. The ending of 'The Voices of Time' is also very strongly evocative of a drug experience, when the protagonist with his increasing perceptions can suddenly perceive every most minute particle of the world, loses all sense of time, and sinks completely under a storm of impressions. This story also came about without drugs, and that, I believe, confirms what I've just said, that the human imagination is incapable of nothing, it doesn't have to fall back on artificial stimulants, on chemicals, to release something that the brain can do even on its own. A fertile imagination is better than any drug.

1982: V. Vale. Interview with JGB

Excerpted from the original, published in *RE/Search 8/9: J. G. Ballard*, San Francisco: RE/Search Publications, 1984

As with David Pringle, anyone who follows Ballard is indebted to V. Vale. As founder of RE/Search Publications in 1980, an offshoot of Vale's punk fanzine *Search & Destroy*, he has worked tirelessly to keep Ballard's name before the American public, which, as many interviews in this collection highlight, has traditionally been indifferent to Ballard's work. RE/Search is known for its avowedly anti-Establishment publishing programme that has consistently sought to uncover esoteric, mythical and buried aspects of Western popular culture. Alongside volumes on Wanda von Sacher-Masoch, sideshow 'freaks', female performance artists, the world of body modification, history's most bizarre pranks and hoaxes, reprinted S&M fiction, industrial music and film, gore and sexploitation films, and Burroughs and Brion Gysin, RE/Search has published four volumes devoted to Ballard. These comprise *RE/Search 8/9: J.G. Ballard* (1984), a book-length edition of the early *RE/Search* magazine; a large-format, illustrated edition of *The Atrocity Exhibition* (1990), complete with extensive annotations by Ballard; *J.G. Ballard: Quotes* (2004), which collects Ballard's most bracing statements from his fiction and vast reservoir of interviews; and *J.G. Ballard: Conversations* (2005), a collection of interviews with Ballard conducted by Vale and associates over a period of twenty years.

The following interview is excerpted from *RE/Search 8/9*. At the time, Ballard was still something of a cult figure, with *Empire of the Sun* still a couple of years away. Besides the main body of his work, he had published experimental fiction in a variety of small-press and obscure publications and had produced several graphic experiments in collage and mock advertising. For the average reader, these were almost impossible to get hold of. One of the great achievements of this volume was to collect much of that parallel body of work, bringing it together with a striking collection of Ballardian imagery by other artists, and the jewels in the crown: two long interviews conducted by V. Vale (accompanied by Andrea Juno), and by industrial musician, now film composer, Graeme Revell.

The Vale interview is extraordinary. Conducted over nine hours at Ballard's Shepperton home on 29 October 1982, it clocks in at over thirty thousand words in the original publication, and covers a remarkable range of topics, signposted by provocative subsections: 'The New Puritanism'; 'Burroughs'; 'The Replica Concept'; 'Deviance'; 'The Future is . . . Boring'; 'The Mental Library'; 'The Information Channel'; 'Crash Injuries'; etc. Ballard is clearly at ease with the underground, industrial-punk concerns of his interviewer, and responds with what may well be the defining interview in this collection, one that seems light years away from the standard science fiction/New Wave/Shanghai concerns of others. [SS]

BALLARD: You espoused punk – that was your sort of key metaphor, as it were. Punk was a stronger movement over here; my impression is that American punk is not quite the same thing at all. Five years ago when the Sex Pistols started going, punk was in fact a genuine anarchic, political movement. Over here, punk was like – I don't want to push the analogy too far – part of the appeal was, say, something like bull-fighting in Spain. For 150 or 200 years in Spain, certainly for this century, it's the only way a working-class lad can make it to the *big time* with nothing except a little courage. I think punk or pop music has something of the same thing. If you're a working-class kid and you've got nothing – no job, no training, no education, no background – what you can do is buy a guitar, or steal one, form a band, and you've got a chance – you may get rich. Or you can use pop music to express whatever your grievances or ambitions or dreams are. So you have these things like Oi! music. *Sounds* magazine, which Jon Savage used to write for, practically invented Oi!, which is National Front/skinhead music that's as politically explicit as *Mein Kampf.* The original punk was political, too – powerful political resentments were being expressed in British punk. I don't know what you do in the States if you're a youngster and you want to scream.

VALE: At one time punk appealed to thinking people; you felt you were going against the grain, rebelling creatively against a boring, stupidly uncomprehending society. Now we're back to conformity and pop fashion; a lot of the original rebellious input has been channelled back into corporate control and marketing.

BALLARD: The United States is really a very conformist and bourgeois country, isn't it? It's a paradox. In fact, in a real sense the US has presented the twentieth century with its greatest excitements, dreams and possibilities – but it's done so within the format of *extreme* conservatism and social convention. So where will the next breakthrough come? It's impossible to say – there may not *be* another one!

That's my big fear, actually. I was talking to my kids and some of their friends, all of whom are in their early twenties, and I was saying that if, as a science fiction writer, you ask me to make a prediction about the future, I would sum up my fear about the future in one word: *boring*. And that's my one fear: that everything has happened; nothing exciting or new or interesting is ever going to happen again. The future is just going to be a vast, conforming *suburb of the soul*. Nothing new will happen, no breakouts will take place. It could happen – that's what my fear is. I don't know what one does about that – opens a vein or something – I mean in the sense of suicide.

I often think that the most radical thing one can do is to *deliberately* choose the bourgeois life – *get* that house in the suburbs, the job with the insurance company or the bank, wear a blue suit and a white shirt and a tie and have one's hair cut short, buy the right fabrics and furnishings, and pick one's friends according to the degree to which they fit into all the bourgeois standards. Actually *go* for the complete bourgeois life – do it without ever smiling; do it without ever winking. In a way, that may be the late twentieth century's equivalent of Gauguin going off to Tahiti – it's possible!

I can remember the *Rolling Stone* in the late sixties, when it was a sort of counter-culture magazine for rebels. And gradually that became a huge corporation to the likes of Time Inc., almost. I remember reading that in the late seventies there were no longer any clacked-up VWs parked outside their offices – just Porsches and new Mercs. Curious the way that happens.

VALE: When Reagan became president, one of his first acts was to terminate the budget for publishing those inexpensive, informative government publications that have been around since the WPA [Works Progress Administration]. We tried to, but couldn't, get the government *Report on the Assassination of Representative Leo J. Ryan and the Jonestown, Guyana Tragedy* – it had over seven hundred pages of hard information.

BALLARD: That was the legislator who was killed?

VALE: Yes.

BALLARD: A lot of people knock the original *Warren Commission Report,* which I think came out a couple of years after Johnson assumed the presidency. I think Gerry Ford was one of the senators who sat on the Warren Commission. Anyway, I bought a copy of the Warren report, and I read it often, because in its way it's remarkable – if it were a novel you'd say it was a masterpiece. And it may very well be a novel, because a lot of its conclusions have been challenged.

I'm amazed that you've never read the *Warren Commission Report* – that is a *gem,* in its way. It's an *amazing* book – absolutely amazing stuff! For political reasons it was discredited shortly after publication, probably because the findings of the report – that Oswald acted alone – did not suit the conspiracy theorists, the people who thrive on the notion that there was this vast army of people out to kill Kennedy. There may have been, but I don't suppose they were actually in Dealey Plaza at the time.

I'll show you the other book which is my 'bible', an amazing book which I recommend you get: *Crash Injuries.* This is a medical textbook on crash injuries – a book to have. I had to write to the States for that. That is the ultimate book – all those comparisons of facial damage in rollover, comparing '52 Buicks with '55 Buicks – bizarre connections. Actually, one can read it without in any way being ghoulish; the way one can read the Warren report. Because one's dealing with fundamental entities like one's own musculature, one's own sort of highly conventionalised response to one's own body, one's tenancy in time and space, things we take for granted, and which are really completely arbitrary. That we are all shaped the way we are is totally arbitrary – a fact we take for granted.

Something like the car crash with its various injuries to, say, the human face shouldn't be a subject of ghoulish fascination, nor the opposite (anybody interested in these things is obviously perverted).

One should approach the material as, say, an engineer approaches stress deformations of aircraft tail-play – as a fact of life which must be looked at, otherwise this plane may crash. The human body may crash, so let's look at it anew. Texts like that are a way of seeing the human self anew, which is very difficult to do. But access to a book like that is not easy. For one thing, you're never told about the *existence* of the book.

That book played a big part in my novel *Crash* – I don't mean that *Crash* would have been substantially different, but it provided the documentary underpinning. Otherwise it would have just been fantasy, which it wasn't. Those two books are really, in their different ways, my two 'bibles'.

VALE: Isn't someone going to do a movie about *Crash* or *High-Rise*?

BALLARD: There are plans, but they've never actually exposed any celluloid to daylight. But maybe they will one day.

VALE: *High-Rise* particularly is so filmic – it's too bad it's not a movie.

BALLARD: Oddly enough, there's something rather comforting about that. I'm glad, really, that *Crash* has not been filmed. Because I can see myself beginning to believe the movie version – my own imagination deformed by the damned thing, squeezed into somebody else's mould.

I've seen a film script of *Crash* by a very good English writer named Heathcote Williams. Some film company wanted Jack Nicholson to star in it. This version was set in Los Angeles with American characters, an American landscape – obviously that's where the money is to make movies. It was a genuine translation, not just of language but of everything. I didn't really like it. It was almost *Disneyfied*: 'Walt Disney Productions Presents *Crash*!'

VALE: What happened to your wife?

BALLARD: She died a long time ago, nearly twenty years ago. I lived here with my three children until they grew up. They were very close in age, so they left home almost simultaneously. If you'd come here three years ago you would have found a very different ambience – kids charging around with their friends, a huge golden retriever. Suddenly, this silence! If you've ever looked after small children for a weekend, and somebody takes them away for half an hour to buy them ice cream, you sit down and say, 'God, what a relief!' Except that when it goes on for ever, you become conscious of a slight vacuum. But it's good; I find I can get on with a lot of work.

VALE: Did you find the Yorkshire Ripper interesting?

BALLARD: I found that case odd – something rather repellent about it. I don't think he was an interesting man in any way. I think he just had this obsessive hatred for prostitutes, and the impression I got was that he was simply reacting to his gut spasm of hatred. He kept a hammer in his car and every so often he would stop in a red-light district and hit one of these woman over the head in the dark. Difficult to feel any kind of sympathy for him whatsoever. Well, one shouldn't feel too much sympathy for any murderer!

In the case of somebody like Oswald, pathetic though he was, one could read his historic diary – there are extracts in the *Warren Commission Report* – and feel that that sad man was in a sense engaged with the largest political issues of the time, and in his own inarticulate way was trying to react responsibly to matters of enormous public concern. But . . . I didn't feel that about Sutcliffe, the Yorkshire Ripper. He was certainly not in the same class of fascination as Hindley and Brady, a very odd pair.

VALE: I saw a book yesterday on the recordings of Constantine Raudive, who claimed to have recorded, in empty rooms, voices of the dead – Burroughs had mentioned him in *The Job*.

BALLARD: I'm sceptical about all that. The whole world of psi phenomena leaves me dead cold. It seems to be less interesting than conventional reality. I mean, the fact that if you pick up that can of beer and let go, it falls to the floor – that strikes me as incredibly mysterious, in a way. Much more mysterious than if it just stayed hovering in midair – that isn't very interesting. The bizarre thing is that we can't communicate with each other telepathically – that's much stranger than any discovery that we might.

I don't think Burroughs has ever been interested in psi phenomena – they don't figure in the novels at all. That's what I like about him. He's very interested in the communications landscape, the onslaught of language and thought manipulation brought about by giant communications conglomerates like Time Inc. His theories of the linguistic basis for the manipulation of news – I think that's a fascinating side to his novels.

VALE: Is porno video as widespread in England as in America?

BALLARD: I haven't got a video machine myself; I think I'm probably the only person on this street who hasn't got either a) a video recorder, or b) a word processor!

VALE: Is this a particularly progressive street?

BALLARD: No, I just mean that everybody has these things, for some reason. A young fellow moved in next door. He said, 'Are you a science fiction writer?' (He reads science fiction; his wife sells Ford cars.) He said, 'Come up to the *computer room*; I'll show you my word processor.' In the maze of this little back bedroom was all this electronic gear; a word processor. 'Do you want to borrow it to write your next novel?' And I know somebody else here who has one. I haven't got a video, but I'm thinking about getting one. So far there's been no policing or censorship at all of video material, not even by the industry – the main commercial distributors of videocassettes.

VALE: Video has made a lot of obscure gore and just weird movies accessible.

BALLARD: There's a lot of horror material of the sadistic kind available, with people screaming in their suburban parlours – it may be doing them some good! And of course there's a lot of porn, which I'm sure is doing them good. I was looking at a display which was open to the street, so I took it to be a *mild* selection of their offerings. There was a certain amount of soft porn; a lot of horror. There was one called *Killer Nun* – nice title, so simple. But it didn't look very adventurous, on the whole. I dare say the 'hard' material was under the counter inside, and that you need to be a regular client. I don't think they display it openly in shop windows here, because the prosecution's too easy to bring on that sort of thing.

VALE: Do you enjoy living here in Shepperton?

BALLARD: I don't really live here – in a way it's just a sort of grid reference on the map. I came here twenty years ago with my wife simply because we didn't have any money. We'd had three children by then, so we moved out, down the sort of price scale, which coincided, by and large, with the distance from London, and found a small house here. Suburbs are nice places to bring up kids in England. I stayed on here out of inertia once the kids went to schools and all the rest of it. It would have been difficult for me on my own to bring up my three kids in Central London.

Also, it's a great place to work. It's isolated. In a crackpot way, I genuinely believe that I like to be where the battle is joined most fiercely, and in a way a suburb like this is the real psychic battleground – it's on the wave front of the future, rather than a city area. I keep an eye on all the social trends that develop – the whole video/word-processor thing – and it's very interesting to watch the fashions. I would almost call it an *airport culture* that's springing up in suburbs like this – a very transient kind of world. It's interesting to watch.

Ten years ago, in the early 1970s, Mercedes gave me a free trip across Germany. They were celebrating the 100th anniversary of Karl Benz's invention of the motor car, or maybe the first car Benz made – it was a big celebration, at any rate. A huge cavalcade of antique cars set out from Bremerhaven in the north and trundled all the way down to Stuttgart in the south of Germany, where they now make VWs. These cars, because they were so slow, couldn't go on the autobahn, which is the only way I'd travelled when I'd been to Germany before. We travelled on all these side roads at about thirty miles an hour, so I had a really good look at the terrain. And suddenly I had this appalling glimpse – it suddenly struck me that if I had to put my finger on what the future was going to be like, it wasn't going to be like New York or Tokyo or Los Angeles or Rio de Janeiro.

The future was going to be like a suburb of Düsseldorf, that is, one of those ultra-modern suburbs with the BMW and the boat in every drive, and the ideal sort of middle-management house and garden. Immaculate suites, not a cigarette end anywhere, with an immaculate modern school and a shopping precinct; a consumer-goods paradise with not a leaf out of place – even a drifting leaf looks as if it has too much freedom! Very strange and chilling, superficially what everybody is aspiring to all over the world: the suburbs of Nairobi or Kyoto or probably Bangkok now.

Everywhere, all over Africa and South America, if you visit you see these suburbs springing up. They represent the optimum of what people want. There's a certain sort of logic leading towards these immaculate suburbs. And they're terrifying, because they are *the death of the soul*. And I thought, My God, *this* is the prison this planet is being turned into.

At this time, the Baader-Meinhof – you know, that armed gang that came out very left politically, robbed banks, killed some American servicemen in a raid, and all the rest – was at its height. Nobody could understand these people. They were all sort of well-to-do, middle-class, well-educated kids from, comparatively speaking, rich families, who took to all this 'absurd violence'. Nobody could understand them. But suddenly I realised, 'My God, *of course* I can understand them.' If you're brought up in one of these suburbs around a German city, where nothing is ever allowed out of place, where because they were so terrified by the experiences of World War II and the Nazi epoch, they'd gone to any length to make certain that everybody is happy, everyone in school or kindergarten is dutifully equipped so there would be no deviance and no problems later. If you have a world like that, without any kind of real freedom of the spirit, the only freedom to be found is in *madness*. I mean, in a completely sane world, *madness* is the only freedom!

That's what's coming. That's why the suburbs interest me – because you see that coming. Where one's almost got to get up in the morning and make a *resolution* to perform some sort of deviant or antisocial act, some perverse act, even if it's just sort of *kicking the dog,* in order to establish one's own freedom. Suburbs are very sinister places, contrary to what most people imagine.

VALE: Cabaret Voltaire used to do collages on paper, but since they've gotten video equipment they do them in real time, on video, using hardcore footage of police brutality, brain surgery, CIA documentaries. Psychic TV is exploring the concept of ambient programming, trying to delve into deeper areas where subconscious decisions are made.

BALLARD: They're making their own programmes. These home-made movies are going to have a big effect on movies, the novel and everything else. The future is going to be like a glorified home movie – people are getting colossal expertise at handling the editing facilities of a home video studio. You've already seen that with these promo videos of the pop music world – some of them are very imaginative.

I don't know if you've ever seen that very early David Bowie video ['Ashes to Ashes'] – it's like an extract from a surrealist movie. Bowie appears as a Pierrot, a clown, one of those circus figures with a ruffed collar. And there's a bulldozer – it sounds terrible, but it's stunning! Because purely with electronics you can suffuse the screen with a pink light, or a blue light, and then overlay something else on, pick it out, turn the whole thing into a kind of planetary landscape. Suddenly all the real trees look like artificial trees, just at the press of a button. You can do extraordinary things.

You're getting a whole new sort of language that doesn't depend on storyline in the old sense, but on ascending scales of sensation, rather like music in a way – a sort of total abstraction. I'm sure all that's coming. Everybody will be doing it, everybody will be living inside a TV studio. That's what the domestic home aspires to these days; the home is going to be a TV studio. We're all going to be starring in our own sit-coms, and they'll be very strange sit-coms, too, like the inside of our heads.

That's going to come, I'm absolutely sure of that, and it'll really shake up everything.

VALE: Just as the word processor is changing writing.

BALLARD: They say you can already tell the difference between a novel that is written on a word processor and a novel written on a conventional typewriter. You'll notice this particularly in commercial fiction – what you have is excellent paragraph-by-paragraph editing, grammar, structure and all the rest of it, but very loose overall chapter-by-chapter construction, and this is because you can't flip through 100 pages on a word processor the way you can with a pile of typescript. So the detailed structure is very tight and elegant, but the overall structure is weak. That is interesting!

This chap next door has only got 35,000 characters (about 7,000 words) on his computer, which creates problems. He was pounding his desk, saying, 'I need *more memory*!' So terribly funny – I thought, 'What's going on here? This world is mad!' I find looking at a cathode screen terribly tedious.

VALE: Do you know Chinese?

BALLARD: I wish I could say I did. Although I was born in China and lived there till the age of sixteen, I didn't learn a word, because it was an area absolutely dominated by the West – by American, British, French and European interests, who ran everything, surrounded by hundreds of millions of Chinese who were desperate to find work, who had to learn English to work for the European or the American businesses, or for their households as servants or whatever. I lived in a house with nine servants, a Chinese chauffeur and all the rest of it – all spoke English. They wouldn't have got the job otherwise. I never needed to learn Chinese. I don't suppose I often heard Chinese *spoken* in the world in which I lived, even though I was living in a city with about five million Chinese – what paradox, that. But life was strange in those days. Shanghai was an incredible place to be born and brought up in.

VALE: The movie *Blade Runner* was supposed to be representative of Hong Kong.

BALLARD: From Philip K. Dick's novel, directed by an Englishman, Ridley Scott, who made *Alien*, a film I also disliked. In a lot of these blockbuster SF movies that come out of Hollywood – the *Star Wars* type of movie – they leave out the imagination. The best SF movies, and this includes those Hollywood movies of the forties and fifties, are stunning because the future seized your imagination by the throat, as it were, the moment the titles started. *The Day the Earth Stood Still*, *Them*, the original *The Thing*. There was one, *The Incredible Shrinking Man*, which was a masterpiece, among the best of all time. Even *Forbidden Planet*, where they were beginning to go over the top a bit. The original *Invasion of the Body Snatchers*.

They were masterpieces because they concretised the idea of a future – time suddenly starts accelerating the moment those films opened. Whereas what you feel with *Star Wars* and movies like that is that the moment the film begins, time stops. These films exist in a kind of time-less continuum that has nothing to do with the future – it could easily be in the remote past. Also, there's no sense of continuity. Watching something like *Star Wars* you don't get the feeling that this is what life is going to be like tomorrow, or, for my kids, the day after tomorrow – it's a completely self-contained world.

One SF movie that did impress me, and colossally so, is *The Road Warrior* [*Mad Max 2*]. That stunned me – I thought that was an amazing movie. The impact of the thing! Also, it was a credible future. I believed that. Technically and imaginatively it's a stunning movie, and judged just as SF I thought it was very impressive.

VALE: Have you seen any other you liked?

BALLARD: I haven't seen enough of the new videos. I don't know if there's a sort of *novelty factor,* which will begin to wear. It's rather like when you see your first porno movies, which I suppose I did about the mid-sixties.

I remember at the ICA there was a private showing of porno movies. I remember seeing about an hour and a half of these films, just screened on to a wall. It was a terribly phoney evening. The then director of the ICA invited a lot of friends and acquaintances; about thirty people were sitting in this room upstairs. He went around introducing everyone, saying, 'What are you doing?' 'I'm writing a book on de Chirico.' 'I'm writing a novel.' Everybody was *doing something* in the arts, in the phoniest possible way, very sixties.

And then these porno films were projected. These were the first explicit hardcore I'd seen, and they had terrific impact – I was stunned, absolutely stunned. Rather like the first pornography I had read, *The Story of O* at the age of nineteen, which rocked me back on my heels; and a little bit of De Sade or something. I was stunned by the novelty of these orgies and other things – some very abstract, arty work which was only at second glance pictures of people having sex. But I noticed that after about half an hour boredom sets in. I'd much rather watch *Kojak* or Cocteau's *Orphée* – almost anything else.

With the resources of video, you can build up quite a large library of images, taping from your own TV set: newsreels, documentary footage – particularly the medical documentaries with very high-definition camerawork showing open-heart surgery or brain surgery or what have you. You can store all those images and use them, with collage/montage effects. Although I wonder whether, as with watching porn, you begin to weary from a sort of *image overload*, and long to get back to something simple like a sit-com.

I think that unless you've got a really powerful imagination – it doesn't matter what the *form* or *medium* is – you will have nothing. But I can well imagine that quite accidentally, you might get some obsessive, say, who finds himself collecting footage of women's shoes whenever they're shown (it doesn't matter if it's Esther Williams walking around a swimming pool with forties sound, or Princess Di) – he presses his button and records all this footage of women's shoes. He might do it without any thought to what he was doing, and it might be possible that, after accumulating 200 hours of shoes, you might have a bizarrely obsessive movie that's absolutely riveting.

All right, you could do it *consciously* – you could begin to, say, store films of car crashes or street executions and the like, but you might get obsessed with people walking through doors or *anything* – *you name it.* You could just start *storing* the stuff, then begin to work on it to tell some *second story* – to overlay, say, the death and disaster footage taken from war movies or Vietnam or the Falklands or riots or what have you; to use that raw play as the *starting point* for your *own* obsessions. I think that unless you've got some idea of your own, you'll get nowhere – you can juxtapose all the bizarre images in the world, but after a while boredom sets in, doesn't it? Unless there's some new myth emerging . . . nothing is more tiresome than yesterday's experimental movie or experimental fiction.

VALE: It's important to analyse horror imagery – to confront and come to terms with the darkest recesses of 'human nature', if there is such a thing.

BALLARD: I agree with you – I've spent a large part of my imaginative life as a writer pushing that idea, in *Crash*, *The Atrocity Exhibition* and so on.

VALE: Well, your works are an example of how to digest and transform all this imagery.

BALLARD: I hope you're right! What would have stopped me in my tracks: I wonder if I would have gone on writing *Crash* if, say, halfway through it one of my kids had been killed in a car crash? But there are moral dilemmas of a rather tricky kind. I think that *to find the truth* is the important thing. The fact is that the medical textbook *Crash Injuries* does tell the truth because it's not primarily interested *in* the truth, in a sense. The man trying to analyse the difference in facial injuries caused by '55 Pontiacs as opposed to '58 Pontiacs in rollover is not primarily interested in anything but what he is pursuing. He's not interested in the effects; the damage to the human face or scalp or whatever is *incidental*, it's the *data* he's after. The point from which he starts, all these figures and comparisons he makes, are going to be made on the basis of people who are already damaged in car crashes – they're taken for granted. So he can leave that; his emotions aren't aroused by the appalling injuries these people have suffered. He is simply analysing, in a scientific way like a man in a lab, the comparisons between different vehicles, different accident modes or what have you. I think one's got to approach it in the same sort of spirit – trying to find the truth, which is often presented quite incidentally.

VALE: We're trying to rid ourselves of clichéd reactions to 'atrocities', as part of the overall aim of deciphering the censorship/control process that restricts the imagination and therefore life.

BALLARD: When you talk about the 'control process', do you mean the whole sort of mental apparatus that *shuts out*, that has all these deliberate filters and shutters, in order to cope with 'life'? The sort of material that very strongly interests me does seem to open shutters, like a sort of Advent calendar with which you open those doors, with which you get a brief glimpse of a different world. If one could have a blinding revelation and *know oneself totally* – the experience of just sitting in that sofa or chair would seem extraordinarily amazing. I mean, these are the sort of visionary glimpses of the obvious that great mystics are able to convey, aren't they?

The mere existence of our own sort of musculatures, the particular skeletal morphology of the mammal, not to mention the whole vast system of inventions and dampers and blocks and subterfuges of various kinds – elaborate mental languages and visa systems that operate on all sorts of borders of the brain, which is in itself an incredibly elaborate structure – if you could only shine a light through the whole of it, existence would seem as bright as the sun! As shocking as a blast of sunlight, or a vast blare of noise.

If you've read any books on neurology and the psychology of visual perception in the optical centres of the brain, in the perception of even something like diagonal crosses as opposed to vertical/ horizontal crosses, huge systems of compensation and adjustment (that are in fact gigantic systems of props and crutches) are at work providing what seems to be our vision of this commonplace object or room. Also, simultaneously, my brain is making all sorts of extrapolations about everything. And social relationships and the human imagination, at the upper end of the scale, are vastly more complicated. But the whole thing is so *conventionalised.* And the brain colludes in a whole system of repressive mechanisms which it willingly accepts in order to make sense of its own identity and of the universe around it, and these mechanisms are *limiting.* It imposes a mass of voluntary self-limitations which allow human beings to go out, sit down, walk down the streets, take planes and lead bourgeois lives with videos and word processors. If you take too many of those shutters away – *boom!* But it's necessary to do it, all the same.

VALE: Surrealists have influenced photography in the direction of inventive manipulation and juxtaposition.

BALLARD: There was a feature in *Time Out* about – I don't know whether she's American or Jamaican – the singer Grace Jones, who's a black singer with a sort of robotic appearance – a very powerful character. She sings a song called 'Warm Leatherette', which I gather is based on *Crash.* Her manager, *eminence grise*, is a photographer who has lived with her for five years. He gave her that image. He takes photos of her in, say, a running pose, and then cuts the photo at various points so that each thigh and leg and arm is cut; next he puts in little inserts that make her arms longer and legs longer, then retouches them so that the woman, in reality, would have to be about nine feet tall. But you don't realise this, because she's posed against naturalistic backgrounds like hotel rooms, and because it's so beautifully done. He's published a book of photos on Grace Jones, and they're extraordinary. She's sitting on a chair or lying across a bed, with an extra three inches of thigh or leg. Bizarre.

VALE: I think of Grace Jones as restoring blatant animality.

BALLARD: She's got a powerful imaginative presence – she does touch *something.* She's obviously manufactured, in the sense that her high-gloss ebony look and her clothes and that strutting manner are very calculated. But she transcends that – she's calculated, but at the same time there's this atavistic power drumming out of Africa, coming at you. You don't often get that mix.

I'd like to turn a photographer like Helmut Newton, whom I adore, on Grace Jones. His photos are like stills from very elegant, slightly decadent movies, aren't they? And you don't need the movies as long as the images are strong – you don't really need video, all you need is a still camera. You feel you've seen the movie when you've looked at one of his photographs; the movie reconstructs itself from a single image. All the images that have gone up to that point, and all those that follow after, are there. That's a marvellous talent to have as a photographer, and there are very few that have that.

Diane Arbus had a bit of that – you felt that the figures were characters in a movie, but a short movie, maybe five minutes long, about maybe a couple of dwarfs in a New York hotel. But with Helmut Newton you feel it's a ninety-minute, very elegant . . .

VALE: . . . *Marienbad*-ish sort of foreign film . . . Where do you go for vacations? Ever go to Barcelona?

BALLARD: Barcelona's a wonderful place. It's worth going to see the big church, the Sagrada Familia. You should go to the Park Güell, which Gaudi designed. And you can walk around the centre of Barcelona and see these apartment houses which he also designed, with their decorated railings. The Catalans have always had their own culture – it's one of the oldest languages in Europe. Both Dali and Picasso came from Catalonia. It's a very lively place – Barcelona's a great city. If you've got a reasonable amount of money, the hotel to stay in is called the Colon, opposite the Gothic cathedral (not the Sagrada Familia) there.

If you can afford to rent a car you can go to Figueras, which is not that far – about a hundred miles. It's Dali's home town, with a Dali museum. If you go about ten miles farther you can go to Cadaqués, where Dali lives, which is worth visiting for its own sake. All the landscapes resemble the giant, lizard-like forms that you get in Dali's paintings – you actually see them: 'My God, he just sat on his porch and just painted those ancient rocks!'

I've been there many times. My girlfriend and I used to take our kids on holiday every summer (not always together). Spain is the place to take a vacation 'cause it's near (Greece is a bit of an effort – it's a long way to drive). Also, I enjoy driving across France. We'd go to a place called Roscas, near Cadaqués, which Dali has used in several of his paintings. It's very near Barcelona. Get a good guidebook before you set out.

VALE: When film first started it was mainly conceived in terms of the theatrical play. Now video is mainly conceived in terms of film, and yet they're very different mediums.

BALLARD: It'll be interesting to see. Certainly one thing, thank God, is that things happen fast these days. You aren't going to have to wait ten years or twenty years – it's all going to happen by next Wednesday! That is really good.

I feel cautious about it, because if you look at the commercial film industry around the world, *that's* actually *sunk* below the point reached, say, in the early sixties – which I think was the end of an era, in a way. I'm not just thinking of American films, but British, French – you name it. Even allowing for vast budgets, the unrivalled resources of today's special effects, high-definition lenses and optimum film stock and processing – how often do you see a film like *Mad Max 2*? They *all* ought to be like that! Why hasn't there been an imaginative follow-through to all those technical resources?

VALE: *Invasion of the Body Snatchers*, made in the fifties, hardly cost anything. The same for *The Incredible Shrinking Man*.

BALLARD: Right, I almost make that my favourite film. That's not strictly an SF movie – the peroration at the end, where the guy stands on the grille looking at the stars, is a high point in imaginative cinema. All one's displacement fantasies – those are powerful fears lurking in the back of one's mind. What would happen if this room were really upside down, or if we were all inside out, or if we were only living in two dimensions instead of four? Those are basically metaphysical questions about the nature of existence – finding yourself a *strange human being*. Everybody recognises you, and I know who I am, but I know I'm not *me*! Those are fears that lurk in the back of everybody's consciousness, and these fears make us realise that consciousness is a very special condition – there's nothing *normal* about normality! That film tapped all those things much more deeply than some 'serious' movie.

VALE: It didn't cop out at the end, either.

BALLARD: Yes, that was good. The film was very efficiently made by Hollywood at its height. The skills of the men working on that 'B' movie were probably far greater than most of those working in the film industry today.

VALE: In the thirties, forties and fifties Hollywood used to produce at least ten great movies every year.

BALLARD: Modern movies are overblown, aren't they? I went to see Herzog's *Fitzcarraldo*, and I thought it was terribly disappointing. Magnificent photography – who could miss, given the Amazon sunsets, the lush vegetation ... But I thought it was overblown, and deficient in story. No Hollywood studio would have *allowed* that movie out of the factory in 1950, because its story was weak. It wasn't nearly so obsessive as his previous movies, like *Aguirre*. That was a stunning film – he thought out his plot and storyline, probably.

VALE: Hollywood made radical films such as *Dead End* with Humphrey Bogart, which starred these tenement kids who lived right next to a wealthy high-rise – incredible class tension. A very strong social critique, yet this was almost run-of-the-mill Hollywood fare.

BALLARD: And a film like *The Grapes of Wrath* was not alone – there were hundreds of movies like that being churned out.

VALE: Like Val Lewton's *Out of the Past, I Walked with a Zombie, The Cat People* – they made films seething with eroticism, as well.

BALLARD: They were great. Presumably, movies just reflect the society that makes them. Life itself may be a bit overblown these days – one never knows. It's an interesting time, much more fragmented than if one lived in the late forties, which I did. Then, if one thought of newspapers, magazines, television in its early days, the cinema – the whole media landscape generally (the world of publishing, the books that came out on topics of the day, political events around the world), they were all part of one *whole* – sort of *graspable* in a way. And it may be that that's going to end. Sections of the landscape will have no connection whatsoever with each other, in the way that many of the fine arts, such as pottery, are more specialised.

For example, glassware like Fabergé ornaments had no connection with the political events at the court of the Tsar for which they were made. Nor did the work of the great ceramic artists of classical China have any bearing on the societies in which they lived or the political currents running through them. You can't reconstitute an epoch from looking at a Ming vase – it stands outside time. It's hard to say, but probably nobody will ever again be fully engaged with a sort of *central experience*. Not in the way people from the thirties can speak of: a shared feeling of everyone being involved in great political currents, when you could see change coming and everybody shared in it equally. Also, great changes are taking place in life in general: the way people live, the standards of living, modern travel. Time will in a sense cease to exist; it won't matter whether you're living in 1982 or 1992 or 2002 – that sense of a single world will go.

Is this your first trip to England?

VALE: Yes. We've just come from Paris – the perfect town for sensual pleasures. The metro is humane; food is cheap and wonderful. Yet it seems to be incredibly bourgeois and conformist.

BALLARD: You're right, France is a *very* bourgeois country, yet in many ways the British, like myself, regard it as a kind of bridge to be crossed to freedom and paradise where the spirit *flies*. And I still feel that as I roll the front wheels of my car off the quay of Boulogne. I start to breathe the air, smelling that mix of garlic, Gauloises, shit and perfume, and it's intoxicating. I immediately think of the whole of French culture from the Renaissance onwards, particularly the late nineteenth century: Rimbaud, Baudelaire, the French Impressionists. Manet and Monet are sitting on practically every street corner in front of their easels. All the great adventures of the human spirit took place there.

I still think, as a lot of Englishmen do, that France is where the spirit takes wing and flies. But in fact France *is* incredibly bourgeois. Life in France, particularly for young people still living with their families, is like being inside a *vice*. One of my daughters did a special French course in school, and had to spend a fortnight with a French family. She'd been to France many, many times, staying in hotels and rented apartments, but she'd never *lived* with a French family. And she was stunned by all the unspoken assumptions about what you *can't do* if you're sixteen years old and living with a French family.

Even though they're all drinking their heads off with the first *pastis* at ten in the morning, it's an immensely rigid life. The domestic observances, assumptions about *everything* – values, one's attitude to work, play, life, responsibilities – my daughter said it was like something out of a Henry James novel. Everything was so straitjacketed, so formalised. On Sunday morning you visited relations – the idea of *not* visiting relations, and, say, going down to the local bar and getting drunk, was unthinkable. You could get drunk with your relations, but you *had* to see them. Incredibly bourgeois and puritanical.

It may be that some of the great artists in France have needed that to give them escape velocity – they *had* to be geniuses, they had to be *Rimbaud* to escape this tightened world which the tourist never sees.

It's a very formal society. I love France, but I visit it as a tourist, and I know that. I may have read Rimbaud, but I'm still a tourist, and I don't delude myself otherwise.

VALE: Your imagery must translate well into Japanese.

BALLARD: My stuff is very popular in Japan for some reason. I have a fairly big following there – they've translated everything. Quite a lot of Japanese over the years have come to interview me. None of them know about me – they think I've lived all my life in Shepperton. Then I drop this little thing in: 'Actually I was born in Shanghai and spent three years in a Japanese camp . . .' There's a *deep silence* – not a word is said for about fifteen minutes. It's terribly funny! So I reassure them that I don't harbour any unpleasant memories.

VALE: When was your car crash?

BALLARD: I had a serious car crash about ten years ago and I took some photographs of the car, but they aren't very dramatic – they aren't in the *least* dramatic. Compared with all those photos of cars that have been totally mangled, say, the car in which James Dean died, or the car in which Jayne Mansfield – *these* photos are not very dramatic. Of course, if they *had* been very dramatic I'd have been dead! It shows what strong cars British Ford makes.

VALE: Was this before you wrote *Crash*?

BALLARD: Actually it was after; many people think the book was inspired by the crash. I *rolled* the car on a divided motorway where there's a continuous island separating the oncoming traffic from the outgoing. A tyre blew out and the car swerved and rolled over and then crossed the central island, demolishing a piece of furniture which I had to pay for.

VALE: Furniture?

BALLARD: In this country, if you demolish a piece of street furniture – a sign saying 'No Entry' or anything, you have to pay for it! You get a bill! I got a bill for £100! I saw the new one they put in – it was a more *advanced model*, illuminated or something, and I realised that all this street furniture was being paid for by people who had had accidents!

VALE: Were you OK after the crash?

BALLARD: I had a bit of a headache, but I was wearing a seat belt.

VALE: That saved you?

BALLARD: It did, it did. I was lying upside down in this car; people were all around me shouting, 'Petrol! Petrol!' running everywhere from the engine – the car was upside down. They couldn't open the doors which were jammed because the roof was down. If the car had burst into flames I would have had problems – putting it mildly! The car was towed away by the police to a pound, and I visited the pound and photographed the car there. Very strange experience, that. But as you see they're not very dramatic.

VALE: Did your head strike the windshield?

BALLARD: It struck the mirror – I got a real headache.

VALE: But the windshield was broken.

BALLARD: That was just the pressure of the roof coming down, because the roof was depressed.

VALE: You weren't in the way of oncoming traffic?

BALLARD: Yes, I crossed the central island and demolished this illumi-nated sign, then continued up the oncoming lane. By a miracle I didn't hit anything, which could have been really nasty.

VALE: Or get hit by an oncoming car.

BALLARD: Or a truck. But I wasn't. That was the biggest piece of luck, and secondly that the car didn't actually burst into flames, since it was leaking all this gasoline everywhere. [Referring to photos] But it just doesn't *look* dramatic. You go to somewhere like Athens – all the cars in Athens look like this! All the cars in Havana look like that! Clacked-out old Dodges used as taxis – there's nothing particularly dramatic about that.

VALE: Did your life flash by?

BALLARD: No, because I didn't think I was going to die, to be honest. All I was conscious of was this overpowering smell of gasoline pouring from the engine, and people shouting 'Petrol! Petrol!' so my one ambition was to get out of the car fast, as I was upside down. It was difficult, as I said, because the roof came down and the doors were jammed. But I wound down a window and got out.

VALE: Are you writing more now that your kids have grown up and gone away?

BALLARD: It's hard to say, actually. I'm certainly not slacking off in any way, simply because I've got so much time on my hands. In 1965, when I was writing *The Atrocity Exhibition* stories, my youngest was only about seven years old. The kids were seven, nine and ten, and it was a full, hurly-burly family life – driving them to school, collecting them, all that sort of thing. I'd write those stories whenever I could find snatches of spare time. And most of my other fiction was like that. Now, I get up in the morning and the day just sort of stretches like the plains of Kansas, with not a speck on the horizon. Which is great, of course!

VALE: I like the fact that your phone hardly ever rings.

BALLARD: That is arranged; I don't encourage people to ring too often! Otherwise you spend all day answering the phone.

VALE: Concentration and sublimation . . .

BALLARD: I think there's a lot of truth in that; I think a certain degree of sublimation does take place. As you get older you can become very obsessive – one gets a sort of closed focus on whatever one's doing – writing a novel, painting a picture, or whatever it may be. Sexual obsession – God, I wish I had that. I have to think back! This close focus shuts out the rest of the world, and in a curious way that includes the world of the senses, too – a way that you at your age would find impossible to believe. But it happens, and it applies to everything. You can become so immersed in, say, a particular paragraph, that when you go out to do the shopping you don't even see the street! It's just a blur. You have to stop and say, 'Come on! Enjoy the sunlight!' That is a danger as you get a bit older: becoming so immersed in what you're doing.

I think you begin to realise that certain things are important to one's self; they provide satisfaction. 'All I want to do is write a certain kind of fiction that I write.' And that's where my particular fulfilment comes from. I haven't got children to bring up, to be involved with on a day-to-day basis. I haven't even got a dog to take care of, so I just concentrate on my work. And that can lead to a peculiar sort of very selective approach to reality, which has advantages . . . and disadvantages. One has to be wary of that sort of tight focus. It's not a problem yet; it could become one in five to ten years' time.

VALE: Do you think it could affect your writing?

BALLARD: No, it's not that intense. I'm not literally staring at the end of my foot all day, in the way that Burroughs described doing when he was on heroin. It's not that sort of obsessiveness. It's really a marshalling of all one's energies to do a particular job at hand. The wider life around one – social life and all the rest of it – does tend to take second place. One begins to apply the principles of cost accountancy to one's social life: do I want to drive twenty miles to make small talk at a publisher's party? Well, the answer is no – why bother, when I can go on with my work instead?

When one's younger, there's a natural tendency to want to meet more people. Straightforward biological reason supervenes, and rightly, I think, so one says: 'To hell with it, let's leave the typewriter and drive thirty miles to make some small talk. [Sardonically] You never know who you may meet!'

I don't know if people get that much fulfilment from painting, or writing a novel, or whatever. In fact, I'm not sure they get any at all! I think it's just a way of unsettling oneself. It's so intangible. Even a painting or a piece of sculpture is really rather intangible. It has a finite form, all right (you can actually touch a sculpture), but nonetheless it's a conceptual object – a conceit. It's very peculiar – I don't know how much fulfilment and satisfaction can come from being 'creative'. I have the deepest satisfaction when I do a job around the house – put in a new windowpane, say. It's enormously pleasing and satisfying – getting that putty in, or getting out the saw and hammer and nails. Very satisfying, a profound feeling of fulfilment.

VALE: And when you finish a book?

BALLARD: It's sort of a nightmare that's briefly stopped; one that will recommence in about three days' time. I don't think I'd do it again if I had the chance offered me. I think I'd become something like a cabinetmaker. I'd opt for a craft, rather than an art!

1983: Sam Scoggins. Ninety Questions from the Eyckman Personality Quotient

Previously unpublished

Here we have the most unusual 'interview' in this collection, a transcript of yes/no answers Ballard gave to film-maker Sam Scoggins in Scoggins' fictionalised documentary about Ballard's obsessions, *The Unlimited Dream Company* (1983). The questions are taken from the Eysenck Personality Questionnaire (announced incorrectly in the film as the 'Eyckman Personality Quotient'), devised by psychiatrist Hans Eysenck to measure personality traits. While the yes/no format was supposed to provoke quick, intuitive answers, the sparseness of the interrogation is actually intimate, and apparently says much about Ballard's character – or about the character of the many 'Ballards' in the public eye. Scoggins asks if he 'locks the house up at night', to which the reply is 'no' (libertarian Ballard). At times he hesitates, as when asked if manners are important ('yes' – old-world Ballard). On other occasions, as when he's asked whether he would dodge taxes if he was sure he wouldn't be caught, he answers quickly ('yes' – subversive Ballard). These responses underscore the slippery nature of his public persona, one that perplexed interviewers for the length of his career: the dichotomy between his gentlemanly manner and the rough grain of the anti-Establishment bias streaked throughout his writing.

There's a sense that this format, as minimal as it is, is far more revealing than some of the interviews later in Ballard's career, in which he seems bored with answering the same questions about Shanghai from journalists looking for easy sound bites. We inhabit Ballard's psychology, stripped to the bone in extreme close-up, with Scoggins' camera inching ever closer as Ballard ploughs his way through his answers, until we are left with an extreme close-up of his eyeball, like the surface of a distant planet.

While Scoggins' film does not record Ballard's results from the test, there is an online version of Eysenck's questionnaire, which contains the ninety questions he answered along with ten more. If Ballard's answers are fed in, along with educated guesses as to what he would answer for the missing ten, the following results are revealed: '63% (12/19) for Extraversion; 5% (1/20) for Psychoticism; 13% (3/23) for Neuroticism; 33% (8/24) on the Lie scale'. As our colleague Mike Bonsall has pointed out, this means that Ballard was 'a stable extrovert: outgoing, talkative, responsive, easy-going, lively, with leadership qualities. He was very well socialised with no tendency towards aggressive or antisocial behaviour and only a moderate propensity for lying.' [SS]

SCOGGINS: Do you have many different hobbies?

BALLARD: No.

SCOGGINS: Do you stop to think things over before doing anything?

BALLARD: Yes.

SCOGGINS: Does your mood often go up and down?

BALLARD: No.

SCOGGINS: Have you ever taken the praise for something you knew someone else had really done?

BALLARD: No.

SCOGGINS: Are you a talkative person?

BALLARD: Yes.

SCOGGINS: Would being in debt worry you?

BALLARD: Yes.

SCOGGINS: Do you ever feel 'just miserable' for no reason?

BALLARD: No.

SCOGGINS: Were you ever greedy by helping yourself to more than your share of anything?

BALLARD: No.

SCOGGINS: Do you lock your apartment carefully for night-time?

BALLARD: No.

SCOGGINS: Are you rather lively?

BALLARD: No.

SCOGGINS: Would it upset you a lot to see a child or an animal suffer?

BALLARD: Yes.

SCOGGINS: Do you often worry about things you should not have done or said?

BALLARD: No.

SCOGGINS: If you say you will do something, do you always keep your promise no matter how inconvenient it might be?

BALLARD: No.

SCOGGINS: Can you usually let yourself go and enjoy yourself at a lively party?

BALLARD: Yes.

SCOGGINS: Are you an irritable person?

BALLARD: No.

SCOGGINS: Have you ever blamed someone for doing something you knew was really your fault?

BALLARD: No.

SCOGGINS: Do you enjoy meeting new people?

BALLARD: Yes.

SCOGGINS: Is making insurance policies a good idea?

BALLARD: Yes.

SCOGGINS: Are your feelings easily hurt?

BALLARD: No.

SCOGGINS: Are all your habits good and desirable ones?

BALLARD: No.

SCOGGINS: Do you tend to keep in the background on social occasions?

BALLARD: Yes.

SCOGGINS: Would you take drugs which may have strange or dangerous effects?

BALLARD: No.

SCOGGINS: Do you often feel 'fed up'?

BALLARD: No.

SCOGGINS: Have you ever taken anything (even a pin or button) that belonged to someone else?

BALLARD: Yes.

SCOGGINS: Do you like going out a lot?

BALLARD: No.

SCOGGINS: Do you enjoy hurting people you love?

BALLARD: No.

SCOGGINS: Are you often troubled about feelings of guilt?

BALLARD: No.

SCOGGINS: Do you sometimes talk about things you know nothing about?

BALLARD: Yes.

SCOGGINS: Do you prefer reading to meeting people?

BALLARD: No.

SCOGGINS: Do you have enemies who want to harm you?

BALLARD: No.

SCOGGINS: Would you call yourself a nervous person?

BALLARD: No.

SCOGGINS: Do you have many friends?

BALLARD: Yes.

SCOGGINS: Do you enjoy practical jokes that can sometimes really hurt people?

BALLARD: No.

SCOGGINS: Are you a worrier?

BALLARD: No.

SCOGGINS: As a child did you do as you were told immediately and without grumbling?

BALLARD: No.

SCOGGINS: Would you call yourself happy-go-lucky?

BALLARD: No.

SCOGGINS: Do good manners and cleanliness matter much to you?

BALLARD: Yes.

SCOGGINS: Do you worry about awful things that might happen?

BALLARD: No.

SCOGGINS: Have you ever broken or lost something belonging to someone else?

BALLARD: Yes.

SCOGGINS: Do you usually take the initiative in making new friends?

BALLARD: No.

SCOGGINS: Would you call yourself tense or 'highly strung'?

BALLARD: No.

SCOGGINS: Are you mostly quiet when you are with other people?

BALLARD: No.

SCOGGINS: Do you think marriage is old fashioned and should be done away with?

BALLARD: No.

SCOGGINS: Do you sometimes boast a little?

BALLARD: Yes.

SCOGGINS: Can you easily get some life into a rather dull party?

BALLARD: Yes.

SCOGGINS: Do people who drive carefully irritate you?

BALLARD: No.

SCOGGINS: Do you worry about your health?

BALLARD: Yes.

SCOGGINS: Have you ever said anything bad or nasty about anyone?

BALLARD: Yes.

SCOGGINS: Do you like telling jokes and funny stories to your friends?

BALLARD: Yes.

SCOGGINS: Do most things taste the same to you?

BALLARD: No.

SCOGGINS: As a child were you ever cheeky to your parents?

BALLARD: No.

SCOGGINS: Do you like mixing with people?

BALLARD: Yes.

SCOGGINS: Does it worry you if you know there are mistakes in your work?

BALLARD: Yes.

SCOGGINS: Do you suffer from sleeplessness?

BALLARD: Yes.

SCOGGINS: Do you always wash before a meal?

BALLARD: Yes.

SCOGGINS: Do you nearly always have a 'ready answer' when people talk to you?

BALLARD: Yes.

SCOGGINS: Do you like to arrive at appointments in plenty of time?

BALLARD: Yes.

SCOGGINS: Have you often felt listless and tired for no reason?

BALLARD: No.

SCOGGINS: Have you ever cheated at a game?

BALLARD: Yes.

SCOGGINS: Do you like doing things in which you have to act quickly?

BALLARD: Yes.

SCOGGINS: Is (or was) your mother a good woman?

BALLARD: Yes.

SCOGGINS: Do you often feel life is very dull?

BALLARD: No.

SCOGGINS: Have you ever taken advantage of someone?

BALLARD: No.

SCOGGINS: Do you often take on more activities than you have time for?

BALLARD: No.

SCOGGINS: Are there several people who keep trying to avoid you?

BALLARD: No.

SCOGGINS: Do you worry a lot about your looks?

BALLARD: No.

SCOGGINS: Do you think people spend too much time safeguarding their future with savings and insurance?

BALLARD: No.

SCOGGINS: Have you ever wished that you were dead?

BALLARD: No.

SCOGGINS: Would you dodge paying taxes if you were sure you could never be found out?

BALLARD: Yes.

SCOGGINS: Can you get a party going?

BALLARD: Yes.

SCOGGINS: Do you try not to be rude to people?

BALLARD: Yes.

SCOGGINS: Do you worry too long after an embarrassing experience?

BALLARD: No.

SCOGGINS: Have you ever insisted on having your own way?

BALLARD: Yes.

SCOGGINS: Do you often arrive at a train just before it departs?

BALLARD: Yes.

SCOGGINS: Do you suffer from 'nerves'?

BALLARD: No.

SCOGGINS: Do your friendly relations break up easily without your own will?

BALLARD: No.

SCOGGINS: Do you often feel lonely?

BALLARD: No.

SCOGGINS: Do you always practise what you preach?

BALLARD: No.

SCOGGINS: Do you sometimes like to tease animals?

BALLARD: No.

SCOGGINS: Are you easily hurt when people find fault with you or the work you do?

BALLARD: No.

SCOGGINS: Have you ever been late for an appointment or work?

BALLARD: Yes.

SCOGGINS: Do you like plenty of bustle and excitement around you?

BALLARD: No.

SCOGGINS: Would you like other people to be afraid of you?

BALLARD: No.

SCOGGINS: Are you sometimes bubbling over with energy and sometimes very sluggish?

BALLARD: No.

SCOGGINS: Do you sometimes put off until tomorrow what you ought to do today?

BALLARD: Yes.

SCOGGINS: Do other people think of you as being very lively?

BALLARD: No.

SCOGGINS: Do people tell you a lot of lies?

BALLARD: No.

SCOGGINS: Are you touchy about some things?

BALLARD: Yes.

SCOGGINS: Are you always willing to admit it when you have made a mistake?

BALLARD: No.

SCOGGINS: Would you feel very sorry for an animal caught in a trap?

BALLARD: Yes.

1984: Thomas Frick. The Art of Fiction

Originally published in *The Paris Review* 94, Winter 1984

In 1983 Thomas Frick visited Ballard at his home in Shepperton, while Ballard was still working on the second draft of *Empire of the Sun*. The mission was to interview him for a highly analytical series then running in *The Paris Review* called 'The Art of Fiction', in which writers were interrogated about their technique, style and working methods. Here, Ballard gave the first hint that his own archive of drafts and preparatory notes – a kind of 'invisible literature' of his own making – might exist. Ballard denied the existence of such, even to his own children, until his death in 2009, once claiming that he burned all his manuscripts in his back garden. The archive has now been bequeathed to the British Library by the Ballard estate, taking its place alongside 'a specimen of Shakespeare's handwriting, one of the earliest surviving Bibles, a Beethoven sonata in autograph and the Magna Carta', as Tim Martin noted in the *Telegraph*.

In Frick's interview, Ballard repudiates postmodern relativism by taking it for granted as an element of our human psychology: it is one of the many perversions, or 'illusions', that the human mind routinely imposes upon everyday reality, whereas in his view the imagination is both the condition of all possibility of such perversions, and the human mind's highest achievement. [DOH]

FRICK: Are you ready to risk the fate of the centipede, who, when asked exactly how he crawled, shot himself?

BALLARD: I'll do my best to examine my hands in the mirror.

FRICK: So, how do you write, exactly?

BALLARD: Actually, there's no secret. One simply pulls the cork out of the bottle, waits three minutes, and two thousand or more years of Scottish craftsmanship does the rest.

FRICK: Let's start with obsession. You seem to have an obsessive way of repeatedly playing out permutations of a certain set of emblems and concerns. Things like the winding down of time, car crashes, birds and flying, drained swimming pools, airports, abandoned buildings, Ronald Reagan . . .

BALLARD: I think you're completely right. I would say that I quite consciously rely on my obsessions in all my work, that I deliberately set up an obsessional frame of mind. In a paradoxical way, this leaves one free of the subject of the obsession. It's like picking up an ashtray and staring so hard at it that one becomes obsessed by its contours, angles, texture, et cetera, and forgets that it is an ashtray – a glass dish for stubbing out cigarettes.

FRICK: So you rely on the magnetism of an obsession as a way of proceeding?

BALLARD: Yes, so the unity of the enterprise is forever there. A whole universe can be bounded in a nutshell. Of course, why one chooses certain topics as the subject for one's obsessions is a different matter. Why was I obsessed by car crashes? It's such a peculiar idea.

FRICK: Yes, why were you?

BALLARD: Presumably all obsessions are extreme metaphors waiting to be born. That whole private mythology, in which I believe totally, is a collaboration between one's conscious mind and those obsessions that, one by one, present themselves as stepping stones.

FRICK: Your work does at times seem to possess a sort of prophetic quality. Are you aware of this as you write?

BALLARD: It's true that I have very little idea what I shall be writing next, but at the same time I have a powerful premonition of everything that lies ahead of me, even ten years ahead. I don't mean anything too portentous by this. I suppose people – certainly imaginative writers – who consciously exploit their own obsessions do so in part because those obsessions lie like stepping stones in front of them, and their feet are drawn towards them. At any given time, I'm aware that my mind and imagination are setting towards a particular compass point, that the whole edifice is preparing itself to lean. In one way, like a great ramshackle barn.

FRICK: Has this manipulation of your obsessions come to feel at all mechanical over the years?

BALLARD: I do exploit myself in a calculated way, but there again one has to remember the old joke about the laboratory rat who said, 'I have this scientist trained – every time I press this lever he gives me a pellet of food.'

FRICK: Perhaps it's a symbiotic relationship.

BALLARD: I take for granted that for the imaginative writer, the exercise of the imagination is part of the basic process of coping with reality, just as actors need to act all the time to make up for some deficiency in their sense of themselves. Years ago, sitting at the café outside the American Express building in Athens, I watched the British actor Michael Redgrave (father of Vanessa) cross the street in the lunchtime crowd, buy *Time* at a magazine kiosk, indulge in brief banter with the owner, sit down, order a drink, then get up and walk away – every moment of which, every gesture, was clearly acted, that is, stressed and exaggerated in a self-conscious way, although he obviously thought that no one was aware who he was, and he didn't think that anyone was watching him. I take it that the same process works for the writer, except that the writer is assigning himself his own roles. I have a sense of certain gathering obsessions and roles, certain corners of the field where the next stage of the hunt will be carried on. I know that if I don't write, say on holiday, I begin to feel unsettled and uneasy, as I gather people do who are not allowed to dream.

FRICK: I believe I once read – perhaps it was in connection with the *Vermilion Sands* collection – that you actually enjoyed the notion of cultural decadence.

BALLARD: Decadence? I can't remember if I ever said I enjoyed the notion, except in the sense of drained swimming pools and abandoned hotels, which I don't really see as places of decadence, but rather like the desert in that I see them merely as psychic zero stations, or as 'Go', in Monopoly terms.

FRICK: But drained swimming pools, abandoned hotels – aren't you inviting the worst sort of psychoanalytic interpretation?

BALLARD: Ah, drained swimming pools! There's a mystery I never want to penetrate – not that it's of interest to anyone else. I'm never happier than when I can write about drained swimming pools and abandoned hotels. But I'm not sure if that's decadence or simply an attempt to invert and reverse the commonplace, to turn the sock inside out. I've always been intrigued by inversions of that kind, or any kind. I think that's what drew me to an interest in anatomy.

FRICK: The current notion of decadence is that it's merely a kind of guilty pleasure.

BALLARD: The guilty pleasure notion isn't to be discounted either, the idea of pursuing an obsession, like the black theme in Joris-Karl Huysmans' *A Rebours*, to a point where it is held together and justified only by aesthetic or notional considerations, beyond any moral restraints. A large part of life takes place in that zone, anyway.

FRICK: Perhaps we can talk a bit about the spiritual mechanics of writing. At this point in your career, you must have evolved a generally clear sense of what the whole process of writing a novel is like.

BALLARD: Writing a novel is one of those modern rites of passage, I think, that lead us from an innocent world of contentment, drunkenness and good humour, to a state of chronic edginess and the perpetual scanning of bank statements. By the eighteenth book, one has a sense of having bricked oneself into a niche, a roosting place for other people's pigeons. I wouldn't recommend it.

FRICK: How does a book take shape for you?

BALLARD: That's a vast topic, and, to be honest, one I barely understand. Even in the case of a naturalistic writer, who in a sense takes his subject matter directly from the world around him, it's difficult enough to understand how a particular fiction imposes itself. But in the case of an imaginative writer, especially one like myself with strong affinities to the surrealists, I'm barely aware of what is going on. Recurrent ideas assemble themselves, obsessions solidify themselves, one generates a set of working mythologies, like tales of gold invented to inspire a crew. I assume one is dealing with a process very close to that of dreams, a set of scenarios devised to make sense of apparently irreconcilable ideas, just as the optical centres of the brain construct a wholly artificial three-dimensional universe through which we can move effectively, so the mind as a whole creates an imaginary world that satisfactorily explains everything, as long as it is constantly updated. So the stream of novels and stories continues . . .

FRICK: So it's more or less a continuous process?

BALLARD: Yes. Presumably, all along one is writing the same book. I'm just finishing the second draft of the China book [*Empire of the Sun*], and although it's a radical departure in subject matter, the way it shaped itself for me and the process of writing it have been no different from anything else I've written.

FRICK: You remarked in an interview some years ago that you yourself consider *Crash* a corrupting book.

BALLARD: I haven't read it for ten years. That interview must have taken place in '73 or '74, when *Crash* and *Atrocity Exhibition* were very much in mind. I've long since moved on to more serene meadows. It's interesting to step, for a moment, into the time machine. Those were heady days, all right, when the sixties were a vivid yesterday, not a vanished epoch. As I remarked just last night to my girlfriend, how dull by comparison seem one's present concerns. *Crash* a corrupting book? I'll take my younger self's word for it.

FRICK: Do you map out your way with any kind of outline or notes before you begin?

BALLARD: Yes, always. With short stories I do a brief synopsis of about a page. In the case of the novels, the synopsis is much longer. For *High-Rise*, it was about 25,000 words, written in the form of a social worker's report on the strange events that had taken place in this apartment block, an extended case history. I wish I'd kept it; I think it was better than the novel. In the case of *The Unlimited Dream Company*, I spent a full year writing a synopsis that was eventually about 70,000 words long, longer than the eventual novel. In fact, I was cutting down and pruning the synopsis as I wrote the novel. By synopsis I don't mean a rough draft, but a running narrative in the perfect tense with the dialogue in reported speech, and with an absence of reflective passages and editorialising.

FRICK: Do you work on more than one project at a time?

BALLARD: I've never worked on more than one novel at a time, though I often break step and write a short story if I'm asked to by magazine editors I know. But I only write them in the evenings or weekends, so that the imaginative continuity and commitment to the novel are unbroken.

FRICK: What are your daily working habits like?

BALLARD: Every day, five days a week. Longhand now, it's less tiring than a typewriter. When I'm writing a novel or story I set myself a target of about seven hundred words a day, sometimes a little more. I do a first draft in longhand, then do a very careful longhand revision of the text, then type out the final manuscript. I used to type first and revise in longhand, but I find that modern fibre-tip pens are less effort than a typewriter. Perhaps I ought to try a seventeenth-century quill. I rewrite a great deal, so the word processor sounds like my dream. My neighbour is a BBC videotape editor and he offered to lend me his, but apart from the eye-aching glimmer, I found that the editing functions are terribly laborious.

FRICK: How many hours a day do you put in at the desk?

BALLARD: Two hours in the late morning, two in the early afternoon, followed by a walk along the river to think over the next day. Then at six, Scotch and soda, and oblivion.

FRICK: That sounds like the schedule of an efficient worker.

BALLARD: Well, concentration has never been a problem, and now there are few distractions. I assume that it is not entirely coincidental that, to the despair of my friends, I live in this remote backwater seventeen miles from London, in a small town where I know almost no one. However, until five years ago I had three adolescent children here, and not much more than ten years ago, at the time I was writing *Crash*, I was still driving them to school, collecting them, and getting totally involved in the hurly-burly of family life as a single parent. My wife died from galloping pneumonia while we were in Spain. But even in those days I kept the same hours, though then I stopped drinking at about the time I now start. At the time I wrote *Crystal World*, and through the five years of *Atrocity Exhibition*, I used to start the working day once I returned from delivering the children to school, at 9.30 in the morning, with a large Scotch. It separated me from the domestic world, like a huge dose of novocaine injected into reality in the same way that a dentist calms a fractious patient so that he can get on with some fancy bridgework.

FRICK: What about your children? Have they been sources of anything that has gone into your fiction?

BALLARD: My children are in their mid-twenties, my son in computing, one daughter in the fine arts, the other in the BBC. They haven't figured at all in my work, which is curious, as I've lived so closely to them for so many years and they were more important to me than my fiction. Presumably the sources of my imagination, at least, run back to a world beyond my adulthood.

FRICK: Are you a note-taker? Before the synopsis, do you jot things down, experiment?

BALLARD: Yes, if I'm not working, I talk over ideas to myself on the machine, by which I mean I type out little ideas, let my mind wander. I generally begin a book with a large sheaf of notes, covering everything from the main themes to the details of the setting, the principal characters, et cetera, all of which I've daily speculated upon in the months before I begin. I'm already doing so now for what may be my next novel. I've never had a creative block, touch wood. I've never had any problems stimulating my imagination. Rather the opposite. At times, I need to damp it down.

FRICK: It sounds as though you're constantly working. Do you rest between books?

BALLARD: I don't really think of it like that. Usually, as at present, as I finish one novel the idea for the next is there – even if as no more than a small piece of grit – and within six months or so, I will be ready to start work on it. But during that period, the work's steadily gathering material to itself, and that probably represents the main effort of imagination I will make.

FRICK: Speaking of stimulation, did any of the psychoactive drugs of the sixties give you any clues for your writing?

BALLARD: I suppose I'm a medium-to-heavy drinker, but I haven't taken any drugs since one terrifying LSD trip in 1967. A nightmarish mistake. It opened a vent of hell that took years to close and left me wary even of aspirin. Visually it was just like my 1965 novel, *The Crystal World*, which some people think was inspired by my LSD trip. It convinced me that a powerful and obsessive enough imagination can reach, unaided, the very deepest layers of the mind – I take it that beyond LSD there lies nothing. Imagination is the shortest route between any two conceivable points, and more than equal to any physical rearrangement of the brain's functions.

FRICK: Back in the sixties, Martin Bax and yourself, as editors of *Ambit* magazine, ran a drug competition.

BALLARD: Dr Bax and I ran a competition in *Ambit* for the best prose or poetry written under the influence of drugs, and it produced a lot of interesting material. In general, cannabis was the best stimulant, though some good pieces came out of LSD. In fact, the best writing of all was done by Ann Quin, under the influence of the contraceptive pill.

FRICK: Dr Bax is a novelist as well, isn't he?

BALLARD: Martin is a physician, a research paediatrician and consultant to a London hospital, and his book *The Hospital Ship* is the most remarkable and original novel I've come across since reading William Burroughs.

FRICK: Burroughs wrote an eccentric and laudatory, in its way, intro-duction to the American edition of *Atrocity Exhibition.* Do you know him?

BALLARD: Burroughs, of course, I admire to the other side of idolatry, starting with *Naked Lunch,* then *Ticket, Soft Machine* and *Nova Express.* I'm less keen on his later books. In his way he's a genius. It's a pity that his association with drugs and homosexuality has made him a counter-culture figure, but I suppose his real links are with Jack Kerouac, Allen Ginsberg and the Beats. Still, I think he's much more of an Establishment figure, like Dean Swift, with a despairing disgust for the political and professional establishments of which he is a part. I have met Burroughs quite a few times over the last fifteen years, and he always strikes me as an upper-class Midwesterner, with an inherent superior attitude towards blacks, policemen, doctors and small-town politicians, the same superior attitude that Swift had to their equivalents in his own day, the same scatological obsessions and brooding contempt for middle-class values, thrift, hard work, parenthood, et cetera, which are just excuses for petit-bourgeois greed and exploitation.

But I admire Burroughs more than any other living writer, and most of those who are dead. It's nothing to do with his homosexual bent, by the way. I'm no member of the 'homintern', but a lifelong straight who prefers the company of women to most men. The few homosexual elements in *Crash* and *Atrocity Exhibition,* fucking Reagan, et cetera, are there for reasons other than the sexual – in fact, to show a world beyond sexuality, or, at least, beyond clear sexual gender.

FRICK: How long does a novel generally take you?

BALLARD: Most have taken a year to eighteen months. *Crash* took two and a half years, as did *The Unlimited Dream Company*; the first because it was a continuing moral challenge – I had three young children who were endlessly crossing the road, and still are – the second because it was imaginatively exhausting, a real set of balancing acts.

FRICK: Do your titles spring naturally out of the work for you, or do you have to hunt for them?

BALLARD: Titles do tend to suggest themselves without being looked for, though in retrospect I feel one or two were mistakes. *The Unlimited Dream Company*, for example, sounds like a jeans emporium. There were also some titles that were strongly urged by the publisher against my better judgement; *Up* was my title for *High-Rise*. I often wrote short stories around titles that intrigued me, though I'm sure I would have written the stories anyway. One title, 'Venus Smiles', inspired me to write a short story, but when it was published I found the editor had changed the title to something else ['The Singing Statues'; 1962]. So I wrote another story with that title.

FRICK: Do you ever get well along and find you have to abandon something? And what's your approach to revision?

BALLARD: I've never aborted or abandoned anything, perhaps because everything I've written has been well prepared in my mind. I write the complete first draft before returning to the beginning, though of course I'm working from a fairly detailed synopsis, so I'm sure of my overall structure. I then do a fair amount of cutting of superfluous phrases, occasionally of paragraphs or pages. Each book is written consecutively, as read, never out of order. I think that the use of the synopsis reflects, for me, a strong belief in the importance of the story, of the objective nature of the invented world I describe, of the complete separation of that world from my own mind. It's an old-fashioned standpoint (or seems to be, though I would argue vigorously that it isn't) and one that obviously separates me from the whole postmodernist notion of a reflexive, self-conscious fiction that explicitly acknowledges the inseparability of author and text.

I regard that whole postmodernist notion as a tiresome cul-de-sac, from which any writer with a strong imagination, or any sense of moral urgency towards his subject matter, would burst forth with immense relief. Of course, I accept that an imaginative writer, like a figurative painter, takes for granted perspective, illusionist space, the unlimited depth of the picture plane, and that with the more extreme types of imagination, such as the surrealists (or myself), a double piece of illusionism is called for – one is asked to accept not only the illusionist space of the picture plane or the narrative text, but the strange events going on within that illusory space. Curious to say, the human mind seems to have not the slightest difficulty in doing this, and even seems designed to work that way, at least, if dreams, myths and legends are any guide. The notion put about by deconstructionist critics – who I hear are all the rage in the States – that there is no difference between a bus ticket and, say, Mr Micawber, that both equally are fictions, seems to me to miss the point that we can't think about Mr Micawber at all without making just that old-fashioned imaginative leap that the deconstructionists are working so hard to dismantle.

FRICK: Aside from your adolescent dream of becoming a psychiatrist, do you have any other pet daydreams about other lives, other careers?

BALLARD: I haven't really had any private fantasies about an alternative life, even in the daydream sense. I rather like the idea of ending my days drinking myself to death on a mountainside in Mexico. I went to the same school as Malcolm Lowry, The Leys in Cambridge, and curiously enough, in September 1939, while waiting with my parents for a boat back across the Pacific to Shanghai, I lived in a rented flat on the same shoreline near Vancouver and Victoria Island where he had his shack – we stayed a couple of months at a time while he was there. His father came from the same Manchester cotton industry background as mine. Bigger mythologies have been built on smaller grounds.

FRICK: Were the classics big among your studies?

BALLARD: Yes, Latin was very important. I was still doing subsidiary Latin when I read English for a year at London University, after ending my medical studies at Cambridge – from one set of Latin tags to another. At school – The Leys – we even attempted Latin conversation. We all agreed that we would far rather take the Latin oral than the French oral, which we detested.

FRICK: Your work has been very well received by critics, but you've had a rough time with publishers in the United States – even though we seem to be in the midst of a science fiction boom.

BALLARD: My own work has nothing in common with *Star Wars* or *Star Trek*, and not much, in a real sense, with written American science fiction, which has veered away into out-and-out escapist fantasy. I don't bring 'Good News' . . . though actually I think I do – for me, *Crash* is a novel with a happy ending. But there's very little my agent or I can do about my work not being in print in the States. Perhaps the economics of US publishing necessitate a larger hardback sale in the short term than my rather quirky fiction can manage. The same is true for paperback. I was published and in print in the States throughout the sixties. I've always tried to be as internationalist as possible, to get away from the parochial view of things summed up in that London *Times* headline fifty years ago or so: 'FOG IN CHANNEL – CONTINENT ISOLATED'. Actually, almost my entire output of eighteen books has been published, reissued and retranslated in Britain, France, Germany, Italy, Spain, Japan and Holland, and it's those countries – all (except Japan) far closer to here than Los Angeles and San Francisco are to you on the eastern seaboard – which give me my sense of a readership.

I think there's no doubt that a new European sensibility is growing, particularly among the college-student young who have grown up in the western European autoroute and high-rise culture of the past fifteen years. They see certain political concerns in my fiction which Americans miss. Perhaps, too, there is a certain amount of fog around Manhattan island. I regret that I haven't had more success in the States, but the Atlantic is very much wider than it was twenty years ago. I sometimes feel that to have a novel accepted in the States again means I will have to write about a bushy-tailed mammal who joins a nature commune and falls in love with a tree. In fact, you and a very nice teenager in New York may well be my only two readers in the States, the way things are going there. Perhaps I should introduce you?

FRICK: Your books are imported by the speciality shops, though they're damnably expensive. The last time I bought one, it was pulled out from behind the counter.

BALLARD: Remaindered copies, under the counter – the next step down the spiral is samizdat, I suppose; a few bundles of grubby typescript will circulate in a clandestine fashion, rooted out one by one by the thought police of the New York publishers. Of course, I'm joking . . . or am I?

FRICK: Could you say more about this new European sensibility?

BALLARD: The young people of western Europe since the sixties have grown up in a remarkably uniform environment, both in terms of the post-war architecture of high-rises and motorways and shopping malls, and also in terms of fashion in clothes and pop music, beach holidays in Spain and

Greece, and their attitudes to society as a whole and their place in it – to the place of Europe between the two superpowers (both of whom, the USA and the USSR, are tolerated but not trusted). I think for the first time in western Europe, one sees a generation which finds itself living in sane, just and largely humane societies – the welfare-state social democracies west of the Iron Curtain – and is deeply suspicious of them, while in fact sharing all the values for which those societies stand. Young people who take for granted that the state will provide free university education, free medical treatment and prosperous consumer-goods economies, but who nonetheless seem to suspect that behind all this lies some unseen conspiracy.

One sees the most extreme example in the Baader-Meinhof group in West Germany, whose terrorist acts seem totally meaningless and irrational. But, of course, that is the very point of those acts – in a totally sane society, madness is the only freedom. I think a lot of my own fiction – *Atrocity Exhibition*, *Crash*, *High-Rise*, for example – taps these feelings of paranoia and desperation. As well, there are all the enormous institutionalised divisions between the social classes, between the meritocratic elites and those on the dole who will never work again, between those making their way into the Silicon Valleys of the future and those left behind in the dead end of the twentieth century. A lot of the youngsters who come to see me and talk about *Atrocity Exhibition* see it as a political work. To them, the voracious media landscape I describe is a machine for political exploitation.

FRICK: I know at one time you put together some collage texts. As a frustrated painter, are you ever tempted to work more visually, in film or television, for instance?

BALLARD: I have, in fact, done a little work in film and television, but nothing I would really recommend to you.

FRICK: How about aleatory methods, à la Burroughs? There was a drawing of you in *Ambit* magazine in which I noticed a pair of scissors on the front of your desk.

BALLARD: The artist requested those scissors in order to cut up his sheets of paper. He then placed them on the desk and incorporated them into the drawing. On the whole, no. I need to rework my material to too great an extent to allow intact found-pieces to appear. However, as in Dali's paintings, there are more elements of collage than might meet the eye at first glance. A large amount of documentary material finds its way into my fiction.

FRICK: Can you give me some examples?

BALLARD: Well, certainly *Atrocity Exhibition*, where I adopt a style of pseudo-scientific reportage closely based on similar scientific papers. And there's the piece 'Theatre of War', in *Myths of the Near Future*, where all the dialogue except for the commentator's is taken from Vietnam newsreel transcripts. There is a scene in *Concrete Island* where the girl Jane Shepherd is berating Maitland. That is a transcript of a secret tape recording I made of my then girlfriend in a rage – well, secret is the wrong word; she was simply too angry to notice that I had switched the machine on.

FRICK: What about the piece 'The Generations of America', which consists entirely of a list of names, connected alternately by the words 'and' and 'shot' – as opposed to 'begat'?

BALLARD: Lists are fascinating; one could almost do a list novel. Those names were taken from the editorial mastheads of *Time*, *Newsweek* and *Fortune* – that was part of the joke, of course, as the first two publications played a large role in the sensationalising of violent death and assassination that I described.

FRICK: You don't seem to mention music very much. What do you listen to?

BALLARD: I think I'm the only person I know who doesn't own a record player or a single record. I've never understood why, because my maternal grandparents were lifelong teachers of music, and my father, as a choirboy, once sang solo in Manchester Cathedral. But that gene seems to have skipped me. I often listen to classical music on the radio, though never as background. I can't stand people who switch on the record player as soon as you arrive for drinks. Either we listen to Mozart or Vivaldi, or we talk. It seems daft to try to do them together, any more than one would hold a conversation during a screening of *Casablanca*. In fact, without thinking I usually stop talking altogether, waiting for the music to finish, to the host's puzzlement.

FRICK: You've been listed as prose editor for *Ambit* magazine for quite some time. Yet the magazine seems mainly devoted to poetry, and, I must say, very bad poetry, too.

BALLARD: I agree. In fact when people ask me what my policy is as the so-called prose editor I reply that it is to get rid of the poetry that infests the magazine. Of course, *Ambit* began life as a poetry magazine pure and simple, and the bulk of its readers, I would guess, are its present and would-be verse contributors.

FRICK: Most of your work is grounded in landscapes, whether real or imaginary. Shepperton and its surroundings play a large role. And certainly the United States, or at least images of the United States, are dominant in many pieces, completely so in your recent novel, *Hello America*. I wonder if you've travelled much in the States, or if you, like Kafka, in *Amerika*, made up your own.

BALLARD: When I travel, it's usually to the Mediterranean, where I go practically every summer. I visited the States in 1939 as a child; and in 1954, when I spent six months in Canada, I made short trips around the Great Lakes, to Detroit, Buffalo, Niagara, et cetera. I've never been to New York or Los Angeles, though I'm keen to visit. I don't think that handicapped me in writing *Hello America*; quite the contrary. Charles Platt recently criticised the book, not on the grounds of accuracy – he said it was wholly accurate – but for lacking authenticity. I feel he has the wrong end of the stick. *Hello America* is about that image which the States has chosen, in this century, to present of itself to the world at large. That image, and no country has been so consistent or effective in presenting an image of itself, is made up of its film stars and gangsters, presidents and their assassins, flashy cars, skyscrapers, Las Vegas, Disneyland, Cape Kennedy, the Mafia, all-powerful advertising, casually owned guns, Coca-Cola, blue jeans, street violence, drugs, and so on. I don't think there's any doubt that these constitute the image that the States has presented, and they would come first to the mind of anyone stopped in the street and questioned in Singapore, Sydney, Sweden or wherever.

Have they anything to do with life as actually lived in the States? Only marginally, I dare say. But I was trying to construct a society using just these images. I suggest you would come up with President Manson playing nuclear roulette in Las Vegas. It's not an incredible thesis, given that we now have a Hollywood actor playing nuclear roulette in the White House, with the latest 'nuclear war is winnable' strategy endorsed by the Pentagon. Contrary to what Platt seemed to think, *Hello America* is pro-American, and ends in the triumph of those old nineteenth-century Yankee virtues embodied in my old glass-airplane-building inventor.

FRICK: In one sense, in the midst of technological decay and overload, you uphold a conservative yet paradoxically pro-technological view . . .

BALLARD: I'm certainly no Luddite. The whole drift of my mind is pretty clearly stated in my work; basically, one has to immerse oneself in the threatening possibilities offered by modern science and technology, and try to swim to the other end of the pool. I think my political views were formed by my childhood in Shanghai and my years in a detention camp. I detest barbed wire, whether of the real or the figurative variety. Marxism is a social philosophy for the poor, and what we need badly now is a social philosophy for the rich. To Americans that means Ronald Reagan, but I'm thinking of something else, some moderating set of values, whether the *noblesse oblige*, the obligation owed to the less fortunate by the old English upper classes, or the Buddhist notion of gaining merit.

Apart from anything else, the modern communications landscape creates a different system of needs and obligations. I've written about that in much of my fiction.

FRICK: What about your reading? Does your writing hamper or dictate your reading?

BALLARD: I think my reading has grown more quirky and idiosyncratic with the years. At present I'm reading and rereading Martin Gardner's *Annotated Alice*, both for the text and for Gardner's brilliant marginal notes, without really realising why. I try to keep an eye on what is going on. I was very impressed by John Kennedy Toole's *A Confederacy of Dunces*, a masterpiece in its way. As far as reading for research is concerned, I've always been very fortunate in my friends. For years, Dr Christopher Evans, a psychologist in the computer branch of the National Physical Laboratory – whom I visited regularly until his death; his lab was just a ten-minute drive away – literally sent me the contents of his wastebasket. Once a fortnight, a huge envelope arrived filled with scientific reprints and handouts, specialist magazines and reports, all of which I read carefully.

Another close friend, Martin Bax, sends me a lot of similar material. The sculptor Eduardo Paolozzi is a restless globetrotter who culls Japanese and American magazines for unusual material. Vale, the San Francisco publisher of the RE/Search series – with excellent volumes on Burroughs and Gysin, and the latest *Industrial Culture Handbook* – is a one-man information satellite beaming out a stream of fascinating things. Readers of mine send in a lot of material, for which I'm grateful. The leader of the rock group SPK [Graeme Revell], who visited me a week ago, told me that he believes that there is a group of some two or three thousand people in Europe and the States who circulate information among each other. Sadly, modern technology, which ought to be so liberating, threatens all this. Already, I've received the first videocassettes in the place of the old envelopes crammed with odd magazines and cuttings. As I don't own a video recorder, the cassettes sit unseen on my bookshelves; the first volumes of the invisible library. One of my daughters reported on one tape, 'It's rather weird, all about autopsies.'

FRICK: One odd thing I've noticed about the varying responses to your work is that some people think it's extremely funny, while others read it in an extremely serious way. I know I've had both responses to the same piece – though usually at different times. What do you think?

BALLARD: A tricky question. I've always been accused of being a humourless writer. *Crash* strikes me as very funny, reading a paragraph aloud used to have me in fits, because in a way it's so preposterous. And 'The Dead Time' has strong elements of a concealed humour of the same kind. But then, existence itself is a very special kind of joke.

FRICK: Now, that old chestnut: do you have any advice for young writers?

BALLARD: A lifetime's experience urges me to utter a warning cry: do anything else, take someone's golden retriever for a walk, run away with a saxophone player. Perhaps what's wrong with being a writer is that one can't even say 'good luck' – luck plays no part in the writing of a novel. No happy accidents as with the paint pot or chisel. I don't think you can say anything, really.

I've always wanted to juggle and ride a unicycle, but I dare say if I ever asked the advice of an acrobat he would say, 'All you do is get on and start pedalling.'

1984: Peter Rønnov-Jessen. Against Entropy

Originally published in *The Literary Review* 74, August 1984

Peter Rønnov-Jessen's interview might equally well have been titled 'Against Dystopia', as in it Ballard repudiates not just the charge of writing 'entropic' fiction but emphasises the utopian fulfilment of his characters' fantasies. The adjective 'Ballardian' – which the *Collins English Dictionary* defines in part as referring to fictions featuring a 'dystopian modernity' – misleads on this point. Ballard's fictions, however apocalyptic their physical settings, generally follow a pattern of psychological self-exploration culminating in the fulfilment of unconscious desire and, in doing so, attempt both to realise in fiction our deepest unacknowledged needs, and to reveal the vulnerabilities of our unconscious desires to manipulation by the media landscape.

It's therefore, perhaps, a stroke of unconscious genius that leads Rønnov-Jessen to ask about the obstructiveness of Ballard's female characters, offering him the opportunity to suggest that his characters, whether male or female, represent, to the unconscious mind, merely a short cut or a cul-de-sac. If our unconscious desires and obsessions are to be decoded, Ballard proposes, we must examine the artificial structures through which we try to transcend the limitations of self, and the limitations of our concept of selves. The interview is also noteworthy for containing a rare discussion of Ballard's excellent novella *The Ultimate City* (1976). [DOH]

RØNNOV-JESSEN: In some of your books you are preoccupied with post-industrial society. In *The Ultimate City* you depict two townships,

Garden City and the Ultimate City itself. Whereas most people would say that the static pastoral of Garden City was an Eden realised, the protagonist obviously prefers the dynamic decay of the Ultimate City – the entropy, to use that catchphrase of the sixties.

BALLARD: I don't think that small section of New York (the city in question, though I never stated it) which he reanimates – trying to recapture something of the dynamism, aggression and freedom for the imagination to soar that was so lacking in the small rural town where he was brought up – is exactly a zone of entropy. Quite the opposite: he sees life in Garden City as imagination stifled, he sees a complete absence of real freedom in this rural paradise. He returns to the ancient city across the bay, a city which holds within itself the possibilities, the tools, the means by which he can release his imagination. Of course, he finds there this old entrepreneur, an architect, an antiquated figure with all his dreams of giant engineering structures. Now Fuller represents the last of that generation who saw through engineering a way to tap man's imagination, a sense of the dynamic possibilities of life. I don't see the city as entropic. I endorse the quest by the young hero to find an alternative to that little paradise across the bay where human imagination is totally stifled. I don't make any moral judgements about it. I think the world will always produce its Buckminster Fullers and people like the boy, who are determined to strike out on their own and who need to release their imaginations in a particularly direct way, who dislike any kind of static society and its values (which are epitomised in the great suburbs of western Europe and the United States: death to the spirit).

RØNNOV-JESSEN: You live in a suburb.

BALLARD: Yes. It's a very good place to work because I'm reminded every moment of the day what the alternative to the imagination is.

RØNNOV-JESSEN: One could say that the dynamism represented by New York is actually the dynamism of decay.

BALLARD: No, I don't accept that. The city is abandoned, and with it, suspended in time, is a whole set of formulae for expressing human energy, imagination, ambition. The clock has stopped, but it will be possible for the boy to start it up again, just as in the novel *Hello America*, where the young hero does precisely the same – except *he* attempts to do it on a continental level. It's basically the same story, though again I point to the inherent dangers.

RØNNOV-JESSEN: There seems to be a sort of relish in the decay, doesn't there?

BALLARD: I don't think there *is* any decay. The America and the Las Vegas that the characters find in *Hello America* is not decayed – it's just abandoned, which is a very different thing. In *The Ultimate City* things get out of hand, of course. It's the classic story of Aladdin with the lamp, the sorcerer's apprentice, and so on. My young hero in both the novella and the novel hasn't realised everything that the *genie* of the human imagination and human ambition is capable of achieving: once you give him the go-ahead, say the magic word and he leaps from the lamp, you may get more than you bargained for. So I'm making a judgement on human ambition and imagination in both works; I'm saying implicitly that the dark side of the imagination emerges. The novel is more specifically about America; the novella is basically about industrialisation and the twentieth century, and it could be set anywhere in any big city – Sydney, Cape Town (though in fact it's New York). I don't see post-industrialism as a matter of decay, either morally speaking or in the literal sense. That's what's interesting about it: it's not that the society based on the machine, on technology, is crumbling in its social structures and moral values, rotting, decaying . . .

No, that isn't what is happening. It's simply that one has evolved completely out of the whole system of values represented by the technological society, just as 150 years ago, at the time of the Industrial Revolution, people left the countryside and moved to the cities. This didn't mean that the agricultural life was decaying, that its moral values were in disrepute. Not at all, it simply meant that people had evolved to a state where they needed the city to fulfil themselves and their possibilities. Just as that has happened, I think people are now beginning to evolve beyond the possibilities of the large conurbations of industrial society – with its built-in conformism of the mass-production line, of the shop floor – and they want more individuality. So a second emigration is going on, certainly in this country and, I think, in the US and most countries of western Europe. People are moving away from the industrial base, in all senses, towards something more reflective and more private. The transformation of the home into a TV studio has taken place gradually – more and more electronic equipment, home video systems, TV cameras, video libraries. People are moving into a more private phase of self-exploration, and leaving behind the mass society that technology created 150 years ago. So entropy is the wrong word to describe the process at work in both *The Ultimate City* and *Hello America*. The clock stopped, but the machine is still there.

RØNNOV-JESSEN: You've said several times that the disasters your characters face lead them to a certain kind of psychic fulfilment. Maitland in *Concrete Island*, Ballard in *Crash* and Laing in *High-Rise* may all be said to have staged the catastrophes themselves, to a certain extent. But what about Sanders in *The Crystal World*, Ransom in *The Drought* and Kerans in *The Drowned World*? To what extent would you consider a reading of these works valid which claimed that the natural disasters depicted are mere externalisations of the characters' subconscious drives and desires?

BALLARD: I think that's very fair. It is quite true that in *Crash*, *Concrete Island* and *High-Rise* the characters almost consciously create the disaster. That's not true in the case of the other three books you mention, because of course it's not possible for an individual to arrange for the icecaps to melt and London to be flooded, or for a drought to turn a whole hemisphere into a desert. But what would have happened to these characters had these global disasters not taken place? It's quite an interesting question. What would have happened to Kerans, Sanders and Ransom if there had been no melting icecaps, no crystallising, or no drought – what would they have done about their powerful compulsions? Presumably they would have contrived crises of their internal universe in some other way . . . but you're right that in my first three novels the external disasters do seem to have been created by the characters in the same way as in the later three novels. It's also a matter of interpretation, isn't it? If you take *The Drowned World*, my hero, Kerans, is the only one to see the significance of the transformation going on. All the other characters in my first three books react as most ordinary people would: if the dam bursts, they run for the hills. It's only the central character who sees the system of imaginative possibilities represented by the disaster.

RØNNOV-JESSEN: In traditional disaster stories the goal of the acting subjects is to subdue the object, the world, whereas your characters seem to want to merge . . .

BALLARD: That's true. That's part of the problem faced by the hero in all three books. Take Kerans in *The Drowned World*: by the time you go back to the sources of your being in the amniotic soup, the primal sea, of course you find the truth about yourself but you lose your individuality by merging into the great undifferentiated source of life. Likewise, the last line of my novel *The Drought* is something like: 'When it started to rain, he no longer noticed that it was raining'. That means the drought is now absolute – the absolute drought endures even when it rains. The psychological process of 'fulfilment' has reached its terminal point when you are no longer aware of the process. Right at the end it starts to rain but Ransom isn't aware of it because the drought is now absolute inside his head. That process is probably at work in all my fiction: ultimately a point is reached where the very process that generated the book in the first place is no longer necessary. But life tends to express itself in that kind of way, doesn't it? People have powerful ambitions and hopes which fade as you reach your fifties (as I have done). One's dreams and hopes seem to fade, and one wonders: 'what's gone wrong with me?' In fact what has happened is that one has achieved those dreams. It's like flying through a cloud: you see this beautiful, clearly sculptured mass of white vapour that seems solid as marble in the sky, but as you approach it disappears and suddenly you're flying through what seems to be just a light fog. That is true of life itself. So I think all those books end at the right point.

RØNNOV-JESSEN: But *The Drought* is different because it actually starts to rain. It's the only one of those three books where the process seems to be reversed at the end.

BALLARD: That may be technically the case. I could have ended *The Drowned World* with the waters subsiding, and the hero still moving through a marine world – mentally. I don't think there is really a difference of substance. In *The Drowned World* it's slightly different, because he is looking for the source of things, the source of himself, moving down his own spinal column, realising that the closer he gets to the source the less there is of him. The notion of identity ceases to exist, so the quest for absolute identity is self-defeating in a way. Well, not self-defeating: you find the Holy Grail but there is nothing there, it evaporates in your hands.

RØNNOV-JESSEN: Your female characters tend to be very alluring, but not very nice people. Would you agree?

BALLARD: That's a fair point. You've got to accept the fact that I'm not writing naturalistic fiction. In fact, I'm writing a very stylised form of fiction. It is almost always about extremely solitary people, a fiction of fabulation. A lot of the women characters, and the men for that matter, have to be seen within the conventions of similar kinds of fiction – in that realm of princesses in castles, the roles that women assume in legends and fairy tales. My fiction really belongs in that sort of terrain. In fabulation women tend to be rather inscrutable (to put it mildly) and their inscrutability is necessary for the efficient functioning of the mythic system, the exploration voyage on which the hero is embarked. A close personal relationship, whether involving sex or not, would destroy that intense privacy the hero needs. It's true of many forms of fiction, and of poetry. The lamia, nightmare Life-in-Death in Coleridge's 'Ancient Mariner', the strange and highly inscrutable characters in, say, Lewis Carroll's *Alice* books (not Alice herself, but the Duchess and so forth), the sort of figures who appear in Edgar Allan Poe – the Annabel Lee phenomenon – where the protagonist *remakes* the women around him, within an image he has assigned to them because they can fulfil certain basic needs.

Women tend to take up those rather threatening, sinister, magical roles. Robert Graves' *White Goddess*: the not necessarily benevolent muse, the almost castigating figure . . . Those archetypal female figures draw on all our responses to the women who shape our view of the world in the early years of our lives. Women do tend to take up a rather threatening role in my fiction, I accept that. But it's necessary, it seals off a whole area . . . the protagonists would never be able to embark on their voyages because the boat would be leaking if they were engaged in warm naturalistic relationships. The relationships between characters in my fiction aren't that important, in a way. All my characters are in the position of Captain Ahab, obsessed with this whale! They are powerfully obsessional, and obsessives tend not to have close personal relationships.

RØNNOV-JESSEN: In most of your fiction the women present a hindrance to the fulfilment of the male characters. There's an interesting mediation in 'Mr F is Mr F', where the protagonist actually does immerse himself in the void, only it happens to be his wife's womb. She takes on a double meaning: she's obviously hostile, but at the same time she is the medium through which he reaches bliss.

BALLARD: Those two strands are present in men's relations with women, aren't they? I think the psychology of that is accurate.

RØNNOV-JESSEN: Most of your male characters don't have any sex life, most of them have left their wives and are now on a lonely quest. But in *Crash* there's a lot of sex . . .

BALLARD: There's *only* sex there. The realm of the affections has been obliterated. That's what the book is about: the transcendence of affection and the emotions, which is what I see as the main achievement of technology. I think we're just on the threshold of this, with modern communications systems, microprocessors, computerised memory storage facilities, visual display, and very easy access to it . . . Modern technology is making possible the emergence of a world where the whole realm of the affections and the emotions will vanish. I think this will happen. A system of values which will be much more strictly moral, in a sense, because it won't be based on emotions, is beginning to emerge. In *Crash* I try to show this happening. Admittedly, in *Crash* it's a perverse new logic which is generated, but it's an instance of a new kind of psychic order which no longer requires the intercession of the emotions.

RØNNOV-JESSEN: You've been likened to Conrad and Greene. Two writers who are never mentioned are De Sade and Georges Bataille. Are they conscious influences?

BALLARD: I've got to make a terrible confession: I've never read a word by either writer, though I'm very familiar with their names. People have in fact, conversationally, referred to my connections with De Sade. I think that particular strand of my fiction, which began with *The Atrocity Exhibition* and culminated with *Crash*, grew spontaneously and wasn't directly influenced by anyone. I am aware of De Sade as one of the inspiring figures of modern surrealism. He interests me, although I've never read a word of him, because of his interest in science and physiology. Perhaps I'm putting my own gloss on De Sade: I've no idea whether his pornographic flights of fancy resemble those in *Crash*.

RØNNOV-JESSEN: They do, to a certain extent. He writes very clinically . . .

BALLARD: Right. As for Bataille, he crops up all over the place but I have never actually read any novels by him. He's one of the members of that invisible library, along with various other surrealist pioneers, that I have not read. I *have* read most of Rimbaud's poems in English, I've read Genet's novels: those two I'm happy to claim as powerful influences on me.

RØNNOV-JESSEN: You're very preoccupied with time. In *The Crystal World* Sanders desires that time should stop, that he should be suspended in time. Entropy. The crystallisation would be zero entropy . . .

BALLARD: No. I don't see that at all. I hope Colin Greenland's book [*The Entropy Exhibition*, about the British New Wave] hasn't misled you. If we define entropy in its strict sense, it is used in physics to describe the lack of energy within a system, the breakdown of complex forms to less organised forms, leading to a state of utter disorganisation and lack of energy. The psychological equivalent of that would be the run-down of fairly complex psychological states of existence into depression, despair, inertia, melancholia, etc. I don't see my work reflecting that, either on a physical or psychological level. Quite the opposite. It's a misreading to assume that because my work is populated by abandoned hotels, drained swimming pools, empty nightclubs, deserted airfields and the like, I am celebrating the run-down of a previous psychological and social order. I am not. What I am interested in doing is using these materials as the building blocks of a new order.

RØNNOV-JESSEN: I use the word entropy as a metaphor, really . . .

BALLARD: But people regularly use the word 'entropic' and have done for the last twenty years in writing about my stuff. I think Kingsley Amis, in a review of an early book of mine, called me a 'poet of psychic entropy', which I felt at the time (and still do) to be a complete misreading of what I am on about. I am not a decadent, celebrating the pleasures of the evening light: I'm much more positive. A book like *The Atrocity Exhibition* is a whole set of complicated formulae, in which the characters are obsessed with building little psychological machines that will generate new possibilities out of everything. Even the most humdrum things, like the angle between two walls, become a kind of psychological machine, a device for opening up possibilities. It's that opening up to a more organised, more complex system of events that runs through all my fiction – certainly through *Atrocity*, certainly through *Crash*. In a sense, I take the most commonplace event, a crash in a car, no more interesting in itself than a burst paper bag, and complicate that metaphor. I don't know what the reverse of entropy is, but I think I produce quite the opposite.

RØNNOV-JESSEN: In *The Unlimited Dream Company*, Blake is almost like the Angel of Death, isn't he? A lot of your characters seem to seek this breaking down of boundaries between the self and the world, the boundaries built up through socialisation, and seek the womb . . . But the dividing line between the womb and death seems to me to be rather thin.

BALLARD: Death takes many forms, of course. A loss of self-consciousness, of the awareness of self, could be regarded as death, but at the same time it's almost an ideal towards which human beings aspire. It's not just the womb. Some of my characters are obsessed with the notion of getting back to the source of their own being, using the systems of biology as a metaphor . . . light plays a large part in my fiction. In the recent novellas I've written [long short stories, technically speaking], 'Myths of the Near Future', 'News from the Sun', 'Memories of the Space Age' – three long stories all about the same theme, really – light plays an enormously important part. Light and time. The characters are trying to build structures through which they can escape from the limitations of self. You could say the sense of ourselves, of our physical bodies, that we all have is in itself a sort of small death – because of its enormous limitations. We find it very difficult to break through that small death to a larger world . . . I don't accept the criticism that there is a negative streak running through my work. Many people have accused me of being defeatist, pessimistic, entropic, and all the rest of it. Death as the end of self, yes! Self-destruction is one of the worst sins you can commit, but of course the destruction of self is necessary to achieve nirvana – freedom from self and identification with whatever you like to call them, the unseen powers of the universe.

RØNNOV-JESSEN: Malcolm Edwards of Gollancz showed me some letters to do with the publication of *The Drowned World*. In a letter to Hilary Rubinstein, Kingsley Amis proposed that the book should be published as an SF novel, whereas Rubinstein wanted it to be published as a straight novel. You seem to have been on the brink of not being launched as an SF writer at all . . .

BALLARD: I think Amis was right. That was an SF novel, and I've always been very keen to identify myself with SF. I know this seems a bit perverse, because the image SF has for most people is that of *Star Wars*, *Star Trek*, nuts and bolts, Heinlein and Larry Niven and so forth. It seems a bit crazy that this writer whose real concerns don't have anything in common with Niven and Heinlein and Asimov should go on saying he is an SF writer. But then I never regarded SF as being restricted to that form of commercial American fiction that flourished between, say, 1940 and the present day. I think of SF in a much wider context, as an important tributary of the river of imaginative fiction, a tributary that has been flowing strongly since Mary Shelley's *Frankenstein*. It's a pity that in the 1930s and 1940s it became dominated by this type of commercial fiction, popular in the States, which is still giving SF its main image. The fact is that I am interested in science, and most of my ideas come from some sort of scientific premise. I think I approach my subject matter very much in the spirit of a scientific investigator who throws out hypotheses to explain the phenomena. At all times it is impelled by a need to find a truth about a situation. So I still consider myself an SF writer.

RØNNOV-JESSEN: What, then, are your feelings about the British SF market? You don't go to science fiction conventions . . .

BALLARD: The SF 'scene' as such is made up of the more traditionalist and nostalgic readership, isn't it? I did go to a convention in 1957. I was so appalled I didn't do any writing for two years. I'm only guessing, but my impression – although there are highly intelligent people in SF now, like Pringle and Edwards and Greenland – is that the dominant influences at these conventions are the Asimov and Heinlein freaks, the *Star Wars/Star Trek* brigade – they actually set the tone. I get invited to a lot of conventions on the Continent, but I don't go to those for the same reason. People say: 'would you come as a guest of honour to this convention in Germany or Yugoslavia or somewhere?' They send me the programme and I see it's the same old movies being screened, and the same panel discussions . . . So I don't have anything to do with them.

RØNNOV-JESSEN: I think it odd that so few critics have touched upon your language. The first time I read you I thought you were American because you tend to use American terms . . .

BALLARD: Well, I'm trying to stress the international nature of my work. I'm denying my Englishness deliberately, in order to avoid parochialism. I've always been conscious of having a readership around the world – a small but international readership. Most of my books are translated into most of the publishing languages in the world. If you read the novels of a lot of SF writers who retain their English identity – John Wyndham, say – there's a sort of Englishness that I particularly dislike: that parochialism, that regionalism. I want to avoid that, and a small token of doing that is to use American terms. Also, it reflects my upbringing. I was brought up in Shanghai until the age of sixteen, which was an American zone of influence. We used words like 'trunk' and 'hood' for parts of motor cars. I still do. We referred to the pavements as 'sidewalks'. It was a Coca-Cola, air-conditioned culture . . .

RØNNOV-JESSEN: It has an odd effect when you are describing a recognisable English landscape – it seems to be transformed in a way.

BALLARD: Very alienating. I like that! That's one of the benefits, isn't it?

RØNNOV-JESSEN: I was surprised to see the Book Marketing Council launching you and Moorcock and Aldiss in their SF promotion [October 1983], because you are the three great names in British SF and don't really need promoting.

BALLARD: We're not quite as great as H.G. Wells, Aldous Huxley and George Orwell, sadly – and never will be. The promotion was a muddle. The *idea* of the promotion was excellent. Dent have sold out their first printing of their reissue of *The Drowned World*, which is a reflection of the promotion. The people in the BMC told me that of all the promotions they've done they had the biggest response to the SF promotion from booksellers, and the worst response of any promotion from the newspapers – which I thought was very interesting. One newspaper, the *Daily Telegraph*, was keen to back the new promotion: 'Glad to help – what's it about? – science fiction? – forget it!' Of course, the BMC relied excessively on sympathetic press coverage of the kind which they got for their previous promotions, and they didn't receive it. In the two most important newspapers here for book buyers, the *Observer* and the *Sunday Times*, I didn't see a single mention of the promotion. So it has been a blunder. They picked too many dead writers and too many

Americans. You can't have a promotion based on twenty writers, only three of whom are actually on the ground in this country. It's a pity, actually, for I think they missed a chance . . .

RØNNOV-JESSEN: Do all your books generally do well?

BALLARD: By what standard? I've never had big sales anywhere. I've been very lucky in that most of my fiction is still around in most of the publishing centres of the world. America is the one exception. I was successfully published there until about five or six years ago. But I'm not the only British writer to suffer. There have been such changes in the American publishing scene. I'm an imaginative writer. I've probably got more in common with Edgar Allan Poe than with George Eliot, say, and it usually takes a long time for an imaginative novel to seize hold of the public mind. I think my books have done reasonably well. *The Drowned World* has been continuously in print. Most of my books are reissued and retranslated, especially on the Continent: small sales, but *repeat* small sales, which is more important in a way. For that I'm grateful. But how many people are there who'd want to read a book like *Crash*? Not many.

A lot of people are put off by my novels because they are imaginative and they demand the reader to suspend the normal certainties with which he or she is familiar. Most people are made profoundly uneasy by imaginative fiction. The funny thing is, if you made a list of the hundred greatest novels of all time probably three-quarters of them would fall into the area of imaginative fiction! *Nineteen Eighty-Four* was an enormous success from the word go, but many were flops . . . *Moby-Dick*, for instance. Poor Melville was a successful writer until he wrote *Moby-Dick*. He died in obscurity, about thirty years later, totally forgotten, and the one book that did that was *Moby-Dick* – it was a disaster for him. That's true of so much imaginative fiction in general.

1985: Tony Cartano and Maxim Jakubowski. The Past Tense of J.G. Ballard

Originally published in French as 'Le passé composé de J.G. Ballard', *Magazine Littéraire* 219, May 1985. Translated by Dan O'Hara

The following interview appeared in *Magazine Littéraire* to mark the publication of the French edition of *Empire of the Sun*. As Tony Cartano and Maxim Jakubowski observe, Ballard was almost the subject of a cult in France, where *Crash* in particular had been read rather more sympathetically than in England. In 1984, Denoël, which had previously published the French editions of *The Drowned World*, *The Crystal World* and *Hello America*, also brought out the first issue of their revue *Science-Fiction*, a special edition on Ballard. He was therefore already riding a wave of critical acclaim in France, and his interviewers here are clearly very well acquainted with his opus, so much so that their use of the adjective '*le monde ballardien*' slips past almost unnoticed. Their questions, too, are subtle and well informed. In somewhat elliptically raising the problem of why there are no car crashes in *Empire of the Sun*, they reveal a real and very suggestive lacuna in that particular novel: the absence of an entire complex of metaphors for one of Ballard's most prominent obsessions. His initial reply is ingenious, if not very persuasive.

What Ballard suggests elsewhere in this interview is that, even when one characteristic theme is absent from a work, the underlying emotion may remain the same, expressed by different means. Choice of metaphor (and in Ballard's anti-realist stories, entire settings, environments and even chronologies can operate metaphorically) is merely a matter of tone, determined in the case of *Empire of the Sun* by the specific psychological apprehensions of the fourteen-year-old protagonist Jim, whose pathology is to perceive the whole of Shanghai as an expression of his own ambivalent feelings about his confinement and the paradoxical liberty it brings him.

By a generation of French readers schooled in the works of Robbe-Grillet, Roussel, Federman, Sarraute, Sollers, Pinget and Butor, and the films of Godard and Resnais, such an approach would be almost intuitively understood. To such writers, to paraphrase Samuel Beckett, reality remains a surface, whereas imagination cannot tolerate the limits of the real. No wonder, then, that French readers were more alive to the terrible affective power of Ballard's 'psychopathic hymn' to the death of affect – *Crash*. [DOH]

CARTANO/JAKUBOWSKI: *Empire of the Sun* is your first 'traditional' novel outside the field of science fiction. Nonetheless, this book contains echoes of your customary universe: there are empty swimming pools, the cadavers of soldiers, archetypal landscapes, as if this autobiographical novel was in some sense going to give us the key to, and the origin of, the Ballardian world.

BALLARD: That's precisely so. I reinvented my past life in the manner of the fictions I had written previously. In Shanghai, one in fact found empty swimming pools, abandoned hotels, all the vestiges of a situation created by technological war. The novels and stories I wrote between 1956 and 1980, that's to say before *Empire of the Sun*, placed the emphasis on my personal obsessions. And that's why in this last novel I look back at my life on two accounts: Jim, my young alter ego, sees existence like a hero who might have read all my books. There's nothing surprising in that my science fiction themes should be at work in *Empire of the Sun*. What writer has not been marked by his adolescence? And suppose that I had pursued the medical career of which I initially dreamt, before starting to write, and that *Empire of the Sun* were the first novel by a fifty-year-old man, well, it wouldn't be the same book, because there wouldn't have been the experience acquired by my work in science fiction. All writers develop a kind of mythology. I simply applied this personal mythology to my memories of my youth. Utilising radical forms in my SF, I had a tendency to adopt a harsher light (the emphasis there is much more violent than in the 'novel') so that the images stand out more forcefully. In *Empire of the Sun* I wanted to make it seem as if these kinds of image were appearing for the first time.

CARTANO/JAKUBOWSKI: How does a science fiction novelist become a novelist, in brief?

BALLARD: Without this personal experience of China during the war, I would probably never have written such a novel. And in the past, I couldn't see myself writing novels that were 'traditional', in the manner of Kingsley Amis or Angus Wilson, for example. I followed without any doubt in the tracks of the speculative novel. But as far as it goes, this conception of the imaginative novel is not restrictive: I readily include works such as *Robinson Crusoe, Moby-Dick* or even *The Plague* by Camus. One thing is certain: I'll never be a naturalist novelist. And perhaps it's that, that separates me from my friend Moorcock today.

CARTANO/JAKUBOWSKI: Yes, like many other ex-authors of science fiction he too has turned his back on his original style to write 'novels' like *The Final Programme*. One could wonder about the significance of other, comparable evolutions. But be that as it may, there is incontestably a continuity of themes and of vision in your own work. *The Unlimited Dream Company*, in which you describe in the realist manner life after death, seems to me a novel close to *Empire of the Sun*. One single exception, perhaps: *Crash*, this novelistic fantasy which stigmatises the influence of the automobile on our civilisation.

BALLARD: It's difficult to define with precision the source of such a singular obsession. It's got nothing to do with real life. The only car accident I've ever had happened two weeks after I'd finished the book. Yet another good example of the fact that art doesn't imitate nature; on the contrary, it's nature that imitates art, and often with questionable taste. The obsessions of *Crash* were not artificial. I didn't at all want to blow the fantasy out of all proportion. Truly, the obsessions which subtend that novel are without a doubt the strongest of all those which run through my work, including *Empire of the Sun*. It's an extreme metaphor for a profound emotion, for a desperate attempt to find a way out of an intimate crisis. The absence of this theme in *Empire of the Sun* has to do with the fact that, in taking power in Shanghai in 1942, the Japanese requisitioned all the cars, thereby annulling all

213

possibility of collision! *Empire of the Sun* is not the synthesis of everything I've written.

CARTANO/JAKUBOWSKI: Up to now, you've sought to invent new narrative techniques: non-linearity, fragmentation of sequences, writing discontinuous with the quantified image of our lives, as you say. Conversely isn't the autobiographical process, by definition, oriented towards a reconstitution of time?

BALLARD: For a long time I thought the opposite, but it's evident that style is determined by the subject. When you take liberties nonetheless, the autobiographical form is constraining, above all if the action rests on autonomous historical events in relation to the characters. Your depiction must of necessity be synchronised with the great clock of history. *Crash* or *The Atrocity Exhibition* were very subjective fictions, in which the reader was invited to penetrate into an alienated universe, one which was at any rate very close to madness. The central personality interiorises, if I can say this, external reality, to the point where the latter becomes an extension of his own psyche. He controls the time, a little in the manner of the mentally ill, of psychotics who live in an entirely subjective temporality. Hence the need to adapt the narrative technique to the psychological structures of the individual. It's very different when you deal with historical facts, the order and signification of which are, in this case, imposed on the individual.

CARTANO/JAKUBOWSKI: One of your stories, 'The Dead Time' [in *Myths of the Near Future*], announced *Empire of the Sun*: for once, the protagonist was an infant, and it was also the first appearance of China in your work. Did you know then that a few years later you would write *Empire of the Sun*, this story being a kind of sketch, a kind of preparatory work?

BALLARD: Yes, that was without doubt the first inkling. 'The Dead Time' dates from 1977. And moreover I always knew that one day I would write *Empire of the Sun*, even if I repeatedly kept putting the project off till later. Approaching fifty, I told myself that the moment had come. To wait longer was to take the risk not only of a failing memory but of the motivation flagging, of an enfeebling of the affective power. That said, and contrary to what I'd imagined, that wasn't at all in evidence.

At the start, I made my principal character an adult. And I quickly perceived that it didn't work. Quite simply because my experience of China was not that of an adult. My memories of that epoch were impressed on me with great force. But this memory belonged to the fourteen-year-old boy I was then. Hence the conscious return to that story written in '77 and the choice of a child as the hero of the book. Without 'The Dead Time', I would perhaps have kept my adult character and the novel would have become something else.

CARTANO/JAKUBOWSKI: A more realist novel, no?

BALLARD: Yes, but also more fictive. The interesting thing about the fourteen-year-old is that he's no longer a child and not yet an adult.

CARTANO/JAKUBOWSKI: The dividing line between autobiography and fiction is a rather subtle question in *Empire of the Sun*. When *The Times* printed extracts from the book before it was published, people who had been in the Japanese camps wrote to the paper to contest your version of the facts.

BALLARD: First of all, I said that the events go back more than forty years. Then, these letters make more sense if one considers the hostility of my protagonist towards the British. These last are ridiculed; they're judged severely. Look, what's of sole import to me is the truth of the imagination which, all things considered, is separate from prosaic truth. Sticking to the pure truth is impossible. Even the most serious of historians are hard pushed to reconstitute this or that event with exactitude, and each of them has his fashion of viewing things. In my 'imaginative' truth, the real is the foundation on which is elaborated a fiction conforming not just to what I knew of Shanghai but to the whole of what happened then in the Far East. Everything evoked in the novel certainly took place, perhaps not in the camp where I found myself, but somewhere in that region of the world between 1937 and 1945. It's a novel and nothing but a novel. The essence consists in awakening a certain emotional sympathy, in touching the imagination of the reader who knows nothing of the events in question. A literal account would hardly manage that. The novel enlarges the vision, it's to do with a hypertrophied truth. The obsessions, the fantasies are almost the only element we're sure of. Our inventions are the only realities left to us.

CARTANO/JAKUBOWSKI: 'The job of the novelist is to invent reality,' you wrote in the preface to the French edition of *Crash*.

BALLARD: That's it. Consider these experiments with unrehearsed, simulated bank raids. You put questions to the public: how many cars were there, how many gangsters, etc. You show them the film of the events they've just witnessed. No one has the same interpretation. So how could you rely on a testimony recalled after more than forty years! A few weeks after the publication of the book in England, some fellow called me. 'Jim,' he exclaimed, 'how are you, old thing? It's been a long time . . .' And he said that he was called Buddy or something of that kind, and that he had been interned in the room adjacent to mine. Just think: I spent three years playing with this boy the same age as me, and I remembered nothing of him! If such a detail escaped me, it proves that one can respect rigour in spirit but certainly not to the letter. And it's true that I didn't have a very high opinion of the British and their conduct in the camps. This most unpleasant aspect of their character came from the class system, the taste for the past, the illusion of grandeur.

Of course, one mustn't generalise. There were also courageous people next to those who didn't face up to adversity, contenting themselves with a comfortable idleness in proportion to their dreams of grandeur incarnated by this British Empire which they had in reality helped to destroy. I think of the invasion of Singapore by the Japanese or the merciless exploitation of the Far East by the West. In the closing lines of the novel, I describe Shanghai as a 'terrible city', terrible in the proper sense, that's to say: that which inspires terror. A similarly systematic exploitation probably no longer exists in our days on this planet. On this point, my novel is very faithful to the reality of the era.

CARTANO/JAKUBOWSKI: Before *Empire of the Sun*, at least in England, your public was not very extensive, yet in other countries, notably in France, you're the object of a kind of cult. How do you explain the success of *Empire of the Sun*, an anti-British novel? Might the English be masochists?

BALLARD: It's a book about the Second World War. That's all. And about the decline of the British Empire. For the rest, I can only take into account this open-mindedness of which you speak, with regard to the great public. Most people don't like the imaginative novel, and they like science fiction still less. Above all if it's to do with the serious novel. That frightens them. They don't want to think too much about what's going to happen in the next five minutes. In general, readers baulk at the allegorical mode; they prefer the naturalist novel, which seems to them to come directly from their own lives. With regard to France, I have to recognise that the reaction of the readers and the critics over fifteen years has given me the greatest encouragement one could have. Although I don't speak a word of French, I've always felt myself close to symbolism or surrealism. Excuse this naïveté, but when my car disembarks at Boulogne, I can't help myself thinking that I've arrived at the Holy of Holies!

CARTANO/JAKUBOWSKI: Might not the acclaim given to your work in France be explained by this unwavering taste of our compatriots for the avant-garde, or everything which resembles it, closely or distantly? Haven't you, for example, been compared with William Burroughs?

BALLARD: You say that but, up to the sixties, England and the United States were subject to spasms of implacable censorship. In France, one could obtain Sade, Henry Miller, Burroughs. Not here. We haven't got this tradition of . . . pornography, or better, the literature of dissolution, in which the writer puts elements of abnormal psychology to serious uses. The books published in Paris by Olympia Press were a godsend. I remember that one day Moorcock brought me several. I was sitting in this same armchair you see me in now, I read *Naked Lunch*. As disheartened as I was faced with the absence of prospects for the novel, I sprang up with a bound shouting 'Hurrah!' At last, a light! England is a very puritanical country. The Protestant notion of moral progress comes to justify the elimination of everything that doesn't accord with that rule. France, in my view, is a country where technology has always had an important influence on the collective consciousness. You haven't only got, as we so often believe here, just the Impressionists or the Ecole de Paris, which is already quite sufficient, I admit. You've also got engineers, and formidable inventors. And that's perhaps the reason that you haven't reduced *Crash* to a simple exercise in style, of erotic and fantastic inspiration.

CARTANO/JAKUBOWSKI: You were a part of the *New Worlds* team, that magazine set up and led by Michael Moorcock, where in the sixties to seventies there appeared the best of British science fiction. Now since, a number of *New Worlds* authors have produced important books: D.M. Thomas's *White Hotel*, Angela Carter and her *The Passion of New Eve* or most recently *Nights at the Circus*, and you yourself today. How do you explain these writers, who ten years ago were considered marginal, occupying henceforth the premier rank of the British novel?

BALLARD: We haven't changed. It's the public who have caught up with us. In England in the sixties and seventies, the novel was secondary, far behind the visual arts as a purveyor of the imagination for a cultivated public. This latter group preferred then to interest themselves in pop art, in David Hockney or Andy Warhol. As far as fiction was concerned, television replaced it. The producers benefited from great freedom. The creative TV shows, the dramas played the role formerly devolved upon the novel, to make observation and commentary upon the most burning contemporary issues. The novel could only decline. The Booker Prize, our most important literary prize, was awarded for the first time in 1969. At first, nobody took any notice of it, not even the editors or the journalists, still less the public. It took ten years for the situation to change. If since five or six years ago there's been an interest in the Booker Prize, it's quite simply because readers themselves are returning to the novel. And at the same time, there's been a noticeable fall in television viewing figures.

This disaffection is partly due to the video invasion, or to the bureaucratisation of channels which've become less and less creative, but that's not the main thing. It's begun to be realised that the novel offers a unique experience: communication with the imagination of a particular individual, and television is incapable of that. Angela Carter, Michael Moorcock, myself, we've accordingly benefited from this open-mindedness. Now, it must be recognised that certain of our novels are not so easy to read. The British public accepts the need to make a little effort, from now on.

CARTANO/JAKUBOWSKI: You're therefore optimistic about the current state of the English novel?

BALLARD: The situation is very healthy. I don't say this solely because of the success of *Empire of the Sun*; more generally the winds are changing. Ten years ago, very few novels appeared on the hardcover bestseller list. Now, they occupy the top places. An extraordinary phenomenon!

CARTANO/JAKUBOWSKI: All the same, you're a very 'visual' writer . . .

BALLARD: Yes. Although I take care of fiction at the magazine *Ambit* and hence I'm led to read numerous manuscripts by young writers, I sometimes prefer contemplation of surrealist paintings. In leafing through an album of reproductions of Max Ernst, Magritte or Dali, the cerebral alchemy which is produced in me preoccupies me much more than the better part of the novels or stories I'm led to read. With the exception of William Burroughs, who helped me to understand how my imagination functions, or rather how the world works. Still today the surrealists guide us towards a discovery of the secret formulas of reality with more certainty than most novels.

CARTANO/JAKUBOWSKI: Yet André Breton announced the death of the novel.

BALLARD: That's true. But literary surrealism is a little forgotten, isn't it? What interests me greatly is surrealist painting. I would have liked to be a painter, you know. My texts are born of a desire to compensate for this frustration. I think and I write in pictorial terms.

CARTANO/JAKUBOWSKI: What you call 'inner space'?

BALLARD: Yes, the surrealist space . . .

CARTANO/JAKUBOWSKI: Television and cinema play this negative role of which you just spoke. But otherwise, these media influence you profoundly. You couldn't write what you write, nor in the manner you write, if television, cinema and video didn't exist.

BALLARD: That's without doubt. The popular consciousness represents the world to itself through the prism of television. The televisual image fashions its vision, its experience of the real. Everything is predigested, as if it were a matter of pre-chopped, packaged supermarket food, which only needs reheating. That's television: it reheats a pre-prepared reality aimed at the audience. It's often said that *Empire of the Sun* is a very cinematic novel. Doubtless that's so, but it doesn't proceed from a conscious and deliberate process. It's certainly necessary that the writer should use the language to which people unconsciously refer in their perception of the world. Even though cinema and television may not be constructed along the same lines, their common grammar defines the language of our times. Nothing is possible without this basic observation. Hence, as I was just saying, the need for me to work in a style and with techniques in accordance with the material treated. The models of the classics don't help me at all: I don't feel obliged to read or reread, for example, George Eliot or Henry James, that's to say the writers of the conscious. For me, the more important tradition through which contemporary consciousness in all its complexity is articulated, is certainly television. The whole question lies in knowing how the writer manages to annex this medium to his literary approach.

CARTANO/JAKUBOWSKI: In *Empire of the Sun*, the eye of Jim, the young hero, works like a camera. He seems to make no judgement on the reality surrounding him. His eye discovers the world. The sole reaction of which he's capable seems to be fascination.

BALLARD: Jim witnesses events as if he was watching a news film or a television magazine at eight o'clock. And it's in exactly this manner that things happened. Most of the scenes evoked in the novel – aerial attacks on the camp, bombardments of Japanese airfields by Mustangs – correspond to what I saw myself. This manner of regarding the world is that of a child. In Shanghai, I led a very protected life, away from the streets, from beggars, and so cut off from a possible emotional reaction. I'd be seated in the back seat of an American car with a chauffeur and governess, fearful of an abduction attempt. I was behind the glass, like being behind the camera – or some television spectator faced with reports on the Indochinese war, or Nicaragua or El Salvador. In *The Atrocity Exhibition*, I had already shown how technology kills feeling. In Shanghai, I was in a similar situation. If I had been a French boy, living with his parents under the Occupation, in a small, familiar town, I surely wouldn't have experienced this feeling of isolation, as I would have been part of a real community. The same had I been a German or Italian fifteen-year-old. In China in the thirties and forties, the Europeans were nothing but tourists. This division, all the more distinct as life in Shanghai was very hard, foreshadowed the death of affect brought about by systems of mass communication.

CARTANO/JAKUBOWSKI: In this sense, the aggressive development of televisual information in the sixties, at the time of the Vietnam war, must not have failed to have an influence upon you.

BALLARD: Certainly. It reminded me of another war I had known. With the exception of the palm trees, the landscapes were almost the same – the omnipresent water, the densely populated town suburbs, the natives who, in both cases, seemed passive, acting as if we didn't exist.

CARTANO/JAKUBOWSKI: In reality, and contrary to your novel, you weren't alone in the Japanese camp; your parents were with you.

BALLARD: Yes, which proves that Jim and I are not one and the same person. I never found myself in a situation as desperate as his. My hero is orphaned. And there lies the impression that the novel is more true than the reality.

CARTANO/JAKUBOWSKI: Jim believes he sees, as if in an hallucination, the light of the Nagasaki explosion. Is it a reminiscence of your obsession with the atomic bomb, such as is expressed in your science fiction works?

BALLARD: It's a subject about which no one is indifferent, isn't it? The nuclear myth has replaced the old religious archetypes. In antiquity there was the destruction of Troy, the fall of Rome. Today we have the breakdown of Western civilisation and nuclear war. We think in apocalyptic terms. What contemporary writer could avoid it? That said, in our Japanese camp we had the conviction that we'd been saved by the bomb. In August 1945, nobody expected to see the Japanese surrender. They would probably never have done so. Remember their hand-to-hand combat in each small island, to the last man. In Okinawa, even the civilians perished at the side of the soldiers at the time of the attack on the island by the Americans. Okinawa was relatively close to Shanghai. And the Japanese contingent was very important in China. If one believed the rumour, the Japanese intended to deport the prisoners to camps in the countryside and dispose of them. There was no more for us to eat.

When the war ended, overnight, like a film which stops abruptly after the last image, my feelings about the bomb – and this goes for all those who were in the same situation as me – were rather ambiguous. Imagine our perplexity. And without a doubt that's the reason I'm in favour of nuclear armament. I haven't the slightest sympathy for movements in favour of disarmament, especially our CND [Campaign for Nuclear Disarmament]. I share the view of the Americans on the matter of nuclear armament. And that goes back to the events I survived in the Far East. The Hiroshima and Nagasaki explosions quite simply saved our lives! Without them, the Americans would have had to invade Japan and the territories in the region of Shanghai. None of us would have escaped that. That's without a doubt. Since then, far from being an instrument of death, the atomic bomb has become for me an instrument of protection. It doesn't embody the forces of destruction, but on the contrary, those of life and creation. It would be an error of interpretation to read the nuclear intervention in my works as a calling-into-question.

CARTANO/JAKUBOWSKI: Another interesting paradox, if I might mention it: in *Empire of the Sun*, Jim seems fascinated by the Japanese soldiers. He must fear them, and he admires them.

BALLARD: Between the ages of seven and fifteen, I had the opportunity to see them at work. Today I'm fifty-four and certainly my view of things is more relative, more moderate. But you have to understand that these intractable Japanese, faithful to their Emperor and to their flag, these Japanese who would never surrender, couldn't help but appeal to the imagination of a young adolescent in need of heroes, whereas in Singapore the English, although well their superior in numbers, were lamentably defeated by the Japanese. The British arrogance was to imagine that it would be sufficient to stop them, after Pearl Harbor, by sending two battleships, the *Repulse* and the *Prince of Wales*, without any aerial cover. The Japanese planes were only made out of bamboo and rice paper, were they not, and their pilots bespectacled incompetents! What do you believe would happen? Well, the Japanese possessed remarkable aircraft at the start of the war, and the pilots were already war-hardened by years of combat in Manchuria and China. In ten minutes, the *Repulse* and the *Prince of Wales* were sent to the bottom. And that fiasco signalled the end of the British Empire in the Far East.

CARTANO/JAKUBOWSKI: One wonders at the end of the novel how Jim will readapt to life in the West, after his return to England.

BALLARD: One nightmare after another! I came back in '46. A dramatic experience! It took me years to do so. And still today I don't feel completely integrated. England is an exceedingly strange country. I've never had the impression of being at home here. A little like compulsory tourism, as if I were part of some diplomatic delegation.

CARTANO/JAKUBOWSKI: Fascinated as you are by modern technologies, have you never thought of living in the United States?

BALLARD: Before going to China with my parents, I spent six months in Canada, I went to Detroit, Buffalo, the Niagara falls.[1] What's more, the Shanghai I knew was entirely within the sphere of American influence: the cars, the merchandise, Coca-Cola, air conditioning, the radio stations, the comics, the lifestyle, it was all American. Today, I'd very much like to go to the United States, but up to now I haven't had the opportunity. You know, I've had to bring up my three children, and that doesn't make travelling easy. And then the America that interests me is that reflected to us in the mass media. The America of cinema, of television, of magazines, of publicity – in a word, the 'models' seem to me more important than this or that aspect of concrete reality, of the type 'the smell of the fields of wheat in Iowa'. No need to travel: these models are sent to us direct by satellite! These days, journeys are practically pointless.

---

1 The French text actually says this, but evidently an error of translation or a misunderstanding has garbled the sense. Ballard was born in Shanghai, and visited the US in 1939. It was much later, in 1954, that he went to Canada with the RAF. It was at this time that he visited the places mentioned.

1986: Solveig Nordlund. Future Now

Previously unpublished

Despite popular opinion, Steven Spielberg and David Cronenberg are not the only film-makers to have adapted Ballard's work for the big screen. In fact, there have been four full-length features: Spielberg's *Empire of the Sun* (1987), Cronenberg's *Crash* (1996), Jonathan Weiss's *The Atrocity Exhibition* (2000) and Solveig Nordlund's *Aparelho Voador a Baixa Altitude* (2002), an adaptation of Ballard's short story 'Low Flying Aircraft' (1976). Nordlund, a Swedish film-maker living in Portugal, brought a European art-house sensibility to Ballard, mixing a striking colour scheme (chemical blues, reds and greens refracted from queasy neon and industrial skylines) with a downbeat, philosophical narrative. The film successfully transmitted the quiet despair of Ballard's story, with its world in which the entire human race has fallen sterile save for a few mutant births each year, and made excellent use of real-world locations, mainly a disused Portuguese resort, to convey its abandoned-resort setting of the future.

Nordlund is a long-standing Ballard fan. The first story of his she read was 'Thirteen to Centaurus' (1964), which she adapted as a short film, *Journey to Orion* (1986), another visually striking work that used the interior of a Swedish passenger ferry for its space-station setting. Just before that, she made a series of programmes for Swedish television about writers she admired, including one on Marguerite Duras and another on Ballard called 'Future Now'. This was the beginning of a friendship hinted at in *The Kindness of Women*, in which Ballard named the family renting the apartment in Spain beside his avatar/narrator 'the Nordlunds'.

This transcript is taken from the 'Future Now' interview. [SS]

NORDLUND: You live alone here in Shepperton, in this house?

BALLARD: If you'd come here five years ago, you would have found three children, whom I brought up myself after my wife died twenty years ago, and this was their nursery, where they watched television and had all their toys. Now I'm alone here, the children have grown up, and so in a way this is my nursery. There's even an exercise bicycle which, sad to say, has the lowest mileage of any exercise bicycle in London. This is where I come in the evenings, but my real existence as a writer is in this room here. This is where my imagination dwells. This is my study, and it's always been my private room. It's at that desk where I've written my fiction. Almost every novel I've written and almost all my entire output of fiction has been written sitting at that desk, looking out on that little garden.

NORDLUND: In *Empire of the Sun*, you write about China, about Shanghai. When the Japanese invaded, did your family continue to live a normal life?

BALLARD: The Japanese occupied all the major cities, though in the case of Shanghai they respected the international settlement, which was a small section in the middle of Shanghai. After Pearl Harbor in December 1941, the Japanese forces rolled their tanks through the streets one morning and took over the city. And *Empire of the Sun* describes the adventures of a boy of my own age called Jim. The book opens on the eve of Pearl Harbor, and Jim finds that, in the confusion when the Japanese enter the city, he is separated from his parents. He returns to his family house, which is now empty, waiting for his parents to return. When they don't appear, he gradually begins to realise that he's on his own. He then is forced to live like a sort of young Robinson Crusoe, almost, in the big houses of the western suburbs of Shanghai, living on cocktail biscuits and scraps left over from the lives led by these now-vanished British and Americans. Eventually, after numerous adventures, he is captured by the Japanese and finds his way to Lunghua camp.

NORDLUND: What is Jim's relationship to the camp?

BALLARD: For Jim it represents complete security. It's the only secure world that he has known, and as the war draws to a close, and it's clear that the Japanese are losing the war, he becomes more and more worried.

He's terrified of what will happen to them when the Japanese are no longer guarding the camp, and this of course is what happened in fact. We in our camp at Lunghua faced our period of greatest danger when the Japanese had surrendered and we were left on our own – two thousand people with no food and no supplies, and the Americans three hundred miles away. There was a very uneasy period of about a month before the Americans finally arrived, and for Jim, his whole attitude towards imprisonment and security and safety is completely unlike the conventional picture that people have of liberation and rescue that we generally see in films about the war.

NORDLUND: Jim doesn't want to be liberated?

BALLARD: Of course, I'm very closely identified with this young hero, who in many respects *is* myself, so I'd like to believe he recognises some kind of truth about the nature of war. He firmly believes, for example, that World War II may have ended but, with its end, and the dropping of the atom bomb, World War III has actually begun, and this is what he feels that none of the adults around him, none of his fellow prisoners, recognise. They are still thinking in old categories of armistice days and red poppies in lapels, and all of these sentimental ideas that people have about war and peace. He realises that war in the mid-twentieth century and in the late twentieth century to come is endemic to the human condition, and that human beings must accept this: that they're deluding themselves by imagining that peace will ever come.

NORDLUND: After the war, you were sent to England to study. Was it a shock for you?

BALLARD: Yes it was. It was a terrible shock from which I've never really recovered. I think the whole of the last nearly forty years has been on my part an attempt to get over the shock. Many people have asked me why it took me forty years to write *Empire of the Sun*, which is a very long time to wait. Partly the reason is that those experiences took a long time to forget, and a long time to remember. They took twenty years to forget and then another twenty years to remember. But also I think that, in a lot of my fiction and a lot of my novels, right from my first novel, *The Drowned World* [sic; in fact *The Wind from Nowhere* was Ballard's debut novel], I was really writing about the war experiences that I went through, but in disguised form.

NORDLUND: You began as a writer of science fiction?

BALLARD: I didn't feel in the 1950s that the English landscape was one I could write about. English society struck me as extremely uninteresting in every respect: class-ridden, obsessed with nostalgia for a vanished empire. I was very aware when I came to England in 1946 that the light here was different – it was much darker, it was much greyer – and that it was a puritanical country where people led extremely rigid and closed lives, and everybody knew his place on the social ladder. And the kind of fiction, the novels that were being written, were all about the English class structure: they were about little nuances of social distinctions, which the English were obsessed with, and to some extent still are. I wanted to write a kind of fiction that broke away from this very old-fashioned, looking-backward sort of fiction. I wanted a fiction that was, never mind about the future, but about the present day. It seemed to me that English fiction wasn't even about the present day.

The fifties, it seemed to me, were a time of enormous change. The world we live in now – the world of international jet travel, package holidays, computers, instalment buying, the whole communications landscape that we inhabit dominated by television, mass advertising, politics conducted as a branch of advertising – all of this was being created in the 1950s. The rails were being laid down along which western Europe would run in the next twenty or thirty years. I wanted to write about this. I wanted to write about change and possibility. I wanted to write about the next five minutes, not the last thirty years, and the only form of fiction that had the vocabulary of ideas to deal with the next five minutes was science fiction. I wasn't interested in interplanetary travel, time travel, outer space; that didn't interest me at all, and I've never written a science fiction set in outer space [actually, he wrote one, 'Tomorrow is a Million Years'; 1966], or millions of years in the future. I wanted a science fiction for the present day. It seemed to me when I started writing in the late fifties and early sixties that the future was a better key to the present than the past. One had to look at the next five minutes to understand what was going on now.

NORDLUND: You don't write traditional science fiction . . .

BALLARD: I'd like to think that I work in the area of myths, dreams, legends, which seem to me to touch the real nature of our experience both as private individuals with our own private dreams and as members

227

of a society. Societies have their dreams too. In fact, what is so strange about the world we inhabit today is the way in which fiction and reality have become reversed. Twenty, thirty, forty years ago, everybody had a clear idea that the world of reality was the external world around you: the world of work, and industry, commerce. The world of fantasy and the imagination was the world inside our heads, our private dreams and hopes for the future. Now that's been reversed. Now the external landscapes of our world are almost entirely fictional, made up of advertising and publicity, an artificial, man-made landscape. The only point of reality we each of us have is the point of reality inside our heads. Our own obsessions are all we have.

NORDLUND: Can you elaborate?

BALLARD: It seems to me that the sort of world we live in needs a certain amount of oil to make the wheels go round. In the sixties sex provided that role. Now, in our landscape, sex is no longer a new frontier: you get the impression almost that sex has died out or doesn't take place any more. Certainly the media landscape that we inhabit, this enormous novel we're living inside, thrives on sensation. It needs sensation to sustain itself. We're rather in the position of some sort of drowsing animal, drugged by some powerful narcotic agent, who needs electric shocks to keep it awake, and the electric shocks are provided by violence today: by violent imagery of one sort or another, whether it's plane crashes or train crashes, hijacks or just car crashes from our local city streets.

NORDLUND: How do you see the future?

BALLARD: It seems to me that what most of us have to fear for the future is not that something terrible is going to happen, but rather that nothing is going to happen. That we may live, or my children may well live, in a boring world, in what I would call an eventless world, a world where nothing happens, and what I fear will happen is that this will lead to the atrophy of the imagination. I felt this very strongly oddly enough a few years ago, when I was taken on a long drive through West Germany. If you want an image of what the future is going to look like, it would be a suburb of Düsseldorf, and that might not be a good thing for the human spirit. One sees that coming over here a bit. If the imagination dies, it may be that the only area that will continue to live will be in the area of psychopathology – psychopathology may become the last repository of the human imagination. In *The Atrocity Exhibition*, I even make the suggestion that psychopathology should be kept alive as the last reservoir – like a nature reserve in Africa – of the human imagination.

NORDLUND: What do you think about the surrealists?

BALLARD: There's no doubt that the surrealist painters have had a far bigger influence on me than any writers have done. I regard surrealism as really the greatest imaginative adventure of the twentieth century. I think the surrealist movement is very misunderstood. People think it's a movement in painting inspired by fantasy, but in fact that's not true. The surrealists were all very interested in science and optics and photography, and their main inspiration of course was psychoanalysis. I think that combination of science and the imagination is very close to my own writing and of course has many affinities with science fiction itself.

NORDLUND: What do you think about science fiction as a literary genre?

BALLARD: In many ways I believe that science fiction is the authentic literature of the twentieth century. I think it's unfortunate that science fiction is boxed off into its own little compartment. It seems to me a little ironic that, after nearly thirty years as a writer, my first real success has been with a book that isn't science fiction, but that is more straightforwardly autobiographical. I mean, I can see the irony of that, but I've always been fairly philosophical about these things, so it doesn't worry me, in a way.

NORDLUND: Has *Empire of the Sun*'s success changed your life in any way?

BALLARD: No, it hasn't. I wish it had. I wish I'd done something like buy a nightclub or run off with a teenage girl. No, my life has not changed at all, and in a way that worries me. It should change, but it shows all the signs of going on exactly as before, although of course these things take a long time to work through the system, and it may be that my life has changed, but I haven't noticed it yet.

NORDLUND: If your life is exactly as before, what is that like, then?

BALLARD: My life? Well, I lead an extremely quiet life. I live about twenty miles to the west of London in a small suburb. Now that my children have grown up and left home, I write during the day, go for a walk along the river in the early evening and then watch TV and drink whisky and soda. And that seems to be the right background for me as an imaginative writer. Perhaps I need invisible surroundings, and this suburb is almost invisible to me. In fact, I went on holiday a few years ago to Greece, and I was there for about a month, and I was standing on a beach in the Peloponnese, and I suddenly forgot where I lived. I couldn't remember. I knew I lived in England, but I couldn't remember where, even though I'd lived then in this house for about twenty years. I actually had to work it out backwards, you know – 'Calais, Dover, London, Hammersmith' . . . 'Shepperton!' I suddenly realised, and then this house.

Obviously this house and this quiet suburb where I work doesn't have a real grip on my imagination. Its great appeal for me is that it is nowhere, that it represents the minimal context in which I can credibly feel part of a landscape, but it's not one from which I draw anything, imaginatively speaking. In many ways I feel like a sort of secret agent who assumes a modest disguise, who pretends to be a bank clerk living in a suburb, and I feel that to a large extent I'm probably doing that. I like to think of myself a bit like the surrealist painter Magritte, who led a very bourgeois life in a quiet suburb of Brussels, took his Pomeranian dog for a walk at the same time every afternoon, drank a little coffee in the local café and played a game of chess, and then went back to this very bourgeois house. I'd like that. I think that's the perfect background for certain kinds of imagination.

1988: James Verniere. A Conversation with J.G. Ballard

Originally published in *The Twilight Zone*, June 1988

Although James Verniere's emphasis at the beginning of this interview is on *Empire of the Sun*, the general tenor of Ballard's argument is critical of mass media and particularly of television. Whereas in 1984, in conversation with Peter Rønnov-Jessen, Ballard saw his fictions as depictions of the psychology of the post-industrial landscape, here he suggests that television is already obsolete, ready to join the urban design of industrial cities and the architecture of high-rises as part of the litter of a past generation's dreams.

In this context, his view of television as a medium that co-opts and represents sanitised versions of both sex and violence, creating a fictional reality in which both of these fundamental human activities exist only in the service of advertising, suggests that we are held in thrall to obsolete visions of futures that never came to pass. The politics of television, Ballard implies, is stuck in the late 1960s, and as such is as much of an imaginative dead end as the politics of totalitarianism. Whether or not he considered modern TV a symptom of capitalism's own frailties, he does not say. [DOH]

VERNIERE: When did you first conceive of *Empire of the Sun* as a novel?

BALLARD: In the back of my mind, I'd always had the intention to write a novel based on my experiences in China during the Second World War. Many people have asked why I waited so long. Instead of being one of my last books, why wasn't it one of my first books? I don't know. It's a difficult thing to explain. Part of the reason is that it took a very long time to forget all those wartime experiences and then a very long time to remember them. Anybody who's read *Empire of the Sun* and some of my previous fiction can see that there are elements of my China background in many of my novels. Some people have even said that *Empire of the Sun* is the key that explains all of my earlier books.

I don't know about that. But the times seemed to be right, and it wasn't until 1980 that my three children grew up and left home. I don't know whether this explanation is fanciful, but I think that all parents are protective towards their children, and in a way I felt vicariously protective towards my younger self. I wasn't ready to expose my adolescent self to all of the hazards of the Second World War again until my own children were safely out of the way.

VERNIERE: *Empire of the Sun* is also your most accessible piece of writing. Was it a conscious attempt on your part to write a mainstream book?

BALLARD: No, I didn't give any thought to that. It was simply the subject matter: the book was semi-autobiographical and the subject matter wasn't invented by me. It was presented to me by my experiences of the war. So that dictated a realistic narrative, whereas the rest of my short stories and novels belong in the category of imaginative fiction.

VERNIERE: Have you come to understand how your experiences in the camp may have influenced your vision as an adult writer?

BALLARD: That's a tremendous question. Writing the book in a sense forced me to take a sort of critical inventory of my whole life and character. Of course, I asked myself the question you've asked many, many times as I was writing because the book cast its shadow over all my previous novels. I've always been tremendously inspired by the surrealist painters, for example, and to some extent the reason is that my adolescent mind saw the events of Shanghai – not just during the war but before it – as part of some huge, surrealist canvas with the normal logic of everyday life suspended: Anything went. There was a tremendous energy and excitement there. It was a place full of paradoxes. In the last line of the book, I refer to Shanghai as 'the terrible city'. It was terrible in the sense that it was a very cruel and brutal place. And it gave a particular kind of spin to my imagination. That spin is still turning.

VERNIERE: How would you describe your new novel, *Day of Creation*? Is it science fiction? Is it mainstream fiction?

BALLARD: Well, it's not science fiction; it's an imaginative novel. But it could be read as a realistic novel. It's set in present-day Africa. It's about a British doctor who's working for the World Health Organisation in a Central African republic being overrun by the Sahara. Drilling for water, he accidentally starts a mysterious river flowing. This becomes a mighty Amazon, which he feels he has created, and it transforms the desert. He then decides to sail up the river to its source.

VERNIERE: Do you feel that people who've read *Empire of the Sun* will also find this new novel accessible?

BALLARD: I think so. That's been the reaction here. Of all my novels, it's probably the closest to *Empire of the Sun*, since on one level anyway it's a realistic story set in the present day.

VERNIERE: In the early seventies, you were referred to as one of the British New Wave of SF. But you've always straddled the fence between science fiction and avant-garde fiction. Do you have problems with such labels?

BALLARD: There is a problem, of course. Those labels are so sticky, and it's almost impossible to get them off. I've spent years trying to peel away the Superglue.

VERNIERE: Perhaps *Empire of the Sun* was the solvent you were looking for.

BALLARD: Maybe, maybe. It is unfortunate, of course, but science fiction has become indelibly identified with interplanetary travel, time machines, *Star Trek* and *Star Wars*, that sort of Buck Rogers/Flash Gordon school. One has to keep reminding people that there's more to science fiction than *Star Trek* and *Star Wars*. A large number of the most serious writers of this century have written what is without any doubt science fiction. Aldous Huxley's *Brave New World*, George Orwell's *Nineteen Eighty-Four*, these are science fiction novels. Many serious writers of the present day have also written out-and-out science fiction novels: Doris Lessing, Anthony Burgess, Kingsley Amis, and many writers in the States.

VERNIERE: And many of the critics who've supported the work of those writers tap-dance around the term 'science fiction' when reviewing the books you've mentioned.

BALLARD: That's true – because they're primarily thought of as mainstream writers, even though in a strict definition of the term somebody like Doris Lessing has written more science fiction novels than I have. *Crash* is not really science fiction. In fact, I think it's true to say – not that anyone is particularly interested – that I haven't written much science fiction since something like 1966, twenty years ago.

But even though I'm probably more identified with a book like *Crash* than with *The Drowned World*, people still think of me as an SF writer. The reason is, of course, that I take a hard, cruel look at the everyday reality around me in western Europe and the United States, and I see science and technology playing an enormous part in creating the landscape of our lives and imaginations. In many respects, we're living inside a science fiction novel, and it's not the SF of *Star Trek*. But, of course, most mainstream writers are working with a set of conventions that haven't really changed since the nineteenth century and early twentieth century, and as a result are rather out of touch with reality.

I have my lonely struggle trying to get a broader definition of science fiction: a definition that incorporates *Gulliver's Travels*, Mary Shelley's *Frankenstein*, Robert Louis Stevenson, on through H.G. Wells, on to that great genius, William Burroughs, who uses huge elements of science fiction in his novels because it's part of the air that we breathe. What I'm striving for is a more elastic definition of science fiction, and I go on beating the drum – but I don't want to bore you to death.

VERNIERE: I recently reread Leslie Fiedler's introduction to the science fiction collection *In Dreams Awake*, and he tackles some of these same issues. In it, he calls science fiction a religious literature. Do you know what he means?

BALLARD: I think that's very true. I haven't read this particular book.

VERNIERE: Well, you're in it, or I should say, 'Plan for the Assassination of Jacqueline Kennedy' is in it.

BALLARD: Well, anyway, I agree. The imagination that expresses itself through science fiction does try to place some sort of philosophical frame around man's place in the universe, if I may quote myself. It's a fiction of paradox. It's thought of as escapist entertainment, but in fact in its naive way it's concerned in all its different varieties with a metaphysical understanding of the nature of human existence, especially at a time of change. Science fiction is the literature that responds to change. It's a dynamic form of fiction, whereas most mainstream fiction (which is very retrospective) is rather static. It visualises a static world, as if society were a large, still photograph in which everybody is set in position and the writer's job is to determine where the moral perspectives lie that link all these figures in the landscape. Science fiction assumes a sort of dynamic flux. Nothing is certain, nothing is sure, everything is relative. I know these sound like grandiose claims.

VERNIERE: They don't. Fiedler also uses the expression 'the eroticised technology of men' in his introduction. Taken to an extreme that 'eroticised technology' might refer to *Crash* and what you've done in some of your other fiction.

BALLARD: I think that's true. Exactly. We're surrounded in our lives by the products of a very high-developed technology, whether it's our motor cars, our hospitals, our homes, jets, the elaborately signalled landscape of the modern highway. You name it. Our individual imaginations tend to overlay all these technological artefacts and systems because that's the nature of imagination. We constantly try to remake the world, and this involves casting the webs of our imaginations over all these artefacts that make up twentieth-century life.

VERNIERE: The tone of your writing is often obsessive and even fetishistic.

BALLARD: I accept that. As a writer I've always had complete faith in my own obsessions. It seems to me that the obsessional approach to life is very much the way in which the twentieth century conducts its business. It tends to stick on to certain subjects, whether it's world war, television, the consumer-goods society, great political movements, in an obsessional way.

VERNIERE: But one might argue that your obsessional tone and your philosophical investigation of the nature of existence are also indicative of religious writing, the writings of certain Christian saints, for example.

BALLARD: I thought you were going to say, 'of Adolf Hitler' [laughs]. Well, I take that as a great compliment. I think the modern imagination does take the whole universe as its subject. It's concerned with metaphysical questions about the nature of consciousness, of experience, of perception. It takes a very large field of enterprise as its arena. As far as the religious-fetishistic thing goes, I accept that because all that this modern imagination has going for it is its powerful creativity. And these things – like crashing cars – do lend themselves to 'fetishisation'; if there is such a word.

VERNIERE: If we could take a bit of a turn here, could you talk about how the popular arts – movies in particular – influence your work? You have often referred to movie stars like Elizabeth Taylor and Marilyn Monroe and to political figures like Madame Chiang-Kai-shek in your fiction . . .

BALLARD: And don't forget my one claim to prescience, which I hesitate to make: Ronald Reagan [laughs].

VERNIERE: That story was on my list of questions.

BALLARD: That was written in 1967 when I think Reagan was governor of California, and I predicted his presidency. The title ['Why I Want to Fuck Ronald Reagan'], I hasten to add, was meant ironically. I may want to visit the States one day and I don't want to be arrested at Kennedy Airport on a charge of perversion relating to the body of the president. Actually, that story was distributed by a group of my readers in San Francisco at the Republican Convention in 1980. They apparently copied the story, deleted the title, and put the Republican seal on it. They then distributed this to the delegates, most of whom didn't blink an eyelid. They thought this was some sort of position paper from some think tank, analysing the unconscious appeal of their candidate. So that's my one little claim to having accurately glanced into the crystal ball. I think the media landscape of the present day is made up of a kind of high-speed mosaic that flashes by, made up of images of public figures charged by our fantasies. It's the texture of ordinary life.

VERNIERE: Which might explain the 'televisionary' aspect of some of your fiction.

BALLARD: Right. I think we're living in a landscape of enormous fictions, of which television is a major supplier. The danger with TV is that it predigests and pre-empts any kind of original response by the viewer. It just feeds the viewer a kind of reality. (It has become, in fact, the new reality, just like processed food has become the staple diet of many people in the West.) This force-feeding makes us rather like a lot of bullocks in a pen. Reality now is a kind of huge advertising campaign, selling television's image of what life is about. The real aim of TV is fulfilling its own needs. Television is no longer an innovative medium here, and I imagine it's probably true in the States as well. It seems to me that film is still very much an innovative medium.

VERNIERE: Not in the US. Like American TV, the American film industry has become a kind of perpetual motion machine, spewing out 'products' to satisfy a need it has created.

BALLARD: It's funny, but I'm probably the last person in his fifties in this country who's still going to the movies. Nobody here over the age of forty goes to the movies. For a man of fifty-six to be going to the movies is practically a social crime. It's unseemly behaviour in the elderly. When the lights come on at the end of the evening, I always feel vaguely guilty looking around, like some middle-aged man hanging around the school playground. But I've recently seen a remarkable new kind of film: films like *Blue Velvet, Raising Arizona* and *Blood Simple.*

VERNIERE: Your fiction often mimics the computer print-outs, charts, graphs and fact-sheets of scientific writing. You've even been heralded as the father of the 'cyberpunk' movement. How much did your background as a medical student who hoped to become a psychiatrist influence your style?

BALLARD: First, it is true that I've tried to reproduce something of the texture of scientific language. I don't mean to say that my fiction is a mass computer print-out of facts. It isn't. But I've drawn heavily in certain books of mine, like *The Atrocity Exhibition* and *Crash*, on the scientific journal or report that covers similar areas and is, in itself, almost a kind of fiction. I mean some of the scientific research that is done in specialised laboratories on topics like the psychology of air-crash victims is – first – horrific beyond parody. But it's almost a kind of nightmare fiction in its own right. It's a kind of pornography of science, issuing from these specialised laboratories which I've parodied in some of my stories.

VERNIERE: You've also shown a fascination for violent death; the assassination of Kennedy is an obvious example. In *Crash*, there is a character who yearns to die in a head-on collision with Elizabeth Taylor. Have you ever come to terms with where that fascination comes from?

BALLARD: To be quite honest, I myself have no desire to die in a head-on collision with Elizabeth Taylor [laughs]. I once nearly bumped into her in a revolving door in a London hotel and that was close enough [laughs]. To be serious, these obsessions with violent death, particularly of well-known figures (presidents, film stars and the like), I take from the world around me. It seems self-evident that people are immensely fascinated by the lives and deaths of public figures and have been since the nineteenth century. I remember reading American magazines as a boy in Shanghai that were full of gory photographs of gangsters and politicians who were gunned down and minor film stars who died in terrible road accidents or shootings in Hollywood. I see Kennedy's death as a kind of catalyst of the media planet that exists now. There was something about the way in which this young president (who was himself a media construction) was dismantled by the same media landscape that created him, that generated a kind of supernova that's still collapsing.

VERNIERE: Are there any contemporary trends that you find interesting or especially disturbing?

BALLARD: In England today, people will not face up to the powerful appeal that violence exerts on the imaginations of almost everyone, whereas in private they do. People love the thrills and spills of grand prix motor races . . .

VERNIERE: And the explosion of the Challenger shuttle . . .

BALLARD: Yes, people stay glued to their TVs, or if there's a car crash in the street, they go out, not to gloat, but they're drawn to violence. We're having a big debate right now over this terrible Hungerford massacre. About three weeks ago a young man in a small English town started walking around shooting people. He killed about fourteen people. It's extraordinary to me to see a complete drawing down of the mental shutters over this. People who ought to know better are absolutely refusing to acknowledge the immense hold that violence exerts over people. It seems to me that it's unhealthy. One should face up to the realities of human nature. That way one can do something about improving it, steering it into safer channels.

VERNIERE: I don't mean to tie this up too neatly, but it seems that what you're saying might be applied to your experiences as a boy. You were exposed to violence in its most extreme form at an impressionable age. Did that experience make you particularly sensitive to its seductive power?

BALLARD: Ah, possibly. But I'm not personally drawn to violence. Quite the opposite. It's true that I witnessed first-hand what most people in western Europe and the United States only witnessed second-hand, if at all. Tens of millions of years of evolution trained humans to react to violence with their nerve endings. But that training is now largely gone to waste. We see violence now purely through film, television and the news media. We experience it almost as part of the entertainment land-scape of our lives. But we've got this huge inherited apparatus for coping with violence – flight or fight, whatever – yet it's being officially denied now that it exists. Violence is being treated here in the same way that sex was treated in the pre-Kinsey era.

VERNIERE: Are you saying that the repression of our natural response to violence might have effects similar to those that resulted from sexual repression?

BALLARD: I think that's the danger. The refusal to acknowledge human nature is a mistake because it will find some other, possibly more lethal, way out. Just as repressive attitudes towards sex generated ignorance and superstition, so the repression of violence will generate an equally unfortunate set of fantasies and delusions. Not only do some of our politicians want to ban violence entirely on TV. (Sometimes I think these people have an extra channel inside their heads that I don't get to watch.) They even want to ban images of violence from the news. They say the news should not be too explicit. You know, reports of an air disaster or car crashes or film from a war zone like Beirut, anything like that. Well, this is a very dangerous kind of censorship.

VERNIERE: There is a line from E.M. Forster's novel *Maurice* that says, 'England has always been disinclined to accept human nature'.

BALLARD: I think that's very true. Profoundly true.

1988: Rosetta Brooks. Myths of the Near Future

Originally published in *ZG Magazine: Altered States*, 1988

ZG Magazine was an alternative art magazine founded by Rosetta Brooks in the early eighties. Like a British version of *RE/Search*, it gave equal space to not only art but also film, music, tribal club culture, sado-masochist tendencies in fashion photography, and so on. Issues were modelled after suitably Ballardian themes including 'Future Dread', 'Icons and Idols' and 'Breakdown'. Later in its life, it was published between London and New York, and documented the street life of both cities. The following interview appeared in the 'Altered States' edition, co-published with Kent Fine Art, New York. The issue doubled as the catalogue for the 'Altered States' exhibition at Kent Fine Art in April/May 1988, which explored how 'concepts of space and time are under-going radical change', and how that change affects culture.

That year, Ballard published his illustrated novella *Running Wild*, a tale of a group of children living in a hyper-surveilled gated community who rebel and murder their manipulative and affluent parents. In much of the interview, although Ballard never mentions the novella by name, the issues and themes with which *Running Wild* would deal are clearly to the fore. Brooks astutely proposes to him that the speed of scientific change is paralleled by cultural change, a point Ballard leaps on hungrily, immediately postulating a late-1980s distinction between the 'TV community' and a new, post-TV generation. Yet he also mentions his short story 'The Intensive Care Unit', a tale in which people do not meet in the flesh, but maintain contact solely via technology. *Running Wild*, although written long before the internet entered the media landscape,

241

concerns the possible future of a post-TV generation who nonetheless co-opt the distance of technology to achieve their own deadly ends. [DOH]

BROOKS: I noticed you have a copy of 'Icarus' up on your bookshelf. The idea of 'Icarus' seems to be rooted in your book *The Unlimited Dream Company*. And, in a sense, flight seems to be one of the most dominant images in your writing.

BALLARD: Yes, that's true. Flight does play a very important part in my fiction – though I never consciously think about 'Icarus' or the Ancient Mariner's albatross or a thousand and one other archetypal images when I write. But that's simply because there's a common pool of archetypal imagery that we all draw on willy-nilly. By and large, we all use the same kind of symbol systems. To mammals like ourselves who are anchored to the ground and yet able to imagine, flight has a whole repertory of powerful meanings. To me it just represents a means of transcending one's own particular time and space and moving to a radically different realm.

I've always felt strongly that there's a profound magic in airports – and even more so in runways. Deserted runways have a tremendous magnetic pull for me. I can stare for ever at aerial photographs of those islands in the Pacific which have abandoned runways – although some of them are still in use by the US army and navy. But they are so powerful as images. The concrete strip just beckons one into new realms. Indeed, any major airport in the world charges me with a powerful sense of inspiration: they offer new points of departure for the imagination.

BROOKS: Do you know the writings of the French theorist Paul Virilio? I mention him because there seems to be a convergence of interests in the ideas of flight and time consciousness. In *Pure War* he talks about Howard Hughes: about how he created a world of temporal habitation for himself in an effort to cheat time itself. But he ended up as a 'technological monk in the desert of Las Vegas', atrophied in a changing world of speed.

BALLARD: That's really interesting. Actually, I've always found Howard Hughes a terrifically sympathetic character. I absolutely endorse his climbing into the penthouse suite of a hotel in Las Vegas and closing the door on the rest of existence. I admired him for doing that. He's a wonderfully enigmatic figure. He embodies all the great myths of the twentieth century in his character and in his life. This young aviator ace was also a great explorer and inventor; bought himself movie studios and airlines; and was extremely rich but untouched by the trappings of wealth. Then there was his obsession with germs. He sort of died of AIDS – not the real AIDS but the imaginary, symbolic AIDS – before his time. He really sums up so many of the obsessions and paranoias of this century. And he was totally American too, in a very attractive way; an utterly democratic man. One can imagine him eating at McDonald's when he was younger – something no European millionaire would ever do!

BROOKS: He reminds me of many of the heroes of your books in so many ways. I associate you and Virilio because you do seem to share a common theme; that time has somehow annihilated space and that, now, time is annihilating itself. It's as though we've reached this state of inertia in which, in a sense, we can now only live within our own constructed worlds. That sounds like a classic description of your stories.

BALLARD: I agree. I think that time, in the strict sense, is dying. The whole progress of the twentieth century has been described in terms of death and decline. But I remember, too, that the late thirties and forties were periods of enormously accelerating change. That was the period when the twentieth century really invented itself. The super technologies, the military technologies and so on; the changes were absolutely colossal. Time just seemed to race past and govern every-thing. And this change continued until after World War II. Since then, however, everything's begun to slow down. Probably the first casualty of Hiroshima and Nagasaki was the concept of the future. I think the future died some time in the fifties. Maybe with the explosion of the hydrogen bomb.

In the thirties and forties people had an intense interest in the future. They saw the future as a morally superior world to the one in which they lived. All the great political movements – the New Deal, socialism, fascism, communism, whatever – were all highly programmatic systems, symptoms of a better future. But there was so much scientific change too; from the discovery of antibiotics, to jet travel, consumer society, television. One had a tremendous sense of the future. Magazines in the thirties were full of articles about the fastest train or the fastest aircraft in the world; of how the first passenger planes would revolutionise life on the planet. Yet some time around the end of the fifties, the future somehow lost its hold. I think it died.

BROOKS: Didn't it just become shorter-term?

BALLARD: Yes, partly. People certainly lost interest in the future. They began to fear the future. And partly, I think, the prosperity in the sixties and seventies induced a kind of infantilism. People stopped dealing with a timescale that lay outside of their immediate present. They began to have no sense of what had happened yesterday or of what would happen the day after tomorrow. So people became immersed in the fulfilment of their own needs and their own satisfactions. They literally lost interest in the future. But by the same token, they also lost interest in the past. These days most people's idea of the past is a rerun of *Casablanca*. They have very little idea of history nowadays. So time has dismantled itself.

I can see a time, probably about midway into the next century, when time will virtually cease to exist. The present will annex both the future and the past into itself. All desires will be fulfilled and people will live in a perpetual present. It may be a bit like the movie *Star Wars* where you have a peculiar surface of events taking place. *Star Wars* is very unlike the science fiction movies of the forties and fifties which always incorporated an intense feel of change; of how technological progress was going to radically alter life on this planet. But in *Star Wars*, events take place in a timeless limbo. They don't impinge on anything outside themselves. The events could be taking place far, far into the future or far, far in the past. I imagine life itself is in danger of becoming like that.

BROOKS: Coupled with your interest in time, your fiction also generates an intense interest in neurology and psychology.

BALLARD: I've written a lot of stories in which one regime of time gives way to another and people find a new world in the imagination. I'm always taking my position from what I've read of experimental psychology, which seems to suggest that the world presented to us by our central nervous system is really a ramshackle construct that serves the purposes of fairly intelligent, bipedal mammals of rather restricted physical and conceptual limits. We may not be able to run as fast as other mammals but we do have stronger imaginations. Our central nervous systems provide us with a kind of modus vivendi. These ramshackle constructs allow us to function within the rather limited ambit provided by our senses and by our limbs. Yet the optical centre of the brain – our visual universe – doesn't accord with what is really out there. The central nervous system conventionalises and irrationalises [sic] reality for us so that we can move through time and space. But I've always felt that one must transcend that space. And there's a way of transcending this rather limited view we have of reality by using the imagination. We've inherited large parts of our view of the world from our forebears hundreds of thousands of years ago, who had much more limited means than we have now. A sense of time gave *Homo sapiens* a way of storing, from minute to minute, information about the world. We may well have outgrown it. Our sense of time itself may now be rather outdated.

But there's an unlimited scope for change and transformation. We can see it now in the sciences. The pace of scientific change is enormous. People aren't aware of it. Most people are scientifically illiterate. The changes that are taking place are only really meaningful to comparatively few specialists in the field. Yet the changes are colossal. Maybe future historians will look back on the twentieth century and dismiss the entire artistic field of fiction, poetry or the visual arts as completely irrelevant and as having no value whatsoever; where the greatest achievements of the human imagination in the twentieth century took place in the sciences. And they'd probably be right.

BROOKS: But the sciences, of course, are providing cultural changes anyway. Scientific and technological worlds are providing us with things that we are only now beginning to conceive of as having any basis in our realities; concepts that were literally in the most way-out realms of science fiction only a few years ago – cloning, *in vitro* fertilisation and so on. How do you think of the world of the fifth-generation computer? Do you think it's going to be McLuhan's Global Village? Or are we going to be our own 'technological monks' in our own self-creating worlds? Is life going to be this fractured experience that it was in the seventies? Or is everyone going to be tuned into *Dallas* for eternity?

BALLARD: The notion of community, which is kept alive now by television and by almost nothing else, may be passing. There's a sort of post-TV generation now who no longer watch TV. They spend their leisure time in various hobby activities like t'ai chi, scuba diving, playing bridge, badminton – you name it. They simply have no time for television. They don't seem to need it any more. So life will become so diversified and different by the end of the century that it will be hard to know if there is such a thing as a national culture. People will have retreated into their own heads.

BROOKS: Do you see this as good or bad? You're ambiguous in your fiction.

BALLARD: A lot of my fiction is cautionary. It deals with possible end points or trends. I wrote a short story called 'The Intensive Care Unit' about a world where people never meet. They simply make contact via TV. Marriage is conducted hundreds of miles apart. And in my story I visualise a man who actually decides to meet his wife and children in the flesh. Of course, it's a disaster. They just cannot bear the sensory overload. On a mere neurological level, they can't bear to be together – rather in the way that we can't bear to be too close to strangers. So I can believe that, in the future, people won't be able to bear to be in the same room as others. Or even on the same street. Of course, it's very difficult to read these kinds of aspects of the future.

BROOKS: It doesn't seem improbable, though, does it, given what is already happening? I mean Michael Jackson walks around wearing a surgical mask because of his obsession with germs. He doesn't like people to touch him. And AIDS has brought about a tremendous fear of touch or contact with other human beings.

BALLARD: Well, exactly. That's another factor, isn't it? There's almost a sinister sense in which AIDS is a metaphor for all kinds of processes – whether you call them diseases or not – that are leading, or inviting, similar separations on the viral level. It's almost as if AIDS is a disease that it was necessary for the human race to discover so as to justify all these alienated processes that are taking place on other levels. It's a curious and very terrifying disease. It's almost like a science fiction disease. It's unbelievable. And I say 'unbelievable' because I'm not even sure whether to believe the statistics. In parts of Africa, for example, they say ten per cent of the population have the disease. And if that's true, the population in that part of the world could be extinct in thirty or forty years.

But the whole thing does seem like a designer disease. It's as though our hour has come. The disease has provided a kind of underpinning to the whole processes of alienation that have been taking place in our culture in the last ten years to my mind. AIDS seems to put a cap on it. Whenever the population density increases, in order to hang on to their mental space, people do tend to retreat into their own inward mental worlds or spaces. It seems inevitable.

1991: Jeremy Lewis. An Interview with J.G. Ballard

Originally published in the *Mississippi Review*, 20: 1/2, 1991

In 1981, Philip K. Dick wrote a letter to Roger Zelazny, describing the moral confusion engendered by the experience of cognitively dissonant images: 'Two items were presented to me for my inspection within a period of fifteen minutes: first, a copy of WIND IN THE WILLOWS, which I had never read . . . A moment after I looked it over someone showed me a two-page photograph in the current *Time* of the attempted assassination of the President [Ronald Reagan]. There the wounded, there the Secret Service man with the Uzi machine gun, there all of them on the assassin. My brain had to try to correlate WIND IN THE WILLOWS and that photograph. It could not. It never will be able to.'

In the following interview, conducted in 1990, Jeremy Lewis provokes Ballard into an incisive analysis of this kind of dissonance as the quint-essential experience of the media landscape. Drawing an analogy between the laboratory scientist and the consumer of pornography, who both isolate the object of their desire from the world of which it is a part, Ballard suggests that the unconscious mind inevitably invents its own narratives from the dehumanised elements of our piecemeal, channel-surfing, sensation-hungry mode of perception. It is Ballard's sensitivity to these unconscious 'hidden agendas' of the media landscape that permits him, eerily and proleptically, to imagine a catastrophe at the World Trade Center – a catastrophe that, by being repeatedly 'marketed' by the media in a predetermined fashion, will serve only to deaden our sensibilities and our sense of the value of the individual. [DOH]

LEWIS: I find *The Atrocity Exhibition* requires an entirely new approach to reading.

BALLARD: What you have got to do is not read more than a chapter at a time, and don't try to read it as if you are trying to read a conventional short story, or a conventional narrative. The dramatic connections between the characters and events are all very important and all have a strong story, oddly enough.

LEWIS: *The Atrocity Exhibition* has a different title in the States. What was the background of that?

BALLARD: It was first published as *The Atrocity Exhibition* in 1970 by Doubleday, but they pulped the entire edition three weeks before publication. I'm told that one of the senior members of the Doubleday firm, Nelson Doubleday, actually opened a copy and saw the Ronald Reagan story and he just sent the order out to destroy the entire edition. Only about six copies survived, of which I'm glad to say I have one, and then one or two other firms thought of publishing it and then finally Grove Press (which had a chequered publishing career) published it in something like 1972 or '73.

They retitled it *Love and Napalm: Export USA* for some reason – against my wishes. They wanted to cash in on the Vietnam War, but I didn't really have much choice in the matter. I protested strongly that was the wrong title, totally wrong. That edition, of course, has been out of print for years.

But I think over the years that the British paperback editions of my books have been available in the States. In fact I was amazed during my book tour in 1988 to find the British editions which shouldn't be there by rights. It doesn't worry me, I'm only too glad.

LEWIS: You've referred in the past to the connections between science and pornography – what you have termed 'the science of pornography'. This connection is central to your fiction, and especially *Crash* and *The Atrocity Exhibition*, where you attempt to interpret such an affect on your characters.

BALLARD: I like to think of *Crash* as the first pornographic novel based on technology. By technology one means science in its practical applications to everyday life. In the case of *Crash* that has to do with the technology of, literally, the vehicle, for the pornographic imagination. But on another level there is a sense in which science and pornography are moving together on a curious collision course. Science is now more and more taking its subject matter not from nature as in the traditional physical sciences, but from the *obsessions* of its own practitioners – particularly in the soft sciences, psychology above all.

This would be true of the last fifty years, but it's much more advanced now. Psychologists decide to develop a *form* of hypothesis for everything! Let's say, there's one in vogue here right now that says watching television dulls the emotional life, or watching images of violence dulls the emotional life. So they set up an experiment in which subjects are exposed to endless images of violence and then they submit them to tests which – surprise, surprise! – reveal that their human responses have been *dulled* by exposure to images of violence!

The same thing is being done by researchers in all sorts of other human fields. The very famous case about ten years ago in which some American psychologist set up a kind of mock experiment in which groups of students were asked to interrogate other groups of students and were given permission to inflict small doses of pain on these students, if they weren't telling the truth. This experiment was designed to test the core of human compassion. Of course, it revealed that gripped by the power of the pain button, young students will lose their heads and become Gestapo-like tormentors.

Now, it seemed to me in all these examples (there are thousands of them) science is moving into an area where its obsessions begin to *isolate completely* its subject under the lens of its microscope, away from its links with the rest of nature. This is always the risk with science as a whole. The pornographic imagination detaches certain parts of the human anatomy from the human being and becomes obsessively focused on the breast or the genitalia, or what have you. That sort of obsession with what I call 'quantified functions' is what lies at the core of science; there is a shedding of all responsibility by the scientist, who is just *looking* at a particular subject with a tendency to ignore the contingent links.

LEWIS: It's an isolation of certain functions outside of time and space . . .

BALLARD: Yes, outside of time and space, and outside the social and human – effective links that normally constrain our behaviour and imaginations.

LEWIS: How can people learn to deal with this, which seems to be everywhere around us, and retain any individual humanist elements?

BALLARD: Scientists are always running the risk of becoming dehumanised. Doctors don't see their patients' faces, they are only concerned with treating the complaint at all costs. I'm told that people who work with laboratory animals admit that, however kindly they may try to feel towards the animals, the time comes where they start to get impatient with the rabbits or guinea pigs or whatever it may be and cross the borderline between sensitivity and insensitivity. That's inevitable.

On a larger field, one sees that tendency underpinning almost the whole of Western life today. The various ecological and green movements are in part a reaction against that. People want to save the whale and the seal because they know that sooner or later the human being is probably going to be next on the list.

The vast commercial, industrial, bureaucratic organisations of the world that virtually run this planet and define everyday reality have no time for the individual, which is inevitable. It isn't necessarily a deliberate callousness. If you design a hundred-storey office block, whatever it is – the World Trade Center, for example – you put in the best possible ventilation system. But if the damn ventilation system conks out, about twenty thousand people are going to be suffocated. I won't say that this becomes an 'acceptable risk'; it's rather like the casualties on our roads. There is a built-in tolerance that is the effect of these systems.

About twenty thousand people a year are killed on the roads in America. Of course, every death is deplored, but collectively it's manslaughter on a gigantic scale; and it's tolerated as part of the price to be paid. Similar tolerances (acceptable casualties) run through the whole of life. There is a sort of built-in deadening of human feeling that is inseparable from the sort of lives we've opted for in the late twentieth century.

You've got to remember to some extent that the communication/media landscape sets the agenda: a media landscape dominated by TV that thrives on sensation. This itself has a numbing effect. One saw this very much during the Vietnam War. And whenever there is a major tragedy – something like the Lockerbie plane crash or famine in Ethiopia – one sees that these images exhaust their own potential to evoke pity in a very short space of time. With repetition the audience of course becomes bored. The whole thing has a numbing effect.

One also gets the hidden agendas beginning to emerge – the subtexts that begin to write themselves into the script. Inevitably you see images of an actress making love followed by an injured child being carried from a crashed car, followed by some African prime minister being shot down, followed by an advertisement for a martini. On the unconscious plain, what sort of scenarios are we stitching together out of these events?

These are the hidden agendas that *The Atrocity Exhibition* is about. Just as the sleeping mind extemporises a narrative form of the random memories veering through the cortical night, so our waking imaginations are stitching together a set of narratives to give meaning to the random events that swerve through our conscious lives. A roadside billboard advertising something or other, to TV programmes or news magazines or the radio or in-flight movies, or what have you.

We are bombarded by this absolute deluge of fictional material of every conceivable kind and all this has the effect of . . .

LEWIS: Killing affect?

BALLARD: Yes. And of pre-empting our own original response to anything. All these events are presented to us with their pre-packaged emotions already in place, so if you are shown an earthquake or airliner crash you are told what to think.

LEWIS: So again how does one become 'objective' or more 'individualised'? In your fiction you draw upon the concept of inner space consistently.

BALLARD: One has to foster one's own imagination to a very intense degree, far more than most people realise. Most people have a huge capacity for imaginative response to the world that is scarcely tapped.

I'm not stressing that we should become a nation of short story writers, novelists, painters and film-makers, but it may be that the information technologies of the near future are going to make possible the tapping of the individual imagination in a way that highly complex, craft demands of home video systems and home cine-cameras have never allowed the individual before. I remember my parents had a cine-camera back in the thirties, but they hardly ever used it. Even the technology of that was too complicated for convenient use.

Video cameras are remarkably commonplace now. This may be only a further step along that road, and I hope they will become even more commonplace because people will really need to look inward far more.

One will not be able to trust the external environment to provide all the necessary cues for a rich and fulfilling life. This has already happened. One sees the way people these days have retreated far more into their own homes, because much less depends on public forms of entertainment, and so on.

The retreat is not just necessarily their own homes, but a retreat into their *private lives* far more than they used to, say in the forties and fifties, when the home was a place where one slept and serviced one's body, while generally speaking one went out to find paid entertainment. You went to the movies or visited a theme park or went on a package tour to somewhere. People are now pulling back from that sort of thing. They want something that expresses their own taste more, and the range of diversity of hobbies and leisure activities is just fantastic. There are huge industries that are satisfying every conceivable whim.

If people are going to survive they will need to do this on the plane of the imagination much more than they have done. Otherwise, they'll simply become a mark on some consumer chart. This has already happened.

LEWIS: The biological function of sex has been changed to become, like everything else, a function of power, money, domination. So sex becomes a reflection of the external landscape.

BALLARD: This is something I cover in *The Atrocity Exhibition*. I point out there in my marginal annotations that the landscape we live in is absolutely saturated with sexual imagery of every conceivable kind.

There's a sense in which we are all taking part in sexual activity, whether we want to or not, and whether we are aware of it or not. We are constantly bombarded by films and TV commercials, magazine advertising, et cetera.

Sex has become a sort of communal activity. It's an explicit element in all sorts of other activities – advertising, publicity, sales promotion, as well as in film and TV, every conceivable thing you can think of.

Elements of sexual imagery are constantly being jolted into the psychological space we inhabit. One has to be aware of these things and the unconscious role they play.

LEWIS: Such excessive imagery that stimulates a character like Vaughan in *Crash*?

BALLARD: Vaughan represents the nth point or terminal destination in the process. It's very important to realise that there is a normalisation of psychopathology taking place. Elements of psychopathic behaviour are tolerated and are annexed into normal life in a way that we are scarcely aware of. I don't mean this in a complicated sense: if you go to a motor racing track, or a boxing match, or any physical contact sport, or things like demolition derbies and so forth, you take for granted a very high level of violence that would be genuinely shocking if it occurred outside those particular arenas.

But in Europe and in the States one sees in film and television a range of violent and sexual imagery being tolerated that would have been inconceivable thirty years ago. On the Continent – not so much in this country where it is heavily censored – you have hardcore porn films, books and magazines more or less freely available and being distributed to the population at large.

The general effect of all this is to normalise the deviant and perverse. We should accept this and not try and fight against this particular tide; instead, to quote Conrad's phrase, we should to some extent immerse ourselves in this destructive element ourselves. This is the environment in which we are immersed, and we might as well keep our eyes open, and try to swim through all this so we get to the other end of the pool; maybe some way will be found of moderating these strains that are present.

LEWIS: You certainly trace this idea of exercising the perverse and deviant in the imagination in all your fiction. This leads to a Nietzschean sense of a new morality and a sense of freedom. The people you've cited as influences – Celine, Burroughs and Genet – were doing the same thing.

BALLARD: That's true. There is a sense in which a 'new morality' (if you would like to call it that) has already started to emerge. People accept moral discontinuities in their lives in a way that older generations would not have done.

Before the Second World War, one felt a continuous spectrum of moral responsibilities ruling one's life in a way that isn't true any more. People are capable of the highest morality in certain areas of their lives, but of complete blanks in others. To some extent this is encouraged by the media landscape. This has always happened – a thoroughly upright parson can deliver a sermon on Sunday morning and then go out on

Sunday afternoon and shoot fifty pheasants out of the sky without a moment's thought.

All of us who eat beef steak know damn well what goes on in the slaughterhouse; the sort of people that are horrified by the bullfight (at least the bull has a chance) think nothing of millions of cattle going to their deaths in grim circumstances. That's always been the case, but I can see the same sort of moral discontinuities coming in people's lives more and more in the future, producing a rather unsettling world where one will need educated feet to be able to make the crossovers from one moral plane to the next. One already sees . . .

LEWIS: This radical increase of freedom also makes us all capable of doing anything at any point, exemplified in the cases of mass murderers wreaking havoc on crowded places.

BALLARD: The functional freedom that anybody can buy a gun and go out and murder a lot of people at a McDonald's is prevalent, yes. But through the effects of TV and interactive video systems and so forth, we'll also have the freedom to *pretend* to be a mass murderer for the evening. I've seen descriptions of advanced TV systems in which a simulation of reality is computer controlled – the TV viewer of the future will wear a special helmet. These sorts of virtual reality projects are obviously going to overpower the viewer. You'll no longer be an external spectator to fiction created by others, but an active participant in your own fantasies/dramas. Obviously these things could lead to all sorts of (one can imagine) nightmarish outcomes, but one might as well be aware of them and not try to fight against them, maybe do something positive with them.

LEWIS: All this strikes me as being very appealing and at the same time very alienating.

BALLARD: Absolutely. Which is a pretty good summary of the late twentieth century, isn't it?

LEWIS: That's why 'educated feet' help a lot.

BALLARD: Yes, they're essential. These are not just abstract, academic matters. People/parents are worried about the way their kids are no longer literate, no longer reading, and just living for a diet of the

255

transient. They're interested in pop music and fashion, not interested in vocational training. They're living in an endless present of clothes, fashions and pleasant sensations. Waiting for a rude awakening.

There is also no doubt that the levels of urban violence have risen enormously. This isn't just a matter of violence being over-reported.

There are huge underclasses who have nothing to lose. Big cities, or specifically their restricted areas, have always been violent; but now you can be mugged walking down Piccadilly in broad daylight. There have been horrendous cases recently in London. A young woman was actually raped on a tube train at four o'clock in the afternoon with other passengers present near Hammersmith. I was concerned because my woman friend lives in Hammersmith and a daughter of mine lives in Chiswick, not far away.

LEWIS: What's the fiction scene like in Britain these days? Is it still dead here?

BALLARD: Of course it's dead. With a few exceptions.

LEWIS: Not as many as in the States?

BALLARD: I'm not sure if there are any exceptions there either.

LEWIS: What are you reading these days?

BALLARD: I'll admit I don't read much fiction. I read pretty widely. I read marginally in the sciences, political history, a fair amount of psychology and biography. But it's a pretty scattered gun. Let's see what I've got here, we'll do a spot test! – *The Science of Art*; Robert Graves' *White Goddess* (a classic); *Primitive Art in Civilized Places*; and a book on the history of wine! That gives you an idea.

LEWIS: Do you see yourself as a 'science fiction' writer?

BALLARD: Not really. The scientific imagination is obviously very, very important in my fiction, which tends to suggest that I am an SF writer. The problem is that SF exists, *out there*, and has changed enormously since I first began writing. It's pretty hard to escape these labels, but they are rather misleading in a way. I certainly don't think of myself as a science fiction writer any more. Back in the late fifties and sixties, I was writing a fair amount of science fiction, most of which was published in SF magazines. I've never regretted that. My early novels, like *The Drowned World* and *The Crystal World* and the short stories I wrote at that time – my early collections – were pretty close to SF, even by the most stringent definitions of what SF is. But they could also be read outside the SF field.

But by the time I got to *The Atrocity Exhibition* in the late sixties, and then went on to *Crash, Concrete Island* and *High-Rise*, and then at the end of the seventies *The Unlimited Dream Company*, I had left behind science fiction completely. Nobody, in fact, ever called *Empire of the Sun* a science fiction novel, but other novels of mine that were not are termed SF (*Crash* is still referred to as a science fiction novel – which is silly, of course).

If you think of the mainstream novel, say, of the last hundred years from Henry James onwards, it has been dominated by realism and various offshoots of realism – the naturalistic consensus sustained the novel throughout the modern movement.

LEWIS: You've obviously been working outside that tradition. Your work has more in common with another lineage – people like Burroughs, Genet and Kafka.

BALLARD: Yes. Parallel with the modern movement and threading its way *through* the modern movement, of course, have been a few mavericks who've been drawing their inspiration from the imaginative fiction of the past three or four centuries. I don't know if Burroughs is the last of the writers of the modern movement or the first of the next postmodern epoch. But Burroughs has more in common with, say, Dean Swift than he has with the naturalistic writers of the nineteenth or twentieth century.

A few of these mavericks have tended to parallel the main naturalistic movement of the last hundred years. Naturalism itself began to break up about twenty or thirty years ago because it just wasn't adequate to come to grips with the realities of either the Second World War or the post-war world. Today naturalism has completely faltered. You only find it in middle-brow fiction. Magic realism gave a whole new lease of life to the novel: other inputs have come from classic surrealism and film, pop art, Andy Warhol and so on.

But the most important novelists are not working within naturalism any more – you think of people like Burroughs, or novels like *Catch 22*,

A Confederacy of Dunces. What else is happening? That's the problem. My mind tends to go blank when I think of other writers. Pynchon. None of these writers are working in the sort of classic naturalistic space, and quite rightly so. I like to think that I am in with those.

LEWIS: In the past, writers would go to certain cities – Paris, New York, Rome – and find a sense of community. It's not like that any more.

BALLARD: The obvious cities to go to are now almost unliveable. A lot of American writers seem to be based around New York, but I can't imagine *working* in New York. It's too oppressive. I think it would be impossible.

One could work in low-rise cities. Something about the horizon, the literal horizon that greets the eye as you look out the window; the horizon is generally visible, down at the end of streets in low-rise cities, according in some way with the larger horizons of the imagination. A high-rise city like New York (I know it is said there that you can see the horizon at the end of every vast canyon, but actually, you can't), exhilarating though it was, I found very oppressive. The physical mass of the buildings and the discontinuity between street life that existed – the two dimensions of the plane on the city floor and the hidden, concealed life going halfway up to the sky – is very constraining.

LEWIS: I would imagine you feel much less of this in Los Angeles.

BALLARD: I loved Los Angeles. I really felt at home there. I regret that I did not make a life for myself in Los Angeles thirty years ago, when I might have done so. It's an infinitely mysterious city, right on the edge of the Third World really, almost bisecting it, practically the capital city of the Third World.

Driving around there I felt that the Mexican/American border, roughly speaking, ran along Wilshire Boulevard. That's not an exaggeration. White Los Angeles or Anglo-Saxon Los Angeles (whatever you'd want to call it) lies north of Wilshire Boulevard, and Hispanic and black Los Angeles lies to the south. And it is a low-rise city, of course.

LEWIS: Why have you never moved from here?

BALLARD: To be quite honest, until I wrote *Empire of the Sun* in 1984, I'd found that, although I'd made a reasonable living, my income wouldn't adequately furnish such a move. I was bringing up three children, you see. I set out originally to be a doctor. Oddly enough, my career and income have more or less matched that of the English GP (until 1984), and English doctors are not that well paid. I could get by and send my children to private schools and through universities, but I didn't have anything left over after that. If I had taken them to Malaga or LA, it would have handicapped them, they wouldn't have received much of an education. So I just couldn't relocate.

Since *Empire of the Sun*, I've had the financial freedom to go and live anywhere, and I have been seriously thinking about it. I may well head for the Mediterranean, but I'm too old to go and live in the States now; I'd have no friends there, I wouldn't know anybody. I'd step off the plane into a completely alien city and the few contacts I have in the film world wouldn't sustain any sort of social life. But the Mediterranean is very attractive.

LEWIS: My own sense is that five or six years in southern California is enough.

BALLARD: Doesn't one get a sort of beach fatigue setting in? It's a slight mental numbing which you notice among British expats living on the Mediterranean. They are *marooned* in a curious way.

LEWIS: You maroon yourself into a form of found utopia.

BALLARD: One's wits are not sharpened or honed on any kind of whetstone, that's the danger. The danger of living in places like that – at least for someone of your age, rather than mine – is finding the material that can be turned into fiction. Whether you can find something to write about in the Algarve is anyone's guess. You might, who knows?

LEWIS: A lot of your fiction, particularly that written in the seventies and onwards (like *Crash* and *High-Rise*), seems to have been inspired by the Shepperton area.

BALLARD: *Crash* is set not in Shepperton but in the area around London airport, which I see as a paradigmatic landscape of the late twentieth century. Wherever you go in the world, the road from the airport is always the same, and that's very peculiar. It doesn't matter whether you are driving away from Madrid airport, or any airport anywhere in the world, what you find is constituted by certain well-defined means: the same facilities, slip roads, architecture, three-storeyed office blocks, all the support services – you name it. They go on for miles and create the same sort of communities around them, composed of dormitory areas for the airport staff and the same transient world of people working in airport catering services, et cetera, et cetera.

My novel *The Unlimited Dream Company* is set here. I've spent a lot of time in Shepperton, which in a way is a paradigm for the late-twentieth-century suburban life. Shepperton isn't anywhere, you see. It exists to some extent in the shadow of Heathrow Airport (a lot of people here work there) and also in the shadow of the film studios. So it's interesting from that point of view.

LEWIS: It's a sort of in-between world. In that sense, it's very like southern California. You don't feel, as in England, that you are really connected to history and its so-called culture. At the same time, this sense makes you feel lost in some ways.

BALLARD: Yes. In the spring of 1988 I did a classic six-city American book tour, promoting my novel *The Day of Creation*. Fascinating, in fact. It wasn't the first time I had been in the States, but it was the first time I had visited cities I had never been to previously – Miami, Chicago, Seattle. I was tremendously impressed by the strength and variety of the whole country. At the same time, there were one or two moments when I stood in those vast shopping malls in suburban Chicago and Seattle and the sense of planetary loneliness came over me, and you realise that this just goes on *for ever*, unchallenging, across a continent. It sends a small chill through the heart. But that may just be a European's observation.

LEWIS: But don't you think this sort of thing is being reproduced in Europe as well?

BALLARD: It's coming. But, of course, Europe is so balkanised, made up of so many small nations with very strong local traditions, that you have a sense of historical past inert in the present. But I have no doubt that it is coming here as well. A large part of my writing is about *just that* – about the superimposition of our autoroute, motorway, airport, hypermarket, suburban shopping mall culture on everything else. Also TV landscapes, which are terribly important to me.

LEWIS: Europe seems to be evolving into a totally homogenised culture. I get the impression that Europe will become a united Europe in a sense of the States.

BALLARD: That will happen, but it will take infinitely longer to iron out. I doubt that it will ever become a *wholly* homogenised culture like the United States. Superficially it will be. Flying into Athens airport (I'm looking ahead thirty or forty years) you will see a landscape, superficially, indistinguishable from flying into the one at Barcelona airport. But once you get below the superficial, you'll find national identities – because of the languages, as these are immensely ancient countries with long-standing traditions. There will be a new two-tiered reality here: the old core nations with their languages and cultures superimposed on to this second tier, which will be this homogenised, internationalised, TV, airport culture. It's already come to some extent.

LEWIS: Have you read Baudrillard's *America*? It's a wonderful book.

BALLARD: Yes, a wonderful book, yes. A lot of Baudrillard that I've tried to read, I've found rather heavy going. He actually wrote a very complimentary essay on *Crash*. I found what he said incomprehensible, and I wrote the book! But I thought *America* was brilliant. I don't think I've ever read such concentrated brilliance, anywhere! The only rival is something like Swift's *Gulliver's Travels* in terms of brilliance. Every sentence, and if not, every paragraph. I've read it about three times, and each time it gets better. *America*, I thought, was tremendous. I don't know what Americans make of it, because of course, what is absent from the book, and I imagine this is rather irritating to Americans themselves, is a *single American*.

LEWIS: I have some American friends who felt he was taking too critical an outlook on the country.

BALLARD: I didn't see too many criticisms. I thought it was a wonderful celebration of the United States and its great strengths. Some of his ideas were brilliantly original – his notion that the United States is the only primitive society on earth in the sense that it is the *only* primitive forerunner of the advanced societies of the future. Everywhere else today is *irrelevant*, but at least the United States represents the early foundation of a stage of the future.

It's very difficult to put one's finger on what the successful formulas of American life are, but it certainly is based upon a whole cascade of successful formulas that together place the United States really on a superior plane to anywhere else. Much as I love France and Italy, there is no question that they, or even West Germany (which in a way is the most American of all European countries), are nowhere near the United States.

Size has something to do with the creation of modern America, but it isn't just size. New York would not be the extraordinary city it is if it were not also the commercial capital of a continent. On the other hand, Seattle is a pretty remarkable city too, and so is San Francisco.

There is something about the States that does represent a quantum leap forward.

1992: Phil Halper and Lard Lyer. The Visitor

Originally published in *The Hardcore* 8, 1992

In 1991, Ballard published *The Kindness of Women*, a sequel of sorts to *Empire of the Sun*. It continued the quasi-autobiographical story of 'Jim' from the point of his post-war departure from Shanghai up to the Los Angeles premiere of the film version of his autobiography about his youth in Lunghua camp. In the final chapter of *Kindness*, Jim observes, 'The clock of my life had come full circle', and the strange oscillations between the book's reimaginings and factual descriptions affect the reader in an equally disturbing way, borrowing their authority and inevitability from the facts of Ballard's known life, while distorting those same known facts through a prism of what Ballard would call 'imaginative truth'.

In 1992, Ballard embarked on a UK tour to support *Kindness*, and at two of those Q&A sessions, in London and Manchester, fanzine *The Hardcore* rather ingeniously sent, as they described it, 'two information terrorists, Phil Halper in London and Lard Lyer in Manchester, to dominate the proceedings and make sure any questions about *Empire of the Sun* and Ballard's childhood were at all costs avoided'. They did not quite succeed. The audience at both events is evidently a mix of Ballard acolytes and neophytes, and one of the most interesting aspects is the way in which Ballard responds to the kind of questions every writer fears, such as 'where do you get your ideas?'. But the advantage of confronting Ballard with his real readers, at this particular point in his career, was clearly that he would be forced to deal with the obscure relation between his own life and the imaginary lives of his protagonists, particularly in *Crash* and *Empire of the Sun*. [DOH]

HALPER & LYER: Did you consider 'Why I Want to Fuck Ronald Reagan' a prediction, or just a story?

BALLARD: Nothing is just a story. I watched Reagan's commercials when he was running for governor of California in 1965, and a lot of these were shown on television because of the novelty value of having a Hollywood actor running for political office. It was seen as extraordinary, treated as a joke by the British media in particular. I thought there was something about Reagan which was a sign of things to come. I can't say I was convinced he would become president, but I thought someone like him would become president eventually, because he understood how the media landscape worked. He realised no one in this huge television audience was listening to what he was saying – all they were interested in was his body language. He came on with this friendly sportscaster manner, or like a Buick salesman, yet he was pitching – at that point, in the mid-sixties – this extreme right-wing image which picked on all these phobias and fears in his audience. He was the first of the new-style politicians who instinctively took the lowest common estimate of their electorate. He succeeded beyond my wildest dreams.

AUDIENCE: You mentioned the sixties and your fascination with Kennedy and LSD. Would you say your artistic loyalties were with the surrealists or with pop art, and have you been to the current pop art exhibition at the Royal Academy?

BALLARD: Well, they're strongly with the surrealists, but pop art was a wonderful source of ideas for me. I remember going to the *This is Tomorrow* exhibition at the Whitechapel Gallery in 1957 [sic] when Paolozzi and Richard Hamilton virtually single-handedly created pop art, long before the Americans got into the act. The British have always had a more analytical approach to the iconography of consumer society than did American pop, which tended to be passive and celebrate the more vacuous elements, although Warhol was of course a genius. But the surrealists were much, much closer to me. I enjoyed going back to the show last week and I was very, very impressed, although the British contribution was played down. The surrealists have been the biggest influence on me, because they anticipated by about fifty years the fact that the external environment can be remade by the mind and that this is the world we inhabit now, where external reality is a complete fiction in every conceivable way.

I can remember days when you saw a balloon in the shape of a hamburger – people would say, 'Oh, that's a publicity stunt.' No one ever says that now. They assume a balloon in the shape of a hamburger is the real thing, not a real hamburger – that's the point. But the fact is this image of a hamburger is real. It is not a publicity stunt but part of the fabric of ordinary life, more real than an ordinary hamburger. When you eat one you think 'Who made this?' It's probably been in storage in a suburb of Düsseldorf for the past three years, whereas the balloon floating overhead does have some genuine authenticity, a genuine uniqueness, and you embrace it as the real. The surrealists anticipated the way the mind can remake the world. Sometime in the seventies the media landscape wrapped itself around the planet and redefined reality as itself, and the amazing thing was that we all went along with it. I think that's a huge shift in the mass consciousness. We accept the fictions of the mass media are real and most of us would be hard put to define what the real is in personal terms. Are they the little obsessions in our head? They're about all we cling to. So we have this doubly fictive universe and I leave it to the next generation of writers to deal with it.

AUDIENCE: Do you think you are a bit guilty of that yourself with the new novel and *Empire of the Sun*, that with a sort of fictionalised look at yourself, in a way you are imagining yourself?

BALLARD: No. *Empire of the Sun* and *Kindness of Women* are novels – they draw on my own life. Had I been born in Godalming, worked on the *TLS*, moved to the BBC and wrote a novel about it, no one would say 'Ah, an autobiography'. That's the perfect Hampstead novel – it would be regarded as a proper piece of fiction. But because my childhood, and, to an extent, my later life in England, is a bit out of the ordinary, people assume it's autobiography. In fact it is substantially fiction. In *The Kindness of Women*, as in *Empire of the Sun*, almost all of the characters are invented. There are no original women in *The Kindness of Women*. I don't want to disappoint anybody. Even the narrator – myself – is to some extent invented. I did many of the things that took place in *The Kindness of Women*, but not quite in the same way they are described because I am trying to reach the imaginative truth, which is more important than the literal truth, drawing on the experiences of a lifetime. To some extent, drama consists of what people say if they had two minutes to think about it. That is a very important point. It's a reworking of life and I think that's what writing is all about.

HALPER & LYER: So was *The Unlimited Dream Company* based on any surrealist painting in particular? When I went to the Max Ernst exhibition . . .

BALLARD: . . . you saw where I got all my ideas. No, I don't think that in particular. I suppose it is a surrealist's vision of Shepperton where I live. But it's a sort of parable of my own life. I fell to earth there thirty years ago and got to work transforming the modest little town into this exotic pagan universe. I wait hopefully every day for the scenarios laid down in the book to come to pass.

AUDIENCE: Do your early apocalyptic novels have any relationship to *Empire of the Sun*?

BALLARD: Well, people who know my stuff well can see the sources in *Empire of the Sun* – well, *Empire* is like a prequel, but written after the rest of the stuff. A large part of my imagination – although not all – comes from childhood. I've never lived in a desert area, although I've written about deserts. Obviously we are all influenced by our childhoods. But mine was, as it happens, particularly traumatic and it has spread itself to my fiction. I think for particular reasons I postponed facing that fiction, and I wrote all those SF novels in my early days, which are kind of disguised versions of that subject matter, and for some peculiar reason I got around to writing about it in the last few years.

HALPER & LYER: Have your children read *Crash*?

BALLARD: Yes, they have.

HALPER & LYER: What did they think of it?

BALLARD: I never asked them.

HALPER & LYER: You describe the bombing of Nagasaki as 'the birth of a new sun' in the chapter entitled 'Empire of the Sun'. Does the novel relate to the nuclear age?

BALLARD: It is related, I suppose, but it's hard to pin down.

HALPER & LYER: In the sixties you talked a lot about your 'optimum sex death'. What would it actually be?

BALLARD: My optimum sex death? The leading character in *Crash* dreamed of dying in a head-on collision with Elizabeth Taylor. I once nearly bumped into the lady in a revolving door in the Savoy Hotel and so I got an indication of what it might be like. Needless to say, *Crash* is to be taken metaphorically.

HALPER & LYER: In *RE/Search 8/9: J.G. Ballard*, you mentioned a Disney version of *Crash*, but now David Cronenberg is scheduled to direct, after he's finished Burroughs' *The Naked Lunch*. How do you feel about that?

BALLARD: Cronenberg is *planning* to direct it. Plans in the film world are like dreams. One has to wait until the first frame of celluloid is exposed to daylight. It is supposed to go into production some time next year, but I'll take that with a pinch of salt until it happens [Cronenberg wouldn't film it until 1996]. If anyone films *Crash*, and many people have been interested in doing so, they'll have to stylise it. Otherwise the director, actors and audience in the cinema will all be arrested – I'll be safe in Patagonia. I think far better it be stylised by a classical film director like Cronenberg, who sticks to the rules of filmmaking where story is paramount and special effects take second place. Better Cronenberg, who has this wonderful, visceral imagination, than say some New Wave director who would make some mad, helter-skelter, kaleidoscope of crazy images and leave the audience totally distracted and looking for the exit. So I'm quite happy. I met Cronenberg and talked about *Crash* with him and he impressed me. Like Spielberg himself, he's an extremely serious man. If you want frivolous, empty-headed people, meet writers.

AUDIENCE: In *The Day of Creation*, did you know that Mallory was going to live at the end of the book? Because it was a great shock to me – I was sure he was going to die. The whole thing felt like a

267

hallucination carried to the extreme, and then it ended naturalistically. You let him off the hook, as it were.

BALLARD: Well, my heroes have a bland version of self-immolation. But I think it is important that he survived his own dream. In *The Day of Creation*, for the benefit of those who haven't read it, a doctor working at an aid station in darkest Africa, on the edge of an approaching Sahara, accidentally starts a stream running and is convinced he has created this river, and becomes obsessed with it, and decides to sail up to its source. You can imagine where that source lies: by the end he is absolutely convinced that this river is flowing from his psyche. And I think it is important that he survives his dream so he can reflect upon it. At the end of *The Day of Creation* the dream disposes of him. As he reaches its source, the river literally dies in his arms, as a tiny trickle. The river is rejecting him and dismisses him, and I think it is important that he is able to reflect upon his dream, which remains ambiguous to the end.

AUDIENCE: Yes, I looked at the ending again, and he's waiting for the girl to come back. He's waiting for the river to come back.

BALLARD: Absolutely, so the cycle will begin again. The whole thing is a vision of his own deepest possibilities and it touches his own imagination.

AUDIENCE: Did you think of *Heart of Darkness* as you wrote it?

BALLARD: I don't think I'm allowed to forget *Heart of Darkness*. If the phone rings, it'll probably be Joseph Conrad, saying, 'Mr Ballard, you stole it all from me.' But to be fair to myself, Conrad in *Heart of Darkness* is not in the least bit interested in the river. The river could be a super-highway. The river is just something that gets Marlow, the narrator, up to Kurtz's station. Whereas the river is all important in my novel, but it is impossible to write a novel just about a river without people automatically thinking of Conrad. I just console myself with the fact that no one will be able to write a novel about car crashes without giving me credit.

AUDIENCE: Well, that brings us on to people calling you a science fiction writer, as people do.

BALLARD: Mustn't despise science fiction . . .

AUDIENCE: I don't, I like it. But to call you a science fiction writer . . .

BALLARD: It's the literature of our age. Mustn't forget that. Change moves at such a rate today that it overtakes almost anything we can anticipate. Certainly in *War Fever* [Ballard's 1990 short-story collection], they're sort of written off of today's headlines. Well, not exactly written off of today's headlines, but in many cases in anticipation of today's headlines. I mean there are hints in one or two of the stories there, hints of the Gulf conflict but written a few years before the event, not that I take credit for that. I like writing about the present, it's always interested me, and I like writing about change. I began writing in the late fifties when SF was interested very much in the sociological topics of the present day. This was the sort of American SF that Kingsley Amis was writing about in *New Maps of Hell*. But sadly in the seventies and eighties American SF has veered to out-and-out fantasy. Perhaps that was a response to the Vietnam War, Watergate, Nixon's problems, and the Americans just wanted to forget about the real world and launch into pure intergalactic escapism – that might be the reason.

Now SF has, I think, shot the bolt. I think it's a form of fiction that has come to an end. I think if I were starting again I wouldn't need to become an SF writer because everything that science fiction has achieved has been annexed into popular consciousness, and many mainstream writers, these days, have written out-and-out SF novels. I'm always telling 'literary' people that Doris Lessing has written more SF novels than I have and people think that I am joking. I constantly see *Crash* referred to as an SF novel, and of course it isn't in any conceivable way. But by calling it SF, it's a way of distancing book from reader. It's a way of not facing up to what the book is trying to say. I think SF has probably come to an end, because it's in the air we breathe. Kingsley Amis, Anthony Burgess, Calvino, Borges, not to forget William Burroughs – there are many, many contemporary writers who use science fiction because it is in the air we breathe and because it is a uniquely able method of dealing with the present day. The mainstream novel, which for the most part is basically a nineteenth-century form, isn't able to do so.

HALPER & LYER: Why is it in your novels, for example *Crash, Empire of the Sun* and *The Drowned World*, the characters always embrace the disaster around them. For instance, Vaughan wants to die in a car crash in *Crash*, Jim runs out on to the runway in the middle of it being bombed in *Empire of the Sun* . . .

BALLARD: They construct private mythologies through their lives and once they create these dreams, they follow them to the end, follow the logic. That's what my fiction is all about: people following their obsessions and their private mythologies to the end, whatever the cost. That way they find fulfilment. I've got a hunch that's how the mind works. It's as close as people can come to happiness. Try it.

AUDIENCE: Do you perceive Freud and Jung metaphorically?

BALLARD: Well, I've always thought of Freud really as a great novelist. Thomas Szasz, the American anti-psychiatrist, describes psychoanalysis, and by implication psychiatry, not as a science but an ideology. I think the ideology underpinning psychiatry is a great work of imaginative fiction. After all, Freud sees the unconscious as a narrative stage on which these archetypal constructs, the superego and the ego, work out, not to mention the Oedipal Complex. They are working out a powerful fundamental drama that takes place in our brains, whatever we have to say about it. Now this is very close to the way in which fiction works. Psychoanalysis has not got a good record therapeutically, and it's not surprising that the greatest concentration of psychoanalysts in the world live in the USA, which is the greatest generator of fiction this century.

I see Freud rather like one of the great surrealists. Whatever you read about the man confirms enormous strengths of character. Very few people have such strengths of character against such adversity, pushing what were absolutely revolutionary notions. He was a completely respectable man – that was the extraordinary thing. It wasn't as if William Burroughs was pushing something new at you. This was a highly respectable Viennese doctor living in one of the most respectable communities that ever existed, actually announcing that children had sexual desires for their parents. It would be like the equivalent today of . . . well I can't think of anything. It would be like approving of paedophilia. It would be as revolutionary as that. One admires him for that but I think, like the surrealists, he integrates the imagination into a logical-rational system which is not scientific but akin to science, which is what the surrealists did. Freud is a vastly greater novelist than I am. But *I* think my fiction is true and might even have therapeutic properties and possibilities. I might market it as such.

HALPER & LYER: Does the angle between two walls have a happy ending?

BALLARD: You tell me. Does the angle between two walls have a happy ending [the phrase originates from one of Ballard's graphic experiments in the late sixties]? Well, it's a serious question actually, which I won't try to unravel at this stage. But everything you see – the man sitting on the stool, people I see sitting on chairs – are all fictions generated by the central nervous system. There are fictions that match so we can all cope with each other. But they are fictions generated by the central nervous system none the less. The angle between two walls is part of that huge image that the brain generates, that explanation for the world that surrounds you. Now, the brain is looking for happy endings all the time. The brain is in the business of finding happy endings, whether it's something to eat or whatever. Does the angle between two walls have a happy ending? It's worth asking.

HALPER & LYER: Is that what you meant when you said 'fiction is a branch of neurology'?

BALLARD: Yes. Yes it is, of course. The brain is generating a huge range of images. I mean the brain is generating a huge range of explanations for what is going on and fiction is a part of that system of explanation. Yes, that is exactly what I meant.

AUDIENCE: Is there any possibility of collaborating with William Burroughs?

BALLARD: I know Burroughs well and have done so for about twenty-five years. He is immensely courteous, but there is a huge barrier between us which I have never been able to breach. He is very Midwestern. He comes from a rich, Midwestern family. But he is the equivalent of a Bournemouth colonel, upper-crust, upper-class, Midwestern provincial American, and his family strata look down on doctors, politicians, lawyers and feel a sort of offhand concern for blacks. He's also very homosexual and very much into the drugs culture, which leaves me out. So sadly, much as I would love to collaborate with William Burroughs, I do not think it will happen – and he's a very, very old man.

AUDIENCE: When you were in China, I was wondering just how much fear you actually felt?

BALLARD: I never remember feeling any fear, either during or before the war. This is something which has absolutely baffled me. I brought up three children of my own. I live in one of the most tranquil suburbs in the Western world, Shepperton in West London. I used to get nervous every time my kiddies ran out to buy a Crunchy bar. I thought they would fall into the hands of some childhood rapist or get run over and I'd never see them again. Whereas I as a child was living in one of the most dangerous cities the world has ever seen. Even before the Japanese invaded in 1937. I was only seven years old. Before then, it was an extremely dangerous place to be. The Kuomintang forces under General Chiang Kai-shek even then were battling with the Chinese communists led by Mao and Chou En-lai, who made their start in Shanghai. There were terrorist bombings and atrocities and the city was full of gangsters of the most ruthless kind. Yet I used to pedal my little bike all over the place. Some sort of magic preserved me. The streets were extremely narrow, and these vast American cars would roar everywhere, and there were violent gangsters who would just kick anyone out of their way, me included, and giant French trams were screaming all over the place. It was widespread with kidnapping and God knows what, but some magic preserved me. I don't know why I'm here at all.

AUDIENCE: Were you aware at the time of having an unusual childhood?

BALLARD: No, of course not – it was the only one I knew. I assumed that the whole world was like that. It was quite a shock to come here, I must say. I mean, people have said to me, 'Ah yes, Ballard, a special case, with this weird childhood.' But in fact the childhood I had was very much closer to the way in which the human race has lived in this century and in previous centuries, rather than life in these very secure enclaves in western Europe and North America. Most people in this century have endured a background of civil war, disaster, et cetera – I observed that and to an extent was part of it in Shanghai. Life in western Europe today is an anomaly. *Empire of the Sun* is much truer to the way most people lived on this planet in this century and in previous centuries than the novels of . . . dare I say it . . . fill in the blanks.

AUDIENCE: But it's unusual because you belong to this side of the world.

BALLARD: My parents belong to this side of the world. My parents were both English, wholly English. I'm making a bit of an effort here, but I still think of myself as a bit of a visitor here after forty-six years. I haven't changed the lino in the kitchen because I'm only staying for Easter.

1993: Joan Bakewell. Memento: J.G. Ballard

Previously unpublished

The following is a transcript of an interview that was screened on Channel 4 as part of its *Memento* series in 1993. It took the strange form of an unintentional parody of *Desert Island Discs*, with Ballard invited to choose a number of his most cherished objects and use them as an opportunity for general discourse. Accompanied by Joan Bakewell, he promenades through a studio set, pausing at each object to discuss its personal significance. The setting lends the whole proceeding a cosy air akin to *Antiques Roadshow*, as if Ballard is being invited to present his treasures and have their aesthetic virtues explained and, more importantly, their monetary value assessed. Yet Ballard's choice of objects seems to Bakewell to be either deliberately grotesque or perverse.

Whether it be owning up to a delight at playing the imp of the perverse, or simple pleasure in the congenial company, Ballard enjoys himself considerably in this interview, and the artificial drama of the set only serves to accentuate his emphatic certainty in his own views. He explains this certainty when discussing the chess set as being a result of his teenage years running wild in Lunghua camp, suggesting that life in Shanghai equipped him to see the true nature of life's events without sentimentalism's distortions. This opposition of sentimentality and truth is surprisingly reminiscent of the rhetoric of realist novelists such as George Eliot, an association to which Ballard would have been reluctant to admit, yet the juxtaposition of the surreal and the concrete, which the format of the interview permits, makes it clear that, for Ballard, an unsentimental perception of the real and an unrestrained imagination are two sides of the same coin. [DOH]

The Chess Set

BALLARD: This chess set is the oldest possession I have, and the only one in fact that links me to my childhood. I walked into Lunghua camp – my Japanese camp – with this set in the winter of '42, '43, and I walked out of it in the summer of 1945, and I've had it ever since. My father and I played chess with this set, and my son and I, years later, used to play chess with it. It's very special, my only link with my past. I think what made me realise that things had changed was the way the adults in Lunghua camp responded to internment. Up till that, till the war, adults had been magisterial, supremely confident creatures. My mother beautifully dressed, my father a sort of distant figure, stepping into the back of a chauffeur-driven car, and all the adults, you know, they were sort of gilded figures who might have been in a movie. Then in the camp I watched, as a boy of eleven, twelve, with the beginnings of an adult mind, the way in which pressures were beginning to erode and weaken their personalities. And *that* was the real education. I think I realised for the first time, which I would not have done otherwise, that adult human beings were fallible, that they could give in to despair, they could give in to petty squabbles, they could give in to weakness. And some could triumph over it despite their own weaknesses, because there were many brave people in the camp who'd triumphed over being rather modest and in many ways rather weak individuals, but they were able to triumph over their weaknesses and survive. That was a great lesson.

BAKEWELL: What about you, though, the growing boy? How were you able to grow up with any set of relevant values? You yourself, as you tell it in *Empire of the Sun*, became a bit of a dealer: you nicked food, you survived. Why haven't you been spoiled by that? Why aren't you a criminal person now?

BALLARD: Well, I probably was spoiled by it, but of course, as I've often thought, life in Lunghua camp and life in Shanghai and the Far East in the 1930s and the 1940s wasn't some sort of strange anomaly – it was much closer to the way the majority of human beings on this planet have always lived, and much closer to the way the majority of human beings still live today. We in western Europe, and in the more prosperous suburbs of our English cities, are living in very artificial enclaves.

BAKEWELL: But you played chess with your father in the camp, you liked games. Did you have rules for getting through from day to day, as a boy?

BALLARD: No. I thoroughly enjoyed my nearly three years in Lunghua camp. It was a huge slum, and the people who really relish life in a slum are of course the teenage boys. They run wild. I ran wild. I was totally out of the control of my parents. And that's why I left them out of *Empire of the Sun* when I came to write the book, because it wasn't psychologically true to have had my parents in the novel. To all intents and purposes in Lunghua camp between the ages of twelve and fifteen, I was a hooligan. I mean, I was a street urchin. As you say, I was out for any deal: how could I get hold of this two-year-old copy of *Popular Mechanics* magazine from these American sailors? Offer them some little service, snatch another extra sweet potato . . . But that's life, you know; that's life on the streets of Cairo, Bombay . . .

BAKEWELL: How did it equip you to deal with life?

BALLARD: Well, I think it's taught me to see the truth of everything, to be unsentimental, and at the same time to guard and value my own imagination and my own pride and what I've decided for myself are the best things in life – in later life, my children and the people I care for. I think it's also given me a freewheeling imagination, of course, that I've put to use as a writer.

The Funeral Horse

BALLARD: This is a replica of a funeral horse that, in classical Japan, used to be buried with the dead, and I've had it for about twenty years. It's made of terracotta. It was given to me by my Japanese publisher, who came to visit me. A very strange present: I couldn't help but think there was an ulterior motive.

BAKEWELL: Was it put in the coffin?

BALLARD: Yes. I've grown to like it, and I think when I die I shall leave instructions that it should be buried with me in *my* coffin, because it's become a sort of constant friend.

BAKEWELL: The Japanese, who put you in prison, and who shot and killed a lot of people around where you were in Shanghai in the war – you admired them. As a young boy you admired even your captors. Now what was that like?

BALLARD: I *did* admire the Japanese. I think there's no doubt about that, I have to be honest. I still do, even though they were extremely brutal and cruel, and any British serviceman hearing me say this will think I'm absolutely mad.

BAKEWELL: Are you? I mean, why do you like them?

BALLARD: I think as a boy, in my naive way, I admired their tremendous courage. I'd seen the Japanese forces fighting around Shanghai in 1937, when they first invaded China. I'd seen them enormously outnumbered by the Chinese armies, fighting on from waterlogged riverbanks, ready to fight to the end. I enormously admired their courage. This is as a child – I'm speaking as the child I was. Now that I'm older I don't value physical courage in quite the same way, and I think the readiness to fight on to the end and kill your prisoners as well isn't something I admire at all now. I think I also admired a sort of melancholy strain in the Japanese. I think in a curious way the Japanese enjoy being sad. It's a strain in their make-up. I was never sad as a child, and I haven't often been sad as an adult, but there's something about that sort of wish for sadness which is very close to a sort of philosophical attitude to life. It's fatalistic.

BAKEWELL: Do you share that?

BALLARD: To some extent. It's curious that the Chinese also share something of that. I mean, people have said – and I thought this as a child – that the Chinese are a very cruel people. I mean, there were public executions in the old city in Shanghai, which took place in what looked like little bullrings. I often used to pass by . . .

BAKEWELL: And see them?

BALLARD: No, I never saw them. No, of course not, because I was protected from that sort of thing. But they would always draw a thoughtful crowd. I think the Chinese, for thousands of years, have been brought up to have very low expectations of life, and the cruelty confirms their rather pessimistic view of existence.

The Dissecting-Room Skull

BAKEWELL: As you travelled out of the camp, you saw a group of Japanese slowly torture and murder a Chinese coolie. And I wonder whether you had seen so much by the age of fifteen that, in choosing a skull, it doesn't have the eerie feel that it does for me, perhaps? Do you feel at ease with the human body in all its sort of vileness, its decay?

BALLARD: First of all, I don't think the human body is vile in any way. I think even the cadavers that I dissected in the anatomy school at Cambridge preserved their dignity – very, very much so. I never felt, dissecting a cadaver, that I was in any sort of superior position. In fact, quite the opposite. You know, these dissection-room cadavers had been donated by doctors before their deaths, and there was something profoundly moving and a great tribute to the human spirit, that these men and women – women doctors, a few of them – had left their bodies to the next generation. I had this skeleton, which I used to study anatomy, and I used to handle the skull almost every day, and the other bones, and examine it, and one couldn't help but sort of find the personality or what seemed to be the elements of a personality, particularly in the skull but of course also in all the other bones. And one developed – I think I developed – a tremendous respect for human beings, however damaged or however ill they were.

BAKEWELL: Do you find from the life you've led, and what you've discovered, that you have a spiritual dimension to human existence, or do you really see man as a mechanical creature?

BALLARD: I think man is a mechanical creature with the soul and mind of a poet. It's our imaginations that allow us to transcend the universe. The universe may be, in the largest sense, a cold and alienating place, but we at least have the gift of the imagination and the gift of the spirit, and that's something the universe *doesn't* have on its own. I think we have a clear advantage there. That skull was once full of dreams, hopes, ambitions: an alternate universe to the one that lay around it, probably in the paddy fields of South-East Asia. However harsh the life this human being led, inside that skull dreams flew.

The Family Photograph

BAKEWELL: This photograph reflects the second catastrophe that destiny dealt you, because when you were married with three young children, happily married, everything to look forward to, things going well, your wife died very suddenly. Now how did you make sense of that event?

BALLARD: Well, it absolutely bowled me for six. It took me a very long time to recover from it, if I ever have. I think I have, with the help of my children. That photograph shows me, about a year after my wife died, with my three children – I think it was 1965. You know, people have said to me, 'How did you manage to bring them up?', and I've always said, 'Well, they brought me up', and I think that was literally the case. They provided the stability and the good sense and the confidence. They're very buoyant, and they swept me along, and I wasn't able to look at the past, because they of course had soon forgotten the past. The years that followed that photograph were very, very happy years. I think I had a second childhood, actually; or rather, I think I had a *first* childhood. I think the childhood I'd not experienced for myself, thanks to the war, I was able to experience for the first time through my own children.

BAKEWELL: Technically, how did you cope?

BALLARD: I made a decision very early on that I couldn't provide anything that remotely resembled gracious living and, as that photograph shows, our life in a semi-detached house in Shepperton was just like a huge, untidy nest, and cleanliness was definitely not next to godliness. In some ways it was a pretty ungodly place, but it was very, very happy. Part of the problem I faced was that so few men in the mid-sixties were looking after children on their own, and it was made pretty clear to me by men and women and even by the local social services, who briefly put their nose around the door, that this was not the sort of thing a man should be trying to do. I think any man trying to do so today wouldn't find that sort of social disapproval.

The Delvaux Replica

BAKEWELL: You were writing science fiction, what you call apocalyptic fiction. Now, this is another of your objects. It isn't science fiction, but it's the height of surrealism, and a lot of the visions, the landscape visions of your novels, are surreal in this way, aren't they?

BALLARD: Yes. The original of this was painted by one of the great surrealists, Paul Delvaux, a Belgian painter, and it was painted in 1936 and destroyed during the Second World War in the Blitz. It had been bought and brought to London. In, I think, 1987 or 1988, I thought, 'I very much want to buy a Delvaux', but his prices then were astronomical. His paintings cost, you know, several hundred thousand pounds, and I thought rather than bankrupt myself by buying an existing Delvaux, what I would do would be to commission another painter to bring to life one of these lost Delvauxs, one destroyed in the war. The original of this one was destroyed in 1940, and it only survived as a black-and-white photograph which I found in a collection of reproductions of Delvaux's works. So I approached an American artist, Brigid Marlin, whom I know, and asked her if she would accept a commission. I think she's really a sort of very religious woman who is a very fine painter of religious topics, and I think she thoroughly disapproved of my choice, but she faithfully executed the painting, which now sits in my living room. I've had it for about five years, and I think in many ways I've gone to live in that landscape.

The Crashed Car

BAKEWELL: Of all the most extraordinary objects, this has to take the biscuit. It is indeed what it looks to be – a crashed American car. Why?

BALLARD: Well, the crashed car, as everyone who's read my fiction knows, has played a central part in it, and I held an exhibition of crashed cars in 1969 as a sort of trial run for my novel *Crash*, which I published in 1972 [sic] and which I think is my most original and best book.

BAKEWELL: It's quite a horrendous book: it's about crashing cars becoming involved with the erotic life of the protagonist, who sees sex and the crashed car as converging, and who gets excited by crashes, by women with scars . . . Now, this is a deeply disturbing book. Were you very disturbed when you wrote it?

BALLARD: I think I was. I think in a way the novel is the record of a sort of mental crash that I had in the mid-sixties after the death of my wife, and I think my interest in car crashes and, to some extent, in media violence – and the late sixties were saturated with violent imagery – I think all of that was an attempt to sort of make sense of, to some extent, my wife's death but also of all those deaths I'd seen in China during the Second World War, which my wife's death reminded me of, and in a way I think if I could sort of turn logic upside down, if I could make black white and white black, if I could prove to myself that the car crash was not a giver of death but a giver of life, that somewhere beyond the collision of the human body and technology, between the human imagination and technology, there was a happier uplands . . . If I could do that, I don't know, in some sort of crazed way I could bring my wife's spirit at least back to life. Many people thought of it as pornographic, and to some extent of course *Crash* is a pornographic novel: the first pornographic novel based on technology. But then we lived in those days in pornographic times.

BAKEWELL: You had the exhibition in 1969, but the sixties were a very lively time for you. You were rather typical of the reputation it has: you took LSD, you were around and about in arty circles . . . Did you enjoy it, or did you have to just come through it?

BALLARD: I found it a tremendously exhilarating time. Of course, most hours of the day I was looking after young children, and in the evenings I would dash off to London – not every evening, by any means – but I also spent a great deal of time watching television, which I think set the agenda of the sixties. It was a violent TV epoch. I mean, people who worry about violence on television now have forgotten what it was like then. We had the most graphic footage from the Congo, Biafra and of course Vietnam, and I felt that a sort of culture of violence was being set up, in which pure sensation was all that counted. There was something very sinister about it. It was like sort of pumping an electric current through the leg of a dead frog: all that mattered was getting this dead muscle to kick, and the whole of our culture was rather like that. *Crash*, I think – the exhibition and the book that followed – grew out of that culture of violence.

The Unicycle

BAKEWELL: This is totally different in mood, and your final object.

BALLARD: This is the vehicle that I would like to ride around in today. My girlfriend, Claire, whom I've known for twenty-five years, bought it for me, as a real surprise, for my sixtieth birthday, and I've always actually wanted to ride the unicycle, and I've been practising ever since she gave it to me. In a way, it was a very shrewd judgement of my character by her, that she should get me this machine. It's a piece of poetry, of course, and that, needless to say, is a very low-mileage model: I've gone about three feet in it so far. But I think it was an interesting judgement on my character.

BAKEWELL: What is she saying, then? In buying you that, what comment is she making?

BALLARD: Well, I think she sees me as a sort of trick cyclist, perhaps: somebody who's determined to defy gravity and is – I hope it's complimentary – capable of staying upright in defiance of all the normal laws of time and space.

BAKEWELL: So, does it sum you up? Are you a one-wheel vehicle?

BALLARD: I think I am, actually. I'm a one-wheel trick cyclist, with a very low mileage.

1994: Lukas Barr. Don't Crash

Originally published in *KGB Magazine*, 1994

Lukas Barr's interview followed the publication of *Rushing to Paradise* in 1994, a novel which, it seemed, was calculated to offend the very political liberals who might constitute Ballard's readership. In it, a ruthless and dictatorial ecological campaigner, who bears a not unfaint resemblance to Margaret Thatcher, creates an anti-nuclear sanctuary for endangered birds upon a Pacific atoll. However, her island paradise becomes a feminist stud farm, and her most recent recruit, a teenage boy, finds that he is participating in the island sanctuary's ecology in a role he did not anticipate. The interview's references to 'cultism' touch upon the ways in which both mainstream politicians and leaders of dissenting movements create realities out of their own psychodramas, and Ballard's conclusion – that puritanism may be the new decadence – seems now all too plausible.

But 1994 was also the year in which the internet began to percolate through society, spreading outwards from its use purely in universities and colleges to a more mainstream user, and in this interview one can see Ballard happily adapting the significance of 'virtual reality' to a Ballardian view that we live 'inside an enormous TV programme', and predicting the advent of distributed personalities in consequence. [DOH]

BARR: Tell me about cultism in your book. We have all sorts of cult news here since the terrorist bombing in Oklahoma.

BALLARD: As far as *Rushing to Paradise* is concerned, there's nothing far fetched at all about the events described there. I mean, in fact, the central action of the book is loosely based on the attempt by Greenpeace . . .

BARR: . . . down in New Zealand.

BALLARD: Right. When the *Rainbow Warrior* was sunk in Auckland harbour by the French secret service agents, it was actually on the way to the French nuclear test islands. They'd made a lot of attempts to get on to these islands, and had been flung back into the surf. So there's nothing unusual about that. We've seen the effects of cults themselves since the Manson gang – what happens when a charismatic leader goes too far – James Reverend Jones in Ghana, Waco, Texas, now these weird militias that are springing up all over the States, or have been there for years, actually, culminating in this Oklahoma bombing. There's something destabilising in the air today. It's worth writing about, particularly as we see extremist fringes popping up all over the place. The feminist movement also has its own extremist fringes, and one could imagine a nightmare scenario of all these extremist cults coalescing, and some very sinister movement emerging.

BARR: You've taken on the left wing, right? You've got environmentalism, feminism, all that.

BALLARD: I don't know where female separatists fit on the political spectrum. They want to destroy the social contract between men and women and replace it with nothing; they seem to believe that all penetrative sex is rape; if a wife loves her husband she's exhibiting a 'slave mentality'. Well, I mean, how do you cope with that sort of fanaticism? Satire seems one way.

BARR: It's the tinges of euthanasia that are the most sinister aspects of the story in *Rushing to Paradise*.

BALLARD: Oh, absolutely, because this is the trouble always: enlightened legislation, or enlightened social activity of whatever kind, does play into the hands of people with agendas of their own, with secret agendas. And, of course, if you legalise euthanasia, you provide a field day for people who like killing other people. And they'll find plenty of reasons for doing so.

BARR: I want to ask you about space, not as in outer space but as in geography, rooms, the space around you. There's that story called 'The Enormous Space', about a man who decides not to leave his house, and gradually shrinks his geography until he's sitting in a cupboard. And then I remember another story. I don't remember what it's called, about a doctor who has a sleep deprivation experiment. He does an operation to prevent his subjects from sleeping, and they're all in this large gymnasium, and by the end they're all huddled together in the middle of the room.

BALLARD: 'Manhole 69', a very early story of mine.

BARR: So talk about the interaction between the interior space of one's mind, and external space of reality.

BALLARD: The thing is we take external reality, our everyday external reality, very much for granted: the room that we sit in, the streets around us, the virtual space of billboards, and movies and TV, all the rest of it, highway networks – we take all this for granted. But in fact it is, literally speaking, an illusion generated by our central nervous system. It's as much a virtual reality as the one the cyber people are working on. I've tried to decode this everyday space. What happens when we see presidents or prime ministers Ronald Reagan or Margaret Thatcher or whoever on television? Within our minds all these different planes of spatial reality are intersecting.

BARR: And they also tend to become flattened in your mind, there's an equality . . .

BALLARD: Yes, they do. Everything turns into a kind of billboard. We're effectively living inside an enormous TV programme. In *Atrocity Exhibition* in particular I've tried to decode, to decrypt, that multilevel space that we create.

BARR: This goes to the heart of what I think is the most impressive quality of your work: once you start to do the decoding either explicitly or not, the subject at the centre of that becomes untethered from any kind of base reality. And has the ability to spin off in any number of directions, into different psychoses. When I read your work, it's a claustrophobic feeling, it's so powerful, so vivid, and it's so moody. You evoke a psychosis, and tell it so straight.

BALLARD: I think your use of the word psychosis is absolutely right. All my characters are trying to escape from whatever situation they find themselves in. They do so largely by – their way out is to construct a

285

psychosis which dramatises their own predicament, and to come to some sort of solution. The man in 'The Enormous Space' who doesn't leave his house is a perfect example of that. In *The Atrocity Exhibition*, the central character is this psychiatrist who's suffered a nervous breakdown. He sets up a whole series of psychodramas, each one of which is a separate psychosis. He wants to kill Kennedy, again, but in a way that makes sense. Now, psychosis is the most dramatic remaking of the mind that one can embark upon. In *Rushing to Paradise*, Dr Rafferty is transforming the island of Saint-Esprit into a huge psychosis of her own. Of course, not all the characters in my fiction, thank God, are as mad as she is. Though I admire her.

BARR: This brings up two other interesting points. Whatever happens in terms of space, in terms of perception, in terms of the mind, you always still have to deal with the body, which isn't subject to the same types of flexibility. So in a way, going back to *Crash*, you can see that the body is one answer to this problem, that you can ground yourself in your body, that you can mark your body, that there's some sort of permanence and weight there.

BALLARD: Absolutely. In the body, and in particular, in pain, and in its sexual activity, *Crash* explores the relationship between sex and technology, and in a sense celebrates the marriage of sex and technology. I agree. In a lot of my fiction I've tried to root the realities of the characters in their sexuality, and in their sexual imagination.

BARR: Well, what about drugs? Because they fit into this as well. You must get asked about drugs all the time.

BALLARD: I'm a bit of a disappointment to people who are into or influenced by the drug culture of the sixties and seventies. You'll be disappointed to hear that I'm very much a whisky and soda man. I took LSD back in '67. Up to that point I'd smoked a bit of pot. When I was a student at Cambridge, I regularly . . . you could then in England buy amphetamines across the counter, in drugstores, without a prescription. And we took them regularly without even thinking about it, if you wanted to work all night, or just feel a bit keyed up. I'd had experiences with drugs, but then I took LSD – I've never taken heroin, never have done. But then I took LSD, and had a classic bad trip, which I won't bother to describe.

BARR: You should, though, tell me about—

BALLARD: I had such a negative trip, a real paranoid journey of despair. It was over in a day, but little vents of hell went on opening for years afterward, as I gather they do. I don't know, it sort of turned me against drugs. And then people started saying about an early novel of mine called *The Crystal World*, which described a crystallising world, going beyond time and space -- ah, that book was written after your LSD trip. I said no, that's not true actually, it was written before my LSD trip. It confirmed, I felt, that human imagination can achieve anything that drugs can achieve. So, I stick to my whisky and soda.

BARR: How would you describe the mood as we head towards the end of the millennium?

BALLARD: It's very strange. I remember years ago, I think in 1984, I said we could expect, as at the end of past centuries, there might be a spread of decadence. But that the decadence might take the form in our case, not of sexual licence, but of a new kind of puritanism. Puritanism of a sort of little-Red-Book-Maoist-guard type. That is exactly what we've seen: a huge rise in puritanical zealousness, in which a whole range of new vices have been invented – people are never happier that when inventing new, or rather exposing new, vices. People are full of puritan relish. We had a bizarre case here, yesterday or the day before yesterday – some animal rights activists attacked a dairy and planted bombs under a whole lot of milk wagons. Those big tankers that drive milk all over the country, like gasoline tankers. They blew up about thirty of these vehicles, protesting the farming of the ox for human consumption. And you know there's another group of weirdos that are anti-car. And they closed off London streets for a mass demonstration against the car, turning them into pedestrian zones. These are not sort of little shopping streets where you can have a cake, these are main thoroughfares.

People believe in nothing. There's nothing to believe in now. All ideology is gone. The great churches are empty, political ideology is finished, there's just a scramble for power. There's this vacuum . . . what people have most longed for, which is the consumer society, has come to pass. Like all dreams that come to pass, there's a nagging sense of emptiness. So they look for anything, they believe in any extreme. Any extreme nonsense is better than nothing.

BARR: What do you predict now? You've just told me what you said in the eighties, how about your predictions for the nineties?

BALLARD: My most successful prediction was made in 1967. I predicted that Ronald Reagan would become president.

BARR: Did you really?

BALLARD: Yes, I did. In *The Atrocity Exhibition* there's a short story called 'Why I Want to Fuck Ronald Reagan' which got me into terrible trouble and had the book pulped when it was first published.

BARR: This is when he was governor of California.

BALLARD: Right, exactly. I took one look at him and thought, 'That man is going to be president.' For reasons I won't go into now but which I explore in the short story. And, as for the year 2000, I'm slightly nervous of making predictions, as I shall then have reached my biblical three score and ten, and might not be around, or might have to answer for my predictions in another place. Well, I think we're well on the track to all kinds of craziness. I think there's no end to what sort of nonsense will come out of the woodwork, and a lot of very dangerous nonsense.

I could sum up the future in one word, and that word is boring. The future is going to be boring. The suburbanization of the planet will continue, and the suburbanization of the soul will follow soon after. At the same time there will be extraordinary unpredictable outbursts, a sort of volatility, largely driven by extremist cults of one sort or another. You know, you may live in a quiet suburb, outside Des Moines or somewhere, and suddenly your local school will be burned down by some gang of fringe fanatics protesting against the use of lead-filled pencils in classrooms. I think that's what we have to look forward to. That plus the internet and virtual reality. People will retreat into these electronic hideaways.

BARR: Virtual reality is such a great tool in the abstract to think about all the things you were talking about earlier: perception, reality, geography, all those things. Yet as it becomes more and more real, and you actually try it out, it just turns out to be an incredible disappointment.

BALLARD: The number of pixels per square centimetre is way below that processed by the human eye, but there is a point where it will equal it and then, conceivably, exceed the processing powers of the human brain and eye, at which point ordinary reality will look rather shabby. And the whole thing raises enormous philosophical questions. Within this world of virtual reality, we will be free to fulfil one of mankind's oldest dreams, that is the ability to play games with our own psycho-pathologies without hurting anyone. You'll be able to run your own concentration camps, assassinate Kennedy, and do it all in a completely innocent way. The mind boggles.

BARR: So, what's your next book?

BALLARD: It's about the nature of crime. I won't tell you any more because with your advanced word processor, you'll be able to tap it out before I can . . .

BARR: How about the two British kids in the papers recently? Kids and crime are sort of an interesting pairing.

BALLARD: You mean the ones in Liverpool?

BARR: There are lots of stories like that. That's not an isolated case.

BALLARD: Absolutely. It happens all the time. It certainly wasn't the first. What was interesting about that case was that it was caught on all those surveillance TV cameras. That was what tapped people's mind. I think people felt as if it were almost a television programme. It was kind of an indictment of TV and its logic in a curious way. I don't know if you've heard of the Moors murders over here twenty-five years ago, a young couple in the north of England strangled a number of kids and buried them on a moor outside Manchester and it prompted incredible interest, quite rightly, there's nothing more horrific than sexual torturing and sadistic killing of children. What was striking was that this couple tape-recorded the screams and preliminary conversations they had with their victims. These recordings were played in court, and everybody's blood just turned to ice. Again it was as if people realised that it was the technological interface between the psychopaths and the public, in the form of tape recordings in their case and in the form of surveillance camera film in the recent one, that grips people. They look at a tape recorder and think, 'My God, this thing has the potentiality of being a murder weapon, in a particular way.'

BARR: Speaking of crime and TV, we're getting a lot of O.J. Simpson coverage. I don't know how it's playing over there.

BALLARD: We get a one-hour summary once a week which I sometimes watch with enormous fascination because the court procedure is so completely unlike all that we watchers of American films and TV series have been led to expect. Where was the incisive cross-examination? It's completely absent.

BARR: Well, we're getting more than an hour a week. It's on all day long live and then all night long on recaps and discussion shows.

BALLARD: It's very difficult for an outsider to judge because looking at it, just glancing in on the thing as it were, you get the impression that these aren't real lawyers. These are the inmates of some institution who are taking part in some sort of remedial psychodrama, where a tragically brain-damaged woman is being given a script and told to behave like a public prosecutor. The judge, it's hard to believe this man is qualified, he seems so totally incompetent. You know he could be . . . it's something like that play *Marat/Sade* – one of those plays that Sade put on in his lunatic asylum using the patients. You'd think that Ito was some sort of brain-damaged Japanese-American who's car crashed, asked to play the part of The Judge. He's the one that doesn't have a script. He fumbles and stumbles. Nobody seems to have a grip on this and it's completely obvious to me that Simpson is going to walk out of that court and be paid a hundred million dollars to star in the film of his life, which will of course include the murder of that poor couple.

1995: Nicholas Zurbrugg. Empire of the Surreal

Originally published in *World Art* 1, January 1995

Nicholas Zurbrugg, who died in 2001, was a poet, artist, academic scholar and literary critic of Swiss parentage. He specialised in postmodernity, and his own eclectic interests in the literary and artistic avant-gardes of the twentieth century permeate this interview. In addition, Zurbrugg's own attitudes towards England and Englishness, and the identification of the writer with nationality, determine the shape of the conversation. In allying Ballard with another writer in whom he was greatly interested – William Burroughs – Zurbrugg was perhaps concerned to explore the personal significance of the exile as a role the writer takes on, but in bringing the issue up, he broaches the question of Ballard's continuing and willing isolation in the suburbs of what is, and must remain, at once 'home' and a foreign country for Ballard.

A heavily annotated, revised edition of *The Atrocity Exhibition* had recently been published by RE/Search Publications with an introduction by Burroughs, and many of Zurbrugg's questions are clearly prompted by the new insights Ballard's annotations offered on that most difficult of his books. [DOH]

ZURBRUGG: Perhaps I could begin by asking you about your feelings as a writer living in England, and the writers and artists you found influential over the years. Do you think of yourself predominantly as an English writer, or as something other, or beyond this kind of categorisation?

BALLARD: I don't think of myself as an English writer. I like to think of myself as an international writer. The writers who helped shape my imagination come from all corners of the earth. In fact few come from England. Most of the twentieth-century writers whom I read, and who I think shaped my writer's role, come from outside England: Kafka, Joyce, writers like Hemingway, Burroughs, French writers like Albert Camus and so on. My writing has also been shaped by the visual arts, in particular by the surrealist painters, who had a much bigger influence on me than any comparable group of writers.

ZURBRUGG: When did you first become aware of some of these writers? I imagine you read Franz Kafka and James Joyce when quite young. But when did you first become aware of William Burroughs, for example, or the art of the surrealists?

BALLARD: I first started reading Burroughs in about 1960, or in the early sixties anyway, so I've read his books from the start. Surrealism, of course, goes back a couple of generations before Burroughs. I was aware of the surrealists when I was still at school. I was very interested in science as a schoolboy, and going on to study medicine. I was interested in psychiatry, so I read a great deal of Freud and psychoanalysis – which was the main inspiration for some of the surrealists.

ZURBRUGG: Did you see much of their painting in England at the time? Were there many shows in London?

BALLARD: Up until the late sixties, I think, the surrealists were very much looked down upon. This was part of their attraction to me, because I certainly didn't trust English critics, and anything they didn't like seemed to me probably on the right track. I'm glad to say that my judgement has been seen to be right – and theirs wrong. Back in the late forties and fifties very few paintings by the surrealists had ever been reproduced in our serious newspapers over here. You were more likely to see something by Dali or Magritte in the *Daily Mirror*, where of course it would be held up to ridicule. But at the same time, there were a large number of exhibitions of work by Magritte, Dali, Delvaux and so on in small London galleries.

And I used to go to Sotheby's and look at paintings there, where surrealist paintings often changed hands. So they had a kind of underground presence, in a sense. They were shown in quite respectable

London galleries, but they were never given major retrospective exhibitions. I think it wasn't until a major exhibition at the ICA [Institute of Contemporary Art, London] on the surrealists – in something like 1968 – that the surrealists at last came to town. And of course, the sixties – with its interest in psychedelia and all the rest of it – were tailor-made for surrealism. Within a few years they established themselves as the most important artistic movement of the twentieth century. Ernst and Magritte are accepted as two of the greatest painters of the twentieth century, and I think Dali will be, too. But the high reputations that they now enjoy were won without any help from the academic or critical establishment. That's all to their credit.

ZURBRUGG: I suppose there were probably one or two people writing about surrealism, such as Roland Penrose.

BALLARD: I think he was chairman of the ICA. He of course had been buying surrealist paintings since the 1930s, but I don't think that he had a very high profile. Surrealism, in a sense, was a victim of World War II. When Breton and the other surrealists returned from America, they found a very cool reception in Paris. I mean, there was a sense in which Hitler and the death camps had explored all the possibilities of the nightmare.

Then there was the rather cool, bleak agenda which the existentialists – Sartre, Camus and so on – were setting out, which matched the postwar mood. And many of the leading French writers, like Camus, had fought in the resistance, and this gave them much more moral authority then Breton – who had sat out the war in New York. But all too soon, a new set of nightmares emerged – above all, the threat of nuclear war – which made surrealism seem relevant again.

ZURBRUGG: Turning to a slightly more basic question, would you think of yourself as a slightly surrealist, or a post-surrealist, writer, in any respect? I think in your notes to the new RE/Search edition of *The Atrocity Exhibition* you say that you've been impressed by surrealist art, but give the impression that you are not nearly so enthusiastic about surrealist writing.

BALLARD: When I arrived in England, there were very few examples of surrealist writing available to me. I wasn't such an enthusiast for surrealist writings that I was prepared to hunt down every last piece about them.

I just took what I could find. There were books on surrealist painting – I mean in every history of twentieth-century art there was a chapter. Usually, it wasn't on surrealist writing. It was very varied stuff, surrealist writing. Most of it was in French and hadn't been translated into English. Also, I've always felt that the literary wing of surrealism seems much less imaginative.

ZURBRUGG: What about Éluard? Did you read much of Éluard's poetry?

BALLARD: As a schoolboy? No. If it had been translated I wasn't aware of it. Also, I think my imagination was powerfully attracted to the visual images of surrealism.

ZURBRUGG: Were you influenced by – or did you find allies in – journals like the *Evergreen Review*? I don't know if you saw *Olympia* or *Merlin* or some of the little magazines that came out of Paris, which probably prefigured the *Evergreen Review*?

BALLARD: I didn't see any of them until very, very much later on – the *Evergreen Review* of the 1960s published in the States. I don't think I've ever seen more than a single copy. My interest in surrealism has always been in half a dozen painters. But I've never been very interested in anything else. The French poetry I read in translation – the precursors of surrealism, Rimbaud in particular – were a very big influence on me.

ZURBRUGG: Lautréamont, perhaps?

BALLARD: Yes. I didn't come across Lautréamont until about 1965 – the New Directions edition, which I've now read many times. I've had that since 1965, but I began writing in the mid-fifties. I'd certainly read Rimbaud since my schooldays. He's a far greater poet – far more revolutionary, and far more appealing to me – than Éluard.

ZURBRUGG: Did you find England rather a bleak place to be writing and trying to do what you were trying to do? Or did that suit your temperament as a relatively independent person?

BALLARD: In the long run it proved a great help to me. But right from the start I did find it extremely bleak, and in many ways still do. I think there was a brief period in the sixties when England became interesting as a fertile breeding ground for new ideas as a result of the sixties explosion, which was powerfully driven by the need to break down the old class structures. I think it was those class structures that seemed to me to strangle all life out of England when I came here in the later forties. There was nothing that I wanted to write about here. And I still feel that.

ZURBRUGG: That reminds me of my own childhood. I grew up in Hampton and Sunbury, near Shepperton – and Shepperton is not New York. I remember trying to work out what it was that set my imagination alight, what were the bridges to other things. And England seems a curious place to be in, in terms of breaking out into other conceptual dimensions.

BALLARD: English writers, of course, don't break out. They're trapped by their childhood. And I think that most English fiction of the twentieth century has suffered grievously from the nature of English life. I mean, one has to be frank. Most of the English writers who have achieved anything this century have tended – if they were born here – to have gone abroad at a very early age. Orwell spent a lot of time in Burma and in Spain, and Greene in France, and Huxley in California, they became virtual exiles. Burgess has lived abroad for the last thirty years, so far as I can see. Those who've stayed here have tended to be fatally constricted by the limitations of English life, and have usually made it their subject matter.

As far as I'm concerned, it may have helped me to have felt completely isolated here – I mean, I still do. I've absolutely nothing in common with most English writers, though I know a few painters and sculptors. And that sense of exile may have given me a certain freedom to explore my own world.

ZURBRUGG: You've mentioned another great literary exile, William Burroughs. What qualities do you warm to or appreciate in his work? What reservations do you have about Burroughs' work, if any?

BALLARD: I haven't any reservations. I feel that Burroughs is the most important and innovative American writer since the Second World War – there's no doubt about that in my mind. I think that in some ways American fiction, certainly contemporary American fiction, is in a bad way. It seems to me that Burroughs' contemporaries – writers of the

1950s and 1960s like Joseph Heller, the author of *Catch-22*; Pynchon and Salinger – represent almost the last generation who had a really large vision, whereas contemporary American writers have a very shrunken notion of what the novel can do, and what its province is. It seems to me that Burroughs meets the twentieth century on its own terms, on its own grounds, and evolves an imaginative response to the twentieth century that's absolutely appropriate to it. You could reconstitute the psychology and inner dynamic of the twentieth century from Burroughs' novels. I think he's revolutionary in all senses – I've no reservations about his work.

ZURBRUGG: Do you think that Kathy Acker's work offers an exception to your general view of contemporary American fiction's shrunken perspective?

BALLARD: Well, she's an interesting writer who's trying to chart the real terrain that lies below the floating surface of everyday life. I think she's a genuine original.

ZURBRUGG: What about William Gibson, the author of *Neuromancer*?

BALLARD: Yes, he's an interesting writer, but in a different way. He's certainly an original voice in the science fiction field, and he and some of the other so-called cyberpunk writers have actually tried to make sense of the information landscape. I give full marks to them.

ZURBRUGG: In your notes to the new RE/Search edition of *The Atrocity Exhibition* you emphasise that you're interested in decoding the secret codes or the subliminal codes of our culture, and suggest that there should be more sex and violence on television as a way of precipitating revolution. At the same time, in *The Kindness of Women* you evoke the sixties as the 'craze years' and as a 'time of desperate strategies', and the main character there finally seems to have undergone a process of 'catharsis' that seems to reconcile him to more immediate, almost domestic, resolutions. Do you sense a conflict at all between your annotations' general appeal for more extreme media content as a form of provocation, and the more modest aspirations of the protagonist in *The Kindness of Women*?

BALLARD: When I write about the protagonist in *The Kindness of Women*, I'm writing about an alternative version of myself. I'm now sixty-one years old [sic] and I've come through my trials of mind, and may well have found myself in serener waters. But when I say that the mass media should be far more free than they are now, and that far from there being less sex and violence on television, there should be more, I'm speaking generally. I think it's important that the generations younger than me should face the world they live in as truthfully as they can. Our domestic television imposes a largely fictitious version of reality. Sex and violence are such powerful catalysts for imaginative change that everything should be done to encourage them in television. I'm talking about legal acts, particularly as far as sex is concerned. I saw a profile in *Time* this week about the American feminist writer Camille Paglia, who appears to be pro-kiddy porn and snuff movies. I'm certainly not in favour of that, but if the acts themselves are legal, there's no reason why they shouldn't be shown.

ZURBRUGG: I suppose the predictable response to that is that there's a danger that an uncritical proliferation of such imagery might lead to something more negative than an integral, truthful appraisal of our condition.

BALLARD: Well, if you go to a country like Holland, where hardcore material is freely shown, there are no signs that the social fabric is disintegrating. It's quite the opposite. People's ability to accept the sexual imagination as a part of everyday life seems surprisingly mature. Over here there's been an extremely powerful backlash against the truth. During television news reports of the Gulf War, you never saw a body. As I say somewhere in *The Atrocity Exhibition*, this encourages the impression – particularly among the young – that plane crashes, for example, are harmless, and that dulls our civic response.

ZURBRUGG: Perhaps I could ask you one final question. Something that I've been looking at a lot are the general accounts of our culture by some of the French theorists, and a lot of them – Jean Baudrillard in particular – tend to offer very apocalyptic diagnoses of a state of crisis and neutralisation that they associate with the last decades. It seems to me that some theorists today overemphasise the negative potential of present times without really suggesting – or acknowledging – that there is any potential for perceptual maturity. Do you have any general comments upon this sort of diagnosis?

BALLARD: I find Baudrillard's *America* one of the most brilliant pieces of writing that I have ever come across in my life. It's an extraordinary book. There are a lot of Baudrillard's other writings, which Semiotext(e) keep sending me, that I find pretty opaque – I suspect through mistranslation. He uses a lot of code words which have probably a very different meaning in French than in literal English translation. He's written an article on *Crash* – my novel – which I've read in English, and I find that difficult to understand. But *America* is brilliantly original. I'm not sure what Baudrillard's overall worldview is. I certainly take an optimistic view. To some extent he sees America [the country] as a huge pop art exhibition. To him, America is an imitation of itself – its imitation of itself is its reality – which I think is true. But he takes an optimistic view of America, and I would do the same about the world as a whole.

ZURBRUGG: I think that comes out again at the end of *The Kindness of Women*, where you talk about the replica of Heyerdahl's ship, the *Ra*, being perhaps more seaworthy than its precursors.

BALLARD: Absolutely – that's an important image. I think that many 'replicas', as it were, are far more seaworthy than their originals. I think America, as a Baudrillardian image of itself, is far more seaworthy than the notional original that most Americans believe in. But I think the old Conradian notion of immersing ourselves in the most destructive element is still true. That's why I'm a strong libertarian – within the constraints of the law – and believe in exploring all the possibilities open to us. I think the logic of the late twentieth century, and certainly the twenty-first, if I'm around to see any of it, is so governed by our information and communication systems that an ever-greater freedom is inevitable. As people have said, once they invented the Xerox machine, totalitarianism – certainly, Russian totalitarianism – was doomed.

1995: Will Self. Conversations: J.G. Ballard

Originally published in Will Self, *Junk Mail*, London: Bloomsbury, 1995

Novelist Will Self enjoyed a friendship with Ballard that lasted from this interview until Ballard's death. In interviews and in print, Self has been an articulate and well-versed supporter of Ballard's work, acknowledging it as an influence on his own writing. This interview showcases Self's knowledge of Ballard's oeuvre, and makes a number of salient points about the significance of Burroughs and Freud as Ballardian touchstones. In turn, Ballard provides detailed insight into his working methods, his views on the American publishing scene, his admiration for Graham Greene and Anthony Burgess, the role of repetition in his work (which could easily apply to a similar technique in the body of interviews he gave), how advanced technology is changing the nature of entertainment, and the ideas and motivations behind his latest novel, *Rushing to Paradise*. [SS]

SELF: Whose idea was it to do the new Flamingo edition of *The Atrocity Exhibition* with the marginalia?

BALLARD: It was suggested by the publishers of the RE/Search volume, Vale and Andrea Juno. They wanted to reissue *The Atrocity Exhibition*, which had long gone out of print in the States, and they had this large-page format, and I thought that there was going to be a sea of white paper because you can't have double columns; the readers' brains would start to frazzle. So I then thought that as this is a largely incomprehensible book it might help to have a few marginal notes. I thought

299

it worked well. So when Flamingo, HarperCollins, got around to reissuing it I suggested using the notes, which they did.

SELF: And how's that gone, has it sold?

BALLARD: I don't know. I wouldn't have thought it would have sold well. I have no idea, I never asked. The American edition has done well, which surprises me. I have always found that America is one nut I have never cracked.

SELF: They have this expression in the States of being 'on the wall', which means that your sales have peaked so that you are always placed on a particular wall, a figurative wall in the bookshop.

BALLARD: *Empire of the Sun* – thanks to the Spielberg movie – did well, but most of my other stuff is just tipped over there. Too pessimistic, too ironic. Everything has been published there but most of it is out of print, I would guess. It is a difficult market to crack, the Americans are so different from us, there is no question about that. There is a strangeness about America, it is not the pop-art aspect of the place, which of course most British visitors are struck by, and the huge advance that the American standard of living represents over ours, but their strange way of thinking. There is something very odd about the place.

SELF: I wonder if I am missing out on something by not finding it as bizarre as perhaps I should. The other thing is that it is so polyglot now, and increasingly polyglot.

BALLARD: I don't think it is bizarre, but their minds move in ways that one can't fathom all that easily. In a different way, the Japanese mind is a very difficult one to read. Whenever I go to the US, I love it, it is a marvellous place, so exhilarating and visually exciting. It is intensely in the present, which is wonderful. We barely touch the present here because of the dead weight of the past, but there the present envelops everything. It is like moving from a small TV screen to a huge cinema screen, you are conscious of a million little details that one can't find in the small-screen world. I am always aware there, after a while, of a missing dimension. I don't know what that missing dimension is – I have thought about it for years – but there is a missing dimension.

SELF: I know that for all sorts of practical reasons you were settled here [in England], but was there a point in your emotional relation to your work where you thought, 'Yes, I am stuck here'?

BALLARD: I am stuck here, and I realised that I was stuck here quite a few years ago, but I think that imaginatively I have always assumed I would be leaving England and settling somewhere abroad, somewhere in the Mediterranean. I have not actually drawn a lot of my fiction from the English landscape so it is rather different in my case. You have to remember I didn't come here until I was sixteen, and the brain is hard-wired by the time you are sixteen. You are constantly aware of what may seem trivial things: the density of light, the angle of light, the temperature, the cloud cover, a thousand and one social constructs, the shape of rooms and the way people furnish them, the way they furnish themselves. All these things, which a true native takes totally for granted and is unaware of, still seem . . . there is still an underlying strangeness for me about the English landscape and there is even about this little town of Shepperton where I have lived for thirty-four years. If you settle in a country after a certain age, after your early teens, then it will always seem slightly strange. In my case this has probably been a good thing, it has urged me to look beyond Little England for the source of what interested me as a writer.

SELF: Most of the interesting English-language writers domiciled here are writing now with a different slant, so perhaps with your background you were a forerunner of that post-imperial and multicultural tendency.

BALLARD: Perhaps. Certainly things have changed enormously. Younger writers of your generation are far more open to the world. Partly I think it is the literary culture which dominated English life since the mid-Victorian period and survived intact until the Second World War. It had laid down through generation after generation the blueprint of what was possible and what was not possible in one's work, one's writing, one's life and one's set of mental attitudes. I never met Graham Greene but I enormously admired him for all sorts of reasons. But I am pretty certain that had I met Greene during the sixties I would have found it difficult to have any sort of close rapport with him because he was so English really, even though he loved travelling abroad and all the rest of it.

SELF: Did you know Anthony Burgess during the sixties?

BALLARD: No, I never met him. I am sorry I didn't, because I admired him tremendously as a reviewer and critic. He had a wonderfully catholic and open mind.

SELF: He would have been *simpatico*, surely, even at that time.

BALLARD: He would have been. I am sorry that I never met him. It is unfortunate.

SELF: You wrote that essay on William Burroughs in the late fifties [sic], at a time when he was languishing and out of favour. Well, I suppose Girodias was just publishing *Naked Lunch* at that time. I was interested in your remarks upon Burroughs. Again, you said that you found it difficult to establish a rapport with him when you actually met him, though judging from the dates when you interviewed him, he was in the midst of a serious smack period.

BALLARD: Have you met him yourself?

SELF: No, I have never met him.

BALLARD: I admire him enormously. I think he is the most important, innovative American writer, and possibly world writer, since the Second World War. But the thing to remember about him is that he is a Midwesterner. He comes from an upper-class, provincial American family and he is not cosmopolitan, he doesn't have the natural cosmopolitanism of, say, a New York writer. It is very difficult to penetrate that almost aristocratic mind-set of his.

SELF: He has gone home to Kansas, he has gone home to die.

BALLARD: Absolutely. We have met a number of times over the last thirty years and we always chat in a friendly way. Obviously I steer the conversation towards those things that I know interest him. But I have

never been able to relax with him, partly because he is a homosexual
... that is an important element, I think, because he comes from a
generation which had to be careful. You could go to jail. This is true of
Angus Wilson too, though he was a very different type, but you sense
with older homosexuals that they have developed a system of private
codes whereby they recognise one another and ease themselves into each
other's company and friendship without endangering themselves in any
way.

Strangers can be dangerous. There is something of that in Burroughs,
complicated of course because he had been a lifelong drug user, at a
time when that too was extremely dangerous. It is difficult for an outsider
like me who is not a drug user, not a homosexual, to penetrate. I regret
that. What is so wonderful about the American literate class is that it
produces unlimited quantities of young men and women, of your age
group, who are so open to the world. But Burroughs is complicated.

SELF: Given your melioristic, if not optimistic, attitude towards the
current period, I wonder if you find it difficult to look at how things
have regressed in the last twenty years. There has been a move back
towards a preoccupation with class, there has been more economic
inequality, there has been a resurrection of Little England.

BALLARD: I agree and I find it deplorable. I thought the sixties – which
you didn't experience at first hand – were a wonderfully exhilarating
and releasing period. All those energies, particularly of working-class
youth, burst out; class divisions, which had absolutely strangled and
imprisoned the English, seemed to evaporate. Those divisions genuinely
seemed to vanish or become as unimportant as they are in America,
where there is a class system but one that doesn't serve a political
function of controlling the population. Here the class system has always
served a political function as an instrument or expression of political
control. Everybody is segregated – hoi polloi at one end of the lifeboat
and toffs sitting around the captain as he holds the tiller – and this
prevents anyone from rocking the boat and sending us all to the bottom.
In America the class system is not an instrument of political control.
When the class system began to ... well, it didn't disintegrate but it
seemed irrelevant in the sixties, I thought, 'How wonderful, this country
is about to join the twentieth century.' And then in 1971 – I think
Heath had just got back into power – I heard someone use the phrase
'working class' and I thought, 'Oh, God, here we go again.' Now, of

course, things are better than they were – I remember England in the late forties and fifties. Hopefully there will be another leap forward. Now we are in the grip of a much larger . . . well, we are not masters of our own fate any more.

SELF: I remember Mike Petty – who, I believe, edited *Crash* – telling me that when he was working on the manuscript he'd lock it in a drawer at night for fear that young publishing colleagues might catch sight of it and be severely traumatised. And I only have to look at a few paragraphs of *Crash* to feel I am in the presence of an extreme mind, a mind at the limits of dark imagination. It imparts a sense of everything having been done.

BALLARD: I haven't reread it since I read the proof so I can't . . .

SELF: You haven't been back to it at all?

BALLARD: No, too frightening.

SELF: You dislike looking back in that way?

BALLARD: I never read my own stuff, the mistakes come off the pages. Oh, God, all those infelicities of style. And one notices little stylistic tricks. Oh, God, no.

SELF: You are never tempted to keep lists of things that must never be repeated or words that have been overused?

BALLARD: I try to do that mentally, because it is such a temptation.

SELF: There is an American writer, Nicholson Baker, who must be the world's greatest anal-retentive, because when he writes a book he compares it with everything he has written before to check there is no repetition of imagery or vocabulary.

BALLARD: I go in for a lot of deliberate repetition, I don't see why not. I like that. They are signifiers for the reader to cross-reference them.

SELF: I was wondering if you felt there was a sense in which a writer's body of work, taken as a whole, is a kind of aerial shot of a foreign territory through which you are conducting the reader. And, further, a sense in which all these topographies join up into some other, numinous parallel world.

BALLARD: They do.

SELF: And the repetitions are, therefore, the switches directing the reader back into this other world.

BALLARD: They are road signs. They point to possible destinations.

SELF: In your most recent novel, *Rushing to Paradise*, the obvious transposition is that the Ballardian hero has become a heroine. Am I correct in saying that this is the first time you have used a female protagonist who has such an obvious affinity with your male protagonists of the past?

BALLARD: Ah, I think that she is probably the first female protagonist. I wrote a number of short stories, a collection called *Vermilion Sands*, and in those stories – although they are all told in the first person by a male narrator – each story is dominated by an enchantress figure. They are the nearest I have come before to a dominant female protagonist. Dr Barbara Rafferty is my first naturalistic female protagonist.

SELF: In a way, the protagonists in *Rushing to Paradise* play out the roles in *The Tempest*: you have a Prospero figure, a Caliban figure, an Ariel figure and a Miranda figure. This is also the case in *Concrete Island*; in fact, it is true of almost all your books. Were you aware, as you were writing it, it would be another island-based book?

BALLARD: Yes, I was. I am aware of my current obsessions because as a writer I have always relied on my obsessions. I have always faithfully followed them. Barbara Rafferty is a new kind of figure for me, but I needed her simply because *Rushing to Paradise* is, in part, a satire on the extremist fringe of the feminist movement. I obviously need a female protagonist. I couldn't have used a lunatic male feminist. Also, the thesis this novel advances – that men are superfluous, there are too many of them, we don't need them any more, or we don't need more than a few – requires a female protagonist. A dominant female figure.

SELF: I wondered if you were inspired by Jack Kevorkian, the American doctor who has been on trial for those euthanasia cases.

BALLARD: I was aware of him, of course: Dr Death. The satire on the animal rights movement – I mean the extremist fringes, because I am all for saving as many pandas, minke whales and dolphins as possible – is fairly straightforward. But the satire on the extremist fringes of the feminist movement is more ambiguous, because I actually take the side of Dr Barbara. That, I hope, gives the book more depth. As the writer, I am as in thrall to Dr Barbara as the boy, the teenager, Jim – oh, what a slip of the tongue! – Neil is. I can see that this is an immensely powerful, strong-willed woman who has all the ancient, ancestral power of women as creators, as controllers, as enchanters of men, as crones, as mothers – all those archetypal female images, which have so terrified and inspired men through the ages, are incarnated in a small way in this character. As a reader of my own book, I respond to her – although on a technical level she is a serial killer – as she is nonetheless immensely appealing. Leaving my book aside, people of that kind are immensely dangerous; they are the stuff of which charismatic leaders are made.

SELF: But the link between extreme environmentalism and extreme feminism is a critique of arationality in political thinking, isn't it?

BALLARD: Absolutely. It is something inherent in the fanatical personality. One of the dangers of these do-it-yourself environmental and similar movements is that they too easily become the vehicles for anyone who wants to get on board, turn the steering wheel and drive off the edge of a cliff. Fanatics are constantly hijacking otherwise sensible political movements, taking control of them and then pushing them in some dangerous or absurd direction.

SELF: Would that be your opinion of what happened when André Breton tried to link the original surrealist movement to Marxism?

BALLARD: Yes, that was an absolute blunder. I don't think Breton ever really understood or responded deeply to the painters who are now seen as the main exponents of surrealism, because he came from the literary side of surrealism, which was much more dominant in the early days. He saw it as a literary movement, and it was much easier to link a literary movement to Marxism than it was to yoke together this strange collection of painters – Magritte, Dali in particular. The whole point of surrealist painting is that it is answerable to nobody. It is unprogrammable because it all comes from the unconscious.

SELF: In *Rushing to Paradise*, the fact that Dr Barbara has been convicted for euthanasia in the past seems to be a reprise of the Ballard preoccupation with the way the progress of technology is once again queering human destiny, whether or not it is mastered. And yet there are images in the book – the defunct camera towers and what they symbolise, for example – that suggest to me that we have arrived in a post-Ballard world which is not dominated by technology. That we have now reached a strange plateau where for a time human ideals and aspirations are mattering again. Am I wrong to see that in the book?

BALLARD: No, I think that is fair enough. Saint-Esprit, the disused nuclear island in the novel, is loosely based on Mururoa, which is still a French nuclear test island. In fact the *Rainbow Warrior*, when it was sunk in Auckland harbour, was about to sail to Mururoa – the Greenpeace protesters later landed on Mururoa, not from the *Rainbow Warrior* but from other craft, and were thrown back into the surf by French soldiers. So I was referring to true-life attempts by animal rightists to defend the turtles. But beyond that, the point is that both the boy, who is myself, and Dr Barbara are, in their very different ways, obsessed with death. My depiction of the young boy, Neil, obviously draws on my own childhood experiences in Shanghai during the Second World War and my own personal obsession with nuclear weapons; these weapons represent a glamorous apocalypse, providing those great mushroom clouds over Eniwetok and Bikini Atoll.

The idea that the human spirit might be somehow transfigured by an apocalyptic nuclear war, even at the cost of hundreds of millions of deaths, that this is a necessary step for mankind – this obsessed me for many years, and it comes through in a lot of my fiction; it informs the mind and imagination of my teenage hero. I provide him with a father who died as a result of cancer that he developed after observing a British nuclear test in Australia many years before. Dr Rafferty is not interested in the nuclear aspect of the island, she has her own agenda. She is obsessed with death but she sees it as some kind of minor detour that we will have to take at some point in our lives. Death for her is a door to safety.

SELF: In one sense, surrealists are the most orthodox Freudians there can be. Neil, for example, needs an extra shot of death instinct, and the fact that his father was killed by the nuclear test gives him that booster injection of thanatos which he needs to be a Ballard protagonist. To what extent do you view yourself as an orthodox Freudian?

BALLARD: It depends on the perspective one takes. As a therapeutic process, psychoanalysis is a complete flop, it doesn't work. But Freud has enormous authority. He has the authority of a great imaginative writer. If you think of him as a novelist . . . if you regard all the aspects of Freud's view of the psyche as symbolic structures, as metaphors, then they have enormous power. I don't think that there is such a thing as a death wish wired into our brains, along with all the instinctive apparatus – the need to reproduce ourselves, the need for physical freedom, the need for food, water, light – I don't believe that there is a death instinct. It might have evolved as nature's way of . . . there may be an advantage to the gene pool as a whole if there are genes that predispose the sick and the dying to wander off to some elephant's graveyard to keep out of healthy people's way.

Now, that could have evolved as a death instinct, a way in which the community cleansed itself of potentially dangerous toxins. But that hasn't happened. Nobody who is close to death wants to do anything but live. Very few people actually look forward to dying. Very few people will their own deaths. On the other hand, death has an enormous romantic appeal, there is no doubt about that. There would probably be more entries in a dictionary of quotations under death than under any other subject. Death has an enormous appeal for the romantic imagination. Obviously it stands for more than just physical dissolution of the body and the brain. It represents something else.

SELF: Does it point up the notion of soul?

BALLARD: Could be. Perhaps by visualising our own death we are cocking a snook at the Creator, we are challenging the unseen powers of the universe with our own small but nonetheless real ability to destroy a portion of that universe. We have very little effect upon the world we live in, but we can catastrophically destroy a portion of it by visualising our own death. By visualising our own death we become godlike. Or, rather, we become satanic. That is part of the appeal. We are playing with ourselves, playing for the greatest possible stakes.

SELF: We are not going to know the answer. But, in theory, if we extinguish ourselves we will know whether realism or idealism is true, whether solipsism is true; we are pushing ourselves to the place where metaphysical questions should be answered by imagining our own death.

BALLARD: But within the safety of the novel or the film we are not really in danger. It is a form of game playing. The imagination takes strange forms. One can dream of dying, and some sort of powerful imaginative adventure is being undertaken by the sleeping mind. And by the waking mind in the large body of romantic poetry and fiction that celebrates or explores death. This huge metaphysical adventure is taking place inside the mind. Freud says, 'In the unconscious, every one of us is convinced that we are immortal.'

Of course, the unconscious is deluding itself. It is very difficult – at my age – to face the imminence of one's own death. I cannot visualise dying, or the notion that my mind will be switched off for ever. It is almost impossible to do so. Perhaps one can only do so by the back door, as it were, through works of the imagination. Cocteau's *Orphée* is an exploration of time and death in all its beguiling qualities. *Rushing to Paradise* is slightly off that particular beat.

SELF: Just to pull you back to Freud, does not the characterisation of him as one of the great twentieth-century novelists explain why the nineteenth-century novel is as dead as you have always said it is, particularly in your introduction to the French edition of *Crash*?

BALLARD: I haven't read that introduction for a long time but, roughly speaking, as I remember it, yes. It probably said some absurd things.

SELF: Not at all. It is something that I always urge people who show any interest in critical theory to read in the hope that it will cure them of the impulse.

BALLARD: I went wrong in two ways in that introduction. First, in the final paragraph, which I have always regretted, I claimed that in *Crash* there is a moral indictment of the sinister marriage between sex and technology. Of course it isn't anything of the sort. *Crash* is not a cautionary tale. *Crash* is what it appears to be. It is a psychopathic hymn. But it is a psychopathic hymn which has a point. The other way in which I went wrong was in all my talk about science fiction. Of course *Crash* is not science fiction.

SELF: I was interested in your categorisation of *Rushing to Paradise* as satire.

BALLARD: Partly a satire, partly not.

SELF: There is an essay I must send you by a young psychoanalytic thinker called Adam Phillips, who wrote a book called *On Kissing, Tickling and Being Bored.*

BALLARD: I have its successor, *On Flirtation.*

SELF: I thought you might like some of his apophthegms, such as 'An artist is a man who has the courage of his own perversions'.

BALLARD: Very good point.

SELF: If you remember, in his essay on Karl Kraus, Phillips says there is a fundamental instability in the satirical mentality. That the satirist, while seeking to locate the moral centre of the text outside the text itself, is at the same time endlessly in search of a moral certainty and dogma. That is the tension that produces a good satirical perspective. But of course it is very dodgy, because the satirist is drawn either towards dissolution or towards religion. So I was wondering if you had felt that tension, felt yourself being pulled in one direction or the other. I would agree with you that there is a strong tone of satire in *Rushing to Paradise.*

BALLARD: I agree. I have written a lot of satire or skits, particularly in my short fiction. And in *The Atrocity Exhibition* with the pseudo-scientific papers at the end: 'Why I Want to Fuck Ronald Reagan' or 'Plan for the Assassination of Jacqueline Kennedy'. These are not satires exactly, although they contain satiric elements. I am satirising the world of laboratory-obsessed researchers who are crashing pigs into concrete blocks, or showing pornographic imagery to disturbed housewives. Many of the things I invented subsequently happened. Atrocity footage has been shown to panels of disturbed housewives to see what the consequences are. There are satiric elements in those pieces, but at the same time, rather like in *Rushing to Paradise*, the frame in which the satiric elements are set works against the satire. The author seems to endorse what is being satirised. The obvious example is that I appear to lend my moral support to Dr Barbara and her activities. Maybe she is right. It may be horrible to think of a world run by Dr Barbara Rafferty and her ilk. This is what I hope the reader will feel when he or she comes to the end of the book.

SELF: You are making a very precise point that the technologies of bio-engineering and contraception enable women to adopt all the necessary roles that men can adopt, so given a few cups of well-preserved semen, the need for men simply isn't there any more.

BALLARD: And this is true, isn't it?

SELF: It is.

BALLARD: There have been news reports from China over the last week or so of a marked imbalance between the sexes. There are several million more men than there are women. When, in the next twenty or thirty years, parents are able to choose the gender of their children I assume most people will choose a boy first. But bearing in mind that a lot of women who have one child never have another for all sorts of gynaecological, social and personal reasons, that will lead inevitably to an imbalance between the sexes. Now if you have high unemployment and a huge army of young men who can't find wives, or even mates, or sexual partners, then that is a recipe for civil unrest on a vast scale.

SELF: A lot of unnecessary testosterone flying around.

BALLARD: Exactly, there are going to be problems. By the same token, in unexpected areas of western Europe or North America – those communities where parents have opted for more girls than boys – one may find havens of social ease, low crime rates, tolerance, a powerful sense of community. More and more people may realise that if you want all the things we ascribe to a civilised way of life, the best thing is to keep down the number of men. These tendencies made possible by the technology of bioengineering touch upon extremely dangerous ground. These are ancient highways rolled through the human mind along which we have progressed for millennia, and when you begin to tinker with these archetypal forces a huge danger lies ahead. The human race is liable to drive off the edge of the motorway if it isn't careful.

SELF: Given your personal experience, as someone who was denied the opportunity to exercise and define your male sexuality through manifest aggression, are you saying that that is all there is to masculinity? And further, that a lot of the traditional divisions between the public life and the private, intimate world were predicated upon men being allowed to go out and kick the shit out of each other somewhere else?

BALLARD: That is true. Of course men, on account of their greater physical strength, were the dominant figures in most social activities: commerce, industry, agriculture, transportation. These activities no longer require man's great physical strength. A woman can just as easily fly a 747 across the Atlantic. A very small part of industry requires brute muscle. A woman computer programmer can control a machine tool that cuts out a car door. A large number of traditional masculine strengths, in both senses of the term, are no longer needed. The male sex is a rust bowl.

SELF: And is in danger of becoming a genetic sport.

BALLARD: Yes. There is another element in *Rushing to Paradise* that is equally important, and that is Dr Barbara's attitude towards sex. She represents the way that women have begun – thanks to the feminist movement in large part – to resexualise themselves. They have begun to resexualise their imaginations. I imagine that Dr Barbara would endorse the pro-pornography feminist lobbyists who believe that women have as much right to make, read and enjoy pornography, to express their own sexual imaginations, as men do. Dr Barbara has resexualised herself. Sex for her is as intense as it is for anyone else. She has not allowed herself to be stereotyped in a way that the traditional middle-class professional women would probably have been. She is a sexual predator.

SELF: Do you think there is anything definitively masculine that is worth preserving aside from aggression?

BALLARD: Well, of course.

SELF: Well, what?

BALLARD: This is a novel that presents an extreme hypothesis, it is not intended to be . . . no more than I am suggesting in *Crash* that we should go out and crash our cars.

SELF: I know, but you speak to my condition. I feel genuinely pessimistic because if you look at the men's movement, the attempt to resexualise and recondition male sexuality, men are considered either effete or aggressive with nothing in between.

BALLARD: Men are going to have to cope with the huge task of deciding who they are. And they are going to have intense competition from the world of women.

SELF: Isn't it arguable that the wilder fringes of the gay movement are one of the phenomena that have sprung up because of the way in which avowedly heterosexual men are afflicted by a creeping sense of impotence?

BALLARD: Could be. And other S&M practices, in particular among homosexuals, are the last survivals of true masculinity. I made the point years ago in *The Atrocity Exhibition* that the psychopathic should be preserved as a nature reserve, a last refuge for a certain kind of human freedom. This applies to the deviant imagination, too. It should be treasured because the imagination itself is an endangered species in this conformist world we live in. The whole planet is turning into a vast Switzerland. This is the other thing I dread; the suburbanisation of the soul. I don't want to give the impression that *Rushing to Paradise*, any more than *Crash*, represents my last word on the subject.

SELF: *The Kindness of Women* was published around the time of Burroughs' *Queer*. It is interesting that both of those books should have been published at that point, because both of them seemed retroactively to humanise your work. A lot of people came to your work through *Empire of the Sun* and, I imagine, read it completely differently from the way I did. I read it and, having known the earlier books, said, 'Ah, that is where all these images of empty swimming pools and people jammed into windscreens come from. This is the great repository of Ballard's imagery.' But it didn't really humanise the earliest books; there was nothing sentimental about *Empire of the Sun*. In fact, it was arguably one of your least sentimental books.

BALLARD: It didn't need to be sentimental.

SELF: It didn't need to be? Elaborate.

BALLARD: Take the image of the drained swimming pool, for example. Way back in the sixties, in some of my earliest short stories, abandoned apartment buildings and drained swimming pools and all the rest of it – these were images that were powerfully nostalgic. I used to set these drained swimming pools and so forth in a nominal future, in some nominal New Mexico, but they were powerfully nostalgic since they looked back to my own childhood. I wasn't aware of it at the time, at all. I had to clothe this rather wistful dream of Shanghai, which I knew I would never return to. I had to clothe these images in some sort of dramatic and emotional disguise to express the anguish I felt. But when I wrote about the real drained swimming pools in my life I could present them as they were. I have often thought that writers don't necessarily write their books in their real order. *Empire of the Sun* may well be my first novel, which I just happened to write when I was fifty-four. It may well be that *Vermilion Sands* is my last book.

SELF: Or *Terminal Beach* [like *Vermilion Sands*, a short-story collection].

BALLARD: Yes, one doesn't necessarily write one's books in their chronological order.

SELF: Similarly, there are no definitive texts, only versions of texts. But then we get to *The Kindness of Women*. One is conscious that it is an autobiographical novel. Everything that had been left out of the earlier books is plugged back into them. Was it a difficult book for you to write?

BALLARD: *The Kindness of Women*? No. It is autobiographical, yes, but it is my life seen through the mirror of the fiction prompted by that life. It is not just an autobiographical novel; it is an autobiographical

novel written with the full awareness of the fiction that that life generated during its three or four decades of adulthood.

SELF: It is retroactively infusing the events with the imagery they
occasioned, plugging that imagery back into the *mise en scène*.

BALLARD: It is the life reconstituted from the fictional footprints that
I left behind me. It was no more difficult to write than anything else.

SELF: I'd like to return to Burroughs, and the subject of his visceral
hatred of women. When he was married to Joan Vollmer in the forties,
he loved her very much – even though he found her physically very
difficult to cope with. She said that he could function as a heterosexual.

BALLARD: I find it hard to believe.

SELF: Couldn't one say that the accidental killing of his wife triggered
his misogyny?

BALLARD: It is a retrospective justification of the act.

SELF: Exactly. And it helps to explain the plunge that Burroughs makes
into the magical world. He describes this brilliantly in the introduction
to *Queer*. It's very easy to see how that experience would tip a man who
was already living far too much within the purlieus of an exaggerated
imagination into a full-blown magical obsession. The parallels with your
own life and fictional existence are obvious, there is no need to recount
them. Why, then, does one have the sense that you are an extremely
rational and well-balanced person?

BALLARD: That's true. It is something I have never understood about
myself, particularly in the years after *The Atrocity Exhibition* and *Crash*
and *High-Rise* came out. People used to come to this little suburban
house expecting a miasma of drug addiction and perversion of every
conceivable kind. Instead they found this easy-going man playing with
his golden retriever and bringing up a family of happy young children.
I used to find this a mystery myself. I would sit down at my desk and
start writing about mutilation and perversion. Going back to Burroughs,
his imagination and mine – I recognise the similarities instantly whenever I read Burroughs. People say I have been heavily influenced by him,

but I don't think I have at all. My fiction is highly structured, I know where I am going, I always plot my novels and short stories very carefully, I always write an extended synopsis. Burroughs doesn't do this at all. I don't think he starts a book with any sense of structure whatsoever; *Naked Lunch* in particular. I have a scientific imagination, my fiction is not generated by my emotions but by a natural inquisitiveness.

SELF: A forensic imagination.

BALLARD: Yes. I am in the position of someone performing an autopsy. Like all of us when we rent a strange apartment and find traces of the previous occupants – a medical journal, a douche bag, a videotape of an opera – and we begin to assemble from these apparently unrelated materials a hypothesis about who the previous occupants were. We carry out an investigation of our own. If we have fairly fluid and loose imaginations we can often come up with very striking visualisations of who our predecessors were. I operate in exactly that way. The environments both internal and external, the outer world of everyday reality and the inner one inside my head, are constantly offering me clues to what is going on. These clues secrete obsessional material around themselves. I then begin to explore various hypotheses: is it possible that car crashes are actually sexually fulfilling? It is a nightmare prospect but it could have a germ of truth – at least on a metaphorical level. I begin to explore the possibilities. How would this erotic frisson be achieved? Then I need to explore that. So let's explore a car crash as if it was an erotic experience. And so I push that out.

I have a speculative imagination that is constantly exploring the interior, mythic possibilities of these ideas. Obviously there is an interiorised mythology that we all have, that gives our lives some sort of compass bearing; we dream that we will go out to New Zealand and become a sheep farmer, or sail a yacht around the world, or open a nightclub in Marbella. We are sustained by these dreams. Now all these things come together in my fiction, but I think my approach is basically a speculative one. Therefore my emotions remain uncommitted to whatever my imagination happens to generate. This is not true of Burroughs. He believes everything he writes. He lives in a paranoid micro-climate of his own; the rain falls and the rain is the condensation of this paranoid climate. The rain is the material of his books.

SELF: *Rushing to Paradise* is classic Ballard, it has the Ballard elements that we have come to expect. Are you someone who thinks about the fictional project ahead? You may work forensically but do you think inspirationally about what you are going to work on next? Do you wait for ideas to come?

BALLARD: Oh, yes, the images and ideas have a life of their own. They emerge through the topsoil of the mind, push forward and make their presence felt. And one then uses them as part of the larger inquiry which every novel or short story is.

SELF: What are your feelings on the role of technology today, when things seem so undefined? I am not asking you to play the Seer of Shepperton . . .

BALLARD: The nightmare marriage of sex and technology that I wrote about in *Crash* may not have taken place. Still, I would maintain that the thesis advanced by *Crash* may be just beginning, if not literally at least imaginatively: with video arcade games, a culture of violence in the cinema, the first hints of virtual reality systems, a culture of sensation for its own sake. We are walking through the shallows of a great, deep sea of possibility; at any moment we are going to feel the seabed drop away beneath our feet. I think we are in a lull before a momentous change that you will see but I won't.

SELF: I'd rather not see it, personally.

BALLARD: I think it will come.

SELF: In conclusion, I'd like to talk about your long-standing interest in visual imagery. What is your view on what contemporary visuals have to offer? Are you stimulated by any of the work that is going on in contemporary art?

BALLARD: The contemporary visual arts are in a parlous condition.

SELF: Aren't they just!

BALLARD: I agree with almost everything Brian Sewell says. I have been to many diploma shows at the Royal College and elsewhere. I went to the show where Damien Hirst exhibited his sheep in the tank. All the installation art was very badly put together. My girlfriend and I compared it to an exhibition at the Hayward Gallery twenty years ago. At the Hayward exhibition there was a lot of installation art – Kienholz's Vietnam War memorial, a huge silver thing with a built-in café; there was even a Coke machine there, and I bought a Coke from it. That's the first time I ever bought a Coke from a piece of sculpture. The Kienholz piece was a beautifully constructed thing. I remember an Oldenburg tableau, a tacky motel room with zebra-striped bedspreads and zebra-striped furniture; it was the American vernacular at its most popular.

SELF: It is amazing that we should be treated to such an appalling derogation. Mind you, I interviewed Hirst for that show. His description of what he was doing was much better than the thing itself.

BALLARD: He is a great novelist; it is his titles that are so brilliant. The shark in the tank isn't a particularly telling image, it is the caption that was a poetic statement. But you have got to bear in mind the question of commodification. Put a sheep in a tank and you can sell it to the Saatchis for twenty-five thousand pounds. Just write the idea down on a piece of paper and you won't get anything.

SELF: The interesting thing about the car is that the car windscreen has been more influential in making us all cineastes than film has itself. The experience of continually driving around confronting a seventy-millimetre frame observing the world like that.

BALLARD: That is a very good point. Recently, I went on Sky TV's books programme, and they sent a car for me. Usually I don't like it when they send cars because it is so boring and they play the radio for hours. But this was a short ride. So I was sitting in the back seat of this Vauxhall Senator, which is about the same size as my car – I have never sat in the back of my car – and it was like watching a movie. The sensation of sitting down at the wheel is slightly different, but I agree with you.

SELF: The way in which we have interiorised the cinematic view has something to do with our dramatic rehearsal of our death, doesn't it? Having internalised the cameraman's perspective, we are then free notionally to annihilate figures on our screen. People of my generation are afflicted with this as if it were a virus; they are not aware of the extent to which their view of their own identity has been compromised by film and the car windscreen.

BALLARD: I absolutely agree with you.

SELF: Which could be another explanation of why the contemporary visual arts seem so sterile.

BALLARD: You are right. The way we see the world, thanks to movies and TV, the car, the presentation of a commodified landscape through thousands of mini-film dramas – I mean, so many advertisements in magazines look like stills from films. It has changed the way we see the world, and the world of the imagination as well. The biggest disappointment for me is the experimental video film. They are so crushingly boring, aren't they? In a way that the experimental cinema fifty years ago never was.

SELF: You just have to go back to early Buñuel.

BALLARD: The video technology is too easy to master.

SELF: There is a facile quality to it. You were talking in *RE/Search* about one of the early Bowie videos, the video to 'Ashes to Ashes', which is superb.

BALLARD: Yes, that was marvellous.

SELF: It was very simple, they weren't exploiting the technology.

BALLARD: There are too many special effects now.

1996: Damien Love. 'Kafka with unlimited Chicken Kiev': J.G. Ballard on *Cocaine Nights*

Previously unpublished

1996 was a busy year for Ballard. Besides Cronenberg's film of *Crash*, his novel *Cocaine Nights* was released. This developed some of the themes from *Running Wild*, principally the implications of public surveillance and gated communities, but transplanted them from Britain to Spain's Costa del Sol region. The resort towns in the Costa del Sol had long fascinated Ballard as a kind of litmus test for the impending leisure society of the future, which he saw as inevitable but with increasingly sinister overtones, in that people become so comfortable they render themselves extremely susceptible to predators. In that sense, *Cocaine Nights'* antecedents go back even farther to his cycle of *Vermilion Sands* short stories written between 1956 and 1970, which depict a stylised future resort where faded film stars and decadent rich people idle away their days, indulging every whim and desire via advanced technology, drugs and psychological warfare.

Here, Ballard explains some of the ideas behind *Cocaine Nights*, including another long-standing obsession: the need for metered doses of violence to kick-start the imaginations of a bored and flaccid society. Elsewhere, he discourses on the extreme reactions surrounding the release of the Cronenberg film and what that says about the nature of censorship and repression in England. [SS]

LOVE: You still live in Shepperton. How long have you been based there now?

BALLARD: Oh God. Since . . . 1960. A long time.

LOVE: And I take it you have no immediate desire to resign to the Costa del Sol?

BALLARD: Oh, no. I have every desire to. I intend to go fairly soon. I think it's time I warmed my old bones in the sun.

LOVE: And settle into the lifestyle you've described?

BALLARD: Well . . . um . . . yes. I wrote the book and then thought, well, it sounds rather fun. I must go and live there. I have been there, of course.

LOVE: What was the genesis of *Cocaine Nights*?

BALLARD: Well, I think watching the growth of the Costa del Sol and similar places along the Mediterranean over the last forty years that I've been going there, and seeing a microcosm of a future that's waiting for us all. You know, these security-obsessed enclaves with tele-surveillance and armed guards and smart cards and all, the whole paraphernalia, like a kind of maximum-security state, reduced to the size of a village. If you know the States at all, you'll know there are masses of similar security compounds. And there have been for many, many years. But they're coming, they're all over Europe now. You can see them out in the Home Counties where I live, to the west of London. People are obsessed with security, at all costs. And you pay a price for it. And I can see this development beginning to isolate people, more and more, behind their triple-security locks, and they'll pay an enormous price, in terms of social cohesion, civic life, you know, just to feel 'safe'.

LOVE: So, do you see any merits in the radical prescription to the problem prescribed by Crawford?

BALLARD: Well, I the author am not suggesting that we all go out and . . . burgle our neighbour's houses, or take up drug trafficking, and the very next day we'll all be practising our violins and forming chess clubs. But I'm saying that it's possible that we're too obsessed with security. Although, anyone who has just been burgled is going to think me an idiot. Quite rightly. But, it's a matter of realising that, you know, certain things have to be bought at a price, and maybe the price is too high. Maybe, to make a pearl, you need a bit of grit in the oyster shell. I think, probably, that the proposition I've put forward in the novel is probably correct.

LOVE: The novel reminded me of the conversation you had with Will Self, about a future of boredom springing up as consumer culture envelops the globe, and these Kafkaesque communities spring up into . . . living death . . .

BALLARD: Yes. Kafka with unlimited Chicken Kiev.

LOVE: The protagonist of the novel, Charles Prentice, is a travel writer, and, as is mentioned, an observer rather than a participant. Why make him so consciously someone who, initially at any rate, observes rather than interacts?

BALLARD: Well, he is an observer. I mean he's a visitor to this strange place. And as a travel writer, he's got a trained eye so that he is, as it were, more aware. More aware of the strangeness of this coast where the Brits have settled over the last thirty years than the average person would be. As you drive along that coast, from Marbella to Malaga, or from Gibraltar to Malaga, you pass all these condominiums and pueblo-style housing estates, and you think, 'Well, they're a bit odd, I wouldn't want to live in one myself.' But you don't realise how odd they are until you go into one, and then you realise that tens of thousands of Brits, along with Dutch and French and Germans and so on – many of them retired there permanently – are all living these very strange lives. I'm not just concerned with the Costa del Sol. What I'm interested in is an emerging psychology where people, for the sake of security or some other social end, are willing to sacrifice a large number of the stresses and strains that are a part of the price one pays for an active and lively and rich cultural mix. I don't say that crime is necessary to kick-start a culture, I'm just saying that one must beware of extreme solutions.

LOVE: Are you – as a person and not a writer, as it were – consciously frightened of a future where people are so obsessed with themselves and their own security, that in a way they cease to be aware of themselves any more?

BALLARD: I think that we're moving in that direction. As living stand-ards continue to rise, as they have done since the war – and I'm sure living standards will, on the whole, continue to rise – people have got more to lose. You know, they've packed their homes with high-tech electronic gear. It's worth burgling the average suburban house, now. Many of them are equipped like TV studios, not to mention things like jewellery. So, one gets this strangely interiorised style of living, where you switch off the outside world, rather like it was some threatening television programme. You do this by treble-locking your front door and switching on the alarm system, and then you retreat and watch videos of the World Cup. And that's not a good recipe for healthy society. Looked at objectively, one could say that cinema, the visual arts, the 'entertainment' culture generally, are in a worse state than they have ever been this century. The cinema is a shadow of what it was in the forties. There's scarcely a novelist worth reading. There's scarcely a painter or sculptor worth looking at. I'm too old to know if the music scene has the vitality that it had back in the sixties, but I don't imagine that it has. And, you know, we're in a culture of substitutes – Elizabeth Hurley. They had Marilyn Monroe, we've got Elizabeth Hurley. Something's gone wrong. Is it that we're engineering a new kind of life for ourselves that has echoes of those that I describe in this book?

LOVE: I take it that, if presented with the choice, you'd have no difficulty in choosing between living somewhere like the retirement pueblos on the coast or somewhere like Estrella de Mar?

BALLARD: Well, yeah. I would opt for somewhere like Estrella de Mar, where it's lively. I mean, it's silly to say this, because I'm not inviting anyone to come and steal my car or burgle my house; but one always assumes that totalitarian states will be imposed from the outside on the average citizen, that they'll be sort of horrific and threatening. But in a way, I've often thought that the totalitarian systems of the future will be actually rather kind of subservient and ingratiating, and will be imposed from within. We'll define the terms of the TV mono-culture which we now inhabit, and it's a pretty empty place. I can imagine, fifty to a hundred years from now, social historians looking back at the closing years of the twentieth century and saying, 'My God, it opened with the flight of the Wright Brothers; halfway through they went to the moon; they discovered scientific miracle upon miracle. And then they ended with people sitting in their little fortified bungalows while the tele-surveillance cameras sweep the streets outside, and they watch reruns of *The Rockford Files*.'

It's a nightmare vision.

LOVE: You mentioned earlier the state of the cinema.

BALLARD: Well, there are exceptions, don't get me wrong . . .

LOVE: Of course. And there's *Crash*. I take it you've seen the film, and reacted favourably?

BALLARD: Oh, very. I think it's a brilliant film, an absolute masterpiece. Cronenberg's best film, I think.

LOVE: Do you think that any of the rest of us in the UK will ever get the chance to see it?

BALLARD: Oh well, I don't know, you see. I don't know whether we're mature enough to cope with such a film. I think the powers that be feel it may give us a rush of blood to the head. I hope that we get a chance to see it. It opened a couple of months ago in France, where it did extremely well. In its first week it was the top-grossing film at the French box office. Pretty remarkable when you bear in mind that it couldn't be farther away from the world of *Twister* and *Mission: Impossible*. I mean, it's a serious film.

We're at a very strange cultural state now. We're so panicky, so fright-ened. So nervous of everything that goes on. Some ghastly tragedy happens, like the Dunblane disaster or Hungerford, when this youth shot about fifteen or sixteen people, including his own mother, and people feel that there must be an explanation, there's got to be some kind of larger reason. Something like that happens and people think, 'My God, there must be something wrong with our society.' And so they find the obvious culprits. After Hungerford people immediately jumped to the conclusion that Michael Ryan, or whatever his name was, had been watching all the Rambo films. Turned out that he hadn't in fact;

he didn't even own a VCR. But people look for desperate remedies to make sense of some desperate tragedy, but it's often the wrong way. I think that the distributors are frightened that there'll be a huge outcry when *Crash* is released and hundreds of overexcited drivers will start crashing their cars into each other. It doesn't seem to have happened in France. As far as I know. I think the film will have exactly the opposite effect, and calm everyone down.

LOVE: Of course, we weren't deemed mature enough as a society to see *A Clockwork Orange*, in that instance by the film-maker himself.

BALLARD: Yeah, Kubrick himself, as you know, pulled that one. You can rent it anywhere else in the world. You can buy it. I bought one abroad, a copy of *Clockwork Orange*. But he decided for reasons of his own. I think he had young daughters at the time and they were threatened, so he pulled the plug on the film as far as Britain was concerned.

LOVE: It seems strange that, in both cases, the country where the source material of the movie was generated is deemed unable to handle the film.

BALLARD: I know. But I mean, this country, we're heavily censored. The sort of films that you can catch on your Adult Movie Channel in any hotel on the continent, we'd never see here in a million years. The sort of videos you can rent freely in the States will never be available here. We're far too nervous. So many of the films we see are heavily cut, particularly on video. We're very heavily censored here. People are frightened. Of course, it's all bound up in the whole political system here – you can't give the plebs too much freedom in one direction, because they might start asking for it in another. Who knows where it will end? You know. I think the film will be shown. It's going to be shown at the London Film Festival in November, and then I think the company will distribute it themselves. I can't believe that a Cronenberg film, starring Holly Hunter and James Spader and Rosanna Arquette, which won a prize at Cannes, is never going to see the light of day.

LOVE: Your work has now been filmed by two very different directors. Do you think this says something about the work itself, or are Spielberg and Cronenberg similar in some way that might not be instantly apparent?

BALLARD: I don't think there really are any similarities between Spielberg and Cronenberg. There aren't any similarities between *Empire of the Sun* and *Crash*, of course. They are very different books. But Cronenberg, Spielberg and myself do share something in common, in that we all spent a large part of our careers in our own versions of science fiction. None of us were working in the mainstream SF field, but in a sort of marginal zone alongside mainstream SF, which we made our own, in different ways. I, in a sort of inner space direction, Spielberg more in the kind of . . . I don't know how I would describe it . . . that sort of poetic SF almost, with something like *Close Encounters*, and Cronenberg in another kind of inner space of his own. So we have that in common. But I've been very, very lucky to have two of the greatest talents in present-day cinema adapting novels of mine.

LOVE: Is it a spurious piece of lazy critical shorthand to draw parallels between the character of Bobby Crawford in *Cocaine Nights* and Vaughan in *Crash*, these deviant messiahs?

BALLARD: No, I think they are rather similar types, now that you mention it. I think they are. They're kind of . . . they are deviant messiahs. They're sort of well-intentioned psychopaths. They're public-spirited psychopaths, a very curious blend. They genuinely want to do good and show people the truth. I know that sounds like Adolf Hitler. But neither Vaughan nor Crawford really want to do harm, to do bad for its own sake. Their idea is to do good. Take the blinkers off, show the truth. They're both small-scale redeemers.

LOVE: It struck me that there are a lot of female doctors cropping up in your work. Is this a conscious, self-referential thing?

BALLARD: Well, I dunno how many there are. I mean, I've written a lot of stuff . . . Of course, I trained as a medical student, and I met a lot of young women doctors, who I probably will meet again, when my time is up. I think I've always been intrigued by the notion of the woman doctor but . . . that's another story. But it's true, there have been a few. There's one in *Crash* and there's one in *Cocaine Nights*.

LOVE: And in *Rushing to Paradise*, too.

BALLARD: That's true, that's the sort of Margaret Thatcher figure. Another messianic do-gooder. Another public-spirited psychopath.

LOVE: Not quite as attractive, though?

BALLARD: Oh, I found her wonderfully attractive. I always had a thing for Margaret Thatcher. Until I grew too old for her.

LOVE: Have you started on another project?

BALLARD: No, I haven't. I'm moving ideas around, having a bit of a rest.

LOVE: Do you have any notion of what might be your place in the British literary scene, how you fit in?

BALLARD: None at all. I don't fit in. I'm definitely outside the castle walls. I gather you have a fairly tight-knit Scottish literary scene. I don't think the English one is like that, it's very scattered. I get the impression that the Scots, rightly, are today very conscious of their national identity, whereas the English are losing theirs. They're a bit lost. It's very large and dispersed. I don't know what part I play in it. I don't think I play any part, actually.

LOVE: Well, time's about up.

BALLARD: Great. You've got enough for about seven lines. It's been a pleasure. Best of luck.

1996: Chris Rodley. Crash Talk: J.G. Ballard in Conversation with David Cronenberg

Previously unpublished

On 10 November 1996, Ballard and David Cronenberg appeared at the British Film Institute in London to talk about Cronenberg's film version of *Crash*. Although the film had received its first public screening in the UK the previous evening, the media circus surrounding it was already in full swing, ignited a few months earlier when critic Alexander Walker attacked the film in the *London Evening Standard*. Walker, whose rant bore the strapline 'a movie beyond depravity', maintained that *Crash* featured 'some of the most perverted acts and theories of sexual deviance I have ever seen propagated in mainline cinema'. Meanwhile, fellow critic Barry Norman branded the film 'repellent', while the *Daily Mail* denounced it as 'disgusting, depraved and debauched', even initiating a campaign for a nationwide ban (*Crash* had already been prohibited by London's Westminster City Council).

For its part, the *Telegraph* reported how Ted Turner – vice-president of Time, which owns Fineline, *Crash*'s production company – was against releasing the film in the States because he was concerned about the effect it might have on teenagers. This led Rodley to wonder to the BFI audience 'if certain critics, and maybe all censors and would-be censors (and even some politicians), demonstrate that they have something very much in common with true psychotics – that they are seriously unable to differentiate between fantasy and reality, or between an imaginary life and a real life'.

Taking Rodley's cue, Ballard and Cronenberg address the role of the press in the controversy and the thorny ambiguity of Ballard's introduction to the novel, in which he professes *Crash* to have a 'cautionary' role. As Cronenberg explains, it is this supposed moral tone that was seized upon by the press, who used it to attack the film, while, Ballard elaborates, covertly using the overarching furore to distort a series of political issues happening at the time. [SS]

CRONENBERG: Someone who was talking to me about the film said, 'Why didn't you call the main character in the movie David Cronenberg? That would have been the true equivalent of Ballard calling the main character in the book James Ballard.' I said it had actually never occurred to me, but in a way you're right and I'm not sure what that would have done to the film. Now, I'd just like to ask you what you would have thought if you had gotten the script and it would have said that?

BALLARD: I think you should have done. If only you'd consulted me on the script, you see, I would have been a big help there! Great moviemakers, I've noticed (and I've worked with two), don't tend to pay any attention to the authors of the original material, but this is one case, David, where you've missed out on immortality. But you've achieved it everywhere else . . . I'd just like to say what a brilliant film it is, an extraordinary film that I think people will realise is a landmark movie in every respect. I think it's much more original than even *you* probably imagine.

CRONENBERG: Well, that's in a way why I wanted to talk about this particular issue, because it'd be interesting to see what you feel the differences are between the book and the movie and what that represents. In your infamous preface to the French edition [and in later editions], you said, amongst other things, that you felt that the book was in some ways a cautionary tale. Like with everything else, the press has really been taking everything out of context and using it for their own particular purposes. What did you mean by that? How literally did you mean that?

BALLARD: It *has* to be a cautionary tale. If not, it's a psychopathic statement. When I was writing the book I certainly didn't think of it as a cautionary tale. I was exploring the apparent links in what I sensed in the very early 1970s in the sort of popular sensorium between violence and sexuality and, in particular, between the car and sexuality. I was just running down a particular glimpse that I'd had of this hare that was running a long way ahead of me. Looking back, though, it seems to me that the book is a cautionary tale where the writer or the film-maker plays devil's advocate and completely adopts what seems to be an insane or perverse logic in order to make a larger point. Swift did it in *A Modest Proposal*, and film-makers like Kubrick did it in *Dr Strangelove*.

CRONENBERG: So you're saying that the cautionary tale aspect was not felt by you as an initial structure or reason for doing it? Because some people would like to interpret that as meaning that you wrote this as a kind of a fable warning people against this and that – which I feel diminishes what the book does and the scope of the book. If it's only something that says, 'Kids, do not do this at home' . . . and that's obviously not how it arose.

BALLARD: No. The book appears to give the impression – and to some extent the film does too – that car crashes are sexually fulfilling. I've *never* said that car crashes are sexually fulfilling; I've been in a car crash and it did nothing for my libido. What I was saying was that the *idea* of the car crash is sexually exciting or intriguing. And by sex I mean all those aggressive sexual energies that impel some young men to chase women drivers who dare to overtake them. The notion that the idea of a car crash is sexually exciting is much more disturbing in a way because it asks much greater questions about who we are. If thinking about car crashes excites us, there's something very strange going on in the human psyche – and that appears to be confirmed by the entertainment culture in which we live, which is saturated and has been for the last thirty or forty years.

CRONENBERG: I had the experience of someone saying to me, 'You know, the car crashes in your movie are not very realistic'. I said, 'Really, what do you mean?' He said, 'Well, there's no slow motion; you're not seeing it from five different angles.' I said, 'Have you ever been in a car crash?' He said, 'No.' So, obviously his understanding of the reality of a car crash was totally formed by Hollywood and that was his new reality, so all I had to do was not use slow motion and we were in another world.

In the same vein, people like to talk about the book being the first techno-porn novel, and that also leaves a lot of room for misunderstanding, especially when that phrase is just taken out of context. You didn't say 'techno-porn' . . .

BALLARD: I said I like to think of *Crash* as the first pornographic novel based on technology. Of course, pornography then had very different connotations: it really just meant explicit sexuality, which was a new card in fiction and the movies, even in the early 1970s. There was very little explicit sex in the novel then. The *Last Exit from Brooklyn* and *Lady Chatterley's Lover* trials here were only just over; people don't realise that the sort of explicit sexual description you get in novels today, or in films for that matter, didn't exist then. Now the word pornography has become all things to all people. It's one of those happily undefined words like fascism that anybody can use for whatever purposes they want.

RODLEY: I was interested in the pornography business, because it's been used very easily over the film. David, have you ever been asked to make a clear case against *Crash* being labelled pornographic?

CRONENBERG: Well, first of all, I'm not against pornography, in fact. So I hate being put in a position where I have to defend the film against being pornographic because the assumption has to be that if it were, that would be a bad thing. However, just for the sake of accuracy, for 'pornography' to mean anything it has to have a very specific definition, and I go back to the Greek roots – *pornographia* – it means writing about prostitutes, originally writing or art of any kind meant solely for the purpose of sexual arousal. It had no other purpose; that was what it was for. So the porn films that one sees are pornography because they don't make any pretensions to do anything else. On that level, obviously, *Crash* is not pornography – in fact people complain, 'Gee, there's a lot of sex in it and I wasn't turned on.' Well, part of that was the point, and part of that was the situation of the characters. Now, of course I would like by the end of the film that your feeling for what was erotic and what was not might well have shifted – because that's what the book did.

The book at first I found to be very cold and clinical and all the descriptions of sex were very medical, there were no passion words, no street sex words, it was all 'anus' and 'penis' and 'vagina' and all that stuff, which is normally a turn-off. But by the end of the book these words, along with the words like 'nacelle' and 'speedometer', were starting to get very sexy, and I thought 'he's really done something to my head here'. And so in that sense I would say you were successful even in those terms, because it was techno-porn, it was arousing . . . it obviously wasn't only for that purpose, though, and that's a whole other discussion. It was erotic, let's put it that way.

BALLARD: I think it's true to say that when you first came across the book and thought about filming it, you were very reluctant, you didn't care for the book. Going back five to ten years, you found the book hard going and didn't really want to film it. Now, what changed your mind?

CRONENBERG: I can only analyse it after the fact. It's similar to you thinking about the cautionary tale after the fact, seeing that that was what it must be, even though at the time you wouldn't have labelled it that. Jeremy Thomas and I had been finishing *Naked Lunch* and he said to me, 'Is there anything that you want to do, is there anything that you're passionate about that we should work together and do another movie?' I said, 'Yes, we should do *Crash*,' then I said to myself, 'Why did I say that?' – I completely surprised myself. Of course, Jeremy ran with it, he said, 'I know Ballard, I'll introduce you. I've already optioned the book in the past' and he got very excited. But I was still left saying, 'Why did I say that?' The only thing I could come up with was that the book had started a process in me that I could only complete by making the film of it, because that is my means of exploring my reactions to things and my understanding of my own life and all that. I still don't really have a better explanation for it.

In the making of the movie, it was beyond liking or not liking, it had become necessary – I needed the book somehow, and at that point it was a very powerful part of my nervous system.

BALLARD: Only a year or two beforehand you'd filmed another very difficult book, Burroughs' *Naked Lunch*; almost unfilmable. It was remarkable the way you overlaid the chronology of Burroughs' life on to this series of cabaret turns that is *Naked Lunch*. It's to your credit that having tackled one monster of a problem in *Naked Lunch*, you went on to another.

CRONENBERG: I thought it would be a similar process. What I'm always struck by so strongly when faced by an adaptation is that, to me, in fact, all books are unfilmable. The old joke is 'How do you film a book? You put it there, you get some lights, and you shoot it'. That is about as accurate as any other description of it, because you have to reinvent them for the screen, and hope that somehow there are legitimate connections between what you've done and the book.

But I did think that I would be faced with making a construct the way I had done with *Naked Lunch*, so I might have come to Shepperton and talked to you about your past and your childhood and things, like I did with Burroughs, and take things from other works and so on, which is also what I'd done with *Naked Lunch*. But in fact when I started to work on the script, it just distilled into the script almost instantaneously. It was actually very easy for me to write, which revealed to me that the book was in some way innately cinematic – much more than *Naked Lunch* ever was. You can see the obvious things – that it has characters who continue from beginning to end, that it's written in the first person and so you have that continuity of at least a consciousness from beginning to end, which *Naked Lunch* doesn't, and there is a plot that develops – even though it's a strange plot. All of those things made it a much easier adaptation.

BALLARD: In a way, I wish you'd been able to persuade Elizabeth Taylor to play herself. She appears in the novel as a target . . .

CRONENBERG: This is where Jim says 'sayonara' to reality. First of all, Liz is about sixty-five; for most of the people who would come to see this movie Liz Taylor is a matronly lady who does AIDS benefits . . . It's worth discussing, though, because it is many people's favourite part of the book, but even Liz is not 'Liz' any more; she doesn't mean what she meant, and the other thing was . . .

BALLARD: I was joking . . . Let me just say this: I think the film is *better* for not having Liz Taylor or a younger equivalent. If you'd introduced a fictional famous actress to become a target, in the way that Dean and Mansfield and Camus are targets, I don't think it would have worked. I think you've extracted the purest essence of *Crash* by dropping the Elizabeth Taylor notion, actually.

CRONENBERG: The other thing was that I really worried that it would diminish Vaughan as a character because he would become a celebrity stalker. There wasn't that category in the early 1970s and it's since become a category; it would be very easy to dismiss Vaughan as a psychotic who is a celebrity stalker, and therefore the other interesting aspects of him would fade into insignificance. You can see what the press would say about that.

James Dean was the safest bet: he was dead, his lawyers were dead . . . fantastic! But I did feel the need for a Hollywood icon at the centre of the movie because that was the part of the Elizabeth Taylor thing that was critical and I think it would have damaged the film if that hadn't been there. Not as a character but as an icon.

BALLARD: Yes . . . I went to the Cannes Film Festival with David and the cast, to the premiere there. I met the cast, and worked very closely with them during the four or five days of publicity, and what impressed me was these very successful Hollywood stars in at least three cases – all of them, in fact, all five of the main actors – were deeply involved with the film. This wasn't just a job. Listening in on the interviews they were conducting, Holly Hunter was fighting her corner – feisty little lady. When these rather bored, but rather cruel, journalists from major news agencies and the like were trying to pick her off, she snapped back at them hard. The same was true of Rosanna Arquette, Deborah Unger, Koteas, Spader – they were all deeply involved in the film, and this was some time after . . .

But I'm interested in how you managed to involve them so passionately in this . . . let's face it, at first sight, rather perverse drama.

CRONENBERG: Drugs and hypnotism. Works every time. I've found that that's the best way to deal with actors . . . Well, of course they had to want to do it, there's no way that you can drag somebody into a movie like this kicking and screaming, or with the lure of money – which we did not have, everybody in fact worked for a lot less than they normally do. It really is like trying to find the right kids to play in your sandbox. I mean, it is very playful; there is that element – you are dressing up in funny clothes and calling each other funny names and putting on make-up. And the set for *Crash* was very funny, very warm, very relaxed, very enthusiastic. You need the balance: the intensity's there in front of the camera, and then the humour and the warmth and all of that is everywhere else.

RODLEY: It sounds very playful and easy, but presumably some of those scenes, one's talking about several takes.

CRONENBERG: It's gruelling, actually, in the sense that I feel that the characters in the movie ultimately go beyond sex. Certainly, the best 'walk-out' moment in the film is when Vaughan and Ballard kiss, because a lot of young men leave at that point. I think it's because they've invested so much of their heterosexual sexuality in this stud James Spader – if they're seeing the movie that way, anyway – and then suddenly he's having sex with a man, and they can't deal with it, they walk out.

In a way, I'm saying that the characters are moving beyond sexuality, beyond sex, beyond gender, to some other thing, which they don't totally achieve by the end of the movie, but that seems to be where they're going, that's part of their experiment, that's part of their escape and their freedom. And in a way that happens on the set. It begins with nudity, what position shall we be in, you have to choreograph it, you have to figure it out. Five hours later, you're worrying about the continuity of the hair on the pillow and you're worried about getting the make-up on the pillow, and it's beyond sex, believe me, and is into some other strange movie thing. And it's very gruelling, and the art is to make it look like it was one take that you just happened to get and it was fantastic, but of course it takes hours and hours – some of those scenes took days to shoot. They were my special effects scenes, really.

BALLARD: I think one of the greatest scenes in the film, one of the greatest scenes in the entire output of the cinema this century, is the car-wash scene. Sound is used in a way that I'd never known before in almost any kind of film. I was saying to Dave half an hour ago that except for *The Tell Tale Heart* – an early 1930s film based on an Edgar Allan Poe story, where the heartbeat mysteriously from this body buried under the floorboards begins to dominate the life of the character – there's no film I know where sound has played such a role. Those whirling rollers hitting the glass and all that foam is an extraordinary combination of all the effects that the cinema is capable of. It's a virtuoso piece of film-making . . . All the rest you could have dropped, actually!

CRONENBERG: It's also the longest car-wash scene in history. When Ted Turner says, 'I rue the day when teenagers will start to do copycat things based on *Crash*,' I'm thinking, 'They're going to take long car-washes with their girlfriends; that is going to be scary.'

RODLEY: Jim, you said at one time that it was your most autobiographical novel.

335

BALLARD: Not literally, but in the mind, of course. I chose to call the narrator in my novel *Crash* by my own name simply because these were my fantasies. I was writing the book in the first person and I thought, why invent a character who's working his way through this extraordinary landscape when I can simply use my own name and give this novel what I think is a degree of honesty that would be absent otherwise? By the same token, you should have called the character 'David Cronenberg'. Of course, you don't have first-person narration in films.

Where David's film is so original is that it introduces this extremely threatening subject matter but doesn't distance it in any way. If you think of films like *Blue Velvet* – brilliant film, a masterpiece in its own way – it's far more violent than *Crash*, and there's perverse sex in it which is at least as perverse as anything in *Crash*. *Reservoir Dogs* is another extremely violent and crude and brutal film, much more likely to incite young men to dangerous behaviour than anything in *Crash*. But in both those films there's a distance: you watch them and you think this is all happening to these perverted nightclub singers and gangsters.

In *Crash* there is no distance: the characters are you in the audience, and there's no way you can escape. When I wrote *Crash* twenty-three years ago, people interviewed me at the time thinking, 'What is this book?' And I said I wanted to write a book where the reader had nowhere to hide, and I think the filmgoer watching David's film has nowhere to hide. The people on screen are the people in the audience. You may say, 'For God's sake, that's all rubbish. I don't get turned on by the idea of car crashes.'

CRONENBERG: Or you might say, 'I'm not as cute as James Spader,' and you might be right.

BALLARD: But I think there's no distance between the characters on screen. That's what's so frightening.

RODLEY: Obviously a lot of the criticisms that have arisen come out of a sort of moral outrage.

CRONENBERG: I don't think it's obvious; I think that's the pretence. But I don't think it's real moral outrage at all. A lot of that outrage is from people who have not seen the film so how can they be outraged? Really, how can they *dare* say those things if they have not seen the film? They're being outraged because other people are outraged and it all goes back, of course, to Alexander Walker, who up until last week was probably the only one in Britain who had seen the film; it all came from his initial 'Beyond the Bounds of Depravity'. Even with that, I had problems because if you're beyond the bounds of depravity then you're not within the country of depravity, you're somewhere else, so he hasn't really told us much.

BALLARD: The first reader of my publisher who came across *Crash* in 1972, the year before it was published, was the first wife of a famous TV psychiatrist – and I think she had some sort of psychiatric training herself – and she said in her reader's report to the publisher, 'The author of this book is beyond psychiatric help.' My reaction was: 'Total artistic success'. I feel the same about the reactions to your film.

CRONENBERG: In fact, you have been beyond psychiatric help, haven't you? Which is fine – it means he's healthy, no problem.

BALLARD: What David doesn't realise is that the screening of *Crash* at the London Film Festival has coincided with this panic that the present Conservative regime feels in the face of almost certain electoral defeat next May. They're climbing aboard every conceivable bandwagon, as they've done in their flustered state for the last couple of years: a child is savaged to death tragically by a pit bull and legislation is immediately cobbled together and enacted in a great flurry of moral righteousness to ban all aggressive dogs; rightly maybe . . . Then there's the tragedy of Dunblane, where sixteen small children are shot dead by this middle-aged paedophile a year ago – a ghastly crime and a terrible thing to happen to the children and their parents. A town councillor is quoted in one of the papers today as linking *Crash*, David's film, in some way to Dunblane and the murder of a school master, Philip Lawrence, earlier this year by one of his fifteen-year-old pupils.

The political parties are really in a degenerate state. You see this in the United States: no one cares who's elected president because it doesn't really matter. We're moving into the irrelevancy of politics; those who occupy the 650 seats or whatever in the House of Commons are desperate to seize the moral high ground; they're climbing on every conceivable hobby-horse. *Crash* has suddenly got on to their radar screen and they've locked on to it. It's a shame in a way because it has nothing to do with the film.

RODLEY: That doesn't totally explain, though, why there was, I assume, less of an outrage when the book was published as opposed to the flak that the film might get. Is that to do with an assumption on behalf of the people who are guiding morals that less people read?

BALLARD: Yes, I think there's no doubt about that. Cinema is the dominant form in which the twentieth-century imagination shapes itself. It's even more powerful I think than television, which on one level has a greater sort of daily influence. TV surrounds us like all those packets of cornflakes in the kitchen and the Mixmaster and the washing machine and the packet of Daz and so on, but film is where the twentieth-century imagination really expresses itself. I think the book – the novel, tragically – is moving towards irrelevance. People are not outraged by novels any more. They were once but not now – film is the dominant medium.

But we and the novel still supply a kind of . . . You can't quite dispense with us yet!

1997: Mark Dery. J.G. Ballard's Wild Ride

Originally published in *Rage*, August 1997

In the 1990s the cyberpunk literary movement, headed by novelists William Gibson and Bruce Sterling, was in full swing, and its cultural influence seemed endless, inspiring a generation of hackers, digital shamans, post-human performance artists and cyber theorists. Within this milieu, *Crash* was frequently hailed as a proto-cyberpunk classic, celebrated for its unflinching, forensic look at the mutant pathologies and sexual deviances incubating under the new neon dawn of computers, virtual reality and techno-fetishism.

In this interview, cultural critic Mark Dery, a leading theorist of the cyber age, engages Ballard in the ongoing controversy surrounding Cronenberg and *Crash*, the novel's confluence with S&M culture and De Sade, the psychology of car design and the poignancy of industrial ruins. Dery even manages to draw from Ballard the most shocking revelation of his career: that he drives a Ford Granada. [SS]

DERY: I wanted to begin with an intriguing remark David Cronenberg made to me in my recent interview with him: he said that during your recent public dialogue with him at the Institute of Contemporary Arts in London, the question of the moralistic tone you took in your introduction to the French edition of *Crash* came up. I've always wondered about that, because it seems out of tune with the book itself, which is flatly reportorial, appropriate to the flattened affect of the characters. Cronenberg said that you confessed to him that you appended that introduction after *Crash* was written, and that you had some doubts about how consonant it was with the book.

BALLARD: The question you've asked is one which was asked by a member of the audience. David made it quite clear that he didn't see the film as a cautionary tale, and I pointed out that at the time that I wrote *Crash*, roughly twenty-five years ago, I certainly didn't see it as a cautionary tale. I was exploring certain trajectories that I saw moving across the mental sky of the planet, following them to what seemed to be their likely meeting point. Moral considerations were neither here nor there; I saw myself in the position of a computer attached to a radar set, tracking an incoming missile. In fact, most of the introduction consists of an endorsement of the non-moralistic view of *Crash*, in that I make the point that an author can no longer preside like a magistrate over his characters and place their behaviour within some sort of moral frame, which is the traditional stance of the author in fiction. Most criticism of the novel sees it as an instrument of moral criticism of life. I mean, that's the *raison d'etre* that justifies the teaching of English literature at universities.

DERY: Well, American tabloid newscasts still follow that script. They always end with what amounts to a scriptural flourish, and there's a Manichaean sense that good has triumphed over evil on the slaughter bench of the six o'clock news.

BALLARD: Absolutely; that's very well put. I think that's true over here, to a large extent, but I think it's more true in the States, because Americans are a very moralistic people for historical reasons we don't need to go into. Most of my introduction disputes this view that the novelist is a moral arbiter, and it's only in the last paragraph that I actually say that I regard *Crash* as a cautionary tale. Which I do, in the sense that *Crash*, whatever else it is, is a warning, and insofar as it issues a warning, it's a cautionary tale. I mean, a road sign saying 'Dangerous bends ahead; slow down' is not making a moral statement, it's being cautionary. In that sense I'd like to think that David's film is a cautionary tale.

DERY: In what regard?

BALLARD: Well, I don't want to invoke Swift's *A Modest Proposal*, because it's so easy to do, but it is possible to play devil's advocate by deadpanning an attitude which seems to be 180 degrees at variance with what one's supposed to be doing.

DERY: This often seems to be lost on critics, especially of the moralistic stripe, who, if they have a common trait, seem to exhibit an almost painful earnestness that vaporises irony on contact.

BALLARD: Absolutely.

DERY: And as a result there's a tendency, there, to take *Crash* literally.

BALLARD: You see, I think this ambiguity is very important. People have constantly asked me over the last year – and they were saying it to me nearly twenty-five years ago when *Crash* was published – 'What are you saying? Do you believe that we should all be going out and crashing our cars? You can't be serious!' But that ambiguity is part and parcel of the whole thing. In *Crash*, I'm taking certain tendencies which I see inscribed in the world we live in and I'm following them to their point of contact. Putting it crudely, I'm saying, 'So you think violence is sexy? Well, this is where it leads.'

But if you say to me, 'Do you think we should all go out and crash our cars?', I would say, 'Of course not!' This is a very important distinction. I've never said that car crashes are sexually exciting. What I have said is that the *idea* of car crashes is sexually exciting, which is very different and in a way much more disturbing: why is it that our imaginations seem so fixated on this particular kind of accident?

DERY: *Crash*'s narrator, James Ballard, says at one point that it took a car crash to snap him out of his terminal emotionlessness: 'For the first time I was in physical confrontation with my own body,' he says. In *Crash*, the car crash functions as a bracing jolt that reconnects us with our bodies – bodies that are part of a material reality that seems to be receding as we spend more and more time on the other side of the screen, be it the computer terminal, the television or the video game.

BALLARD: Of course, it's the idea of the car crash which jerks us out of our apathy; this is the important thing. One mustn't take brief episodes from a novel and try to generalise a complete moral universe from them, because these are just cogs in a machine whose purpose is unknown to the cog. I mean, the characters' roles within *Crash* have to be seen as

341

fully integrated into an imaginary drama, and it's the drama as a whole that one should look at.

DERY: Robert Towers, in his *New York Review of Books* review of *The Kindness of Women*, takes you to task for the 'lack of inwardness and psychological depth' he sees in your writing. But I think he and others like him miss the point that your fiction constitutes a psychoanalysis of the postmodern self. To my mind, you're one of the first novelists to offer a science fiction premonition of the postmodern ego – a decentred self, to use the cultural critic Fredric Jameson's term, disoriented by the generic placelessness of malls and retail chains and the vertiginous whirl of free-floating facts and images peeled loose from their referents. Does this resonate with your thinking?

BALLARD: Absolutely. For the last thirty years, ever since I started writing the pieces that made up *The Atrocity Exhibition*, I've been saying that we live in a world of complete fiction; so much of what used to be an internalised psychological space within an individual's head – his hopes, dreams, and all the rest of it – has been transferred from inside our individual skulls into the corporate sensorium represented by the media landscape. You see people, these days, who give the impression that their minds are a complete vacuum; no dreams or hopes of any importance – even to themselves – emanate through the sutures of their skulls, as it were. But that doesn't matter, in a sense, because the environment itself is doing the dreaming for them. The environment is the greater sensorium generating these individual hopes and ambitions, signs of the cerebral activity that has been transferred from inside the individual's skull into the larger mental space of the planetary communications landscape.

Now that's a very dramatic shift, because it means that Freud's distinction between the latent and manifest content of a dream now has to be applied to the outside world. You can't just say that these huge figments and fantasies that float across the planet and constitute our real sky can be taken at face value; they can't.

Exactly thirty years ago, when I wrote my piece 'Why I Want to Fuck Ronald Reagan', when Reagan was governor of California, I was trying to – I won't say deconstruct, because that's a horrible word – analyse what Reagan really represented. Part of the problem that some critics have with the apparent lack of depth in my characters arises from the fact that my characters, right from the earliest days when I started writing fiction, were already these disenfranchised human beings living in worlds where the fictional elements constituted a kind of externalised mental activity. They didn't need great psychological depth because it was all out there, above their heads.

DERY: You and Cronenberg seem to share an interest in psychology in general and Freud in specific; have you two discussed psychology in relation to the characters in *Crash*?

BALLARD: Not really. When I first met David, I'd seen all his films, but I think in many ways we were so closely tuned to each other that we really didn't need to talk about our respective work. But there are a surprising number of resonances between Cronenberg's work and my own. I've always thought, from the beginning, that he was the perfect choice to film *Crash*. What's so interesting is that *Crash* is in many ways unlike any of his other films. So many of the Cronenbergian tropes, the biomorphic horrors and the pulsating washing machines and so on, have all been abandoned because they're not necessary any more. The biomorphic horrors are implicit within the ideas being portrayed in the most realistic way. Likewise, you know, if you've got something as dramatic and contortionist as the car crash, you don't need to play around with the everyday structures of material things.

DERY: Watching the film, I was struck by the extent to which its pathological surrealism has come true. The whole idea of the sexuality of scars is enacted now in the so-called 'modern primitive' subculture, where those on the far fringes of youth culture have taken up scarification as a fashion trend and a tribal totem. *Crash* seems less and less like 'an extreme metaphor for an extreme situation', as you call it in your introduction, than a laboratory study of an increasingly pathological culture.

BALLARD: Well, at the ICA conversation in London, I said to the audience that *Crash* illustrates what I call the normalising of the psychopathic – the way in which formerly aberrant or psychopathic behaviour is annexed into the area of the acceptable. This has been proceeding for probably a century, if not longer, but certainly it has gathered pace tremendously in the last thirty or forty years, and it's been aided by the proliferation of new communications technologies: television, home videos, video games, and all the rest of that paraphernalia, which allows the anatomising of desire. The normalising of the psychopathic is most advanced, of course, in the area of sexuality. Sexual behaviour that my parents would have deemed a one-way ticket to a criminal insane asylum is now accepted in the privacy of the bedroom, tolerable if both parties are in agreement. We're much less shocked than we used to be by deviant behaviour. I mean, the tolerance of male homosexuality and lesbianism and the huge range of what, previously, would have been regarded as out-and-out forms of psychopathy are now accepted. And this extends beyond sexuality, into other realms as well. To take a trivial example, among my parents' generation, shoplifting was one of the most reprehensible things the ordinary person could do, and if you were arrested, it would lead to social ostracism. Nowadays, if your neighbour was arrested for shoplifting, one would be sympathetic: 'Poor woman, her husband's been having all these affairs, she's been very unhappy.' We're extremely tolerant of behaviour that would have outraged our parents' generation.

DERY: Again, in the introduction to *Crash*, you write that 'the demise of feeling and emotion has paved the way for all our most real and tender pleasures . . . in the excitements of pain and mutilation'. In *Crash*, sex, although unencumbered by the trappings of S&M, is characterised by a ritualised brutality that is undeniably sadomasochistic. What do you make of the strip-malling of S&M, in the basement scene in *Pulp Fiction*, in Madonna's *Sex*, in Gianni Versace's bondage collection, in *Batman Forever*, and so on? S&M seems to be emerging as the talismanic sexuality of millennial culture.

BALLARD: It's puzzling, because if you don't share a particular sexual proclivity, it's rather difficult to get worked up about it. But I agree with you; it's everywhere – in magazines, advertising, and the like. And one wonders what the subtext really is; whether it's purely a sort of style, introducing a bawdy fascism – the glamour of the jackboot, the thrill of the psychopathic and the forbidden – or whether it's a kind of personal theatre in which one sees a preview of pathological virtual reality fantasies. I don't know. It strikingly dramatises all sorts of moral ambiguities; it's a wilful mimicry of activities that in any other space would be regarded as near criminal.

DERY: The surrealists were great fans of De Sade, and enshrined him as an honorary surrealist. Didn't you, at one time, immerse yourself in him?

BALLARD: Immerse myself in De Sade? What a thought! [laughs]

DERY: [laughing] I don't mean bodily, I mean mentally.

BALLARD: Well, he was, in his way, a genius; I once described *The 120 Days of Sodom* as a 'black cathedral of a book'. De Sade is an enormously important influence on us today, and has been for a long while. He constructs a highly convincing anti-society which defies bourgeois society and liberalism by constructing a community based on torturers and their willing victims. Now, that's a prospect that the liberal conscience just cannot cope with. I'd like to think that *Crash* is a movie De Sade would have adored.

DERY: You seem to enjoy nettling ideologues and moral crusaders at both extremes of the political spectrum, and yet, in your review of Maurice Lever's *Marquis de Sade* [included in Ballard's *A User's Guide to the Millennium*], you raise the moral flag yourself, noting that 'the jury will always be out' on De Sade, whose 'novels have been the pillow-books of too many serial killers for comfort'.

BALLARD: Well, that's a worry, isn't it? One can see, on one hand, that De Sade is an enormously important figure in European and American thought. On the other hand, he has been the pillow reading of too many psychopaths – the Moors Murderers, Ian Brady and Myra Hindley, who killed children, for example.

DERY: Like De Sade, they're practically pop stars now.

BALLARD: Yes, and I'm not sure that's a good thing, either. One of the surrealists – Breton, I think – said that the ultimate surrealist act would be to take a revolver and fire at random into a crowd. Now, one can salute the brilliance of that insight, but at the same time if somebody actually found a revolver and put that insight into practice, one would have to deplore it. This same ambivalence, this ambiguity, is at the heart of something like *Crash*, and this is what people find difficult to cope with – that there's no clear moral compass bearing. I'll be very interested to see how the film is received in the States.

DERY: Throughout the novel, there is an almost 'paranoiac-critical' confusion, to use Salvador Dali's term, of bodies and the built environment, of flesh and commodity fetishes. There's an obsessive repetition of geometry, as in, 'My right arm held her shoulders, feeling the impress of the contoured leather, the meeting points of hemi-spherical and rectilinear geometries'. Disappointingly, we catch only fleeting glimpses of this Euclidean eroticism in the movie. I kept looking for signature images like 'the conjunction of an air hostess's fawn gabardine skirt . . . and the distant fuselages of the aircraft', but they weren't there.

BALLARD: One or two people have pointed that out. But to be fair to Cronenberg, no film can possibly contain the whole of a novel in a couple of hours. The important thing is to concentrate on the nervous system of the novel. I think David has done that; he's gone to the heart of the obsessional world that *Crash* describes. I've seen the film three or four times, now, and I constantly see things in it that I hadn't seen before. The performances are wonderful, and the film itself is very artfully constructed. It's ostensibly quite naturalistic, but in fact it inhabits a strange penumbral space. There's something deeply premonitory about it, deeply prophetic. Just as some films cast a light on the past, this one seems to cast a light into the future.

DERY: I'd like to end with a few obvious questions. One of Cronenberg's earliest feature films was a movie about cars, *Fast Company*, and the first movie he ever made was an eight-millimetre documentary about auto racing in which a CBC producer was killed when his Triumph TR3 rolled over. Have you and he talked about cars?

BALLARD: We talked about his Ferrari, and the differences between American Indy car racing and European Grand Prix racing, over dinner in Cannes. He's a great car buff, which I'm not. People think I'm a car fanatic, but in fact I'm not in the least interested in cars, really, although I am interested in the psychology of automobile design, car styling as a barometer of the public imagination. Fluctuations in American automobile design over the decades seem to reflect the state of the American psyche: the enormous baroque and confidence of the Eisenhower years, and then, after Kennedy's death, the puritanical slab, flat sided and undecorated – the American car was in mourning. No, not in mourning – it was in denial, to use the latest jargon. But now it's started to get more exuberant, hasn't it?

DERY: There seems to be a proliferation of postmodern compact cars – downsized versions of Raymond Loewy's aerodynamic roadsters of the thirties. How do you psychoanalyse this neo-streamlining vogue?

BALLARD: I think it reflects an awareness of the future. Thirties design was strongly influenced by the sense that one would be living in the future, and I think people are getting more aware of the future as the countdown to the year 2000 comes. Maybe the human race is trying to escape. It can't go into outer space, because that's basically inaccessible, and it's already tried to escape into inner space through drugs and mysticism and, to some extent, the internet. Maybe it's going to try to escape into another realm altogether. God knows what it will be.

DERY: Your characters are always trying to tear loose from the time–space continuum. I wonder if, in a weird way, the car crash is an attempt to tear through the fabric of reality – to 'break on through', as the sixties catchphrase has it.

BALLARD: I think so, absolutely. As I've often said, we live in a world of manufactured goods that have no individual identity, because every one is like every other one, until something forlorn or tragic happens. One is constantly struck by the fact that some old refrigerator glimpsed in a back alley has much more identity than the identical model sitting in our kitchen. And nothing is more poignant than a field full of wrecked cars, because they've taken on a unique identity that they never had in life.

DERY: One could imagine the crash as the car's desperate attempt to establish – if only for a fleeting moment – a sort of selfhood, even at the expense of its existence.

BALLARD: Exactly. Very strange, that; paradoxical. Also, there is a deep melancholy about fields full of old machinery or wrecked cars because they seem to challenge the assumptions of a civilisation based on an all-potent technology. These machine graveyards warn us that nothing endures.

DERY: One last question: what sort of car are you driving now?

BALLARD: Oh, this will shock you! I drive a Ford Granada.

DERY: Dear Lord.

BALLARD: I know. But again, I'm not interested in cars.

DERY: You had a rollover right after completing *Crash* – did the novel in a sense impel that? Was that the final plot twist, an instance of the book leaking into reality?

BALLARD: Well, had I died in the crash, two weeks after completing the manuscript, people would have said that this was a willed death, expressing the essence of the book. I think it was pure coincidence, actually, because I found writing the book a very fearful experience. I had three very young children crossing the road a hundred times a day, and never at any point during writing that book did I ever envisage putting that psychosis into practice. I was too frightened by what I was uncovering to want to test out the theories the book seemed to embody. So I certainly don't think I had a blowout because I wanted to. I think it was a case of nature imitating art. An extreme case.

1997: Richard Kadrey & Suzanne Stefanac. J.G. Ballard on William S. Burroughs' Naked Truth

Originally published in *Salon*, 2 September 1997

Ballard's admiration for William Burroughs is a consistent thread throughout this collection. Tirelessly throughout his career, he spoke of the impact of reading *Naked Lunch* for the first time and of the importance of Burroughs' appropriation and reworking of science fictional tropes to comment on the control systems of technological societies. Burroughs' genius, he often explained, validated his own decision to develop a science fiction of the present rather than of the distant future.

In this interview, novelist and photographer Richard Kadrey (who interviewed Ballard three times in total) and journalist Suzanne Stefanac allow Ballard to exclusively reflect on what Burroughs meant to him, and on Burroughs' legacy to literature and the creative arts. [SS]

KADREY/STEFANAC: William Burroughs was someone who was suspicious of language and words, but his whole life was defined by them. Do you see a contradiction here? Perhaps the essential writer's contradiction?

BALLARD: I think Burroughs was very much aware of the way in which language could be manipulated to mean absolutely the opposite of what it seems to mean. But that's something he shared with George Orwell. He was always trying to go through the screen of language to find some sort of truth that lay on the other side. I think his whole cut-up approach was an attempt to cut through the apparent manifest content of language to what he hoped might be some sort of more truthful world. A world of meaning that lay beyond. In books like *The Ticket that Exploded* and *The Soft Machine*, you see this attempt to go through language to something beyond. If there is a paradox, I think it lies somewhere here.

KADREY/STEFANAC: How did you first encounter Burroughs' work?

BALLARD: I think it was in something like 1960. A friend of mine had come back from Paris where *Naked Lunch* had been published by the Olympia Press, which was a press that specialised in sort of low-grade porn, but also published what were then banned European and American classics. Henry Miller, for example, was first published in the Olympia Press. And Nabokov's *Lolita* was first published by the Olympia Press.

Anyway, it was a rather low time for me. I had just started out as a writer. I hadn't written my first novel. And this was the heyday of the naturalistic novel, dominated by people like C.P. Snow and Anthony Powell and so on, and I felt that maybe the novel had shot its bolt, that it was stagnating right across the board. The bourgeois novels, the so-called 'Hampstead novels', seemed to dominate everything.

Then I read this little book with a green cover, and I remember I read about four or five paragraphs and I quite involuntarily leapt from my chair and cheered out loud because I knew a great writer had appeared amidst us. And I, of course, devoured the book and every Burroughs novel. I think there were about three or four then in print from Olympia Press. I knew that this man was the most important writer in the English language to have appeared since the Second World War, and that's an opinion I haven't changed since. It was an encouraging moment. I mean, although my writing has never been along the lines that Burroughs set out, his example was a huge encouragement to me.

I first met him in the early sixties in London. I visited him in his flat in Piccadilly Circus. I'm not sure that he got up to a great deal of writing there. He didn't seem that happy.

This was in a street called Duke Street, literally about a hundred yards from Piccadilly Circus. And, of course, this was of interest to him because that's where all the boys used to congregate, in the lavatory of the big Piccadilly Circus Underground station. They had completely taken it over. It was quite a shock for a heterosexual like myself to accidentally stray into this lavatory and to find oneself in what seemed to be a kind of oriental male brothel. He obviously found that absolutely fascinating.

I think these big cities aren't all that different, really. Burroughs roamed around the world throughout his youth and middle age without ever really stopping anywhere for very long. I think the closest he probably felt to home was Tangiers. He certainly did his most important writing there. I mean, he wrote *Naked Lunch* there, and I think he found a very sympathetic community of homosexuals and drug users and, of course, an unlimited availability of boys and young men.

This was Interzone, of course. Interzone was based on Tangiers, so I think he was happy there. Happier than he seems to have been in New York. Or, for that matter, during his days as a would-be farmer. I think he must be one of the strangest men ever to set out to raise a cash crop. I remember reading his collected letters a few years ago and he's describing how many carrots and lettuce he's planted and you can tell that this isn't going to work out.

KADREY/STEFANAC: When critics look at both your work and Burroughs', they often point to the severity and even a sense of dissociation. Sometimes they even call your works antisocial. Do you see any truth in that?

BALLARD: Severity, yes. Honesty is what I prefer to call it. That has a much more satisfying ring to it. Burroughs called his greatest novel *Naked Lunch*, by which he meant it's what you see on the end of a fork. Telling the truth. It's very difficult to do that in fiction because the whole process of writing fiction is a process of sidestepping the truth. I think he got very close to it, in his way, and I hope I've done the same in mine.

The bourgeois novel is the greatest enemy of truth and honesty that was ever invented. It's a vast, sentimentalising structure that reassures the reader, and at every point offers the comfort of secure moral frameworks and recognisable characters. This whole notion was advanced by Mary McCarthy and many others years ago, that the main function of the novel was to carry out a kind of moral criticism of life. But the writer has no business making moral judgements or trying to set himself up as a one-man or one-woman magistrates' court. I think it's far better, as Burroughs did and I've tried to do in my small way, to tell the truth. So I don't object to the charge of severity at all.

KADREY/STEFANAC: So you think the writer is more interesting as a reporter than as an artist?

351

BALLARD: I mean he's reporting not just on the external world, but on his own interior world because he's telling the truth about himself. It's extremely difficult to do. Most writers flinch at the thought of being completely honest about themselves. So absolute honesty is what marks the true modern. When the modern movement began, starting perhaps with the paintings of Manet and the poetry of Baudelaire and Rimbaud, what distinguished the modern movement was the enormous honesty that writers, painters and playwrights displayed about themselves. The bourgeois novel flinches from such notions. It's difficult to tell the truth about one's own fantasies and obsessions and equally difficult in a different way to reflect honestly on the external world.

And mankind can't bear too much of that sort of honesty. Certainly Burroughs revealed, with absolute honesty, his own obsessions. I mean, teenage boys ejaculating as they die on the scaffold. Pretty grim stuff, you know, socially objectionable, I dare say. But at least he was honest about his own obsessions.

KADREY/STEFANAC: And he made it a little more palatable, and I see this in your own work, by the use of black humour.

BALLARD: Absolutely. I mean he's one of the greatest humorists who ever lived. His books, particularly *Naked Lunch*, are hilarious from the word go. They never let up. *Naked Lunch* was written largely in the form of a long series of letters to Allen Ginsberg, in which Burroughs practised these routines which were sort of skits or cabaret items in which he introduced characters like Dr Benway. They were these extraordinary comic routines.

KADREY/STEFANAC: You're both often misunderstood, however. You're both read as darker, more sombre writers and not often given the credit for the humour in your work. Is this because of the subject matter?

BALLARD: My humour is rather different. It's much more deadpan. I suppose there's an element of tease in my writing. I mean, I've never been too keen to show which side of the fence I'm on. And all the controversy that's grown up over David Cronenberg's film of *Crash* has tended to centre on 'Do you or do you not actually believe that people should find car crashes sexually exciting?' People think I'm being evasive sometimes, but it's that ambiguity that's at the heart of everything. I try to maintain a fairly ambiguous pose, while trying to unsettle and provoke the reader to keep the unconscious elements exerting their baleful force. But you're right, I don't think I've been given enough credit for the humour I have.

KADREY/STEFANAC: Both you and Burroughs have been dogged by censors your entire careers. What is it about both of your works that inspires this venom on the part of the censors?

BALLARD: Well, it's such a huge question. In Britain, it relates back to insecurity of a desperate kind. *Crash*, the film, is still banned from central London, the West End. Westminster Council controls, I don't know what the equivalent would be in New York or San Francisco, the central entertainment district where most of the major movie theatres are. This is generally subsumed under the term West End, which also includes, of course, the Houses of Parliament and the main government district in Whitehall. And they banned the film from the West End of London. So it's only being shown in peripheral areas and sometimes in a ludicrous way. There's the council that's directly adjacent to Westminster on the north-east side called Camden, and it passed the film. So there's this very peculiar sensation that there's a sort of invisible frontier much like the one that existed between East and West Berlin. One could cross this set of traffic lights, literally about thirty yards from the Camden theatre, and you enter the forbidden zone of Westminster. It was like going through Checkpoint Charlie in the old Berlin.

But it all reflects the same thing. Not unlike the trouble Burroughs had with *Naked Lunch* when it was first banned from publication in the States. Just like Henry Miller's novels, which were banned from publication in America for decades. It's a deep insecurity, a fear that once you allow the populace at large to enter any kind of forbidden rooms, God knows what they may get up to next. So one's got to keep the lids severely jammed on these nefarious books and films. Meanwhile, allowing people to go and see the latest *Die Hard* film, or piece of designer sex and violence from Hollywood. Very, very curious.

KADREY/STEFANAC: Both you and Burroughs write very visual narratives and you've both painted. Do you find a resonance between writing and creating something visual?

BALLARD: Burroughs did take up painting in his later years. I took up painting in my youth and found I hadn't any talent for it, but I always really regretted that I didn't, because I think I would've been far happier as a painter. I don't think that's true of Burroughs. I think he was a writer from the word go. In conversation he chose his words very, very carefully. He thought quickly, but spoke rather slowly. Obviously words were immensely important to him and the framing of ideas, thoughts, wasn't something to be just done at the drop of a hat.

In a way, he adopted a kind of adversarial relationship with the word, with the printed word, seeing how easily it could be manipulated for sinister reasons. My approach has been quite different. I would love to have been a painter in the tradition of the surrealist painters, who I admire so much. Sometimes I think all my writing is really the substitute work of an unfulfilled painter. But, you know, there we are.

KADREY/STEFANAC: Both you and Burroughs studied medicine. This seems to have had a profound effect on the work you both produced.

BALLARD: I studied medicine for a couple of years before giving it up, as a great number of writers have done, curiously. I think Faulkner even spent a small amount of time as a medical student. But Burroughs was intensely interested in the mechanisms involved in any kind of process. Right across the board. And he was intensely interested in psychology and psychiatry. He was interested in all kinds of obscure things. I remember the very first time I met him, this was the early sixties, his boyfriend had 'love' and 'hate' tattooed on his knuckles, which was quite startling then.

Once, while the boyfriend carved a roast chicken, Burroughs began to describe the right way to stab a man to death and he was graphically illustrating it with this large carving knife. His head was filled with all sorts of bizarre bits and pieces culled from 'Believe It or Not' features and police magazines and all kinds of obscure sources. But he was very interested in scientific or technological underpinnings. I think, in a way, I share that with him. I've always felt that science in general is a way of ordering one's imaginative response to the world.

KADREY/STEFANAC: It's also a separate language, too, isn't it? Books such as *Naked Lunch* and your *Atrocity Exhibition* use scientific language to break down the novel into something that people hadn't seen before.

BALLARD: I think that's true. I've always used a kind of scientific vocabulary and a scientific approach to show the subject matter in a fresh light. I mean, if you're describing what happens when, say, a car crash occurs and a human body impacts against a steering wheel and then goes through the windscreen, one can describe it in a kind of Mickey Spillane language with powerful adverbs and adjectives. But another approach is to be cool and clinical and describe it in the way that a forensic scientist would describe what happens, or people working, say, at a road research laboratory describing what happens to crash test dummies. Now, you get an unnerving window on to a new kind of reality. I did this a lot in *The Atrocity Exhibition*.

The same applies to, say, describing a man and woman making love. Instead of using all the clichés that are marshalled wearily once again in most novels, approach it as if it were some sort of forensic experiment that you were describing. An event that is being watched with the calm eye of the anatomist or the physiologist. It often prompts completely new insights into what has actually happened.

So yes, I've done that and Burroughs did that in a different way. His novels, particularly *Naked Lunch*, are full of almost footnote material explaining the exact route to the central nervous system taken by some obscure Amazonian poison on the end of a dart as it pierces its victim. He was very interested in that sort of thing, the exact mechanisms by which consciousness was altered by drugs of various kinds. I think I share that with him too.

KADREY/STEFANAC: If there is one thing that you think we should, as readers, take away from Burroughs' work, what would that one thing be? Or that you would hope we would take away, perhaps?

BALLARD: It's difficult to say, because I think he's a writer of enormous richness, but he had a kind of paranoid imagination. He saw the world as a dangerous conspiracy by huge media conglomerates, by the great political establishments of the day, by a corrupt medical science, which he saw as very much a conspiracy. He saw most of the professions, law in particular but also law enforcement, as all part of a huge conspiracy to keep us under control, to keep us down. And his books are a kind of attempt to blow up this cosy conspiracy, to allow us to see what's on the end of the fork.

1998: Zinovy Zinik. Russia on My Mind

First published in the Russian literary magazine *Pushkin* #9, 1998, in a Russian translation. The English version was published in *The London Magazine: A Review of Literature and the Arts*, February/March 2003

Although this interview was conducted in 1998 and first printed in a Russian magazine, the interviewer, Zinovy Zinik, has been based in London for over thirty years, working for the BBC. In being confronted with the real and vivid contrast between Soviet totalitarianism and American consumerism, Ballard rises to the defence of American super-fluity, emphasising that food and transport are real basic needs, even if at the same time he demonstrates considerable ambivalence towards American values.

The interview is exceedingly rare in that Zinik presses Ballard on the hard details of his political ideology and forces him to offer more than a sound-bite critique of the various ideologically driven regimes of the twentieth century. It's clear the seeds of what would become his 2006 novel, *Kingdom Come*, were already germinating in Ballard's mind, as here he outlines its plot in miniature – a dictatorial messiah emerging 'from the wilderness of the vast North American and European shopping malls'. [DOH]

ZINIK: Has the end of communist Russia marked the end of two centuries of social engineering?

BALLARD: The end of social utopia? Yes, and many of my left-wing friends felt a distinct pain when it all ended with the collapse of the

Berlin Wall, etc. I did so too myself, since heroic experiments have to be admired despite sometimes vast human cost. I even remarked to my ex-CP girlfriend, 'Now's the time to join the Communist Party,' only to be told by her rather bitterly that there wasn't one to join – in the UK. (I was actually a great if partial admirer of Margaret Thatcher for her attempt to Americanise the British people.) Bourgeois life has triumphed, and the suburbanisation of the planet and the universal acceptance of the shopping mall have now virtually put an end to politics. What we have is the commodification of everything, including ideologies, and government by advertising agency – as in Blair's New Britain.

I think we've now gone beyond politics into a new and potentially much more dangerous realm where non-political factors will pull the levers of power – these may be vast consumer trends, strange surges in the entertainment culture that dominates the planet, quasi-religious eruptions of the kind we saw at Diana's death, mass paranoia about new diseases, aberrant movements in popularised mysticism, and the growing dominance of the aesthetic (which I prophesied twenty years ago). The only ballot box common to all these is the cash register, an extremely accurate gauge of consumer preference in the very short term but useless beyond the next five minutes.

All this leaves the human race extremely vulnerable to any master manipulator. I've remarked elsewhere that messiahs usually emerge from deserts, and I expect the next Adolf Hitler or Mao to emerge from the wilderness of the vast North American and European shopping malls. The first credit-card Buddha, at its best, or, at its worst, the first credit-card Stalin.

ZINIK: To what extent was Soviet communism unique – or was it rather yet another example of the tyrannical manipulation of human idealistic urges and instinct for survival, too familiar to the Western mind through two thousand years of Christianity? With your childhood experience in China under the Japanese, how familiar does the proverbial Soviet horror seem to you?

BALLARD: Tyrannies usually self-destruct in years rather than decades, at least in the modern epoch, and the survival of the old Soviet Union for the greater part of the last century is a remarkable event. Stalin dominated much of that time, and he was lucky to have had so many enemies. I see him primarily as a war leader, first raging [sic] war against large elements of his own people, then leading the battles against Hitler and the unbeatable USA. Presumably the Soviet system delivered more than people give it credit for – the whole country organised like a vast internment camp, with all the boredom and dulling of hope and enterprise but an underlying sense of security.

Despite World War II, a reasonable level of prosperity reached the Russian masses, but of course the constraints of the system prevented them from ever moving beyond the subsistence level. I remember driving through Yugoslavia in 1962 and seeing a complete new town of handsomely landscaped apartment blocks, all modelled on the enlightened post-Corbusier pattern, with the ground floor divided into a dozen or so shopping units. Unhappily these concrete cells were empty, since the consumer infrastructure didn't exist. It was a desperate place and the dirt-poor people would stare at the European cars on their way to Greece, dreams of the West in their eyes. But after a while the dream either breaks free or dies, and people settle for the third best. Six months after the end of World War II British internees were still living in my camp outside Shanghai, subsisting in their shabby quarters on a diet of American C-rations. They had been institutionalised.

ZINIK: Most of your novels deal with different types of black utopia, with the transformation of human society and human nature into something unpredictable, mostly monstrous. Has Soviet communism (as an example of social engineering gone wrong) ever been on your mind when you contemplated such transformations in your novels? What is your attitude to anti-utopian classics such as Aldous Huxley's *Brave New World* and Orwell's *Nineteen Eighty-Four*?

BALLARD: It was difficult for a writer like myself, who began in his career in the 1950s, not to be aware of the Soviet Union, and Orwell's *Nineteen Eighty-Four* confirmed one's fears that tyrannies can play upon people's deep-rooted masochistic needs. One could see the Soviet Union as a kind of Sadean society of torturers and willing victims.

In the same way the Nazis seem to have exploited the latent docility of their victims. Everyone who has served in the armed forces knows that there are military bases where the regime of discipline and brutality is far more excessive than it needs to be, and yet doesn't provoke any revolt and may even satisfy some need to be brutalised. The whole socialist project may fit into the same scheme. Where socialist systems endure for decades, as in China and the Soviet Union, they do so because people unconsciously want things to get worse, rather than better.

Brave New World, a masterpiece of a novel, takes the process one step farther and is uncannily accurate in its prediction of the society we are now becoming: soma, feelies, test-tube babies. I've always suspected that the Soviet Union was the last of the old-style authoritarian tyrannies. The totalitarian systems of the future will be obsequious and subservient, plying us with drinks and soft slippers like a hostess on an airliner, adjusting our TV screen for us so that we won't ask exactly where the plane is going or even whether there is a pilot on board.

ZINIK: The Soviet utopia, unlike the utopian dreams of the English sectarians of the seventeenth century, was born out of the French as well as the German idea of the collective, of the state being responsible for the individual. You have witnessed the collective dance of the 'flower power generation' in the swinging 1960s in London, as well as French intellectuals' obsessions with the Chinese notion of the rule of the collective. Did it affect at all your mode of thinking? Reading your novels, one comes to the conclusion that the human mind, with its innate propensity for barbarism, is always in need of some kind of irritant drug, some black territory of total anarchy, and a zone in which it could play out its fantasies, including social experiments. You once said that we live in the age that gave birth to the cross-breed of reason and nightmare. The Soviet nightmare was very much an illustration of this idea. How come you never refer to the Soviet experience in your prose?

BALLARD: If I haven't referred to the Soviet experience it is partly because I've never been there, and chiefly because I've been more interested in the latent pathology of the consumerist West, which is where the entire planet seems to be heading.

Also I am not sure if the Soviet Union was a special case. Did Russia industrialise too quickly? Did it educate its population too quickly? Did it place too great a reliance on science? Did it make a mistake abolishing religious practice? Its tragedy was that it was obliged to fight the bloodiest war in history against an advanced nation in the grip of ideological madness. But for Hitler and the Nazis, could Stalin and the Soviet leaders have maintained their brutal grip for so long?

Is a communist system inherently dependent on the creation of enemies to justify its repressions, given that communism runs counter to almost all human social tendency? If you want to destroy the economy of an advanced nation, introduce it to socialism, say American supply-siders led by Milton Friedman et al., and they may well have a point.

In addition, the monolithic tyranny of Stalinism seems to me to be un-European, but to owe more to Asiatic despotism. Whenever I saw photographs of Stalin and his henchmen standing atop the Lenin mausoleum, I couldn't help thinking of Chiang Kai-shek and his gangster generals of the Kuomintang reviewing their massed armies, and of their Japanese war counterparts.

ZINIK: Do you see Russia as one of those zones where the Western mind can go and experience something which is unacceptable in one's own country? How would you describe the type of society that attracts minds which are usually either bored, lonely, excited, disrespectful of moral implications, or naive and idealistic, blind to the nastiness behind the bright façade?

BALLARD: One has to remember that despite the antagonisms of the past half-century and the threat of nuclear war, a huge reservoir of goodwill towards the Russian people exists in the West. This is quite unlike some Western responses to the Germans, who are not much liked by their European neighbours and certainly not trusted. Memories of the Franks go back a long way, all the way to the Romans, who never conquered them and, if I remember correctly, received a chilling shock when several of their legions made the mistake of crossing the Rhine and were massacred to the last man.

But Russians are perceived in a very positive light, as affable and likeable people. I have known a good number of Russians in my life: during my Shanghai childhood I had several White Russian nannies, and many White Russian men were employed as garage owners, dentists, doctors and so on, as well as foremen and drivers. They were all likeable characters. If Western visitors are going to Russia to gaze at the relics of socialism for reasons of nostalgia, that amazes me.

ZINIK: Could one speculate about some kind of energy points ('G-spots' in social structures) without which humankind withers and dies in passivity? Is Russia one of those points on the political map of the world, which provokes, like infection, self-destructive urges in some people? Is it possible to describe such a temperament? Do you recognise among your characters those who might be attracted to Russia?

BALLARD: I suppose, from the standpoint of evolutionary biology, there must be a reason why a huge and diverse nation with a highly educated elite should choose to enslave itself for seventy years, but it's hard to find one. Perhaps, historically, Russia was very late in developing a middle class, so that until the start of the twentieth century there was almost nothing between aristocracy and the rural and urban working class, a set-up that stops the clocks, as you can see in any banana republic or oil sheikhdom. The USA and Japan are the exact opposite, almost entirely composed of the middle class, who are intensely insistent on their civic rights, like any Whig mercantile class. I'm afraid my characters would not be attracted to Russia, since all my heroes are mavericks.

ZINIK: You once remarked that Marxism is a philosophy for the poor and that we need to develop a philosophy for the rich. We shouldn't forget, of course, the fact that the ideas of the French Enlightenment and French Revolution are as much responsible for the creation of the Soviet utopia as they are – in a more immediate sense – responsible for the birth of the United States of America.

The cherished Russian notions of suffering and sacrifice in the name of collective welfare were historically juxtaposed in the twentieth century to those of American self-promotion and happiness. One could say the Cold War was fought over the wrong interpretation of Jean-Jacques Rousseau. Do you see these two types of ideals as mirroring each other? Is the brainwashing by commercial advertising comparable to that by Soviet ideology, the living dead of American consumerism not dissimilar to the victim of the Soviet totalitarianism?

BALLARD: You use the word 'utopia' a lot in connection with Soviet history, but this only applies in the most abstract and notional sense. For most of the time the former Soviet Union was a dystopia of alarming durability. Having myself experienced cold, hunger and disease during the war, I can't imagine how they could ever serve a glorious end, and there is no way in which Russian suffering is some kind of mirror image of American consumer plenty. Eastern Europeans and Russians, like people from the developing world, have always been astonished by American plenty, by vast supermarkets and shopping malls crammed to the ceiling with a king's ransom of consumer goods.

They fail to realise that Americans themselves are not in the least awestruck by their own superabundance, and in fact take it completely for granted. They expect a refrigerator to have an automatic ice-cube maker, just as they expect a car to have a powerful heater and a four-speaker sound system. The richest society is one where everyone is a millionaire but is unaware of the fact; a state that already exists on the Upper East Side of New York.

Sadly, Russians will probably still feel poor even when surrounded by a lavish consumer culture. There are Marxist interpretations of American consumer culture, which believe that American capitalism has entrapped and pacified the working class by beguiling them with the opium of meretricious consumer goods. But this analysis seems desperate to me and ignores the fact that the basic needs of the working class, e.g. for personal transport and food refrigeration, are fully genuine needs, and the cars and refrigerators in question are superb functional examples of their kind.

The same applies to advertising, which people in the developing world assume Americans are brainwashed by. In fact Americans are scarcely aware of the advertising around them. Today's Russian intelligentsia would make a huge error if they equated American consumerism with Soviet totalitarianism. They would make the same mistake if they assumed that Americans, Europeans and others in the developed world are brainwashed by the dominant entertainment culture of Hollywood films, TV and popular music. All this is merely a sea in which everyone floats.

In fact, I often wonder if people here are really immersed in this sea at all. It forms the background to their lives, like a TV set left on in a room that no one is watching. This explains the apparent contradiction of these comments with those I made in answer to your opening question. The consumer and entertainment landscape dominates everything, but it's nothing but wallpaper.

ZINIK: On the other hand, what about the need for an enemy which satisfies the no less acute urge for self-righteousness among us? With the end of the Cold War, what would replace Soviet totalitarianism in the role of intellectual enemy?

BALLARD: The real problem is that it (the consumer and entertainment landscape) is the only wallpaper – every other form of competition for people's attention and imaginations has been vanquished. If people were alert and critical of their consumer environment there would be some hope that they might change or penetrate it.

Similarly, if there were a conspiracy by manipulators behind the scenes there would be the hope that people might wake up. But there is no conspiracy. This leaves people in a valueless world, wandering like aimless Saturday crowds through the great supermarket of life. Under the placid surface of their minds, dreams stir the strange phantoms and pseudo-religions that we spelled out earlier.

1999: Iain Sinclair. J.G. Ballard's Cinema in the Slipstream of Discontent

Originally published in Iain Sinclair, *Crash: David Cronenberg's Post-mortem on J.G. Ballard's 'Trajectory of Fate'*, London: British Film Institute, 1999

Like Will Self, writer Iain Sinclair has been a tireless supporter of Ballard's work, and both he and Self have incorporated Ballard into their individual resurrections of psychogeography, the nebulous political/urban/literary programme formulated by Ivan Chtcheglov and Guy Debord in the 1950s. But while it may be superficially easier to locate Ballardian themes in Self's work, it is less so in the case of Sinclair, despite Ballard's appearance in *London Orbital*, Sinclair's narrative about walking around the M25, and in the film of the book, directed by Sinclair and Chris Petit.

Many commentators place Ballard and Sinclair in a simple narrative of compatible writers and thematic consistencies, yet their relationship is rather more complex. As Sinclair has often emphasised, Ballard celebrated the edges of cities, seeing in suburbia, shopping malls, airports and motorways a sense of liberation and freedom from mainstream thought. For the most part, Sinclair's writing seeks to destroy such terrain, to explode its eventless surface to rediscover an archaeology of the recent past, all the haunted stories, places and people that ritually coalesce when cities evolve. Yet just as there is a latent, reverse critique in Ballard's appreciation of urban 'non-space' (he is against extremism in any direction, heritage or modern), Sinclair, it seems, cannot help but be drawn to such terrain, despite his surface opposition. Ballard's appearance in Sinclair's work, then, serves as a kind of grit, forcing Sinclair to assess and come to terms with his own relationship to time, space and place.

In 1999 Sinclair interviewed Ballard for Sinclair's short book on Cronenberg's *Crash*. The fruits of that conversation were fragmented throughout, and are collected and expanded upon here for the first time. Prompted by Sinclair's singular interests, Ballard discusses Cronenberg's intentions, the ritual nature of celebrity, the genesis of *The Atrocity Exhibition* and *Crash* and the side projects associated with those works: Ballard's 1969 exhibition of crashed cars and the obscure 1971 BBC short film *Crash!*, directed by Harley Cokliss, in which Ballard starred alongside Gabrielle Drake. [SS]

SINCLAIR: Could you deliver a short autobiography, in terms of the films you've seen?

BALLARD: I was born in 1930. I started being taken to the movies in Shanghai when I was about six or seven years old. I've got a feeling that the first film I saw was *Snow White*. A pretty shocking film, actually. Frightened me out of my wits. I've never forgotten it. All that 'mirror, mirror, on the wall'. Pure evil vibrating across the cinema.

Filmgoing was in its absolute heyday. My mother, during the school holidays, would often say, 'Would you like to go to the cinema?' I'd say, '*Yeah!*' I and the White Russian nanny – we had a whole succession of them – would pile into the car and the chauffeur would take us to downtown Shanghai. And we'd sit in one of those vast empty auditoriums and watch some Hollywood movie.

As a small boy I *hated* sitting alone. The funny thing is that now I love it. We'd go into the circle. I used to nag my nanny – if I spotted a couple fifty yards away – to get us sitting *right* next to them.

I saw a lot of films, all the films that Hollywood churned out. Then there was a break during the war. I went to school in Cambridge, at the Leys School, a boarding school . . .

SINCLAIR: Malcolm Lowry went there.

BALLARD: Yes, he *did*. We came from a similar background, quite mysteriously. Manchester. Cotton brokers. Very odd that. . . . But, anyway, Cambridge. I used to sneak away whenever I could. I saw French and

Italian classic films at the Arts Cinema – '46, '47, '48, '49. I left school and went to King's Medical School. This was the heyday of Hollywood *noir* movies. I remember going to see *T-Men*. Which only cineastes have heard of. Hard-edged, really tough gangster film. I remember watching that and thinking it's much more important to see *T-Men* than to go and listen to Dr Leavis, or even my own anatomy lecturers. I *knew* that was part of the emerging culture.

SINCLAIR: Did you read pulp novels at this time?

BALLARD: Not really, no. Not until much later. I think I read Chandler as his books were published. I've always *loved* Hollywood thrillers. My idea of a perfect evening would be watching *Point Blank*. I actually bought the original of *Point Blank*, the book by Richard Stark. The novel is just a pale shade of the film. So I've never really liked reading thrillers, but I love the films.

SINCLAIR: Did Alain Resnais, Chris Marker and the French New Wave directors influence your writing? The jump-cuts, fractured narratives, the relish for the city, the enthusiasm for comic strips, posters, petrol stations?

BALLARD: I don't think they did, to be honest. My first short story was published in 1956/57. And the other stories for the magazine *New Worlds* were also written around that time. I think I was exploring my own space. I don't know whether cinema had much influence.

I remember going with Claire [Walsh, Ballard's girlfriend] in '68, whenever it came out, to a special showing of Godard's *Weekend* – this was before I wrote *Crash* – at the ICA. I remember thinking: 'He's got it wrong. Godard's got it wrong.' He sees the car as the symbol of American capitalism, and the car crash as one of the wounds inflicted by capitalism on the docile purchasers of motor cars; people whose lives are completely modified by Wall Street. Whose sex lives are reduced to the kind of banal banter that you get in advertising commercials. I thought: 'That's the *wrong* approach.' He's missed the point. He doesn't see that the car is, in fact, a powerful force for good in its perverse way. And even the car crash can be conceived of – in imaginative terms – as a powerful link in the nexus of sex, love, eroticism and death, that lies at the basis of our own sexual imagination. With its heart wired into the central nervous system of all human beings. I knew Godard didn't get it – because he saw the car crash in rather old-fashioned Marxist political terms.

I felt when I started to write *Crash* in about 1970 – when I'd finished *The Atrocity Exhibition*, which contains a lot of forward references to what would become *Crash* – that I was on a totally different tack. The Godard approach was very specialist. But then *Alphaville* was a brilliant film, a masterpiece. No question about that. The interior space of *Alphaville* is so wonderful. I wish I could say *that* had influenced me. I hope it did. I love all those chrome hotels – and the *great* Akim Tamiroff, in his overcoat, sitting sadly on his bed. Eddie Constantine, the glamorous super-hunk. I think originally Godard was going to call it *Tarzan vs. IBM*. I loved that film.

SINCLAIR: You've described the assassination of President Kennedy as an 'energising event'. Would Godard have seen it in those terms?

BALLARD: No, I think the political perspective would have prevented him from doing that. The Kennedy assassination of '63 could be regarded as a detonator. We move from a pre-electronic world, in imaginative terms, into an electronic world. TV really arrived here, colour TV in particular, at that time. You saw things *live* on television in the mid- to late sixties. You saw the Vietnam War virtually live. Oswald was shot dead *live* on TV.

I remember watching TV with my parents in Manchester in something like 1951. There was only one channel. We looked at a screen the size of a light bulb. The idea that TV plugged into reality seemed absurd. By the mid-sixties, TV was a window into the world. It was an unfolding in *real time*.

SINCLAIR: Is *Crash* a novel of the suburbs?

BALLARD: There's a huge bias in the English novel towards the city as subject matter and setting for the novel. I take quite the contrary view, needless to say. I regard the city as a semi-extinct form. London is basically a nineteenth-century city. And the habits of mind appropriate to the nineteenth century, which survive into the novels set in the London of the twentieth century, aren't really appropriate to understanding what is really going on in life today.

I think the suburbs are more interesting than people will let on. In the suburbs you find uncentred lives. The normal civic structures are not there. So that people have more freedom to explore their own imaginations, their own obsessions. And the discretionary spending power to do so. There's a sort of airport culture – with its transience, its access to anywhere in the world. Social trends of various kinds tend to reveal themselves first in the suburbs. The transformation of British life by television in the sixties took place, most of all, in the suburbs, when VCRs came in. In the suburbs you have nothing to do except watch TV.

An inner-London, or an inner-city, version of *Crash* would be impossible. The logistics just aren't there. The traffic moves too slowly. One doesn't have the imaginative freedom.

SINCLAIR: Were you happy for Cronenberg to move the story to Toronto?

BALLARD: Jeremy Thomas [the film's producer] and Cronenberg told me, about six months before they started shooting, that they would shoot in Toronto. I think at other times they, vaguely, thought of shooting it around London. The original setting. But I thought Toronto was just right, the paradigm of North American cities (although it's not recognised like all the others). 'Oh, my God, a bit of *The Rockford Files*, *The Streets of San Francisco* and *Kojak*, coming up again.' Toronto is anonymous, and most of Cronenberg's films have been set there. Part of the eeriness of his early Toronto films is because you don't know where you are.

SINCLAIR: The names of the characters in *Crash* seem coded to me. Is that wishful thinking? Catherine Ballard obviously derives from Catherine Austen (sometimes Austin) in *The Atrocity Exhibition*. Names that float playfully between two great female literary traditions of the nineteenth century: the necrophile romanticism of the Brontës and the domesticated irony, the control, of Jane Austen. With a bit of a nudge in the direction of the car. Seagrave, surely . . .

BALLARD: Seagrave, of course. There was a land-speed record-breaker in the thirties. Yes, yes. I think you're probably right. I don't know about the origin of Vaughan. I think I just wanted a name that was *different*, you know. That didn't have any obvious associations. This created problems for the French because they can't pronounce it. They pronounce it 'Vogan'.

368

Claire won't mind me saying this, because I've said it in public: Claire is the basis of the character Catherine. Catherine Ballard. I remember, when I was writing the book, I said, 'Shall I call the character based on you "Claire"?' She said, 'Mm, perhaps not.' So I called her 'Catherine'. When we met Deborah Unger [who played Catherine in *Crash*], when we arrived at Cannes, I said, 'Deborah, by the way, this is Claire. Claire is the basis of your character.' Poor Deborah Unger, who is a former philosopher, a student of philosophy from Vancouver University, more or less *collapsed* in panic.

SINCLAIR: What about the Travis/Travers/Traven mutations in *The Atrocity Exhibition*?

BALLARD: That was very self-conscious, based on – Jesus, what was his name? – the German/American . . . Yes, of course. B. Traven. He was used as a mysterious figure. So it was a wonderful name to give to a character who was himself disintegrating into multiple identities. Basically a psychiatrist having a mental or schizophrenic breakdown. I just multiplied variants on his name. Tallis and Traven and so on. But, no, I don't know where Vaughan came from.

SINCLAIR: He turns up in *The Atrocity Exhibition*. He was there before *Crash*.

BALLARD: *Does* he? Yes. He was a sort of psycho. I never *read* my own stuff. It must have come from there. There was a connection between the two.

SINCLAIR: Yes, but how did he arrive the *first* time? If there is a first time, because I'm convinced all your work is one book.

BALLARD: Well . . . Yes, of course it is. Of course. That's true of all readers. One doesn't want to irritate. Yes, yeah, yes. I think I said years ago that fiction was a brand of neurology. I still believe that. There's always spare processing capacity in the brain. We see that when we sleep, dream . . . I did record dreams at one period. I based one or two, not many, short stories of mine on dreams. I used to dream, when I was younger, very strangely plotted, story-driven dreams. Some of them made what I felt were good strong story ideas.

SINCLAIR: Does it matter that the principal character in *Crash* shares the author's name, his public identity?

BALLARD: It's *meant* to be disturbing. But also partly meant to be serious. To be *honest*. To root the book, as much as I can, in my own true self.

SINCLAIR: In the *New Worlds* days, Kingsley Amis was a big supporter.

BALLARD: I was published by Cape for twenty years and I don't think Tom Maschler ever *really* understood what I was doing. But he paid attention to people he felt were significant opinion makers. People like Kingsley Amis – who was a great fan of my early stuff like *The Drowned World*, my early stories, and hated *The Atrocity Exhibition*. He *loathed* it.

I had a very close relationship with him. He was quite a sharp man, very astute. I don't want to speak ill of the dead. In a way he followed the Arnold Bennett trajectory. The boy from the provinces comes to London. Has a huge integrity and then gets seduced into a world of yachts and the south of France, the Greek islands. That happened to Kingsley, a bit.

When I first met him in '62, I'd just written *The Drowned World*, my first novel. He was then in Keats Grove in Hampstead. With Elizabeth Jane Howard. I remember we ate meals on our knees. When I'd meet him in London, we'd meet in pubs.

And then, in about two or three years, he started to change. We had to go to hotels and have pink gins. Things were changing. *The Atrocity Exhibition* was a book he could never get on with. That never worried me. I just went on doing my own thing. There's not much element of conscious choice, you know. One tends to follow one's obsessions, hunches. It's all laid down years in advance.

SINCLAIR: The huge success of *Empire of the Sun* gave mainstream literary commentators the opportunity to 'understand' and re-evaluate you in autobiographical terms. Yet, paradoxically, *Empire* is more of a fictional construct, less the story of the development of your imagination than *Crash* or *The Atrocity Exhibition*.

BALLARD: People think *Empire of the Sun* is straight autobiography and that therefore they can go back, if they're interested, through my early fiction and reinterpret it. 'Oh, now we *know* . . . the swimming pools.'

Of course in a city like Shanghai there are a lot of drained swimming pools. But I hardly noticed them at the time – any more than the abandoned houses and ruined buildings and the rest of it. *Empire of the Sun* is my life seen in the mirror of the fiction prompted by that life.

I was fifty-five when *Empire* was published. As they say, there are no psychopaths after the age of forty. I mean nobody becomes psychopathic after the age of forty. It may be that one calms down a bit. It's a *wonderful* time to write, when you are really young. But after *Empire of the Sun* and Spielberg, my life hasn't changed. I live in the same house. I think people expected me to start jet-setting around the world. My life didn't change at all. Claire and I have gone on in the same sort of life I've always lived. I think it's a matter of temperament.

SINCLAIR: Were you happy with the film of *Empire of the Sun*?

BALLARD: Yes, I was very impressed by it. It's a very imaginative film. It packs a powerful punch. I don't think the Hollywood film has ever come to terms with war – because war runs counter to the whole ethos, the optimistic, positive ethos. Every camera angle, every zoom, the language. The grammar of the Hollywood film is diametrically opposed to the rhythm and grammar of the experience of war: most of the time nothing happens, then something happens that makes everything even worse. But, bearing that in mind, I think *Empire of the Sun* was a remarkable piece of work.

SINCLAIR: How do you feel about Michael Moorcock's account of the period between *The Atrocity Exhibition* and *Crash*, the drinking, the Westway driving, visits to wreckers' yards, a dark night of the soul? Was this one great fiction writer attempting to colonise the life and work of another?

BALLARD: Mike's a mythologist. People need to *authenticate* works of the imagination. People believe that a writer must be his book. It's not true. *Crash* was an extreme hypothesis. The mock scientific paper of *The Atrocity Exhibition* is a chromosome that contains the main themes of the subsequent novel, of *Crash*.

SINCLAIR: According to Moorcock, the exhibition of crashed cars you held was 'pretty dull. Two or three crashed cars. That's about it. I think he had a Chrysler. He couldn't find the American cars he wanted. The biggest one he ever owned was a Granada. He wouldn't let that car go. He insisted I go with him one day to the wrecker's yard. He's arguing with the blokes and he gets the car back. It's not running, it's rumbling along. It stinks of death. It reeks of damp and mould. We're doing about ten miles an hour, everything steaming and banging. And he's insisting it's all right.'

BALLARD: Oh, that's a bit of myth-making – but I think he's probably telling the truth. What happened was . . . I had an accident, about a week after finishing *Crash*. My Ford Zephyr, a big English Ford, had a front blowout at the foot of the Chiswick Bridge . . . rolled over, crossed the dual carriageway. Ended up on its back. The windscreen was shattered. The car was dragged to a police pound and it must have rained, because the upholstery – which I assume was made of plastic – must have contained some wool. Of course it smelt musty. That's what Mike remembers. I had the car repaired.

SINCLAIR: How did the Cokliss film come about?

BALLARD: It was *before* the book was written. The film was based on my interest in the car crash – as it emerged through the pages of *The Atrocity Exhibition*. It was made in the early seventies. With Gabrielle Drake. She was quite a serious actress in her early days, but then she moved off into *Crossroads* or something. She was very sweet. I met her a few times on the set, as it were, chasing around multi-storey car parks in Watford.

There are an enormous number of multi-storey car parks in Watford, I discovered. It's the Mecca of the multi-storey car park. And they're quite ornate, some of them. They played a special role in *The Atrocity Exhibition*. They were iconic structures. I was interested in the gauge of psychoarchitectonics. The multi-storey car park and its canted floors, as a depository for cars, seemed to let one into a new dimension. They obviously decided they had to beautify these structures. They covered them in strange trellises. It was a *bizarre* time.

SINCLAIR: Was it a legitimate tactic to press real people, real names, into your incantatory texts? ('You: Coma: Marilyn Monroe'; 'Plan for the Assassination of Jacqueline Kennedy'; 'Why I Want to Fuck Ronald Reagan'; 'The Assassination of John Fitzgerald Kennedy Considered as a Downhill Motor Race').

BALLARD: Yes. Once they become so famous that they have become fictionalised by their own fame, then I think they are part of the common property of the shared imagination of today.

SINCLAIR: Would it bother you if some other novelist pressed your life into a sinister fiction? Could 'public' figures be projected into any scenario, however perverse?

BALLARD: Absolutely. They are like gods. Princess Di and Thatcher were the last of them, the only English ones. We aren't important enough as a country. We don't generate the myths of the age. Most of them come from America. America is one huge dream generator.

SINCLAIR: It was inevitable, with Di's crash in the Paris underpass, the ultimate marker in the Ballardian trajectory of fate, that the brighter hacks would invite you to comment. So were you responsible? Was this the curse of prophecy? Does the visionary/paranoid writer, in the heat of composition, somehow fix the future?

BALLARD: Well, a lot of people were ringing me up after Di's death, more or less accusing me of stage-managing the whole thing. I didn't say anything at the time, because I think there's no doubting the fact that she died in a crashed car, pursued by the furies – like Orestes. A classical death, if there is one. The fact that she died in a car crash *probably* is a validating – in imaginative terms – signature. To die in a car crash is a unique twentieth-century finale. It's part of the twentieth-century milieu. The deaths of car crash victims have a resonance that you don't find in the deaths of hotel fire victims, or plane crash victims.

SINCLAIR: Is satire still possible?

BALLARD: Yeah. Why not? I think so. I think anyone in the public eye is – horrible phrase – fair game. If they are that famous they've already incorporated themselves into our dreams.

2000: John Gray. 'Technology is always a facilitator': J.G. Ballard on *Super-Cannes*

Previously unpublished

In his 1999 review of Iain Sinclair's book on Cronenberg's *Crash*, the political theorist John Gray considered Ballard the 'most gifted and original living writer' in Britain, on a higher plane than Conrad, Greene, Burroughs and Wells. Ballard is central to Gray's worldview. In his 2003 book *Straw Dogs*, an attack on humanist beliefs, he writes in the acknowledgements: 'Reading and talking with J.G. Ballard sharpened my view of the present and the near future.' Ballard repaid the compliment, offering a blurb for *Straw Dogs* that claimed: 'This powerful and brilliant book is an essential guide to the new millennium . . . [It] challenges all our assumptions about what it is to be human, and convincingly shows that most of them are delusions. Who we are and why we are here? John Gray's answers will shock most of us deeply.'

Straw Dogs quotes *Cocaine Nights* and *Super-Cannes*, highlighting Ballard's depiction of enervated leisure- and business-driven enclaves and their jaded residents, who become re-energised by the subliminal marketing of violent acts as life-affirming entertainment. Gray picks up the thoughts of a character in *Super-Cannes*, who asks: 'What else can drive the bizarre shifts in the entertainment landscape that will keep us buying?' For Gray, after violence has been exhausted and can no longer sell, the answer is 'morality', which will be 'marketed as a new brand of transgression'.

In the only published article to date that examines their relationship

374

in any detail, Mike Holliday suggests that Ballard and Gray share common concerns, including the view that Western lives are dominated by chance and fragmentation rather than conscious choice and intent; that violent psychopathy provides a latent reminder of our primate past, ready to surface and explode at any time; and that shared reality is an illusion, a construct of media fictions. Paradoxically, both Gray and Ballard also admired Margaret Thatcher, despite seemingly anti-capitalist convictions in both.

In this interview, a transcript of a 2000 discussion originally broadcast on BBC Radio 4, Gray talks to Ballard about *Super-Cannes* and the themes Holliday identifies are clearly essayed, providing an intriguing insight into the evolution of Gray's thought in the lead-up to *Straw Dogs*. [SS]

BALLARD: In a way, the Shanghai of the 1930s and forties was a preview of the world to come perhaps twenty, thirty or forty years down the line. Shanghai was a brutal and cruel city. Unrestricted venture capitalism was going full blast there twenty-four hours a day. It was a vast metropolis, human life was worth absolutely nothing – if you fainted with hunger on the streets of Shanghai and fell to the pavement you lay there until you died. But at the same time it was a sort of media city. There was no television, but there were about a hundred radio stations in every conceivable language.

GRAY: It must have been almost the most modern city in the world.

BALLARD: It was certainly the most important city in the Pacific area, far more than its nearest rival, Los Angeles, on the other side of the sea, because it was a major political centre. There were huge struggles throughout the twenties and thirties between communists and the very right wing Kuomintang regime under Chiang Kai-shek. Bitter battles were being fought. Mao and Chou En-lai were both active there.

GRAY: I'm interested that you mention these revolutionary movements because they must have gone on side by side, not only with this brutal venture capitalism but also with a lot of organised crime. What strikes me about many of your writings is that you see a subtext of violence – violence itself, either dream violence or actual violence – as being woven into very modern societies. In other words, as we get more modern, as we get more rational, it's not the case that violence disappears, it's rather the case that it emerges suddenly, like the bombing of a supermarket, or in the form of serial killers, or in the form, maybe, of the stylised violence that permeates the media. So it seems that Shanghai embodied that, that it was a kind of augury of the modern society we live in.

BALLARD: I think it was an extremely modern city, in that it was full of American cars. It sounds antique now, but it had the latest trams, all these radio stations going full blast all the time. I think if you introduce elements of the latest technology – it doesn't matter whether it's the motor car, or the jet plane, or the fax machine, or email – you're facilitating a much larger exchange of human ambitions, motives, hates, fears, fantasies, aggression, paranoia, political ambition, criminal violence. All this is made possible by advanced communication technologies.

GRAY: In *Crash*, you pointed to the fantasies embodied in the private motor car. Not only the fantasies – or even the reality – of personal freedom – going where you want, doing what you want, when you want it, and not being dependent on other people – but also the fantasies of release in sudden death, of an almost erotic relationship with the car in which you're travelling. Right through your writings is the theme of the way the most basic, and even unconscious, human needs, emotions and instincts interact with our most modern and innovative technologies, including those in everyday life like the motor car.

BALLARD: Certain activities and certain objects do tend to become the focus of all kinds of human impulses, dreams and ambitions. The motor car was probably the biggest example in the twentieth century. If you wanted an image that summed up the twentieth century, it's probably not a soldier guarding a concentration camp. I think it much more true to the twentieth century, with its dreams of freedom and promise, for it to be a man or a woman at the wheel of a car driving along a super-highway.

Technology is always a facilitator, not only of the manifest content – the obvious message, when you pick up a telephone or use a fax machine or send an email – but also of the latent message. Freud made the distinction, looking at dreams, between the manifest and the latent content: what's the secret message of this particular dream? I think that technology has to be approached in the same kind of way. On the superficial level, aircraft are crossing the skies taking tourists to holiday destinations, emails are sending messages all over the world, cars are rolling down superhighways. But then there's a secret, latent world where all kinds of ancient human anxieties and dreams are stirring constantly and the danger is that we don't recognise it.

GRAY: We tend to think of technology as a toolkit, don't we? A bag of tools which we use for particular purposes to meet particular needs. But what you're suggesting, and what all your work shows, is that technology manifests this deeper part of ourselves. It's not only a set of tools but also a set of symbols, of ciphers, of dreams. Technology is ourselves dreaming awake, a lucid dream in which we act out impulses, desires, fantasies and needs of which we're not conscious.

BALLARD: Yes, and I think we have small inklings of what these dreams mean. We move into rather dangerous territory. Let's say, when you buy yourself a new car, you suddenly find that this car allows you to overtake slower drivers with complete safety and ease. And then you notice in yourself that there are certain – perhaps I won't say sadistic, but, maybe, misogynistic – strains of aggression. Particularly when you overtake a woman driver, or anyone my age driving a car very slowly in the left-hand lane. I watch a theatre of the road taking place as young men in their hotted-up cars overtake young women in their hotted-up cars. You can see that the technology is facilitating all kinds of suppressed aggressions.

GRAY: In one aspect of your writing, you suggest that the facilitation of aggression and fantasy can actually be a route to freedom for individuals. That's to say that individuals can use technology – you might even say toy with it, play with it – to follow their own obsessions, to toy with their own madness, to get a kind of freedom that isn't available to them in the hyper-rational, well-administered types of societies that are coming about in the whole of the world.

BALLARD: Yes. I think if you look at the world that's emerging in the first years of this century, despite the wars that are going on – the civil unrest, the desperate poverty of the Third World – the West on the whole is enjoying unprecedented prosperity. It's also a deeply conformist world. We all subscribe to the humane and liberal values of our welfare-state democracies, we all accept enormous interventions in our lives by the state: the right way to bring up our children, the right way to treat our wives and husbands, the right way to behave in the office. Our lives are circumscribed by enlightened legislation almost every minute of the day. The purity of the food we eat, the water we drink, the sorts of plants we can grow in our gardens virtually: all are legislated out of this benign and sensible and caring administration that governs the Western world. And we're suffocating under it. Human beings are not the sane, sensible . . .

GRAY: . . . peaceable . . .

BALLARD: . . . creatures that we imagine we are. You only have to turn off all the water supply in England and three days later people would be killing each other around the Serpentine. We're potentially extremely cruel and violent and this is not deeply buried like some ancestral past back in the Palaeolithic era 30,000 years ago, this is very close to the surface, as you saw in the former Yugoslavia during the terrible civil war there, as you saw in Rwanda where two rival African tribes murdered each other in the hundreds of thousands. The potential for violence is extremely great; these impulses are just below the surface. And they come out, at football matches, at boxing matches, all those brutal contact sports we've enjoyed for a long time.

GRAY: In other words, they come out in the most peaceable, most well-administered, most enlightened societies, because the human animal will never be fully domesticated.

BALLARD: On the whole we derive enormous benefits from behaving ourselves, from acting in a civilised way. We don't, by and large, obey speed limits and traffic signals because we're frightened of the police arresting us; we do it out of self-interest. We know that if we all cooperate we're going to get home safely. But this breaks down. We inhabit a house in which there are rooms that have never been unlocked, down in the basement. Now and then we've had a glimpse in these rooms and there are strange old cabinets and odd musical instruments. What sort of tunes do they play, one wonders, lying in the dust? All sorts of odd photographs that we've had a look at briefly show interesting things about out grandparents and their parents, which tell us that there is more to us than perhaps we think of as we sit back in front of the video recorder and watch a Merchant-Ivory film. There is a darker corner of the human psyche which intrigues us, and which we feel might benefit us if we started to explore it. It's almost a kind of murder-mystery investigation. A crime happened perhaps, or some strange event in the human past, and we are drawn to try and understand what happened.

GRAY: Much of your recent work, including *Super-Cannes*, seems to be about this individual need to explore what's hidden in us, to descend into the parts of ourselves that are not fully sane, that even contain a certain element of real madness. It seems to be about this kind of individual self-exploration that can be co-opted by business, by government, so that types of behaviour and fantasy that in the past were forbidden become almost light entertainment, part of a new industry where we're fed with brilliant, violent, strange, surreal imagery – but with the goal not of emancipating us, but of keeping us at the job, keeping us working. In other words, the liberation that comes with wealth, affluence, freedom of choice can be used as a tool of social control. Is that a paradox that you recognise?

BALLARD: Yes it is, and it's really what *Super-Cannes* is all about. I think, if you look back on the twentieth century, that it was above all the century of large organisations. In previous centuries, you never found anything equivalent to General Motors or ICI or any of the other giant corporations that manufacture the goods and services we all depend on. And I think that these giant corporations have underpinned the liberal, humane view of the world, the social contract we establish when we all become responsible citizens, when we vote every four years or whatever it may be, when we stop at red traffic lights, try to bring our children up as decent citizens. The giant corporations of the world, who sell us all the products that make up our lives, have endorsed this sane and rational view of human nature. But I wonder whether this is going to come to an end.

It may be that the appetite that we all displayed during the twentieth century for more consumer goods, for more international jet travel, for bigger and better houses, for bigger and better cars, has become a little dulled. Simply out of familiarity. I mean, how many cars can the average family cope with, how many TV sets do we really need? Now, to keep the consumer society consuming, it may be that the giant corporations of this world, inevitably, even without being aware of it, will begin to try to tap other strains in our character. And, as in *Super-Cannes*, it may be that they'll turn to a very old, dark friend of human nature, the taste for cruelty and death that benefited our remote ancestors because it helped them to survive. A taste for cruelty, for the subversive, for the deviant, for the perverse.

GRAY: The reason that business might, even without realising it, be forced to explore the possibility of marketing this dark side of human nature, and of satisfying its needs, is that very rich, affluent societies like ours face a problem of satiated desire, a problem in which the existing staples of consumer life leave people bored. So, the companies which are exploring more markets have to dig deeper and deeper into the human psyche to get beyond the surface desires we all frankly and candidly reveal, to the deeper, as you say, almost psychopathic side of human nature, and aim to satisfy that. That's one of the central themes of *Super-Cannes*.

BALLARD: Absolutely. I think that's a real fear. And we've seen, after all, a very good example of this process at work in the political field. You could say that fascism and Nazism during their terrifying reign over Europe were an example of the way in which a political system, under Hitler, motivated people by appealing to psychopathic or violent strains in their make-up.

GRAY: Many of the characters in your writing seem to be seeking to escape, from memory, from regret, from the shallow time that passes in their personal lives, to something else, to, sometimes, a kind of deep time of the nervous system, and sometimes what they're trying to do is put the past aside in order to inhabit the present better. It occurred to me that your more autobiographical writings, *The Kindness of Women* and *Empire of the Sun*, could almost be read in that light, as a way of bringing to light some of your own memories and turning them into something illuminating, instructive and beautiful so that you yourself could be free of them.

BALLARD: I think that's absolutely true. Time has been a very important strand in my fiction, partly because of the sort of dislocations I knew as a child, when what appeared to be, on the one hand, a very settled and stable childhood existence in pre-war Shanghai suddenly came to an end after the Japanese attack on Pearl Harbor and wartime internment and so on. I suddenly saw time come to an abrupt stop, and a very different and ugly sort of clock begin to tick. It was disconcerting for a twelve-year-old to go and visit friends and then find an empty house with windows open and half filled suitcases lying across beds. I think that jolted me into realising that the comforting progress of the clock hands around the day, measuring out our lives, was a huge illusion, and along with it was a huge set of illusions about who we are and our relationships with each other. Many of the characters in my short stories and novels have sudden glimpses into what they realise is a sort of larger reality, that there's a deeper past to the human race, when the everyday clock has stopped and there are much larger clocks whose movements are virtually imperceptible but which cover giant periods of time as the human race evolved. So that all of us, in our brains and spinal columns, carry the memories of the human race as it emerged from its primitive forebears and began to develop consciousness, beginning, for the first time, to dream. My characters try to remythologise themselves to recharge the batteries of their imaginations. They're trying to decode reality.

GRAY: Many of your characters discover that the choices they thought they'd made were really ciphers of symbols already written, in a sense, in the geometry of their lives. Although we think of our lives in terms of choice, decisions – of intending to do things, forming plans and then achieving them – your characters often find themselves discharging hidden assignments, and only later do they see the geometry of their lives as a whole.

BALLARD: Yes. There's a way in which all my characters are rather like someone who begins to notice odd, suspicious details about his or her life. They suddenly find some documents in a desk drawer and hear a mysterious phone call left on the answer machine and then realise: 'I'm a secret agent, but I don't quite know my assignment'. And then you begin to investigate, you begin to explore: 'What is my assignment?' Now, in a sense, that's what all of us are doing in our lives. We all feel, at times, a kind of unease and emptiness about our lives. You know: 'Do I really want to be a professor of history? Do I really want to be a novelist, dentist, accountant? Perhaps I'm playing the wrong role. Perhaps I've got a deeper role and what I do normally is a kind of disguise.'

GRAY: And that disguise is what broke down in Shanghai. The kind of everyday, superficial, social, professional, vocational, marital roles that we perform in our lives – they're the roles that are so fragile, that can easily be kicked away. But kicking away isn't all a negative matter of disillusionment or breakdown . . .

BALLARD: No, it may be a very positive first step to a new kind of life. It's extremely difficult for people to remake themselves, particularly if they've got husbands and wives, jobs, children. It's very, very difficult to throw everything up and embark on a completely new reappraisal of yourself. But, I think, sooner or later, all of us have to do that. Mostly I think we do it vicariously, by reading novels, by going to films and so on. We allow others to be our deputies in making some kind of radical shift, stealing a million dollars from a bank or whatever it may be. But I think we all feel a powerful need to make this change, to rediscover who we really are and what our real assignment is.

2003: Hans Ulrich Obrist. 'Nothing is real, everything is fake'

Originally published in the catalogue for the 'Beck's Futures' exhibition, Institute of Contemporary Arts, London, 2003

The catalogue in which this interview was printed was part of the 2003 ICA 'Beck's Futures' exhibition, an annual contemporary art prize sponsored by the German brewer Beck's between 2000 and 2006. The interview was conducted by curator and art critic Hans Ulrich Obrist, who had developed a special interest in the interview as a medium of unique significance, and who continues to publish volumes of a vast series of interviews with contemporary artists, called *The Conversation Series*.

Obrist's characteristic style of interviewing, determined by his notion of 'conversation', shapes the whole discussion, which barely touches upon Ballard's fictions, instead focusing upon the influence that specific artists, architects and exhibitions had upon him. Tellingly, most of Obrist's quotations in the interview are not quotations from Ballard's works, but from earlier interviews with him. [DOH]

OBRIST: I'm interested in knowing about the transition between your childhood years in the Far East and your arrival in England just after the war. You've said before that those years in China have greatly influenced your writing – all the abandoned cities and towns and beach resorts that you keep returning to in your fiction are related to these spaces in China that the Japanese had abandoned during the war; as well as the semi-tropical nature of the place, with its lush vegetation. When you came to England, it was a place totally exhausted.

You said: 'The war had drained everything. It seemed very small, and rather narrow mentally, and the physical landscape of England was so old.' I'm wondering how this experience of post-war England as a very dull place compared to China has influenced your later work as a (science) fiction writer. You later said, 'Why I became a science fiction writer was because the future was clearly better and the past was clearly worse.' And also: 'I came from a background where there was no past. Everything was new – Shanghai was a new city.'

BALLARD: Yes, I don't think it's possible to escape from one's past. The brain and the imagination are imprinted for ever with the images of one's first years. I think puberty is an important turning point, as it is in the case of language acquisition. I lived in Shanghai until I was fifteen, went through the war and acquired a special 'language', a set of images and rhythms, dreams and expectations that are probably the basic operating formulae that govern my life to this day.

Shanghai was almost a twenty-first-century city: huge disparities of wealth and poverty, a multilingual media city with dozens of radio stations, dominated by advertising, befouled by disease and pollution, driven by money, populated by twenty different nations, the largest and most dynamic city of the Pacific rim, an important political battleground. In short, a portent of the world we inhabit today. The significant thing for me was that all this was turned upside down by war. Friends suddenly vanished, leaving empty houses like the *Mary Celeste*, and everywhere I saw the strange surrealist spectacles that war produces. It taught me many lessons, above all that the unrestricted imagination was the best guide to reality.

OBRIST: You studied medical science at Cambridge and then spent time in the RAF in Canada before coming back to England to become an editorial assistant of a science magazine. At the time you had already started writing fiction. Were your interests in science, technology, the predicament of the individual in a highly mechanised society, and the way in which certain symbols and images can precipitate complex chain reactions in the imagination there at the very beginning? Could you tell me about the way you honed your work and your style?

BALLARD: Yes, I think that my imagination was fully formed from the beginning, though that is probably true for most painters, novelists, poets and so on. I've always believed in the radical imagination that sets out to change reality – probably a doomed ambition. I wasn't interested in accepting the social consensus. I wanted to unsettle and unnerve, to provoke the reader. I never consciously shaped my ideas or my style. I simply followed my obsessions, and was confident that they would take me to strange destinations beyond the edge of the map.

OBRIST: The same year that you published your first texts, in London the Independent Group organised the exhibition *This is Tomorrow* [at the Whitechapel, London, in 1956], which startled everybody with its flood of popular imagery, undiluted in scale and treatment: films, advertising billboards, car styling, consumer goods and comics.

You said about your experience of this exhibition: 'To go to the Whitechapel in 1956 and to see my experience of the real world being commented upon, played back to me with all kinds of ironic gestures, that was tremendously exciting. I could really recreate the future, that was the future, not the past. And abstract expressionism struck me as being about yesterday, was profoundly retrospective, profoundly passive, and it wasn't serious. *This is Tomorrow* came on a year before the flight of the first Sputnik, but the technologies that launched the Space Age were already underpinning the consumer-goods society in those days. How much of this did abstract expressionism represent? If an art doesn't embrace the whole terrain, all four horizons, it's worth nothing.' Could you tell me more about your memories of this show?

BALLARD: At the time I didn't see *This is Tomorrow* as an aesthetic event. For me it wasn't primarily an art show, just as I didn't see exhibitions of Francis Bacon, Max Ernst, Magritte and Dali as displays of paintings. I saw them as among the most radical statements of the human imagination ever made, on a par with radical discoveries in neuroscience or nuclear physics. *This is Tomorrow* showed how the world could be reperceived and remade.

Very few people today are old enough to remember how traumatised Britain was by the Second World War (which in many ways we had lost). The British were locked into an exhausted present, and were trying to find their way back into the past, where they hoped they might be happier and discover their former certainties. A hopeless quest. A new future has to be built from scratch, and *This is Tomorrow* was a start. What impressed me was that it was a confident art.

OBRIST: Did you befriend Richard Hamilton and Eduardo Paolozzi there, or did you know them before? You've always said that you had been influenced as a writer by certain artists, painters and even that novels like *Crash* for instance were composed as visual experiences, 'marrying elements in the book that make sense primarily as visual constructs'. Could you tell me more about that and about the influence of these artists? I'd like to know also about how you perceived their interests in science fiction writing, *New Worlds* and in your stories in particular. Did you play the role of a visionary writer? What was the nature of the relations between you? One of cross-fertilisation?

BALLARD: I didn't meet Paolozzi until 1966, and Hamilton somewhat later. I admired their work greatly, but I think the surrealist painters had the biggest influence on me – De Chirico, Ernst, Dali and Delvaux. These are all painters of mysterious and disconnected landscapes, through which the few human beings drift in a state of dream-like trance, which had a direct and powerful appeal for me.

I admired many of Hamilton's paintings, such as *Homage to the Chrysler Corporation* (1957) and his masterpiece, the collage *Just what is it that makes today's homes so different, so appealing?* (1956), and I also admired Paolozzi's great early sculptures, the totemic figures constructed from machine parts, and his brilliantly original screen prints. I don't think I was any kind of influence on them. They were much more interested in American science fiction with its high-technology images.

OBRIST: The ICA was a powerhouse of experimental exhibition practice at the time, a laboratory for interdisciplinary dialogues. Could you tell me about how you saw it at the time and why it worked? What can we learn now from this experience for the present? In an interview I conducted with Richard Hamilton he told me, 'The main reason for the ICA's success as far as I was concerned was that the institution was small enough to be like an intimate club.' Would you agree?

BALLARD: The ICA has always been enormously important as an ideas laboratory, not only in the days of the Independent Group in the 1950s but also in the late 1960s after it moved to its present home in the Mall. There were many important exhibitions devoted to surrealist and installation art, and the ICA was a hothouse where people with original ideas met to exchange ideas. In the last few years it's regained its old flavour.

Part of the problem it faces is that the avant-garde is now the new establishment. The new is in danger of becoming the new old. But today's ICA seems to be successfully repositioning itself as a post-2000 ideas lab.

OBRIST: Could you tell me about the exhibitions that you designed, such as the one in the sixties at the New Arts Lab with the crashed cars (a crashed Mini, an A40 and a Pontiac which had been in a massive front-end collision – a Pontiac from the last grand period of American automobile styling around the mid-fifties, with huge, flared tail-fins and iconographic display). You called it New Sculpture.

I know that this show encountered massive hostility, that the cars were attacked. In a conversation with Eduardo Paolozzi published in *Studio International* in 1971 you said about this exhibition: 'The whole thing was a speculative illustration of a scene in *The Atrocity Exhibition*. I had speculated in my book about how the people might behave. And in the real show the guests at the party and the visitors later behaved in pretty much the way I had anticipated. It was not so much an exhibition of sculpture as almost of experimental psychology, using the medium of the fine art show. People were unnerved, you see. There was enormous hostility.' So, did you consider the exhibition medium to be a unique tool in this respect?

BALLARD: My show of crashed cars was held at the New Arts Lab in 1969. It was an art show designed to carry out a psychological test, so that I could decide whether to write my novel *Crash* – begun in 1970 and finished in 1972. I wanted to test my own hypothesis about our unconscious fascination with car crashes and their latent sexuality. One could argue that today's Turner prize, and the exhibitions of work by Hirst, Emin and the Chapman brothers, perform exactly the same role, that they are elaborate attempts to test the psychology of today's public.

Going farther, I'm tempted to say that the psychological test is the only function of today's art shows, and that the aesthetic elements have been reduced almost to zero. It no longer seems possible to shock people by aesthetic means, as did the Impressionists, Picasso and Matisse, among many others. In fact, it no longer seems possible to touch people's imaginations by aesthetic means. People in London flocked to the Barnett Newman show out of a deep nostalgia for a time when the aesthetic response still mattered.

OBRIST: In 1971 you also said: 'Violence is probably going to play the same role in the seventies and eighties that sex played in the fifties and sixties. There's what I call in my book *The Atrocity Exhibition* the death of feeling, that one's more and more alienated from any kind of direct response to experience. And the car crash is probably the only act of violence most of us in western Europe are ever going to be involved with, is probably the most dramatic event in our lives apart from our own deaths, and in many cases the two are going to coincide.' What do you think of that statement retrospectively? What about now?

BALLARD: Violence does seem to play a dominant role in our imaginations, perhaps for good reasons, a symptom of our need to break down the suffocating conventions that rule our lives. Human beings today display a deep and restless violence, which no longer channels itself into wars but has to emerge in road rage, internet porn, contact sports like hyper-violent professional rugby and US football, reality TV, and so on.

OBRIST: This interview is meant to be published in the catalogue of Beck's Futures 2003. Are you familiar with and interested in today's art? You said, 'the tradition in fine arts is the tradition of the new. The main pressure on the sculptor or painter is the pressure of the new. The new to the new. But in literature the main tradition is the tradition of the old. Where Eduardo and his fellow painters and sculptors are expected to find something new to say, my fellow writers and myself are expected to find something old, and to go on saying it.' What are your favourite artists and writers of today? What do you think of the ways artists maintain relations between art and the future today? And what about the relations between visual arts and literature? (It's something that has practically disappeared, don't you think?)

BALLARD: I take a keen interest in what today's painters and sculptors are doing. On the whole my views coincide with those of the great Brian Sewell, but I see the young British artists of the past ten years or so from a different perspective. They find themselves in a world totally dominated by advertising, by a corrupt politics carried out as a branch of advertising, and by a reality that is a total fiction controlled by manufacturers, PR firms and vast entertainment and media corporations. Nothing is real, everything is fake. Bizarrely, most people like it that way. So in their installations and concept works the young artists are rebelling against this all-dominant adman's media landscape. They are trying to establish a new truth about what an unmade bed is, what a dead animal is, and so on. Our mistake is to judge them by aesthetic criteria. By contrast, the novel resists innovation, and is much closer to the TV domestic serial.

OBRIST: In this same interview of 1971, you said, 'I think that the biggest need of the painter or writer today is information. I'd love to have a tickertape machine in my study constantly churning out material: abstracts from scientific journals, the latest Hollywood gossip, the passenger list of a 707 that crashed in the Andes, the colour mixes of a new automobile varnish. In fact, Eduardo and I in our different ways are already gathering this kind of information, but we are using the clumsiest possible tools to do it: our own hands and eyes. The technology of the information-retrieval system that we enjoy is incredibly primitive.' It's really a premonition of the internet! Are you a big user of the internet? In your opinion, how did it change the way artists and writers look at and interact with the world?

BALLARD: Yes, it was a premonition of the internet, which I relish for the unlimited information it provides, and the unlimited possibilities. Large sections of it strike me as remarkably poetic. It may turn out to be more important and more innovative than television. It's a kind of collective lucid dreaming.

OBRIST: A lot of young artists are fascinated by your novels and stories and I know of at least one dialogue, the one with Tacita Dean. You wrote a short piece on her work that was included in a book published by Tate in 2001 where you concentrated on her *Trying to Find the Spiral Jetty* (1997), and *Teignmouth Electron* (2000), a series of photographs of a derelict trimaran which belonged to yachtsman Donald Crowhurst, who sent false radio signals giving the impression he was undertaking a round-the-world race, while in fact he was preparing for death in the Atlantic Ocean. Could you tell me more about this dialogue between the two of you?

BALLARD: I met Tacita at the opening party for Tate Modern, and was immediately charmed by her, as everyone is. I saw her films and was very impressed by them, especially the film made in the rotating

389

restaurant above the Berlin TV tower. It's her masterpiece so far, and a deeply moving effort of the imagination that I haven't yet come to terms with. Above all it displays the foundation structure of reality – the movement of time through an imperceptibly moving space, the passage of light and dark, and shows that human beings are the briefest visitors to the universe that is all around them but of which they are barely aware. Tacita follows her obsessions and, fortunately, it is impossible to guess where they will lead her.

OBRIST: I just read Mike Davis's latest collection of essays, *Dead Cities*. It's interesting how social commentators in recent times have been asked to or themselves willingly play the role of prophets. Do you share any of Davis's analyses of all the wreckages caused by the city's growth, his comments on white flight, deindustrialisation, housing and job segregation and discrimination, and what he calls 'national sacrifice zones'? What about his prophecies on the future of life and cities in the face of catastrophic terrorism, global warming, runaway capitalism and fears of all kinds?

BALLARD: I have just read *Dead Cities*, and am a great admirer of Mike Davis, especially for *City of Quartz*. Perhaps he is a little too nostalgic for an idealised America dominated by clean rivers and civic responsibility. I feel that he hasn't come to terms with the form that late twentieth- and early twenty-first-century cities have taken – unrestricted urban sprawl, the decentred metropolis, a transient airport culture, gated communities and an absence of traditional civic pride. The problem facing planners and architects is how to accept and make the most of this.

OBRIST: In your books you have long questioned the state and especially the 'normality' state institutions indoctrinate and protect. What do you think of the current prevalence of surveillance, dataveillance, the loss of civil liberties and increased state control?

BALLARD: Deplorable. I've long said that the totalitarian systems of the future will be subservient and ingratiating, the false smile of the bored waiter rather than the jackboot. We see this subservient Stalinism in London mayor Ken Livingstone's plans for controlling central London traffic. Hundreds of spy cameras, an army of wardens, a computerised surveillance system out of *Alphaville* – in short, an Orwellian nightmare come true, but disguised as a public service. Of course, there should be no parking or traffic restrictions of any kind. What we need are more roads, a huge system of overhead freeways on the Los Angeles pattern. But we are too brainwashed to demand this.

OBRIST: Do you see the recent shift of 'acceptable' societal behaviour into increasingly conservative norms as one more potentially dangerous form of such control?

BALLARD: There are swings and roundabouts. The loss of freedom in the surveillance society is balanced by the huge gain in freedom and possibility found in the internet. On the whole there is a loss in freedom, and the danger is that people may move into the area of psychopathology in order to enlarge the scope of their lives and imaginations.

OBRIST: Of course, it is somewhat implicit in my last questions, but I'm tempted to question you specifically about September 11 and this new history into which we've found ourselves projected since. And now there are so many geopolitical reshufflings. How does it feel to be a (science fiction) writer – or more generally an artist – in light of these developments? Do you think the artist has a duty to be critical in some way of global or political events?

BALLARD: September 11 changed America, one of the few countries in the past century that has never been bombed from the air. I feel that the US is still trapped in the twentieth century, and is still trying to solve its problems by twentieth-century means – carriers, field armies and bomber groups. Of course writers should speak out.

OBRIST: The other day you mentioned that you saw *Cities on the Move* at the Hayward Gallery.

BALLARD: It was a remarkable exhibition, one of the most impressive I have seen for many years, and I am still digesting it.

OBRIST: The urban metropolis is often much more than a mere backdrop and becomes a character in itself in your novels. What is it about the metropolis that prompts this? Regarding your research and experience of writing *Empire of the Sun*, can you tell me how much memory you have of the city of Shanghai?

BALLARD: The 'urbanisation', which has replaced the city of old, is where most people live, and its contours shape their minds. Patterns of urban life are constantly shifting, and constitute a script that we all have to perform. We're allowed a certain freedom to improvise, but our roles are written by the city. I went back to Shanghai in 1991 for the first time in forty-five years, and found that my memories were remarkably intact, though the city is a forest of high-rises and TV towers and has expanded far out into the countryside. In due course it will become the most important city of the Pacific rim, eclipsing Los Angeles and Tokyo.

OBRIST: The Chinese architect Yung Ho Chang ran an architecture studio based on your book *Crash*. For him, the moment a crash occurs can be considered to be very architectural. Can you discuss the importance of the architectural for your thinking? I read that your favourite hotel in London is the Hilton at Heathrow Airport. Can you tell me why that building, and what relationship or dialogue you have more generally with architecture or architects?

BALLARD: The Heathrow Hilton designed by Michael Manser is my favourite building in London. It's part Space Age hangar and part high-tech medical centre. It's clearly a machine, and the spirit of Le Corbusier lives on in its minimal functionalism. It's a white cathedral, almost a place of worship, the closest to a religious building that you can find in an airport. Inside, it's a highly theatrical space, dominated by its immense atrium. The building, in effect, is an atrium with a few rooms attached. Most hotels are residential structures, but rightly the Heathrow Hilton plays down this role, accepting the total transience that is its essence, and instead turns itself into a huge departure lounge, as befits an airport annexe. Sitting in its atrium one becomes, briefly, a more advanced kind of human being. Within this remarkable building one feels no emotions and could never fall in love, or need to. The National Gallery or the Louvre are the complete opposite, and people there are always falling in love.

OBRIST: What is your favourite museum and why? What do you think of the evolutions undertaken by museums in the last few decades? In your view, what role do museums play today? And ideally what do you think their role should be?

BALLARD: I like traditional museums, the less frequented the better. All the changes in the past fifty years have been for the worse. I remember the Louvre in 1949 when it was completely deserted, whereas today it is a theme park where you can enjoy 'the Mona Lisa experience'. This isn't only a matter of funding. Museum directors enjoy being impresarios, guru figures manipulating the imaginations of the public. Museums shouldn't be too popular. The experience within the Louvre or the National Gallery should be challenging and unsettling, and take years to absorb. The Italians had the right idea. Most of their paintings were in dimly lit churches, uncleaned and difficult to see. As a result, the Renaissance endured for centuries.

OBRIST: I'm currently working on an exhibition project investigating the significance of the notion of Utopia today; we are gathering all kinds of comments, ideas, utopistic (Wallerstein) works, projects and concrete utopias coming from various disciplines. I cannot help asking you what utopia means for you and if you think the term has resonance today?

BALLARD: Sadly, I think that the notion of a utopia died at some point in the twentieth century – two vast utopian projects, Soviet Russia and Nazi Germany, turned into the greatest nightmares the human race has ever experienced, and people now are understandably sceptical about any future utopia. We're still living in the aftermath of an extremely dangerous century. People today are rightly sceptical about any proclaimed intentions to build heaven on earth. We now live in the present, unconsciously uneasy at the future, and this short-term viewpoint does have dangers. We know that, as human beings, we are all deeply flawed and dangerous, but this self-knowledge can act as a brake on hope and idealism. I look forward to seeing your exhibition.

OBRIST: I also want to ask you who or what in your mind – in the present or the past – has come closest to realising a utopic project. In many of your novels ambiguity seems a prevalent feature. I've read an interview in which you spoke about the importance of being ambiguous in your work (for instance in relation to your book *Crash*: should or can people find car crashes sexually exciting; you leave multiple readings open ended). Could you tell me more about ambiguity in your work? Do you think ambiguity could be characterised as a central theme, a 'red thread' or strategy that connects your diverse works?

BALLARD: There were times in its history when the United States came close to suggesting what a utopian project might be, but the less appealing sides to American life now seem to be in the ascendant – there's a self-infantilising strain that gives America the look of Peter Pan's never-never land. However, the future may well be a marriage between Microsoft and the Disney Company – an infantilised entertainment culture imposed on us by the most advanced communications technology. What I fear for my grandchildren is a benign dystopia of ever-present surveillance cameras watching us for our own good, a situation in which we will acquiesce, all too well aware of our attraction to danger. I hope everything I have written is ambiguous, reflecting the paradoxical faces that make up human nature.

OBRIST: The second law of thermodynamics concerning the irreversibility of process, otherwise known as entropy, is a recurrent, indeed maybe the recurrent, theme in many of your novels. What made this such an important concern for you?

BALLARD: I think of it as the loss of energy in a system; the move from an organised to a disorganised state. War is a good illustration, but it affects relationships, marriages, one's perceptions of oneself – this is how time says farewell to us.

OBRIST: Was pop art and its critical fascination with mass culture, television and the media, and its own theorisation of the media, important for you?

BALLARD: Yes, because the mass media have turned the world into a world of pop art. From JFK's assassination to the coming war in Iraq, everything is perceived as pop art. Nothing is true. Nothing is untrue.

OBRIST: Is the archive an important site for you, either physically or symbolically?

BALLARD: There are no Ballard archives. I never keep letters, reviews, research materials. Every page is a fresh page.

OBRIST: In many of your stories, and *The Drowned World* is just one example that comes immediately to mind, the protagonist is a scientist. What for you is the link between literature and science?

BALLARD: Science is a new religion waiting to be born. Infinitely more important than literature, which is an old religion – poetry – waiting to die.

2003: Chris Hall. 'All we've got left is our own psychopathology': J.G. Ballard on *Millennium People*

Previously unpublished

The context for this interview was the publication of Ballard's 2003 novel *Millennium People*. Journalist Chris Hall, who had previously interviewed him on two occasions, was concerned with uncovering some of the real-world inspiration for the events described in this satirical work, with its portrayal of a disenfranchised London middle class and their efforts to kick-start a class war via low-level terrorism and targeted pranks. Ballard discusses *Millennium People*'s place in the trilogy of gated-community narratives that includes *Cocaine Nights* and *Super-Cannes*; the nihilism of British politicians, including the 'slightly unstable' Tony Blair; his old bête noire Alexander Walker; and the threat of terrorism in London.

This is the full, unpublished version of the interview, although fragments previously appeared in *Time Out* and *Icon*. [SS]

HALL: This novel seems somehow more personal – unusually the protagonist has some kind of an emotional life, and I found it funnier in a different way from most of your stuff, not black humour but warmer somehow. Plus some of the names . . . were you conscious of using Kay Churchill and St Mary's hospital as names? [Claire Walsh was JGB's partner of forty years – her married name had been Churchill; his wife, Mary, died in 1964.]

BALLARD: I wanted an unexpected name for this film studies lecturer and rebel – names creep up on you. It's a peculiar thing, you think, 'Oh, I'll change it later', but by the time you're finished writing the first draft, you're kind of stuck with it . . . Johnson, no! With *Crash* I wanted to peg the whole drama as firmly into reality as I could, and I thought I wanted to 'tell the truth', and since I was inventing all this, I thought I may as well make the narrator myself. But this is different – the names aren't significant, I'm sure of that.

HALL: Are you aware of the flash mobbing phenomenon?

BALLARD: Where they're all congregated in a furniture shop in the West End for no reason, and that was the reason – flash mobbing. These are demonstrations that have no purpose, and I thought immediately, 'My God, this is where I came in!'

HALL: Is it fair to see *Millennium People* as of a piece with *Cocaine Nights* and *Super-Cannes*, focusing on gated communities of the mind?

BALLARD: I think that's probably true. They're all looking at exploring the psychopathology of everyday life and trying to undercover those secret engines which keep us moving, which are often very different from what we take to be the case. With *Millennium People*, the middle classes – and that includes about ninety per cent of the population – do have something to complain about. You could call it the last volume in a trilogy.

HALL: There's a bit [in *Millennium People*] set at the Olympia cat show, where the protesters are chanting 'Moggie, moggie, moggie . . . out, out, out!' That seems like a very un-Ballardian joke . . .

BALLARD: Have you been to the Olympia cat show?

HALL: I'm allergic to cats . . .

BALLARD: That's a shame. I recommend it, an amazing phenomenon in anthropological terms. You don't have to be a cat lover to be absolutely staggered by the human race – not to mention the cats, they're pretty amazing too!

HALL: How do you respond to critics who say that you're writing the same book over and over?

BALLARD: I'm not sure that that's true. I used to think that all writers wrote the same – there's just one book and they rewrote it in endlessly different ways, but I'm not sure that's true. Although all Kafka's novels seem to be the same, all Dickens's novels seem to be the same, Shakespeare's comedies seem the same. But every writer is locked into the sort of room of his or her mind. A room with no doors, so you sit there and write. You can't escape the basic elements of your own character, but if you've got a strong imagination you can transcend those. The previous two books were set in the Mediterranean; this one is set in London. There are big differences.

HALL: Even the weather is catching up with you . . .

BALLARD: Yes, it is getting more Mediterranean; still, we've got a long way to go on that score. But big cities create their own weather, don't they? Paris, doesn't matter what time of the year you go there, it's always spring. London, it's always autumn, I think, in a curious way.

HALL: I hear you haven't been very well recently – did that affect how long the book took to write?

BALLARD: My illness started about three years ago, just after my last book. Some mystery virus – I had to stop for nearly a year, but I pulled out of it, thank God. I hope the book is all the better for that – the more time you have to think, the better. I was too weak, I had these fevers every day for about six months – kind of an extended bout of flu. Weird. I'd written about half the book before that – I was glad to get back to it.

HALL: Do you still have an impulse to retire to the sun one day?

BALLARD: I'm trapped in Shepperton! I'm leaving it a bit late, but I would like to retire to the sun – locally, the sun is coming north to meet me, to meet all of us. One of these days I'll call it a day, and that's when I'll pack my suitcase. At the moment, I have no shortage of ideas and a peculiar kind of compulsion to get them down. Not that it makes a damn bit of difference, but there we are . . .

HALL: How do you mean?

BALLARD: I mean, you know, when you're a younger writer, you want to change the world in a small way – when you get to my age, you realise that it doesn't make any difference whatsoever, but you still go on. Strange way to make a living; strange way to see the world.

HALL: I disagree profoundly! Your work has had a huge influence on all kinds of writers, film-makers, artists over the past four decades. Likewise, readers who have had the way they view the world transformed. I think of it like the Velvet Underground – even though a relatively small number of people saw them, most of those who did formed their own bands – it inspired them massively.

BALLARD: Well, that's a great compliment if that's true. When you're the organ grinder turning the handle as the writer does, occasional passers-by flick a peanut at the monkey, throw the coin into the hat. If I had my time again, I'd be a journalist.

HALL: Really?

BALLARD: Writing is too solitary. I think journalists have more fun.

HALL: As you get older, does it get harder anticipating the next five minutes, as you put it?

BALLARD: As one gets older one's supposed to get more conservative and entrenched in one's ways. I haven't found that – I've got more left-wing as I've got older. I don't feel in the least entrenched. I'm still very conscious of shifts in public mood and public behaviour all the time – I don't mean trends, I'm not good at spotting trends. But the world seems to be changing just as much now as it was fifty years ago, and I'm just as interested as I was. At times, I think we're going through quite a critical period. I don't mean September 11, Iraq – they're a part of it – I mean what we have is . . . consumerism dominates everything now. It's all we have. There are signs, I think, that people aren't satisfied by consumerism that . . . People resent the fact that the most moral decision in their lives is choosing what colour their next car will be.

HALL: Ha!

BALLARD: It's true! Whether they should buy this or that brand of trainers – it all comes down to what you're going to buy next. I think people realise that they are so many hamsters turning round on these little money wheels and it isn't enough. It's quite a dangerous state of affairs. Out of the desert we'll come walking – towards someone who'll be offering a more exciting ideology. The message of the last three books, this trilogy, is that all we've got left is our own psychopathology. It's the only freedom we have – that's a dangerous state of affairs. I keep repeating that in a totally sane society the only freedom is madness. Now, we're nowhere near being a totally sane society – we're expected to behave in a totally sane way, and there is a danger that we could veer off into some kind of socialised madness. It seems very volatile. Politics is so totally discredited. We have a prime minister, Tony Blair, who seems slightly unstable. He's got this powerful evangelical commitment to what he believes is right, and he invents the truth when he can't find it out in front of him as he did over the Iraq war. That's a dangerous state of affairs. I don't think he's aware of this either, which is worrying.

HALL: I presume you've been following the Hutton Inquiry in all its labyrinthine detail?

BALLARD: The detail is intended presumably; it's a wonderful smoke-screen that hides the real question – why did we go to war? The Iraq war itself was an outbreak of psychopathology on a political scale. Why Blair took us into that war is a great mystery – it's not clear at all. I mean, Bush's motives are completely clear – the American leadership wants to take charge in the Middle East, stabilise the situation there, to control all that oil. But what Blair's motives are, we don't know. Maybe it doesn't matter – better to be seen doing something extravagant than doing nothing at all. He's a sort of actor-manager. Finds himself putting on a rather dull, second-rate show and decides to liven it up with some spectacular opening flashes. I think we're living in dangerous times, and most people aren't really aware of it. They're worrying about asylum seekers or abortion or paedophilia or God knows what.

HALL: There have been plenty of anti-war demonstrations, not least in London, of course.

BALLARD: It was a very impressive turnout and it was really ignored – that was a dangerous thing to do. We can probably expect more of these apparently wrong-headed political decisions as part of the break-down of the rational. Dictators through the ages have appealed to the irrational, to mobilise populations. We're beginning to see apparently rational governments – the US, the UK – stepping into these very murky ponds. Worrying. But we'll see.

HALL: Do the events described in *Millennium People* have anything to do with the new millennium, with a new consciousness?

BALLARD: We're on the cusp of a new millennium. As the clocks ticked away to midnight 1999, the last midnight, people for years have been saying, 'What's going to happen in the next millennium?' as if there'd be thunder and lightning in the heavens, as if there'd be some huge psychic shift, but, in fact, that didn't happen. It was an event confined entirely to the calendar, particularly after the flop at the [Millennium] Dome. But I've got a feeling there are shifts in the unseen tectonic plates that make up the national consciousness. In *Millennium People*, I tried to nail down a certain kind of nihilism that people may embrace, and which the politicians may embrace, which is much more terrifying – they have the power to go to war, whether we like it or not – all tapping into this vast, untouched resource, as big as the Arabian oilfields, called psychopathology. They can dip into that – it's a high-octane fuel that could lift the whole human race into orbit. You can see that happening. The British tabloid press is a daily reminder – those screaming *Daily Mail* headlines. The tabloid press represents the unconscious mind of the British people, and you can see what its real obsessions are.

HALL: Do you read them?

BALLARD: In the supermarkets I cast my eye over them. At the time Cronenberg's *Crash* came out, led by Alexander Walker – film critic of the *Standard* – the *Daily Mail* really went to town. It was extraordinary and bizarre. It was out of all proportion to the reality of what is after all an art film. To get cabinet ministers calling for bans is extraordinary. I know the Major government was in its last few months desperate to climb on the moral bandwagon – it was looking for an enemy. Cronenberg's *Crash* featured on the *front page* of the *Daily Mail* something like six times – quite extraordinary. *What's going on?* You can't take that at face value. And the same things happen with asylum seekers and whatever else. 'Stop this vile—' and you fill in the blank.

HALL: There is this impression of you living a kind of self-imposed exile out in Shepperton and never venturing out, but that's clearly not the case, is it? I mean, in *Millennium People*, London is very well rendered indeed.

BALLARD: I know London very well. I spend two or three days a week in London. My girlfriend lives in Shepherd's Bush. My two daughters live in inner London – my son lives in Birmingham – with their families. In a way, it isn't me. It's not my favourite city, I'll admit. Andy Warhol went to Rome and was reported to have said, 'That's what happens when buildings are allowed to last too long.' I think the same is true of London in a way. A lot of late nineteenth-century speculative building, which makes up most of the residential housing from South Kensington all the way around through north London to Lambeth, is speculative housing that wasn't meant to last very long. It's been artificially propped up by the fact that it's become a secondary banking system. People put their money into bricks and mortar. The fact that the bricks are mostly dust now – one push and the whole lot would fall over – doesn't matter. It's our own South Sea Bubble. It's expanding, almost exponentially, but I'd like to see the whole thing levelled. Or chrome-plated! But that won't happen.

HALL: Were you thinking of *The Third Man* with *Millennium People* and on the cover [which features the Millennium Wheel]? I've always thought that Harry Lime's famous lines about 500 years of democracy and peace in Switzerland producing the cuckoo clock were very Ballardian. Did you do that deliberately?

BALLARD: Oh God! I didn't actually. I could have brought that in – yes! I wasn't thinking of that actually, but I could have been.

HALL: Are there any films based on your novels or short stories in development at the moment?

BALLARD: There are a lot in development. *Super-Cannes* and *Cocaine Nights* have had scripts written for them by Paul Mayersberg, the guy who did *The Man Who Fell to Earth* and this new Mike Hodges film, the follow-up to *Croupier*. And I hope Jeremy Thomas can get going with Vincenzo Natali, whose film *Cypher* has just opened here – he's got the rights to *High-Rise*, has big plans. And I've heard that H2O films in LA have supposedly got Samuel Jackson for *Running Wild*, a novella of mine.

[We are interrupted by a call from the *Time Out* photographer, who appears a minute later]

BALLARD: Street photos are so much more interesting. My God, all that equipment! Fuck! Come on, smash and grab . . . Ten to fifteen minutes. I think outside is best.

HALL: I presume you know this hotel pretty well . . .

BALLARD: I used to come here a lot because there was a Japanese restaurant called the Hiroku for many years. I used to park in the basement garage and as you climb the steps up into the lobby, into this area round the corner, I often used to say to Claire, 'It would be impossible if you didn't know which city you were in to identify your location' because of all these Japanese tourists. People from all over the world would come here, Americans, you name it. Genuinely international – it's quite extraordinary.

HALL: Do you still have the metallic palm tree in your study [as seen in *RE/Search 8/9: J.G. Ballard*]?

BALLARD: I think the metallic palm tree is in my bedroom now – ha ha! They help me to dream.

HALL: Is London holding its breath for a terrorist attack?

BALLARD: Yes, I do feel that. I think that's very true. It's worrying. I worry for my daughters and my four grandchildren as well as friends and so on, because there's so little we could do about it. I mean, the IRA proved that over the years. That's why Blair's decision to take us into war may be a costly blunder, costly in human lives – he's helped to destabilise the UN, he's split us away from our partners in Europe, he's helped to alienate the Arab world and the Muslim world and beyond. It was a bizarre thing to do. It looks like they have achieved the very instability and breeding ground for terrorism that they were supposed to eliminate. Quite incredible. September 11 was obviously deeply unsettling – these terrorists are not illiterate gunmen squatting in a hillside in Afghanistan with a rusty Kalashnikov – they were highly educated, middle-class architects and engineers, mostly Saudis, who were drinking coffee in shopping malls in Hamburg and north London and, even more bizarrely, travelling to take their flying lessons in the country they were going to attack – it's quite incredible.

My book doesn't take in September 11 or the Iraq war or anything like that – international terrorism. I'm more concerned with the home-grown variety – trying to get to grips with these very strange cases that have been going on . . . The University of Texas library tower massacre of the 1960s where some disaffected youth climbed to the top of the library tower in Austin, Texas and started shooting at random at people below. And, since then, there have been these mysterious, random attacks by people, primarily in America. There was a guy who walked into a McDonald's in San Diego and started to fire at random. We had Hungerford: Michael Ryan got up one morning and killed about fifteen people, including his own mother. Motiveless. Absolutely motiveless murder as far as we can see. Even the Dunblane killing, the tragic killing of those small children, had no motive. Hamilton supposedly resented some decision by the local authority to ban him from leading a scout group or whatever. But that's a pretty tenuous explanation. Events like the Jill Dando murder . . . I never mentioned Jill Dando [in *Millennium People*] . . . What all these murders have in common is that they appear to be meaningless – there are no motives.

HALL: She wasn't even a celebrity.

BALLARD: Not even a celebrity – right! When she was killed, I'd never really heard of her. I never watch morning or afternoon television and there's a huge army of speakers and presenters and chat show hosts that operate only during the early daylight hours before darkness falls. But these are utterly meaningless murders. This is what *Millennium People* is about – it may be the fact that they are meaningless that is their great appeal, as one of my characters, Richard Gould, says. And that's a danger. There's a danger that protest movements similar to the one I describe here may reach a point of desperation which you see in the animal rights protest movement of the last ten years. People who will give their own lives to protect laboratory animals from suffering are nonetheless prepared to kill lab workers and scientists in pursuit of that end – putting bombs under cars, etc. There's a kind of desperation where meaningless acts by virtue of their lack of meaning have a sort of desperate purpose – and that's worrying.

It's part of the suburbanisation of the planet – living out in Shepperton gives me a close-up view of the real England. That's the real England – the M25, the world of business parks and industrial estates and executive housing, sports clubs and marinas, cineplexes, CCTV, car-rental forecourts. That's England. To his credit, I think Tony Blair realises that. Most British writers suffer from the handicap that they live in inner London, and they subscribe to a kind of traditional view of what England is. They think it's somewhere between Bloomsbury and Muswell Hill, that England is still the England of heritage London, that it involves the heritage sites like St Paul's and the Tower of London, and the Houses of Parliament and Bloomsbury, which is another heritage site, all held together by a dinner-party culture. But that isn't the real England – the real England doesn't go to dinner parties, it's living out in Staines and Slough on brand-new executive estates. That's where boredom comes in – a paralysing conformity and boredom that can only be relieved by a violent act, by taking your mail-order Kalashnikov into the nearest supermarket and letting rip. That's not far fetched.

HALL: I see that there's a BBC4 season dedicated to you coming up.

BALLARD: Which will be watched by an audience of seven . . .

HALL: Seven very important people . . .

BALLARD: Seven important people, yes, of course!

HALL: Do you feel neglected as a writer, because of your relative lack of awards and so on? Or do you concur with Will Self that only pets win prizes?

BALLARD: I don't feel neglected at all. My novels and short stories have been published all over the world. Lucky to have a huge success with *Empire of the Sun*, and these recent novels have done rather well sales wise. Most of my stuff is still in print, which is saying something these days, I can tell you. Prizes tend to be rather conservative – they don't like mavericks. Burroughs and Genet would never have won the Nobel Prize.

HALL: At *Icon*, the architecture magazine I write for, they've been running a lot of stuff about how to improve the road network.

BALLARD: I'm glad to hear it!

HALL: They've recently run a piece about potential automated systems for driving. In the future will we be considered insane driving our non-automated cars?

BALLARD: Probably the case. On the whole, I'm very pro-car. The anti-car movement of recent years strikes me as deeply sinister. There's something totalitarian about Livingstone and all these Orwellian cameras. People aren't protesting – quite incredible. What we need isn't fewer cars, but more roads. London is a low-rise city of vast area rather like Los Angeles – it's about the same size. LA built the freeway system, and that's what we need – a freeway system all over London – roads up in the air, carrying people free of the ground so that the ground is left for local traffic as it is in LA for the most part.

2004: Jeannette Baxter. Reading the Signs

Originally published in *Pre-Text*, Volume 9, 2004, and in the *Guardian*, 22 June 2004 (retitled 'Age of Unreason')

With the publication of *Millennium People*, Ballard shifted his focus in his 'crime' novels from the British expatriate enclaves of southern Europe to middle-class revolt fomented in the high-security gated communities of central London. Jeannette Baxter, who has edited two academic collections of essays on Ballard, and who in 2009 would publish her academic study *J.G. Ballard's Surrealist Imagination*, emphasises in this interview the influence of the surrealists upon Ballard, clearly linking his revolutionary imaginings with the politically transformative claims made both for and by the surrealists.

In a previous interview in 1984, Ballard said that: 'The world economic systems are so interlocked that no radical, revolutionary change can be born any more, as it was in the past. It may be only from aesthetic changes of one sort or another that one can expect a radical shift in the people's consciousness.' Twenty years later, in this interview, he repeats that assertion, but it takes on a sinister hue as he suggests that the aesthetic changes occurring in twenty-first-century Britain are merely the precondition of, and prelude to, the appearance of an opportunist politician – or perhaps a media 'messiah', as in *Kingdom Come* – equipped with the potential to encourage us towards self-defeating, transgressive 'extreme possibilities'. [DOH]

BAXTER: You admit to being more of a voracious consumer of visual texts than literary ones. When did your interest in the visual arts begin and to what extent did this impress upon the trajectory of your writing? What's your impression of the contemporary arts scene?

BALLARD: It began soon after I came to England, in the late 1940s, while I was still at school. There were no museums or galleries in Shanghai, but I was very keen on art – I was always sketching and copying, and sometimes I think that my whole career as a writer has been the substitute work of an unfulfilled painter.

In the late 1940s in England a certain controversy still lingered over Picasso, Braque, Matisse, while the surrealists were utterly beyond the critical pale. The surrealists were a revelation, though reproductions of Chirico, Dali, Ernst were hard to come by and tended to be found in psychiatric textbooks. I devoured them. The surrealists, and the modern movement in painting as a whole, seemed to offer a key to the strange post-war world with its threat of nuclear war. The dislocations and ambiguities, in cubism and abstract art as well as the surrealists, reminded me of my childhood in Shanghai.

I read a great deal too in the late 1940s, but from the international menu (Freud, Kafka, Camus, Orwell, Aldous Huxley) rather than the English one. But there was a defeatist strain in the modern novel (which quite appealed to me as a moody sixteen-year-old). A huge internal migration had taken place from Joyce onwards, and there was something airless about *Ulysses*. By contrast, the great modern painters, from Picasso to Francis Bacon, were eager to wrestle with the world, like the brutal lovers on one of Bacon's couches. There was a reek of semen that quickened the blood.

I don't think any particular painters have inspired me, except in a general sense. It was more a matter of corroboration. The visual arts, from Manet onwards, seemed far more open to change and experiment than the novel, though that's only partly the fault of the writers. There's something about the novel that resists innovation. In the late 1940s (and for decades later) I was desperate for change. England, Cambridge, the professional middle class needed to be laid on the analyst's couch.

Today's art scene? Very difficult to judge, since celebrity and the media presence of the artists are inextricably linked with their work. The great artists of the past century tended to become famous in the later stages of their careers, whereas today fame is built into the artists' work from the start, as in the cases of Emin and Hirst.

There's a logic today that places a greater value on celebrity the less it is accompanied by actual achievement. I don't think it's possible to touch people's imagination today by aesthetic means. Emin's bed, Hirst's sheep, the Chapmans' defaced Goyas are psychological provocations, mental tests where the aesthetic elements are no more than a framing device.

It's interesting that this should be the case. I assume it is because our environment today, by and large a media landscape, is oversaturated by aestheticising elements (TV ads, packaging, design and presentation, styling and so on) but impoverished and numbed as far as its psychological depth is concerned.

Artists (though sadly not writers) tend to move to where the battle is joined most fiercely. Everything in today's world is stylised and packaged, and Emin and Hirst are trying to say, this is a bed, this is death, this is a body. They are trying to redefine the basic elements of reality, to recapture them from the admen who have hijacked our world.

Emin's beautiful body is her one great idea, but I suspect that she is rather prudish, which means that there are limits to the use she can make of her body and its rackety past. Meanwhile, too much is made of conceptual art – putting it crudely, someone has been shitting in Duchamp's urinal, and there is an urgent need for a strong dose of critical Parazone.

BAXTER: In *Millennium People*, you make the point that the middle-class revolution in Chelsea Marina will become part of the 'folkloric calendar . . . to be celebrated along with the last night of the Proms and the Wimbledon tennis fortnight'. If revolution is inevitably repackaged, then where does it leave us? Can art ever be a vehicle for political change?

BALLARD: The revolutions that are repackaged tend to be pseudo-revolutions, or those that were media events in the first place. The destruction of the World Trade Center on 9/11 has not yet been repackaged into something with more consumer appeal, I notice. Another revolutionary event, the assassination of JFK, was rapidly defused by the intense media coverage, the endless replaying of the Zapruder film, and the vast proliferation of conspiracy theories. But Kennedy was himself largely a media construct, with an emotional appeal that was as calculated as any advertising campaign. His life and death were both complete fictions, or very nearly. A real revolution, as 9/11 was in its way, will always come out of some unexpected corner of the sky.

The point about the middle-class revolution in *Millennium People* is that it was pointless, that it failed. For all their efforts to throw off their chains, the revolution achieved nothing, and the rebels returned to Chelsea Marina, resuming their former lives, even more docile than before. What I'm arguing in *MP* is that in our totally pacified world the only acts that will have any significance at all will be acts of meaningless violence. Already we have seen signs of this – random shootings, the lack of motive for Jill Dando's murder, suicide bombings that achieve nothing, as in Israel. As *MP* tries to show, even a political revolution may be pointless. All this, it seems to me, means that the main danger in the future will not be from terrorist acts that advance a cause, however wrong headed, but from terrorist acts without any cause at all. Dr Gould in *MP* articulates all this more fluently than I can. I agree with him.

Can art be a vehicle for political change? Yes, I assume that a large part of Blair's appeal (like Kennedy's) is aesthetic, just as a large part of the Nazi appeal lay in its triumph-of-the-will aesthetic. I suspect that many of the great cultural shifts that prepare the way for political change are largely aesthetic. A Buick radiator grille is as much a political statement as a Rolls-Royce radiator grille, one enshrining a machine aesthetic driven by a populist optimism, the other enshrining a hierarchical and exclusive social order. The ocean liner art deco of the 1930s, used to sell everything from beach holidays to vacuum cleaners, may have helped the 1945 British electorate to vote out the Tories.

BAXTER: The majority of your novels can be read as provocative celebrations of the transformative and transgressive powers of the imagination. In *Millennium People*, however, the imagination is spectacularly lacking. Your cosy phrase 'the upholstered apocalypse' gestures, rather worryingly, towards an imaginative and critical impasse of sorts, doesn't it? Is this decay in the life of the mind a terminal state of affairs?

BALLARD: Nothing is ever terminal, thank God. As we hesitate, the road unrolls itself, dividing and turning. But there is something deeply suffocating about life today in the prosperous West. Bourgeoisification, the suburbanisation of the soul, proceeds at an unnerving pace. Tyranny becomes docile and subservient, and a soft totalitarianism prevails, as obsequious as a wine waiter. Nothing is allowed to distress and unsettle us. The politics of the playgroup rules us all.

The chief role of the universities is to prolong adolescence into middle age, at which point early retirement ensures that we lack the means or the will to enforce significant change. When Markham (not JGB) uses the phrase 'upholstered apocalypse' he reveals that he knows what is really going on in Chelsea Marina. That is why he is drawn to Gould, who offers a desperate escape.

My real fear is that boredom and inertia may lead people to follow a deranged leader with far fewer moral scruples than Richard Gould, that we will put on jackboots and black uniforms and the aspect of the killer simply to relieve the boredom. A vicious and genuinely mindless neo-fascism, a skilfully aestheticised racism, might be the first consequence of globalisation, when Classic Coke and California Merlot are the only drinks on the menu. At times I look around the executive housing estates of the Thames Valley and feel that it is already here, quietly waiting its day, and largely unknown to itself.

BAXTER: Am I right in thinking that one critique which your latest novel throws up is that, in the glare of the consumerist spectacle, we have lost all sense of critical distance to the realities of capitalism and globalisation? I'm thinking specifically here of the reality of terrorism. John Gray propounds a similar thesis in *Straw Dogs* (your chosen book of the year for 2003) when he suggests that al-Qaeda is 'a byproduct of globalisation, it successfully privatised terror and projected it worldwide'. What's your feeling on this?

BALLARD: I agree with John Gray, and was very impressed by both *Straw Dogs* and his al-Qaeda book. What is so disturbing about the 9/11 hijackers is that they had not spent the previous years squatting in the dust on some Afghan hillside with a rusty Kalashnikov. These were highly educated engineers and architects. There was certainly something very modern about their chosen method of attack, from the flying school lessons, hours on the flight simulator, the use of hijacked airliners and so on. The reaction they provoked, a huge paranoid spasm that led to the Iraq war and the rise of the neo-cons, would have delighted them.

BAXTER: The BBC comes under intense scrutiny in your latest novel. The media and the government, you suggest, are conspiring bedfellows (politics is conducted as a branch of advertising) which disseminate certain knowledges and selected truths. Your critique of the fabrication of historical reality through political spin has particular resonance as we await the outcome of the Hutton Inquiry. Do you anticipate that the Hutton report will initiate any serious moves towards curbing the media-political machine? Or do we run the risk of placing too much faith in a legal narrative the likes of which we've seen before – a 'sexed-down' version of the *Warren Commission Report*?

BALLARD: At the time I write this,[2] 25 January, I can only guess at the Hutton report, but I'm sure there will be no threat to the political status quo, certainly not from a judge who has spent his career serving the state (and in Northern Ireland). I'm sure that knuckles will be rapped, the BBC and MoD admonished, suggestions made for a 'tightening-up' of chains of command, etc.

But nothing will change. The links between the media and politics are now hard-wired into the national sensorium. We couldn't behave in any other way if we wanted to. Incidentally, I am not hostile to the BBC, or to the Tate Gallery (my daughters, one of whom went to UEA, worked for them for many years). The BBC helped to shape our national culture, and may well be the greatest source of education and enlightenment the world has ever known, with the possible exception of the Roman Catholic church, for all the latter's failings. But social and political change of a radical kind are now virtually impossible here.

BAXTER: Your latest cluster of novels tests the controversial theory that transgression and murder are legitimate correctives to social inertia. If we are at once disquieted yet invigorated by acts of violence and resistance, then what implications does this lack of moral unity have for the reader?

BALLARD: The notions about the benefits of transgression in my last three novels are not ones I want to see fulfilled. Rather, they are extreme possibilities that may be forced into reality by the suffocating pressures of the conformist world we inhabit. Boredom and a deadening sense of total pointlessness seem to drive a lot of meaningless crimes, from the Hungerford and Columbine shootings to the Dando murder, and there have been dozens of similar crimes in the US and elsewhere over the past thirty years.

These meaningless crimes are much more difficult to explain than the 9/11 attacks, and say far more about the troubled state of the Western psyche. My novels offer an extreme hypothesis which future events may disprove – or confirm. They're in the nature of long-range weather forecasts. As I've often said, someone who puts up a road sign saying

---

2   The interview was conducted by fax.

'dangerous bends ahead' is not inciting drivers to speed up, though I hope that my fiction is sufficiently ambiguous to make the accelerator seem strangely attractive. Human beings have an extraordinary instinct for self-destruction, and this ought to be out in the open where we can see it. We are not moral creatures, except for reasons of mutual advantage, sad to say . . .

BAXTER: Little comment is made on the varying textures of humour in your work yet your novels are littered with jokes – from the deadpan confrontations of *The Atrocity Exhibition* and *Crash* to the wry observations of *Millennium People*. Why is humour important to you? And why do some readers find it so uncomfortable to laugh at your work?

BALLARD: I'm delighted you think that. People, particularly over-moralistic Americans, have often seen me as a pessimist and humourless to boot, yet I think I have an almost maniacal sense of humour. The problem is that it's rather deadpan. Readers say that *Millennium People* made them laugh aloud, which is wonderful news, but then there is something inherently funny about the idea of a middle-class revolution. But perhaps that in itself is a sign of how brainwashed the middle classes are. The very idea that we could rebel seems preposterous.

BAXTER: You recently turned down a CBE. Is this a move, in part, to retain your integrity as an artist?

BALLARD: No. I just don't want anything to do with all that nonsense, a Ruritanian charade that helps to prop up our top-heavy monarchy.

BAXTER: In your introduction to *Crash* you diagnosed 'the death of affect' as the culminating disease of the twentieth century. What's your prognosis for the twenty-first century?

BALLARD: A century is a long time. Twenty years ago no one could have imagined the effects the internet would have – entire relationships flourish, friendships prosper on the email screen, there's a vast new intimacy and accidental poetry (from the osprey-tracking site to tours round old nuclear silos and the extraordinary aerial trip down the California coastline and a thousand others), not to mention the weirdest porn. The entire human experience seems to unveil itself like the surface of a new planet.

Whether the internet or any other technological marvel can halt the slide into boredom and conformism I seriously doubt. I suspect that (as I pointed out in *Super-Cannes*) the human race will inevitably move like a sleepwalker towards that vast resource it has hesitated to tap – its own psychopathy. This adventure playground of the soul is waiting for us with its gates wide open, and admission is free.

In short, an elective psychopathy will come to our aid (as it has done many times in the past) – Nazi Germany, Stalinist Russia, all those willed nightmares that make up much of human history. As Wilder Penrose points out in *Super-Cannes*, the future will be a huge Darwinian struggle between competing psychopathies. Along with our passivity, we're entering a profoundly masochistic phase – everyone is a victim these days, of parents, doctors, pharmaceutical companies, even love itself. And how much we enjoy it. Our happiest moments are spent trying to think up new varieties of victimhood . . .

2006: Toby Litt. 'Dangerous bends ahead. Slow down': J.G. Ballard on *Kingdom Come*

This version is previously unpublished, although excerpts first appeared in *Waterstone's Book Quarterly*, 7 September 2006

Like Will Self and Iain Sinclair, novelist Toby Litt often takes the opportunity to champion Ballard's work in his journalism and reviews. In a 2007 interview, Litt said that because *Crash* had so inspired his own writing, he put it in the acknowledgements to his novel *Corpsing* 'because I felt the influence should be openly acknowledged'. In 2009 he declared: 'When I read J.G. Ballard, I go into a particular kind of trance.' In this interview, conducted at Shepperton on 10 July 2006, Ballard discusses the role of the middle classes in his final novel *Kingdom Come* and in its predecessor, *Millennium People*. He also explores the latent fascist tendencies in consumerism and the concomitant death of religion, and his feelings about his father, which fed into the creation of *Kingdom Come*. [SS]

LITT: I'm here to talk to you about *Kingdom Come*. I enjoyed the book very much. I reviewed *Millennium People*, and this seems a less humorous book.

BALLARD: A lot of people found that very funny, and I'm glad. Humour is something I've always been accused of lacking. There's a lot of humour in my novels and short stories, but it's of a rather deadpan kind.

415

LITT: I don't think it's lacking in anything you've written. But I did find that *Millennium People* took a slightly more slapstick approach. Whereas in *Kingdom Come* it's slightly more sombre but also more directly political. Was that the aim of the book?

BALLARD: I think that's right. The thing about *Millennium People* is that there's something inherently comical about the middle classes claiming to be the new exploited proletariat. I mean, one can't help but laugh at the absurdity of the notion. The fact that we laugh is a measure of the degree, perhaps, to which the middle classes have been conned into thinking that they represent the upper echelons of society, which in fact they don't any longer.

LITT: If with, say, *Millennium People*, it's a ridiculous idea that the bourgeoisie should see themselves as revolutionary, so in *Kingdom Come* we have the – not really the bourgeoisie – the slightly lower middle class seeing themselves becoming fascist.

BALLARD: The new middle class of the motorway towns.

LITT: Why is that less ridiculous?

BALLARD: I think it's less ridiculous because we see uneasy, sort of, tremors fluttering all those St George's flags. I mean, had you come here a week ago, every bloody shop in Shepperton had a large St George's flag. Many of the houses around here had flags fluttering. Every other car had more than one flag. You know, you can't help but think the excitement over the World Cup was about more than mere sport, I feel. I don't say that it's the first sign of a fascist takeover, but . . .

LITT: In the RE/Search book, *Conversations*, that's just come out, you say: 'Consumer society is a collaborative soft tyranny which most people are happy with. Others like me would call it the new Dark Age!' And in *Kingdom Come* you have the Dr Maxted character say: 'The danger is that consumerism will need something close to fascism in order to keep growing'. And slightly later: 'The consumer society is a kind of soft police state'. So, he's not exactly quoting you, but he's you speaking through a character. When you say 'fascism' in the novel, one of the issues is that the führer doesn't really want to be the führer. Is that a defining characteristic of fascism, that it needs

416

the leader, and that that's the only thing missing at the moment for England?

BALLARD: I think fascism does need a leader. But the leader may take an unexpected form. And I suggest in the book that our equivalent of the ranting führer is the cable channel chat show host. The thing about führers and messiahs is that they always come out of the least expected places – deserts, usually. But of course the shopping malls and retail parks in England in 2006 are a desert by any yardstick you care to apply. I mean, consumerism itself is a vast desert. A desert without a single oasis as far as I can see. But the point one of the characters makes, several times, is that we don't need a ranting, jackbooted messiah. It's almost a fascism lite – horrible phrase, but you know what I mean. But the underlying motivation is probably the same.

I mean, one sees what people are looking for is their own psychopathology. They're looking for madness as a way out. They're bored, and they want to start breaking the furniture. They are, you know, the tribe of chimpanzees who are tired of chewing twigs and decide to go on a hunting party. And to do so they first work themselves up into a blood-curdling state of rage, and then they go and tear a lot of monkeys limb from limb. And I'm suggesting a similar sort of mechanism may have been at work in the fascist Germany of the 1930s. No explanations I've seen are ever convincing of why cultivated and intelligent people like the Germans and Italians should plunge into this insane worldview. And that's the sort of comparable thing, in a lower note – the other end of the piano – that might take place here.

LITT: You have a clinical background in understanding insanity or psychopathology – or, at least, more than the layman does. But when you say 'mad' or 'insane' you don't really diagnose very often. You wouldn't say that one of your characters was paranoid schizophrenic, or, more recently, bipolar. You say they're 'mad' or 'insane'. Why is that?

BALLARD: Well, firstly, I'm not a psychiatrist. And secondly, I prefer to leave it open. Because these psychiatric definitions seem to shift around. I mean, they take many forms, whereas we all know what 'mad' or 'insane' means. I mean, one look at Hitler and his henchmen – one look at the Pol Pot brigade, one look into Stalin's eyes – and you can see something very dangerous is going on. The normal constraints of civic feeling have no role to play. These people were trading on their own psychopathology. Somewhere in his diaries, Goebbels more or less admits it. He says that he and the Nazi leaders had merely done in reality what Dostoyevsky had done in the novel. So, anyway, we all know what madness is.

A lot of psychiatric categories are defined by patients who present themselves to psychiatrists in institutions, and these are people who may not be self-maintaining in the community at large, who are actually ripe for sectioning. But the sort of people that I'm talking about are not: Hitler, for example, and the Nazis; Mussolini; even Stalin and his henchmen; Mao and his colleagues. But we know that most of them were completely mad by the larger standards that the lay public applied. I'm not making any clinical diagnoses. That would rapidly lead me into trouble.

LITT: But it leaves it open, in a way. People could write about the uses of 'mad' in *Hamlet* or *Macbeth*, where it could at one point mean 'very, very angry' or 'unable to control oneself', and at another something closer to 'clinically insane' or 'schizophrenic'. But are you splitting a sort of political madness – the madness of the powerful from the madness of the powerless. Because if someone is just on the street shouting and hearing voices, that's a different thing.

BALLARD: Well, he's going to be sectioned fairly soon. Whereas if someone stands on the street saying it's all the fault of the Muslims or the Jews or whatever, he probably won't be. I mean, some new bit of legislation might lead him to the nearest magistrates' court. But in general, one can hold extremely deranged ideas – someone like Le Pen, I think, does – without the men in white coats arriving on the scene.

LITT: Have you ever felt that your own sanity was threatened? Not that you were coming close to holding those views, but that you were close to losing your rational mind?

BALLARD: No, I never have, actually. Maybe it's lucky I became a writer.

LITT: Have people thought that of you?

BALLARD: Well, I think some people have. Particularly in respect to books like *Crash*. That's such an obvious one. I don't think the madness thing is a big issue as far as *Kingdom Come* is concerned, because this is a warning. I'm trying to say: 'Dangerous bends ahead. Slow down'. The point is that what I see as threatening about the all-pervasive and all-powerful consumer society is that it's not any specific individual who is responsible for anything nasty that may happen in the future. This is a collective enterprise. All of us who are members of consumer society; all of us are responsible, in a way. I think that these are sort of almost seismic movements that drift through the collective psyche and which facilitate the emergence of ultra-right-wing groups like the Nazis and the fascists in Italy. Or even the communist regime under Stalin. There you have extremely threatening political organisations which come to power with the complicity – that's the extraordinary thing – of the populations they rule.

People still think that Hitler and his henchmen imposed Nazi Germany on the German people. I don't believe they did for a moment. All the eyewitnesses at the time suggest that Hitler and the Nazi leaders were extremely popular. Once they'd got into the saddle they were able to manipulate radio and the mass media, film and the like, and the Germans, you know: unemployment started coming down, people prospered, and they had certainty in their lives for the first time, and the unpleasant undercurrent, involving killing large numbers of Jews and Slavs and Russians and God knows what else – that was sort of played down. The Germans went along with the regime to the end. There was no serious attempt, as far as I can make out, to reject the regime. And the same thing was true in Stalin's Russia. I think it may be that in the future we'll be dominated by huge masochistic systems. Soviet Russia was an example of this. I mean, people tolerated their own abuse because for some reason they wanted to be abused. Someone says in this book that the future is a system of huge competing psychopathologies. I'd say that was true of the twentieth century. It sort of sums it up, in a way. So I'm not talking about an individual impetus that will drive the engine. This engine has been assembled, and will be started by everyone probably working unconsciously.

LITT: I went to a reading recently by American writer George Saunders, and someone asked him from the audience – and it's a fairly bland way of putting it – 'Are you an anti-capitalist?' So, are you an anti-capitalist?

BALLARD: No. Not really. I mean, I was a great supporter of Margaret Thatcher. I thought economic freedom was the one thing this country desperately needed. I think her economic policies were right, almost to the end. I think her social policies got out of hand, and she paid the price. I rather supported Tony Blair in his early days. I thought he was a con from the word go. I think I wrote to that effect in the *Statesman*. I think we wanted to be conned. We wanted this nice young man with his people-carrier and his suburban wife and kids. We wanted him. Out on the M25 – that's where I live – I could see that people wanted the new suburbia. And Blair promised a sort of blandness. He just played mood music, but we like mood music.

LITT: A lot of your books open up what a Shakespearean critic might call 'carnival', where everyone goes into the forest and everyone goes mad for a bit, but they tend to zip it back up at the end.

BALLARD: As human beings tend to do.

LITT: You don't see things as getting exponentially worse?

BALLARD: No, I don't. They might get worse for extended periods. The point is that all societies base civic order on a trade-off between various dominant forces, which may take many different forms. In the old days, we had monarchy, we had Parliament – the world of Westminster politics – we had the armed forces, which played a big role in keeping the British Empire together, we had the Church of England and we had the capitalist system insofar as it flourished in a real way post-1945; it certainly did in the period previous to that, from the Industrial Revolution onwards. The point is that all these powers in the land played off against each other. But they kept the show on the road. What has happened now, as I try to explain in the book, is that almost every one of these former powers in the land has been discredited. The monarchy inspires no loyalty, except for a very small number of people. I don't know if you're old enough to remember people lining the docks at Plymouth, or somewhere, as our boys, the navy, sailed off for the Falklands. That war was an election campaign, as I imagine Thatcher realised at the time. She tapped into a powerful nationalist spirit. We wanted our boys to come back safely. We wanted them to win.

I know there's nothing quite comparable in Iraq and Afghanistan, but you can't feel any pride in what our soldiers are doing out there. That's why the bereaved relatives are so indignant. Their sons and husbands are dying for nothing – dying for some PR whim of Tony Blair. No pride in the armed forces. No pride in the monarchy. And politics totally discredited. I mean, people aren't that outraged by Tony Blair lying to get us into the second Gulf War. If we're not outraged by that, why should we be outraged by John Prescott's far less grievous sins? The monarchy is just a huge dysfunctional family. God knows whether Charles will rise to the challenge when his mother goes. I've no idea. He doesn't show many signs of realising the damage he's done. That just leaves the only steady ingredient, the only steady element in our lives, the only one that offers hope and the probability of a better world, if we do what the advertisements say: consumerism. That has finite goals and finite means for achieving those goals: 'Buy this new microwave and you will cook delicious suppers and your husband will love you all the more'. And you'll probably find it's true. I mean, most of our lives are dedicated to consumerism in one form or another, and it seems to work.

What I'm saying is that, left on its own, without the constraints of the other great former civic powers, it could get out of hand. Because consumerism makes inherent demands, it has inherent needs, which can only be satisfied by pressing the accelerator down a little harder, moving a little faster, upping all the antes. In order to keep spending and keep believing, we need to move into the area of the psychopathic. That's the fear. You see it with the World Cup. Maybe I'm just old, but it does seem to me all a bit over the top. 'What's next?' – that's what I'm asking. I don't think there's a little group – Mohammed Atta and his boys sitting in a Hamburg shopping mall – thinking, 'This is our chance, chaps. We hijack some airliners.' I don't think there is. I think the need comes from within us all. We want more exciting lives. There are limits to the number of TV sets you can have at home. There are limits to the number of cars you can own. Once you've got all those things, what happens next?

LITT: So, in the book, the reader reads *Kingdom Come*, the title, and will have associations of Anglican religion and the King James Bible . . .

BALLARD: I quote from the Lord's Prayer.

LITT: And then the opening paragraph: 'The suburbs dream of violence, asleep in their drowsy villas, sheltered by benevolent shopping malls, they wait patiently for the nightmares which will wake them into a more passionate world'. So 'passionate' suggests the Passion, the Passion of Christ. So the people would want something verging on the religious.

And, towards the end of the book, they are making shrines in the Metro-Centre [shopping mall]. But the book isn't about religion. More central is soft fascism and sport.

BALLARD: I don't feel religion could act as the catalyst. Could it become the end in itself? Could we get a religious response? It's hard to imagine because I think we're a secular society. We've fallen out of love with the notion of the supernatural. In fact, somebody says [in *Kingdom Come*], the two sickest societies are the two most religious societies, America and the Middle East. And they're getting sicker. Now, it's very worrying. You see in America another direction being taken, towards a sort of religious fundamentalism. So that could easily swing back into some sort of fascism. I think basically America is too corrupt, in a sense. I mean, it's a very corrupt place. You know, it is obsessed with the almighty dollar. It's the only thing that makes sense of American lives, really.

Why are we so interested in sport? It's a very puzzling question. I don't ask it in the book because you can't squeeze everything in. But why are we so obsessed with sport? Particularly as the sports we're most obsessed by, we're not good at. You know, we're no damn good at football. There's this huge myth that Beckham and his boys are going to win the World Cup. Everybody knows they're not going to win. Maybe they know and don't care, they just want the feeling that he might win. Likewise, you know, we're not much good at cricket. We're no damn good! I don't want to sound too much the amateur psychiatrist; I try to steer away from that. But it does make you think, you know, what the heck is going on in these people's lives? Something strange . . .

But the appeal of sport, you see, in this book, of course, is that it does facilitate a lot of quasi-fascist activity. The sense of, you know, 'we're all marching together'. The arms and legs swinging like windmills. The health thing, a very important part of the whole Nazi creed. But also the sense of constant expectation, of challenge, that we're all in this together, we've got to fight the enemy, et cetera, et cetera. All of this is sort of tied in to the consumerist thing. All these loyalty cards and cable channel programmes and the whole stadium lights blazing. I chose that route, which I think is truer to this country.

LITT: But if someone were to read your book, and take it as a warning, and they were living somewhere up or down this street . . . What might you want them to change in their behaviour, in their life?

BALLARD: Well, nothing. I would not ask the people of Shepperton to change a thing, because they're not typical of it. I wanted somewhere that didn't really exist. If Brooklands [the fictional town in *Kingdom Come*] is anywhere, it's somewhere like Kingston. It's a ghastly place. I hate Kingston. It represents the absolute nadir of English consumer and suburban life. It is just one vast mall. Put a dome over it and you would have the Metro-Centre. Or somewhere like Staines, also pretty ghastly.

What would I say to these people there? Quite a question, because the obvious answer is: 'Stop buying things'. You know, the whole economy is going to collapse. This is part of the problem, of course. The engine is now revving so fast that you can't apply the brakes. You'd just tear off the brake drums and hurl the whole vehicle into the ditch.

LITT: Do you think you've changed? Do you think if the author of *Crash*, yourself at that age, were sitting next to you, you would disagree on this point? That he would be saying, 'It's false to assert that there can be any slowing down. Therefore the only thing is to speed up until you miss the bend.'

BALLARD: I've got a feeling that, were the author of *Crash*, thirty-five years ago, to tackle this subject, I don't think he would necessarily approach it in a different way. I think I would write the same book, even though I'm much older. It's hard to know. The thing is, I am not offering a grand answer to all societies' problems. I leave that to others. I'm issuing warnings. And I can't anticipate how people will respond. They may well say, 'Oh, this consumerism and all this football – it's driving us crazy. Let's turn to something else, you know. Let's teach ourselves to play the piano and take up glass-blowing and look for less drama in our lives rather than more.' It's possible.

You know, war – the inter-European wars, and the wars associated with maintaining empires – has always had a sort of moderating effect: 'Right, now, we've survived this terrible encounter, but we've lost all these men, our civilians. We must now calm down for a bit and rebuild and try to find a better world.' We don't have wars any more, in that sense. You could almost say that the Gulf War will be the last war. It's the last roll of the dice by an old style of politician: Blair and Bush, you know, who think they can beat the patriotic drum, and this will rally everyone. Well, people haven't been rallied. And I think that's quite interesting.

LITT: One of the things I find most deeply appealing about your books is your insistence on people's perversity.

BALLARD: I think we're a mix of things, a mix of impulses, you know. We're civilised but we can be very uncivilised. We're governed by reason, obviously, but not all of the time. Much of the time, we're not governed by reason. Much of the time, we exploit that fact. A world entirely governed by reason would be a nightmare. That's one dystopia I would never embark on. You know, I don't think that there's an innate decency about human beings. I don't think there is.

I think there are dangerous things going on. That's basically what I'm saying. Markets are no longer contributing much to social cohesion. This is a dangerous time, because if all we're going to rely on is consumerism, we may play to the worst states in our own make-up. You know, the need for more excitement or thrills. This is an important fact, I think, a daunting fact to face, but we are vastly more tolerant today of – whatever you like to call them – deviant and perverse strains in our make-up than we were, say, fifty years ago. Look at something like the evolution over six or seven years of the *Big Brother* series. It has evolved in an extraordinary way. The opening series, which I watched, actually, out of curiosity, was practically a university department by comparison with today! But now, what is interesting is that all these people have obviously been recruited because they are going to humiliate themselves. But they know that. And we know that. And nobody cares. But this is how people become rich and famous, by humiliating themselves. There's something rather nasty about the way that we are, in a sense, sort of looking through the bars of the old eighteenth-century asylums and jeering at the inmates. It's not much superior to that, now.

Morally, I don't see any difference whatsoever. Because for every sad case paraded on the TV screen for our amusement, there are ten thousand or a hundred thousand sad cases who will never make it to fame and fortune. And yet they cling to this big hope. There's a coarser texture to life today, there's no doubt about it. Self-restraint is not admired. It'll get you nowhere.

LITT: You wrote about the sixties as basically a crisis point – a time when something new happens. And 'new' is a word which comes up a lot in *Kingdom Come*: the idea that something new is happening in the Metro-Centre; a new kind of people. But do you think they are new compared to 1966, say, or 1968, when I was born? Do you think that there is a qualitative difference? That there is an essential difference between this stage of consumerism and that? Or is it merely an acceleration?

BALLARD: You said '66. What happened then?

LITT: Well, I was just picking a point when the sixties had got going. But then I was thinking that if you take the Kennedy assassination as important, then maybe you need some time for the effects to be felt.

BALLARD: There's a kind of appetite for more horrors waiting below the surface. I mean, the response after Di's death . . . Most people agree – I did – that she was wonderful, absolutely wonderful. When she appears, briefly, on the screen today, I think, 'Gosh! She had something, that young woman. There was some sort of magic there.' But at the same time I thought the collective response was bizarrely over the top. It was saying something, I don't know what, but it was saying something loud and clear. You could find a hundred examples.

LITT: You were quite restrained when it came to public comment after that, I seem to remember.

BALLARD: One or two Fleet Streeters rang me up and said, 'Do you feel you've made her death possible?' [Holds up hands to ward off imaginary journalistic onslaught.] Whoa! Slow down! You know: 'The death only makes sense, a true sense, a real sense, a larger sense, if we see it in Ballardian terms . . .' No thanks. No. There's no doubt, I think, that James Dean's death in a Porsche Spyder did help to generate the huge myth which sprang up about him. But then driving fast cars and killing yourself was part of his world. It wasn't part of Diana's world.

LITT: And you couldn't psychopathologise it for her, because she wasn't driving. And she wasn't sexually involved with the person who was driving, as far as we know. It didn't tie in to her story, in that sense. But the reaction of the people to her death was . . .

BALLARD: Bizarre, I thought. I thought it was incredible. I don't know what it said, but I think it shows how bored we are, frankly. I mean, if the Queen were to die the lamentation would fill the land and silence every television set.

LITT: Can I ask about *Kingdom Come*'s main character, Pearson? Because he's more involved in a way with things than some of your previous main characters. Firstly, the scene where he goes to his father's house, and his father is dead so the job of clearing it out has devolved to him – it's much more moving, in a sense, and much more straightforwardly moving, than a scene you would allow other characters to be involved with. They seem very disengaged from their affairs, often; affairs with women, if they're men. But also they tend to go to less emotionally charged places. Were you aware of that? It's quite gentle, really.

BALLARD: I think it probably reflects my rather ambivalent feelings towards my own father, who died in the 1960s, but from whom I was pretty estranged, I think. Something that went back to the war, actually, as I've said. You know, one effect of being interned in a camp for nearly three years with my parents was that estrangement. I never really felt that close to my parents afterwards, because my parents, like all the other adults with children, could not feed me, clothe me, keep me warm, give me any hope for the future – they were often frightened, more frightened than I was. I mean, I didn't know the likely outcome. The Japanese traditionally killed all their prisoners before making a last stand, and they planned to make a last stand at the mouth of the Yangtze. And well-developed decisions had been made, and plans had been laid out for the marching – for emptying all the civilian camps around Shanghai, and marching us all up country out of the way, and getting rid of us. My parents, I think, knew this – this had been talked about – and were obviously worried sick.

But I think one effect of civil war of any kind is that children look to their parents. I see this when watching the news from the Gulf – you see children looking to their parents, sort of, 'Why didn't you stop this? Can't you do anything now?' And if the parents are powerless, and they usually are, civilian parents, they can do nothing. And that's damaging. Very damaging. I came to England in '46 with my mother, went to school here, became a medical student. But by the time I saw my father, it was the early fifties, and I'd made a lot of important decisions in my life. Coping with England for a start. I didn't have any help from him, there. And it was a very strange place. You know, this was a country that had lost the war, in effect, though nobody admitted it. I don't think anybody realised it, you know, just how badly we'd come out of the war. When I saw him in the 1950s, it was too late. I'd made all these deci-sions – to become a doctor or whatever – and as soon as I left school

I knew I wanted to become a writer. These are decisions I never talked over with him.

So the central character, Richard, has never really known his father, which is something he shares with me, for different reasons. That sort of rediscovery of one's parents is something that I went through. And I think it shows through. It's just by a matter of coincidence. It's not central to the book but it drives him, of course. It drives him. Had he known his father well, he'd probably have said, 'Oh God, this ghastly place. I've been here a hundred times. Never liked it. Sad that he should get shot by some lunatic in a shopping mall, but that's that. And now we thankfully leave.' Well, he doesn't. He stays on. Partly because he wants to discover more about his father and more about himself. And so he's helped create, as an advertising man, this vast mall.

LITT: In terms of how you position him as a character, he's implicated, and he supports what's going on. He draws back when it comes to racism. But a lot of the rest of it he still goes along with.

BALLARD: He turns a blind eye to it.

LITT: He's not a drifter, as are some of your other characters. I mean, in film-script terms, he has a very strong motivation that any Hollywood producer would recognise: avenging or discovering the truth about the death of his father. It's a good, solid motive. So he's powered by that, but, as you say, he seems quite unengaged with the morality of what's around him, apart from the racist attacks. That seemed also quite explicit. You're not saying this is something that you could see as morally neutral in any way. It's something that you condemn in the book. But there could be other things that could be seen maybe as quite as bad, in moral terms, in terms of violence or how much they damage people. You've written about them in other books, but they aren't condemned. So, is there something different about racism? Or is it something that you think is a moral absolute?

BALLARD: Well, I don't think any of the narrators or substitutes for myself in other books have shown any tendency to support questionable behaviours, you know.

LITT: But Pearson seems to say that consumerism is OK. But the things that stem from it – and the logic of the sport coming out of that . . .

BALLARD: He's slightly seduced.

LITT: He says, 'I want the elephant. But I don't want the left hind leg.' And that's part of the elephant. It can't walk without it. And the reader knows that. The reader knows that all these things are working together – they have synergy, to create what's going on. So, throughout the book he is not recognising that fact. He's fighting against it.

BALLARD: I think it's clear to the reader that he's a dissatisfied advertising man who had this notion . . . I mean, he anticipates the logic that the psychiatrist, Tony Maxted, unfolds for him later on. He's got this idea, his slogan: 'Mad is Bad. Bad is Good'. He wants to know, 'How do we get people to buy our bloody products? We can't tell them this car is more powerful, this washing-machine washes whiter. They're bored with that.' They need a deeper appeal, an appeal to their darker sides, you see. And he tries to bring this off, but it doesn't work. He loses his job. Then when he gets to Brooklands, he begins to sense that here is a chance, particularly when he meets David Cruise, the chat show host – he realises that this is a wonderful chance to test out his original theory.

And he devises these brief commercials which present Cruise not as a sleek chat show host – you know, traditional afternoon TV – but as a sort of *noir* hero who looks as if he's going to drop dead at any moment. This is a chance to try this out. And there's his father's apparent involvement with these violent sports groups; he doesn't realise at this stage what his father's motives actually were – he thinks his father supported them. He doesn't go along with this National Front stuff, but the fact that his father seemed to be interested almost sanctions him getting involved with the nastier sides of people's characters. So he's seduced by the possibilities – particularly when they seem to work so well. What he hasn't anticipated – and he's constantly being warned by the young woman doctor, by the headmaster, and by Maxted – is that, you know, 'you're playing with fire, you're going to get burned'. These impulses are damn dangerous. Just because we haven't got a strutting führer and a lot of guys in black shirts doesn't mean that the suburban version is going to be any less dangerous. He's warned, but he's seduced by the possibilities of what is a marketing plan. He's using psychopathology as a marketing device. Now, he doesn't have a vast, all-encompassing world-view. He's not St Thomas Aquinas. He's an advertising man who sees a chance. And he learns his lesson the bitter way. At the end he realises, 'What a fool I've been!' So, in a way, an experiment has been carried out on him. He doesn't realise, but he's carrying out an experiment on himself.

LITT: About Shanghai – I've been there two times recently and it's almost completely gone. Trying to find something old there is futile, really. I was led round by a Chinese writer, Chen Danyan, who is a bestselling author there. She writes about old Shanghai in the twenties and thirties. She tried to take me to somewhere old, but we ended up in a Starbucks. Actually, we ended up in a coffee house opposite a Starbucks, because I didn't want to come all that way and end up in a Starbucks. And we were in a road that was meant to be a similar architectural style to old-style Shanghai, and she said, 'Do you see that piece of stone up there? That's original.' That was it. That was all that was left.

BALLARD: Because the Chinese themselves don't have any feeling for the past, curiously. They're the oldest continuously civilised nation on the planet, and yet they're not the least bit interested.

LITT: The thing is, we have cathedrals as our venerable buildings. But if they have a Chan temple, it's made of wood and they rebuild it anyway – they rebuild it every couple of hundred years. So, they have no equivalent. Even the things that were the most venerable . . .

BALLARD: I think the explanation is that the culture of Chinese society is fixed, now, in the kind of role of the family, the role children play with respect to their parents, to elders and betters. Chinese society hasn't changed. Go to a big Chinese restaurant in London. They're usually run by families. I think they don't trust anyone outside the family to handle the cash. You don't get large firms because you reach a size where, inevitably, you've got to bring in an outsider who's going to count the cash. 'Ugh! We know what that leads to.'

But if you go to a big restaurant in London and look at the family running it, although they were probably all born here – and, if not, born in Hong Kong – their lives are no different from the lives they would have had had they been brought up in Shanghai or Hong Kong. You know, it's all absolutely set in the cement under their feet. Whether they'll change a great deal, I don't know. It's very hard to say. I mean, communism was never going to work there. I didn't have to think about it for ten seconds. It's preposterous. Everything is dominated by the family. They can't feel any loyalty to anything outside the family, and it's taken for granted.

LITT: I'm going to stop there.

BALLARD: Thank you.

2006: Simon Sellars. 'Rattling other people's cages'

Originally published on ballardian.com, 29 September 2006

My own interview with Ballard took place just after the publication of *Kingdom Come*. Although I could see the book had flaws (I agree with Iain Sinclair's suggestion that it might have worked better as 'a series of savage essays or presentations'), I responded to the brilliant social critique at its heart. For Ballard, consumerism's interlocking colonisation of demand, supply and desire was so complete, so airtight, that the logical extension was the packaging of violent desire as the latest must-have 'product'. In that sense, I saw *Kingdom Come* as the end point of *Crash*'s themes but with an updated charge, highly relevant to the new terrain of shopping malls as virtual city-states, and, analogously, to the micro-pockets of communities that were fragmenting within nation-states ('micronations', to all intents and purposes), organised around shared psychopathologies and antisocial impulses.

At the time, the Cronulla beach riots were a hot topic in Australian daily life, with their defence of micro-national patches of turf and orgies of flag-waving and ritualistic nationalistic fervour. I was therefore interested in how Ballard might place such events within the framework of *Kingdom Come*. [SS]

SELLARS: I've been keeping up with the *Kingdom Come* reviews: people are criticising you for repeating the template of your last three novels. But it seems to me you're actively parodying your own style.

BALLARD: I think there's an element of that. But I think there always has been in my novels. I can't resist having a dig at myself.

SELLARS: A character describes the narrator, Pearson, as 'beyond psychiatric help'.

BALLARD: Ah yes – that is a deliberate little in-joke for those who are interested. The publisher's reader for *Crash* made that comment years and years ago, so I couldn't resist inserting it. [The reader's verdict: 'This author is beyond psychiatric help. Do not publish'].

SELLARS: Perhaps the most obvious shift in your style occurs in Pearson himself: he's more active in shaping the events around him than equivalent characters in previous books.

BALLARD: The thing is, I wanted the protagonist – the narrator – to be more involved professionally, and emotionally, in the events that are unfurling. If you go back to my previous novels, something like *Super-Cannes*, the narrator of that finds himself in this strange business park in the south of France by chance, really, whereas the narrator in *Kingdom Come* is directly involved. I wanted to show how disaffected and deracinated intellectuals often get drawn into political conspiracies that turn out badly. We have a clear example at the present time with many of the leading American intellectuals who are involved with President Bush and his neo-cons – someone like Fukuyama, although I think he's recanted. These think-tank intellectuals in America provided a lot of the rationale for the whole neo-con response to 9/11. And earlier than that, you see people like Joseph Goebbels – a fully fledged intellectual, without any doubt – becoming the propaganda chief of the Nazi regime. Albert Speer's another one. I wanted to show how rootless intellectuals do get involved in these conspiracies.

And so we have Richard Pearson – this advertising man, who's been trying to liven up the advertising business with a bit of psychopathology and has failed – arriving at this huge shopping mall and seeing a chance to put his theories into practice. He finds David Cruise, a third-rate führer running a cable TV show, and gets to work, not realising quite what he's doing.

SELLARS: The reviews have been mixed.

BALLARD: They haven't been all that great, to be honest. There have been some good ones, but on the whole they've been rather downbeat. And that's something one just has to live with. But also I just get the vague feeling that this is a subject that the sort of people who review books would rather not look at too closely. Perhaps I'm deluding myself there, but after all, *Kingdom Come* is a full-frontal attack on England today. I think in many ways this country has lost its direction, lost its purpose, and there are some very strange things going on under the surface. And that's what I'm writing about – I have been for years.

SELLARS: The book's themes travel beyond England, though.

BALLARD: Well, my feeling about this country – that we have nothing left but consumerism – does, as far as I know, translate to other consumerist societies like America and Japan. My impression is that Australians, however, have got other things to do with their spare time. They're not besotted with shopping, because the country's so large and there are so many opportunities for recreation – that's probably another delusion of mine, I've no idea. But I've been to Canada several times and no one would call Canada a consumerist society, because people have got more things to do – there's more space. The peculiar thing about England is that we're so densely populated. When I say there's nothing to do except go shopping, that's almost the truth. You know, you can't climb into your car and drive off into the wilderness. Shopping is all we have. But I think, translated overseas, the general principle of *Kingdom Come* will hold: there is something about consumerism and late capitalism that is too close for comfort to fascism. There are echoes.

SELLARS: Well, we like to indulge in a little cathartic violence here in Australia, too. I don't know if you heard about the riots on Sydney beaches last year . . .

BALLARD: Oh yes, I did. Rival gangs attacking immigrants.

SELLARS: Yes, surfer gangs versus the Lebanese community. *Kingdom Come* resonated with me because its clockwork mobs were so reminiscent of this incident. Except instead of football, it was organised around surfing – a typical Aussie touch.

BALLARD: I think sport is the key catalyst. England doesn't have a very good soccer team, but we've always had world-class hooligans. And I think the English take a certain pride in that.

SELLARS: Why is that? To compensate for loss of empire?

BALLARD: I'm not sure it has anything to do with that. The British Empire was lost a long time ago, and most British people didn't benefit directly from empire. In fact, there are economic historians who claim we made a loss from the British Empire – that it cost more than we gained from it. Most British people didn't share in the empire at all, and I don't think the loss of all these possessions scattered around the world was a tragedy for the British. It was probably a relief when it collapsed. It's like when you read accounts of the Republican movement in Australia, which has my 100 per cent support, of course . . .

SELLARS: Mine, too.

BALLARD: I can't understand why an English queen is the Australian head of state. It's bizarre. I mean, why not have a Japanese head of state? A Swedish head of state? I can see that there are ties to Britain, and perhaps one shouldn't make light of these things, but most English people wouldn't be in the least bit upset if you decided to have your own head of state and declare Australia a republic. I don't think the end of empire is such a big thing, now. It might have been true thirty or forty years ago, but not now.

SELLARS: Nationalism, though, plays a big part in the events you describe in *Kingdom Come*. Same as with the beach riots: they were propelled by an intense nationalism – republicanism taken to its logical extreme.

BALLARD: Well, that does happen, doesn't it? People will seize on any symbol or banner or slogan that comes in handy. Like here, during the World Cup a couple of months ago: English supporters seized on the St George's cross, a flag that was virtually unknown ten years ago. It was only when the National Front, the ultra-right party, started draping themselves in the Union Jack that the possibility that a flag might sum up one's ambitions came into play. I live in a very quiet suburb, absolutely docile, and a couple of years ago – it may have been during the European football championship – I looked out of an upstairs window and saw that two of my neighbours, about a hundred yards away, had erected flagpoles in their garden and were flying the St George's cross. It sent an odd feeling down my spine, because it was clearly saying something. You don't go to the trouble of buying a flagpole – and these were real flagpoles, much taller than the bungalows next to them – and then put a big flag on it without it meaning something. I wouldn't even know where to buy one!

SELLARS: At Ikea, perhaps? Were the 2005 riots at the Ikea store in London another influence on *Kingdom Come*?

BALLARD: Well, the Ikea riots happened when I was writing the book. 'There we go,' I said to myself. Yes – that was an incredible event in many ways. It fed into the novel. England is a much more socially divided, unstable and violent place than people realise. This is not some sort of Switzerland floating in the North Sea. We're not a Scandinavian country, like Norway or Sweden. We ought to be part of that bloc, but we're not. I don't know what we are. That's the problem.

SELLARS: *Kingdom Come*'s theme of violent consumerism seems to be an update of some of your earlier work. I'm thinking of your short stories 'The Subliminal Man' and 'The Intensive Care Unit'.

BALLARD: Those stories were so long ago . . . Yes, perhaps there are elements in them. Maybe you're right. I hadn't thought of it.

SELLARS: Why don't you write short stories any more? That's an aspect of your work appreciated by many.

BALLARD: The problem is that there's nowhere to publish them. Very few magazines or newspapers these days carry them. It used to be very common in the English papers fifty years ago – some papers had a short story every day. But also, if you're going to write them, you've got to cast your mind into the short-story mode and think in terms of short stories. You can't just turn that on for one piece. Every so often I get rung up by a newspaper or magazine, and they say, 'We're doing a special number with three or four short stories, specially commissioned. Would you write one?' But they want something very short to start off, and mine tend to be much longer, and then they want something rather conventional – something that's not going to unsettle the advertisers.

Well, I've tried to devote my entire career to rattling other people's cages and it's difficult to do that these days with a short story.

SELLARS: Iain Sinclair said that '*Kingdom Come* could have been stripped down to be a series of savage essays or presentations about the motorway corridor with dramatized events happening in the middle'. This got me thinking in reverse: perhaps your non-fiction writings – the short journalistic pieces you do for newspapers – have taken on the characteristics of your short stories.

BALLARD: Yes, I think there's a germ of truth in that. I mean, people have long complained that my book reviews have nothing to do with the book in question! And that's something I apologise for, because it's extremely irritating to the author.

SELLARS: You once said the key image of the twentieth century was the car. What do you think the key image of the twenty-first century will be?

BALLARD: That's interesting. It's hard to tell – it's so early. If I had to pick an image now, it'd probably be an internet screen. It obviously plays a big part in people's lives. But it's pretty early – contact me in fifty years' time and I'll update that!

SELLARS: I was at a talk you gave in London in 1996, where you said your dream would be to hook up to the internet and download every psychiatric journal ever published.

BALLARD: Lovely thought.

SELLARS: It's nine years later: have you done it yet?

BALLARD: No. I don't have a PC. I'm not on the internet and I think that's a matter of age. I'm nearly seventy-six now and I think the personal computer and the internet really came in about ten years ago. And by then I was an old dog and the internet was a new trick. I mean, I still write my novels in longhand and type them out on an old electric typewriter. I don't have any modern appliances. I have a mobile phone but I hardly ever use it. And all these things like iPods and BlackBerries – I am interested in them, but I'm too set in my ways.

436

SELLARS: Technology in your writing is broken, isn't it? It's burnt out. So much so that when people discuss your work, they tend to focus on images of urban decay, flyovers, car crashes, all that – even the *Collins English Dictionary* definition of 'Ballardian' highlights 'bleak man-made landscapes'. But there's a body of work from your early career that seems just as relevant today: the environmental quartet of *The Wind from Nowhere*, *The Drowned World*, *The Burning World* and *The Crystal World*. I wonder why that aspect of your work doesn't get as much attention as *Crash*?

BALLARD: I suppose it's because the kind of urban disaster imagery that I wrote about in *The Atrocity Exhibition*, *Crash* and *High-Rise* is closer to people's lives. Not many people have visited a jungle recently, or a desert. People are very concerned about ecological damage to the planet, but it tends to be something you see on television, whereas decaying, inner-city ghetto blocks, high-rise blocks and car crashes are part of everyday life if you live in a big city in the West – or in the East, for that matter.

SELLARS: And yet the ecological vision in your earlier work is getting a bit too close for comfort. The psychological aftermath of Hurricane Katrina was reminiscent of *The Drowned World*.

BALLARD: Yes, it did remind me of *Drowned World*. An extraordinary event, really – that something like that could happen to the most advanced nation on Earth.

SELLARS: How do you feel about having your own dictionary adjective, 'Ballardian'?

BALLARD: I'm surprised, actually, but I suppose it's a compliment. It's a shorthand phrase, but the trouble with shorthand phrases is that they often conceal more than they state. Take a term like 'Orwellian': it immediately sums up *Nineteen Eighty-Four*, but of course there was a lot more to George Orwell than *Nineteen Eighty-Four*. In fact, most of his books are not 'Orwellian'. *Animal Farm* is not Orwellian in the sense that *Nineteen Eighty-Four* is. But, no – it's a huge compliment. I do take it as a compliment.

SELLARS: According to *Collins*, 'Ballardian' is also defined as 'resembling or suggestive of the conditions described in J.G. Ballard's novels and stories, especially dystopian modernity'. But surely your writing is far too playful to be branded 'dystopian'. I find your characters and situations affirming, for all the darkness they willingly surround themselves with.

BALLARD: I'm glad you said that. I think my work is superficially dystopian, in some respects, but I'm trying to, as you say, affirm a more positive world-view. I lived through more than two-thirds of the last century, which was one of the grimmest epochs in human history – a time of unparalleled human violence and cruelty. Most of my writing was about the twentieth century, and anyone writing about the twentieth century writes in a dystopian mode without making any effort at all – it just comes with the box of paintbrushes.

You know, to be a human being is quite a role to play. Each of us wakes up in the morning and we inhabit a very dangerous creature capable of brilliance in many ways, but capable also of huge self-destructive episodes. And we live with this dangerous creature every minute we're awake. Something like *The Atrocity Exhibition* sums up my fiction: the attempt by a rather wounded character – in this case, a psychiatrist having a nervous breakdown; there are similar figures throughout the rest of my fiction – to make something positive out of the chaos that surrounds him, to create some sort of positive mythology that can sustain one's confidence in the world. Even something like *Kingdom Come* is affirmative, where I show a clear and present danger being dealt with, and one of the key figures responsible realising the error of his ways. So in that respect, I agree with you completely: my fiction is affirmative.

SELLARS: *Playboy* thinks so, too. They recently voted *Crash* the fifth-sexiest novel of all time.

BALLARD: [incredulous] *Who* said that?

SELLARS: *Playboy* magazine.

BALLARD: *Playboy*?

SELLARS: Yes.

BALLARD: [disbelieving] *Playboy* magazine?

SELLARS: Yes!

BALLARD: You mean Hugh Hefner's magazine?

SELLARS: Yes – Hugh Hefner!

BALLARD: God! I'm amazed.

SELLARS: Me, too.

BALLARD: I'm genuinely *amazed*.

SELLARS: It came in at number five.

BALLARD: Well, I take that as a compliment. Usually, crashing expensive sports cars would not figure highly in the *Playboy* lifestyle. What you want instead is a glamorous blonde in the seat next to you and a martini cooler in the rear seat as you drive at 150 miles an hour. And no talk of crashing!

SELLARS: What do you know about the film of *High-Rise* that Vincent Natali's working on?

BALLARD: I think it's in the early stages of development. I think there is a script, and they're still working on it. 'In development' in the film world generally means that they're looking for the money. We'll see.

SELLARS: Before I knew Natali had signed on, I remember seeing his film *Cube* and thinking he'd do a great job filming *High-Rise*. The themes and obsessions seemed to parallel your book.

BALLARD: Yes, very similar. I agree with you. I've seen *Cube* and I liked it. I thought it was original. I think he can bring something fresh to the idea.

SELLARS: What other films have you seen recently?

BALLARD: Oh . . . Well, I live in a small town called Shepperton, with just a single high street and about forty shops, two of which were DVD and video rental stores. I patronised them regularly – I used to see about three films a week. I was tremendously up with what was going on in the film world, but over the past couple of years, both those stores have closed down. And this means that I've stopped renting. So I've hardly seen any films at all for a long while. I mentioned this to someone recently, and she said, 'Ah, this is because people are downloading films from . . .' I couldn't make out what she was talking about, actually . . . from their mobile phones, it sounded like. Downloading from somewhere – they don't need to go to video stores any more. I also think people are moving into a kind of post-TV, post-film world, where they've got so many other things to do. Recreation of every conceivable kind. The idea of passively watching a screen seems to be passing. I think that part of the appeal of the internet is that it's interactive – an obvious thing to say, of course. But also, films are so bloody awful these days.

SELLARS: And just plain *bloody*, too. What do you think of the trend in horror films towards hyper-real scenes of torture and sadism like *Wolf Creek*, *Hostel*, *Severance* and so on?

BALLARD: Horrible. I've never liked horror films.

SELLARS: Why?

BALLARD: Oh, I don't know. Fear of death or something. The earliest horror films I saw were Dracula movies – never liked those. The whole idea of horror, particularly wrapped up in touches of the occult – ugh. They're saturated with the fear of death and displaced sexual anxieties. No, thank you. Not for me.

SELLARS: Well, they're much more sadistic these days. It really is 'violence as spectator sport', to quote yourself.

BALLARD: Absolutely. You see this dimension of anatomical frankness even in popular TV programmes like *CSI*. Every one ends with a cadaver being cut up and a heart or a brain being removed and held up to the light. Pretty frightening stuff. But I think we're anaesthetised – our sensibilities are dulled. There may be all this frankness on the screen, but most people, in England anyway, wouldn't have seen a dead body, let alone an autopsy. Put it all down to the diseased brain that helps to run human affairs.

SELLARS: I know you feel differently about science fiction than you do horror: you once said SF was 'the only true literature of the twentieth century'. What about today?

BALLARD: Well, if you were some sort of cultural historian looking back at the popular fictions of the twentieth century, you'd have to consider certain phenomena: the detective story, the *film noir*, James Bond movies, and you'd have to look at science fiction, which seems to respond with a huge vitality to the enormous changes taking place, particularly in the mid-twentieth-century, which has more or less created the world we live in now. This popular fiction had its serious fringes, largely inspired by people like H.G. Wells at the start of the century, but then it began to dominate Hollywood cinema. It infiltrated huge areas of popular entertainment: television, books, advertising – you name it. It would be foolish to deny the power of twentieth-century science fiction, to respond to and energise people's fears of science and technology, and their hopes for the future based on science and technology.

Science fiction created this extraordinary fiction of anticipation. Now, the problem is that at the heart of science fiction was novelty: it was predicting the new all the time. I remember reading science fiction magazines from the 1950s and one was constantly excited by the vision of the future dominated by television, advertising, space travel – the modern world, in short. As far as I can see, science fiction has lost that sense of the new, because its vision has materialised around us. We take it for granted. The future envisaged by science fiction is now our past, and the result is it's probably come to a natural end. That doesn't mean that one can't continue writing it: one just has to move into a different terrain.

SELLARS: You once said you were becoming more left-wing as you got older. Does that still fit?

BALLARD: I think it probably does, actually. I don't know about Australia – it strikes me as a pretty wonderful place, from everything I've read about it – but here, the gap between rich and poor is widening to such an extent that, particularly in London, it's begun to shift the whole demographic. The middle class, the people who sustain modern society – the nurses, junior doctors, teachers, civil servants and so on – are being forced out because vast sums of money are pouring into the housing market and distorting it. Gated communities are springing up everywhere, and the moment they can, people are opting for private medicine, private teaching, private hospitals – cutting themselves off from the rest of society, and that's not a healthy development. One thing I've always liked about America, and I think it's probably true of Australia, is that the children of well-to-do people and the children of people on modest incomes go to the same schools. I think that's good. It's not true over here and that's bad! A class-ridden society with huge divisions – that's bad. Something ought to be done about it, but I'll leave that to another generation.

SELLARS: Well, things are becoming more divisive in Australia. Our prime minister wants to test immigrants for 'Australian values'. It's worryingly undefined so it could be anything – Australian slang, Australian songs and so on – as the PM has hinted. Maybe people will be deported if they can't say 'you bewdy' or talk like Paul Hogan with conviction.

BALLARD: God.

SELLARS: Things are changing all over.

BALLARD: And not necessarily for the better.

2006: Mark Goodall. An Exhibition of Atrocities: J.G. Ballard on *Mondo* Films

Originally published in Mark Goodall, *Sweet & Savage: The World through the Shockumentary Film Lens*, London: Headpress, 2006

Mark Goodall is an academic film historian at the University of Bradford, and the author of *Sweet & Savage*, a scholarly study of the 1960s 'shock-umentary' trend spawned by Gualtiero Jacopetti's *Mondo Cane* and its many sequels and imitations. Like *The Atrocity Exhibition*, the *Mondo* films were presented in quasi-factual form, purporting to be documentaries about the ubiquity of, at least to Western sensibilities, horrific, bizarre and often brutally violent customs and practices throughout the world. As Ballard notes, their audience in the sixties was relatively select, and the films were shown only in small cinemas in the West End of London. In the 1980s, with the advent of home video players, the *Mondo* films found a new audience, as did their successors, such as the primitivistic horror film *Cannibal Holocaust*, and became condemned as part of the 'video nasty' furore whipped up by the British yellow press.

Goodall's interview focuses upon Ballard's own reactions to and memories of the early screenings of the Jacopetti films, yet there is also a clear analogy between the knowing primitivism of such films and Ballard's own depictions, in such novels as *High-Rise*, of the regression of middle-class professionals into a state of barbarism. Goodall suggests that the genre might have had a specific influence upon *The Atrocity Exhibition*, and indeed the hidden echo of George Orwell's 'atrocity pamphlets' in *Nineteen Eighty-Four* does emphasise the notion of

Ballard's novel as an examination of our own pathological revulsion for, and simultaneous attraction towards, the mirror image of primitive violence portrayed in the *Mondo* films. The idea that the framed portrayal of the barbarities of the other can function as a reflexive comment upon our own unconscious self-hatred is very much at the core of *The Atrocity Exhibition*. [DOH]

GOODALL: What were your initial impressions of the films of Gualtiero Jacopetti: *Mondo Cane, Mondo Cane 2, Women of the World, Africa Addio*, etc. Where did you see them, and what was the audience like?

BALLARD: I was very impressed by Jacopetti's films – I saw all of them from 1964 or so onwards. They were shown in small cinemas in the West End, to full, or more or less full, houses, and my impression is that the audiences completely got the 'point'. As far as I remember, the response of the people sitting around me was strong and positive. I think there was comparatively little sex in the first *Mondo Cane*, and I can't recall even one dirty raincoat. The audience was the usual crew of rootless inner Londoners – the best audience in the world – drawn to an intriguing new phenomenon. At the time, some twenty years had gone by since the war's end, and everyone had seen the World War II newsreels: Belsen, corpses being bulldozed, dead Japanese on Pacific Islands and so on. All grimly real, but safely distanced from the audiences by a sign that said 'horrors of war'. What the *Mondo Cane* audiences wanted was the horrors of peace, yes, but they also wanted to be reminded of their own complicity in the slightly dubious process of documenting these wayward examples of human misbehaviour. I may be wrong, but I think that the early *Mondo Cane* films concentrated on bizarre customs rather than horrors, though the gruesome content grew fairly rapidly, certainly in the imitator's films.

But the audiences were fully aware that they were collaborating with the films, and this explains why they weren't upset when what seemed to be faked sequences – they might have been real, in fact – started to appear in the later films. There was almost the sense that they needed to appear 'faked' to underline the audience's awareness of what was going on – both on screen and inside their own heads. We needed violence and violent imagery to drive the social, and political, revolution that was taking place in the mid-1960s; violence and sensation, more or less openly embraced, were pulling down the old temples. We needed our 'tastes' to be corrupted, and Jacopetti's films were part of an elective psychopathy that would change the world – so we hoped, naively. Incidentally, all this was missing from the way audiences – in the Curzon cinema, I think – saw another 1960s shockumentary, *The Savage Eye*, directed by Joseph Strick. When I saw it, I, like the audience, shuddered but felt no complicity at all. A fine film.

GOODALL: Can you recall any critical or other 'professional' reactions to Jacopetti's films when they were released?

BALLARD: I remember the critical/respectable reaction to the Jacopetti films was uniformly hostile and dismissive. As always, this confirmed their originality and importance.

GOODALL: Jacopetti has distanced himself from the films that later copied *Mondo Cane*, labelling them 'counterfeit'. What were, or are, your impressions of the copies of his films?

BALLARD: I can't remember any specific imitations, though I must have seen one or two. They were too obvious, ignoring the delicate balance between 'documentary' footage on the one hand, and on the other the need to remind the audience of its role in watching the films, and that without its intrigued response the films wouldn't function at all. The balance between the 'real' and the ironic simulation of the real had to be walked like a tightrope.

GOODALL: How did *Mondo* films influence your own work, ideas and thought processes, in particular *The Atrocity Exhibition*?

BALLARD: For me, the *Mondo Cane* films were an important key to what was going on in the media landscape of the 1960s, especially post the JFK assassination. Nothing was true, and nothing was untrue, and *The Atrocity Exhibition* tried to find a new sense in what had become a kind of morally virtual world: 'Which lies are true?' I think that Jacopetti was genuinely important, and opened a door into what some call postmodernism and I call boredom. Screen the JFK assassination enough times and the audience will laugh.

I was a great admirer of *Mondo Cane* and the two sequels. We, the 1960s audiences, needed the real and authentic – executions, flagellant processions, autopsies, etc. – and it didn't matter if they were faked: a more or less convincing simulation of the real was enough and even preferred. Also, the more tacky and obviously exploitative style appealed to an audience just waiting to be corrupted – the Vietnam newsreels on TV were authentically real, but that wasn't 'real' enough. Jacopetti filled an important gap in all sorts of ways – game playing was coming in. Also they were quite stylistically made and featured good photography, unlike some of the ghastly compilation atrocity footage I've been sent. It is lovely to think that he had his retrospective in a British university – as in *The Atrocity Exhibition*, which is not set in the US, as some think.

GOODALL: Do you think the films have any relevance to the present day, or to the future?

BALLARD: I suspect they're very much of their time, but that isn't a fault, necessarily. But there are many resonance's today, as in the Bush/ Blair war in Iraq: a complete confusion of the simulated, the real and the unreal, and the acceptance of this by the electorate. Reality is constantly redefining itself, and the electorate, the audience, seems to like this – a prime minister, religiously sincere, lies to himself and we accept his self-delusions. There's a strong sense today that we prefer a partly fictionalised reality on to which we can map our own dreams and obsessions. The *Mondo Cane* films were among the first attempts to provide the collusive fictions that constitute reality today. Wartime propaganda, and the 'Ripley's Believe it or Not' comic strip of bizarre facts in the 1930s, were assumed to be largely true, but no one today thinks the same of the official information flowing out of Iraq, or out of 10 Downing Street and the Pentagon, and significantly this doesn't unsettle us.

2006: Jonathan Weiss. 'Not entirely a journey without maps': J.G. Ballard on *The Atrocity Exhibition*

Previously unpublished

Jonathan Weiss is the director of the 2000 film version of *The Atrocity Exhibition*, an independent production which Ballard praised much more fulsomely than any of the other adaptations of his work, commending it as a 'poetic masterpiece'. The transcript below is taken from Weiss and Ballard's audio commentary on the DVD release. Weiss based his film upon the annotated RE/Search edition of *The Atrocity Exhibition*, seeing it as a ready-made 'shooting script' for a film, yet Ballard's conception of the central theme of the book – as Weiss describes it, a 'psychiatrist who is going insane in a world that is itself insane' – was already implicit in the original publication. What is made especially clearly in this interview is the way in which Ballard's discontinuous narrative structure emerged from a personal struggle with the tragic death of his own wife in 1964.

The central character in *The Atrocity Exhibition*, whose identity slips between a number of proximal names – Traven, Tallis, Travis, Talbot – serves as a cypher for the distributed and dissociated personalities of Ballard himself, whose own self-determined task in the 1960s was to make sense of the meaningless death of his wife in the context of other equally tragic deaths which, so the media landscape seemed to insist, had much greater 'meaning': the Kennedy assassination, the death of

447

Marilyn Monroe, the many deaths of the Vietnam war. Ballard's enthusiasm for Weiss's film, which faithfully renders the world of the book, free from narrative logic and the explanatory sequence of cause followed by effect, only accentuates the degree to which one becomes aware through this interview that *The Atrocity Exhibition* is the most personal of Ballard's works. [DOH]

BALLARD: In making the film of *The Atrocity Exhibition*, you faced problems that neither Steven Spielberg nor David Cronenberg faced, in that it's never clear in the course of the book what exactly is going on. And I think readers who really persevere with the book begin to grasp the underlying logic.

WEISS: Well, it's not a narrative logic; it was your only non-narrative book that I'm aware of, your only non-narrative novel.

BALLARD: It's not a narrative logic but the reader wants to know, like the viewer of the film, where exactly he or she is, and I think it becomes clear as you read the book, and as you see the film, that you're partly inside the mind of a psychiatrist who's having a mental breakdown. Now, when I started writing the pieces that made up *The Atrocity Exhibition* – and I think I started writing the first piece in 1965 – we were living through a very charged decade, dominated by the assassination of President Kennedy but also by the Vietnam War, by the space race, by the explosion in the counter-culture, the drug culture. A completely new world was ushered on to the stage.

WEISS: And also the media that brought the revolution in technology . . .

BALLARD: Yes. We'd moved from a sort of print-dominated world of newspapers and magazines into an electronic world dominated by television. The Vietnam War was transmitted live, or virtually live; we didn't see Kennedy assassinated live, but I think we saw Lee Harvey Oswald shot dead three days later virtually live on television. There was a sense that all the rules had changed and also that we were living in a kind of madhouse, that the world had become a sort of deranged psychiatric institution. When I was writing the book, it struck me that the one figure who best expressed this madness would be a psychiatrist who was having a mental breakdown.

WEISS: So, regarding this theme of the psychiatrist who is going insane in a world that is itself insane – that's the central theme of this book . . .

BALLARD: Yes, I think it is the central theme of the book. I'd like to say, incidentally, that when I started writing the separate chapters that make up *The Atrocity Exhibition* – written over a period of about four years, from something like 1966 to 1969 – I had no clear idea in my mind of the overall architecture. I was following a number of imaginative obsessions, because I've always had complete faith in my own obsessions – they're about the only thing I have trusted about myself – and I had a feeling that this central figure, whom I called Travis, though he has a number of variants on that – Traven, Tallis, and so on, Talbot – I thought he expressed the sort of dilemma of any thinking person of the 1960s when faced with this huge overload of sensational mass media, of Vietnam, the Kennedy assassination, the whole counter-culture, drugs. The global apple cart had been completely overturned, and apples – bloody apples – were rolling in all directions. It seemed to me that you feel that a psychiatrist is a sort of last hope for mankind, someone who can explain what is wrong with the human soul. When the psychiatrist himself is suffering a mental breakdown, things have really come to crisis point. I felt that my Traven character, the psychiatrist having a mental breakdown, was the right figure to express all this.

Now, the book took the form of a series of – I suppose you could call them – psychodramas, which this unhappy man, this psychiatrist, absolutely at the end of his tether, stages, each based around some significant event: the Kennedy assassination, the war in Vietnam, the space race, the death of Marilyn Monroe, among others. What he's trying to do is to restage these tragic events but in a way that makes sense.

WEISS: Because in the manifest way we know them, they don't have the meaning that we need. Is that it?

BALLARD: Right. Most of them either were absolutely nightmarish crimes like the assassination of Kennedy, tragic human mysteries like the death of Marilyn Monroe, or events of very sort of questionable aims like the space race, and so on. All these contributed to the mystery of a world out of joint. Traven's intention is to stage a series of private dramas using whatever materials come to hand, perhaps some old car crash footage, perhaps film of plastic surgery, clips of the space race, Vietnam, and the Kennedy assassination, deserted runways, geometric models, empty hospitals, strange corridors, odd rooms where the conjunction of walls and floors seems to speak a secret language.

And everything to Traven, the world, seemed coded, everything had to be sort of decrypted on the psychological plane. And then with luck, the pieces of reality would begin to fit together in a way that makes sense. So that he could see Marilyn Monroe's suicide, assuming she did commit suicide, or Kennedy's assassination, not necessarily as negative events – they would be positive events. And I think that this probably tied in with my own life. My wife had died in 1964, tragically of pneumonia, while we were all on holiday, three children and ourselves in Spain. It happened very quickly and I think I was never able to come to terms with it properly. Even when the grieving process was over, a year or two later, I was faced with this huge conundrum, why? Why had nature committed this terrible crime against this young woman who was then only about thirty-three or thirty-four with three young children.

An appalling crime been committed – was there any way conceivably that this death had some sort of positive aspects to it? And I think I used that tragic death as a sort of template which I could apply to these larger tragedies in *The Atrocity Exhibition*, like the Kennedy assassination and so on. And if the Traven figure in *The Atrocity Exhibition* could solve the mystery of, say, Kennedy's assassination, or the war in Vietnam, or what have you, that could be used in some way to unlock the mystery of my wife's death. I think that underpinned it. *The Atrocity Exhibition* was never just an imaginative or mental construct like most of my other novels; it drew on deep roots and deep obsessions.

WEISS: You were able to work on them in a much more immediate way? Without all the narrative structure?

BALLARD: Yes, I wanted to get away from the 'A plus B plus C' kind of narrative because it didn't reflect the world in which we actually lived. We were being bombarded with imagery of a very intense kind from advertising, TV, magazines, cinema, commercials. Life had become more and more discontinuous. The kind of discontinuities that are built into living in a city, in any age, where you meet people for five seconds, or five minutes, and then move on and meet someone else from a totally different corner of your life – those discontinuities had been enlarged a hundredfold, and I wanted a narrative flow that reflected all that. Now, people take so-called non-linear narratives for granted – you get films where you jump from the present into the past or even into the future.

WEISS: Right, but that's just reordering of a narrative. This just does not have that kind of narrative basis – the book does not have that kind of underlying narrative.

BALLARD: Yes, I agree with you. *The Atrocity Exhibition* isn't a reordering of narrative at all. Reality is already reordered, if you like. The world *is* discontinuous.

WEISS: That's why to me the book always felt very close to life.

BALLARD: That's what I wanted. I find that watching your film, the kind of jumps from, say, a washbasin in a bathroom to . . .

WEISS: . . . an airstrip . . . or a character who hasn't been in the film before, who hasn't been explained . . .

BALLARD: These things are part and parcel of the way we actually live. All of us in our daily lives today, never mind in the 1960s, take an awful lot for granted. I mean there's no sort of central ordering principle which each of us feels – we don't sort of say halfway through the day, 'Right! I am a character in, as it were, chapter three,' who has a narrative assignment determined by some sort of larger, evolving process, like a character in *Hamlet*.

WEISS: But we demand that out of our literature, certainly in cinema.

BALLARD: Yes, we do, particularly from cinema. And everything has got to have a motive, cause and effect have got to apply – nobody opens a door without there being a reason for it, whereas in ordinary life we're constantly opening doors without having any clear notion as to why we're doing it.

WEISS: The 'T' character in the book, from beginning to end, is in a mental breakdown – that's always the way I've understood it. He's going through this process, which really is the basis of art itself, isn't it? Creating all these situations, dramas, in an attempt to make sense of life. How would you compare the way in which the film deals with this with the book?

BALLARD: I think the film is totally faithful, actually, to that aspect of the book. I think it's surprisingly faithful. I think the temptation to impose some sort of narrative, some sort of evolving character who learns from the last five minutes or the last ten minutes, as characters tend to in films – that temptation is resisted. I hope it never was much of a temptation.

WEISS: It wasn't. It was never a temptation. Absurd; no!

BALLARD: I think if it had been a temptation, then you would never have set out to make the film. I'm very impressed by the film, by the way, and I always have been. And I'm impressed by the dedication that you've brought to it. But it may be that you have more in common with the Travis character than you realise, and I'm speaking quite seriously. In a way, the making of the film may be as much an act of therapy, maybe one of those psychodramas.

WEISS: Well, actually, I look at it the other way around; making the film has put me on to a ten-year . . . [laughter from both] . . . I don't want to go into it, this is your commentary, not mine . . .

BALLARD: Jonathan, I think we can say that when you began to make this film ten years ago, you suffered from all the human stresses that the rest of us suffer from. Ten years later, one consequence is that you are completely *sane*! Making the film has been a huge therapeutic exercise.

WEISS: Well, I still don't know what it really means to be sane in an insane world.

BALLARD: Well, exactly, and that question is one that is posed by *The Atrocity Exhibition*, both book and film. And I think that ultimate mystery is very much clearer in the film than it is in the book, because so much of the imagery in the book is strongly visual, but of course it's handicapped by the fact that I'm merely describing visual scenes of one sort or another, whereas in the film you're showing them directly.

WEISS: It's one of the things I really liked about the book: it's the way it has to be, there's no interior psychological analysis or investigation of this character. The book reads like a film script for this film. It was very easy for me to adapt it because from the very first page that I read of *The Atrocity Exhibition*, this was something that you see in your mind's eye. It's very different from your other books, but you've never been an author, not to my knowledge, who'd go into a lot of psychological detail, from an interior perspective.

BALLARD: That's true. In my fiction as a whole, I've always tried to avoid too much novelistic analysis of character, motive, behaviour, and the like, because I think it's better, and more true to the way we live, if you can externalise these elements. I think it's better, for example, rather than discuss through a given character someone's human unease about the sensitivity of the human face, it's almost better and much more powerful to do what you do in the film. That is, to show directly an operation of plastic surgery going on, where you suddenly realise just how sensitive the human face is, and how what we think of as the absolute essence of our personalities insofar as the everyday world is concerned, the expressions we have, our reactions to affection, to shock, the to and fro of everyday life – how sensitive they are to a pair of scissors. We think of some sort of inner core that is our soul, that is the essence of our interior personalities, but all we have to show the world is our faces. They're enormously important to us, yet they are as much an image on a canvas, canvas stretched across bones, stretched across our skulls, as any painting by Manet or the Impressionists. That's where I think your film is so impressive because what were, as you say, scripted outlines, scripted intentions, in the book, are actually brought into the real world in the film. It's one thing to talk about crashed cars, it's another to show newsreel footage of people barely alive in the mangled remains of their Buicks.

WEISS: The way relationships are described in the book, they are described almost always in terms of, literally, of architecture, of planes and geometries and spaces, things that we never think of in terms of inner psychology. At one place in the text itself, in *The Atrocity Exhibition*, and perhaps in the notes that you added years later [the annotations in the RE/Search version], you talk about the fact that the inner psychological world becomes literally externalised and manifest architecturally and geometrically, and of course this was the basis for all the 'T' characters discussing it in terms of politics, economics, sexuality, and the angle between the walls and the ceiling. This is something that is to me an incredibly powerful aspect of the book because it's psychologically true, it's not speculative.

BALLARD: Well, I think it's very true of people with certain kinds of mental abnormalities. Autistic children, for example, are hypersensitive to the shapes and contours of furniture, of the rooms around them, and they can react with panic if a particular easy chair has been moved. All the research in the neurosciences in the last fifty years shows that unknown to us large areas of our brains are continually assessing the input of information received, largely by our eyes but also by our balancing organs and by the postures we assume as we move around. A huge amount of information is being assessed by the brain and then assembled into constructions that are, after all, mental – they exist inside our heads, not out there as most of us assume. The brain is assembling these stage sets which for everyday purposes are completely convincing; we look at the walls around us, we look at the walls and ceilings, chairs, streets, our cars moving around, and so on, and we feel 'Yes, this is reality', but of course it is a construct of our central nervous systems.

Where things go wrong, where there's a sort of mismatch between the input and the ability to assemble a meaningful stage set out of that input, as it seems to with autistic children, or for the rest of us when we have a bit too much to drink, or have taken a narcotic drug that heightens or disorientates our senses, then we realise 'My God, this *is* a stage set!' So when Traven asks 'Does the angle between two walls have a happy ending', this is not just a joke. He's absolutely serious, because he's applying that to the most basic experiences of life, establishing who we are: 'I am me', standing or sitting in this room, but is this an ongoing narrative? Yes, of a kind. If it is a narrative, where is it leading and does it have a happy ending? The sort of question an autistic child might ask. Does this room, do these walls, have a happy ending? And this applies to the angles in our faces.

WEISS: Yes, the whole relationship between personal psychology and the external world has been completely flipped around. But what's actually very disturbing, if you think about it, is that these characters, who are supposed to be sane, or authority figures within this so-called institution, they take everything that he's doing absolutely seriously, as if it's taking place in the real world. Which suggests that there is absolutely no basis for saying that somebody's sane or not. Actually

I think the character Dr Nathan says that the question isn't valid any more.

There's the whole psychopathy sexuality thing that's going on – sexuality is everywhere but in sex itself, the sex kit that Travis devises. When this was written in the sixties, you had of course this whole so-called liberation thing going on . . .

BALLARD: Well, I felt at the time, and I still do feel, that in a way sexuality was migrating away from our own bodies, from our relationships, physical and affectionate, that we had with other people, to the environment around us, in the advertising imagery, the X-rated films where sexual frankness was everywhere . . .

WEISS: Sexual attachment to objects, especially cars.

BALLARD: Right – the deliberate engineering of, say, car design, particularly car interior design, of imaginative elements that clearly tapped, or tried to tap, half-conscious sexual feelings – the tactility of certain surfaces in furnishings for the home, in new fabrics – the correct assumption that human beings couldn't process the enormous flood of sexualised imagery with which they were being bombarded every moment of their lives, and that therefore the manufacturers or entertainment industries controlling this flood could absolutely inundate the individual consumer's mind and push in a message that the individual would never realise he was receiving. So you got this kind of drowned world where we all suddenly became rather silent aquatic creatures floating in this space, unaware of the direction of the current that was carrying us along.

And this is one of the obsessions that Traven is constantly trying to understand. He explores what most people would regard as pretty frightening pornographic imagery; he explores with the eye of a forensic pathologist. He treats sexual desire as if it was something stretched out on an autopsy table. He takes a woman's body and dismantles it – not literally, but almost literally – and constructs a kit which is literally that. I mean, inside his suitcase, as you show in the film, he has a set of the key elements that we respond to when we become sexually aroused – a pair of latex breasts, nipples, detachable pubic hair . . .

WEISS: The reification . . . Maybe you could talk a bit about pornography, sex, science.

BALLARD: Traven sees pornography as a kind of hyper-analytic response to sexuality. Normally, traditional sexual activity involves a sort of warm bath where physical activity and a world of mental affections blur into each other, and give rise, of course, to a huge number of problems. Traven takes the view 'What is actually going on?' He sees the sexual identity of his own body, and the body of his wife and of his on-off girlfriend, Karen Novotny, as a mystery that needs to be decoded and dismantled. He sees pornography, which is emotionally neutral – pornography is sex with the emotions deleted – as a useful technique for exploring what exactly is going on when two people copulate, when a penis enters a vagina, when a hand embraces a breast, when fingers explore clefts, which are obviously geometric structures which powerfully cue innate responses laid down in the central nervous system a hundred thousand years ago. Pornography is a way of dismantling all the excrescences that have grown around this sexual activity at its most basic, and finding the actual sort of operating elements.

WEISS: With the emotional content gone. That's what science does, obviously.

BALLARD: That is *exactly* what science does. The scientist feels no emotion when he is trying to find the boiling point of lead, or working out how some area of the rabbit's brain responds to vertical patterns as opposed to horizontal patterns. Science continually dismantles the world and feels utterly free of any emotional entanglements that cloud reality. And Traven sees science and pornography moving on a kind of collision course; eventually they may meet and fuse, and oddly enough in the thirty years or so since the book was written, one begins to see that what were thought of as parodies at the time that I wrote them – the chapters at the end of *The Atrocity Exhibition*, which appear to be scientific papers on various themes –have long since moved into the realm of the actual, in laboratories all over the Western world, where panels of housewives are indeed being tested on their responses to atrocity films or images of violence or destruction. The scientific investigators who are trying to look at some aspect of human psychology are in fact like pornographic impresarios. And I think that's a theme that runs through both your film and my book: that science, far from a being a sort of neutral and independent force for good, is in fact one of the elements that has led to this huge confusion.

WEISS: Is Traven, Travis – whatever – a product of it? Is he a victim of it? Or is he a knowing explorer of it, an investigator of these forces that you're talking about?

BALLARD: Well, he's both victim and investigator.

WEISS: Do you see him as liberating? Or liberated?

BALLARD: Yes, I think he works his way out of the mental crisis in which he finds himself at the beginning of the book. The last of the principal chapters of the book is called 'You and Me and the Continuum' and there he sees himself almost as a kind of second coming of some kind of messiah-like figure. A character who emerges on to the media landscape and is clearly possessed of almost supernatural powers, who seems able to transcend time and space and is maybe in transit between this world and some distant galaxy, whose arrival may have been prefigured in the great legends of Gilgamesh and the Middle Eastern myths that were absorbed into the Christian religion. He lies somewhere between Christ, as he himself quotes, riding into Jerusalem on an ass, and those cosmic space vehicles which may have been seen approaching Earth two thousand years ago. I think some sort of transcendence begins to operate . . .

WEISS: Transcendence was a very important thing for me.

BALLARD: Right. He's begun to understand that this is not entirely a journey without maps. Traven is making small discoveries along the way. Each time he sets up one of his psychodramas, each time he sees Kennedy killed, he's learned something, he's begun to assemble a new language out of radio telescopes, neurosurgical equipment that is used in the hospitals, car crashes, mysterious signals that he picks up on his car radio – all these are being assembled into a new world. That world, curiously, is very like the one we all live in, except that for most of us that world is screened from us by the kind of 'A plus B plus C' needs of day-to-day existence.

WEISS: The outlining was always something that worked at a very deep level for me – the character's obsession with drawing outlines around his subjects, which then remain after the subjects disappear.

BALLARD: They are an attempt to fix the flow of movements. Our central nervous systems are not powerful enough to memorise all these details of postures and movements and the emotions that go with them, and this is an attempt by him to, as it were, photograph the most commonplace events in day-to-day existence and get them to leave an indelible record, rather like those shadows left by the Hiroshima bomb of people running along bridge parapets. I think the cumulative effect is that he does begin to make sense of this atrocity, which is everyday life.

WEISS: Here's a question which may seem a bit ridiculous: do you think it's possible in the real world – in other words, in our quotidian reality – when we walk out of the theatre, when we turn the television set off, when you and I leave this recording studio, to have any relationship between what this character is doing and our own lives?

BALLARD: Even for those of us who aren't psychiatrists, let alone psychiatrists having mental breakdowns, the life Traven leads is very close to those that most people in cities lead today. I mean the discontinuities, the mysterious empty spaces in our day-to-day existences, the flood at the same time of imagery that we haven't initiated or called for, that pour out of our television sets and personal computers, movies, and the like. Every time we turn the pages of a magazine we're being bombarded . . .

WEISS: But he reacts to images differently. We're very passive in the way we accept media, whereas the one thing you can say about this character is that he's very active – isn't he?

BALLARD: Yes, he's on a quest to make sense of the world, and I think he realises that it's not so much he himself who's having a nervous breakdown as the world itself which is having a kind of virtual nervous breakdown. Reality, the external world, seems to be governed by the rules that govern mental breakdowns rather than by rules that govern sanity, and he is reordering this disordered reality to try to extract a set of rules that will allow it to become something closer to sanity. Now, that's a huge struggle obviously, but the attempt may, towards the end, come off.

WEISS: It's the coherence of the poetic role rather than the coherence of the rational role.

458

BALLARD: A photograph of sand dunes in the Egyptian desert may have much more connection with our own bodies seen in a bathroom mirror than seems obvious at first sight. On the unconscious level, where primary circuits of the brain are establishing a kind of stable sense of reality, on that level they may be almost interchangeable.

I get a very strong sense from the film that modern industrial societies are themselves constantly staging a series of psychodramas, where the stage sets are assembled into some kind of vast shopping mall, which twenty years later is then abandoned and left to rust, like a forgotten, open-air theatre staging of *Hamlet* – this is Elsinore. You get that sense, particularly when you see abandoned airports . . .

WEISS: In your work, abandoned airports, swimming pools, motorways are always far more powerful than when the thing is in use.

BALLARD: Well, it's that old paradox, that a rusting refrigerator thrown out of somebody's pick-up truck into a ditch beside a road has a unique identity that no showroom model, or even the working model in your kitchen, anywhere near approaches. There's nothing more poignant than a field full of abandoned cars, because all the logic that states that a car rolls forward on its four wheels, takes people on journeys, helps people to conduct their lives, gets them to destinations, collects children from school, offers a site for lovers to have sex – all these narratives that are implicit in every car, rusting in a field, are still there. These are not ghosts, they are presences, like photographs of radar screens.

WEISS: *Crash* came out of this book . . .

BALLARD: That's right. Most of the themes present in *Crash* are present in *The Atrocity Exhibition*.

WEISS: Actually, there are lines from both books. We both use them, Cronenberg used them – they're verbatim, little speeches.

BALLARD: It sounds like self-plagiarism. Some people think it's a great crime; I've never looked at it from that point of view. It wasn't self-plagiarism: these are sort of mantras that have to be repeated until they glow in the dark. The curious thing is that people have said to me, many times, why have you not written a follow-up? It's a fair question because the world of the seventies or the eighties wasn't that different from the world of the sixties: all those media overlays and confusions . . .

WEISS: You could argue it makes even more sense today, because today, the effect of media being what it is – the omnipresence of media – you could even argue that reality is completely a construct of this media.

BALLARD: I have actually tried once or twice to start a follow-up to *The Atrocity Exhibition*, but I never got very far.

WEISS: Is it more difficult to write this way?

BALLARD: No, *Atrocity Exhibition* wasn't difficult; I think it has something to do with the time in which it was written. You were on the sort of cusp in the mid-sixties of a transformation from the old print-dominated world of newspapers and magazines to the electronic world of television, above all, and I think it was that sense of emerging from one medium on to the beach, as it were, of another medium that was a very important impetus with *The Atrocity Exhibition*. We were breathing a new kind of air. We had lungs, as it were, for the first time. We'd moved from a world where the past was constructed anew every week, every day, by newspapers and magazines, every month, into a world where past and future had been concertinaed into a much more compressed and charged present. And that's what *Atrocity Exhibition* is about. Reading *The Atrocity Exhibition*, or seeing your film, one senses there is no past and no future.

Everything has been condensed into a kind of high-pressure present where it's almost impossible to visualise anything new happening; it's impossible to think in terms of the day after tomorrow. Elements of the past exist but they've all been reduced to kits, outlines on walls, crashed cars, elements in a sort of huge exhibition.

WEISS: What you're talking about is a shift into a new world where the understanding of past, present and future is radically, irreversibly changed. Is *The Atrocity Exhibition* a testament to that, a harbinger?

BALLARD: Yes, I think that's probably true. I think people's sense of past and future is radically different from, say, my parents' and grandparents' generation. I remember vividly as a child in the 1930s, the intense curiosity and excitement about the future you found in popular encyclopaedias, and in magazines like *Popular Mechanics*. All the American and British magazines I saw as a boy in Shanghai were filled with accounts of another land-speed record broken, or the fastest train, or a plane that can fly at two hundred miles an hour. Next year it will be three hundred miles an hour, and within five years we may be able to fly around the world in a day. That excitement really extended into almost every aspect of life.

This constant extrapolation into the future, which incidentally of course was the huge engine of science fiction – the future was anything with a fin on it, everything was streamlined. That was art deco for you, of course, streamlined teapots. And also, of course, people were very well aware of the past, perhaps conscious that the great European colonial empires were coming to an end, everyone was very aware of their national histories. That's gone today, no one's interested in the future. I think the future died in 1945 with the atomic bombs at Hiroshima and Nagasaki. People were frightened of the future, and for the first time, too, they became frightened of science. Science became almost an abusive force, manipulating the gene structure, threatening new diseases, playing around through brain surgery with the central nervous system – there was a danger humankind would lose its soul, that the soul would literally be cut out of our brains by advanced neurosciences. Likewise, we've completely lost interest in the past; the past is a programme about Hitler on television. Most people have only the haziest idea of, say, the First World War, and the nineteenth century might as well be ancient Athens.

We live in a kind of enormously expanded present, which is just packed like a tenement city with images from the past, and to some extent the future, which have been commandeered, ransacked out of the years past and the years to come, and *The Atrocity Exhibition* really describes just that world. Traven is making a desperate bid to understand what all these elements that are no longer linked by time mean: if they are not linked by time, what are they linked by? Maybe the central nervous system in the deep levels of the brain has its own sort of architecture, that it's assembling a different world. Maybe the film he makes is an attempt to show a world where he offers a replacement for time, just as to some extent he offers a replacement for the emotions, in his relationships with his wife and his lover.

WEISS: Because there's no emotions whatsoever, not in the book and not in the film.

BALLARD: He's offering a substitute for emotions, which are difficult to describe in words because they're so powerfully visual. He's offering a kind of ongoing drama. Dramatic tension takes the place of emotions, and spatial awareness takes the place of emotions. The unity of apparently disparate things – balconies on a Hilton hotel, and the operation scars on Elizabeth Taylor's throat after her tracheotomy – these have a clear relationship, and Traven is offering these relationships to take the place of emotions. So that we are no longer constrained by our appetites and fears, but have a much more expansive and open sense of a world where everything is connected to everything else by a new kind of algebra, a new kind of geometry. And that's very evident, I think, in the film.

WEISS: Do you think something like that is actually happening, outside of the non-world of the film, in the world of reality?

BALLARD: Yes, I think so, I think it is happening. I think in many ways people have such information-rich lives today, partly thanks to the internet, and partly thanks to the mass media, which they have enormous access to, and I think information drives out emotions in a way, so that a new kind of logic begins to intervene. Traven is searching for that logic, and the film is his attempt to define that logic . . .

I think we'll call it a day. Call it a day?

WEISS: Sure.

2007: Hari Kunzru. Historian of the Future

Previously unpublished

With the imminent publication of what would turn out to be Ballard's last book, his memoir *Miracles of Life*, the Anglo-Indian novelist Hari Kunzru interviewed Ballard at the London home of Ballard's girlfriend, Claire Walsh, where Ballard was increasingly living owing to his poor health. The interview, conducted on 31 October 2007, was intended for the in-house magazine of Waterstones bookshop, and throughout there's a tangible tension between the kind of questions Kunzru clearly wants to ask for himself, and both his and Ballard's awareness of the 'middle-brow' target audience. In this sense, Kunzru actually acts out the 'thin veneer' he describes as separating social convention and unconscious desire. Similarly, Ballard himself lets forth a deluge of candid comment – perhaps with too much candour – about the self-important delusions of the English.

Yet Ballard is also keen to emphasise that his real interest is not in any one class or nationality, but 'in what lies inside the animal', and the echo of Emile Zola points to his fiction as a kind of post-Freudian naturalism. His loss of faith in science fiction, as a means of connecting the imagination with the future, is here proffered almost apologetically, yet it accords with his abandonment of the genre in his later career, especially from the late nineties onwards. [DOH]

KUNZRU: What's the relationship between *Miracles of Life* and the two novels based on your early life, *Empire of the Sun* and *The Kindness of*

Women? I read those books at the time as if they were quite straight-forwardly autobiographical.

BALLARD: Of course, those two books are novels. I never pretended everything in them was literally true. Quite the opposite. They are novels that draw on my life without in any way trying to be a literal account of what I had for breakfast in 1935. At the time *Empire of the Sun* came out, I went to great lengths to point out there were substantial differences between my life and the life of Jim. The obvious one is that my parents were not in the camp. I justified that by saying that in a way it was psychologically truer. There was a sort of estrangement between myself and my parents, just as I say in this new book that there's an estrangement in any large slum, or bidonville – whatever you want to call it; cardboard shacks – between teenage boys and their parents for the reasons I set out. Parents have no control of any kind. They can offer no treats. And so on.

KUNZRU: They have no stake in society, even if it's the society of the camp. As a teenage boy you're just floating around, you're an outsider.

BALLARD: Absolutely. In any slum it's the teenage boys who run wild, who have the greatest freedom. And who have the energy too. Where I got the energy from I don't know.

KUNZRU: The pleasure you mentioned is, I suppose, most surprising to the reader. You relished a lot of your experiences there.

BALLARD: Yes I did. I think if children – and I was a child – that if children are in the presence of other adults they know they don't have any fear. There are amazing accounts of children in the Nazi extermination camps who were happily playing cowboys and Indians. If, as a child, you're with your parents you feel a sort of security. I think also by leaving my parents out of *Empire of the Sun* I was trying to mythologise my own younger self and I think in a way leaving Jim on his own in the camp was true to what was going on there. The events in *Miracles of Life* are drawn as I remember them. It's not a work of fiction in any way.

KUNZRU: You've resisted interpretations of your work that say it all stems from experiences in Shanghai, but in *Miracles of Life* you seem to be noticing things like empty swimming pools, things you see as significant to your later work. I was very struck by your description of climbing into the derelict casino with your father – the ruins of a previously highly organised social space which has been suddenly and catastrophically evacuated. The image seems to be a fairly obvious key to understanding your work.

BALLARD: We're all shaped by our childhoods, but if your childhood takes place during war, enemy occupation or for that matter civil war, famine, drought . . . You can imagine the experiences of a twelve-year-old boy in New Orleans during the flooding – you'd be marked for ever by that, not in a bad way necessarily, but it would be a reference point throughout your future life.

KUNZRU: And a reference point in a very particular way. With regard to the casino you write, 'reality itself was a stage set which can be dismantled at any moment'.

BALLARD: I think that's something the war taught me. The adult world always has enormous prestige for a child: parents are respected, their friends are respected, teachers, doctors, all the rest of it, and when the adult world is radically undermined, even demolished, this has a huge effect on the way one sees reality. The fact is, Shanghai was a stage set.

KUNZRU: Even before the catastrophe of the war?

BALLARD: Yes, I think it was. There was so much space given over to vast advertising displays, stunts of various kinds – I give several examples in *Miracles of Life*. One that sticks in my mind is the fifty hunchbacks that the management of the Grand Theatre hired to form an honour guard – Chinese hunchbacks recruited from the backstreets and slums of Shanghai – I can't remember whether they were dressed up in seventeenth- or eighteenth-century costumes or whatever. There were all these stunts going on. Shanghai was a vast engine of illusions of various kinds. Venture capitalism going full blast twenty-four hours a day. And that sort of city is very easy to switch off, because there's no fall-back position. If you take away the skywriting aeroplanes and the hunchbacks . . .

KUNZRU: . . . and the generative motor of capital that's driving it . . .

465

BALLARD: . . . then there's nothing left.

KUNZRU: It's very striking throughout your work, this sense of the thinness of the social, and the fragility of convention. To me that makes you strikingly un-English as a writer.

BALLARD: That's very sweet of you. I think that's a huge compliment.

KUNZRU: At certain points you mention your dislocation from the notion of Englishness, and that seems to be at the heart of it for me. One would traditionally think of the English novel as a mining of this infinitely thick layer of social sediment – but for you it can always be swept away at any point, and there's the skull beneath the skin, the psychopathology that underlies this thin veneer.

BALLARD: Absolutely.

KUNZRU: So what is your relationship to Englishness? You talk about it in very disparaging terms.

BALLARD: The England I'm very disparaging about is the one I came to in 1946 which is sixty years ago, and the country has changed enormously. That England was absolutely dominated by its class system. I'd been misled by all those *Chums* annuals and *Boy's Own Paper* annuals, by *Just William* books and A.A. Milne – even *Peter Pan* – giving the impression that the whole of England was based in Knightsbridge and South Ken, with one or two offshoots like Godalming and St James's Park, and the confident attitude that went with all of that. It didn't take more than five minutes to realise this was a huge self-delusion and the people who were being deluded were not outsiders like myself but middle-class English who believed that this was the true nature of the realm. They didn't really accept that in those days 80 per cent of the population was working-class, very poorly educated, very poorly housed, very poorly paid, and really being exploited in the most ruthless way – in the way that the Chinese workforce in Shanghai was exploited. I just found it impossible to come to terms with after the reality of previous years.

It just seemed preposterous to maintain this huge body of largely nostalgic illusions about what England was. We hadn't even got our basic facts right – most people thought we had won the war with a little help, sometimes more of a hindrance, from the Americans and the Russians. In fact that couldn't be farther from the truth. There's no doubt that England changed over the next twenty or thirty years. The consumer society arrived and a post-war Labour government instituted the National Health Service, huge programmes of public housing, better education and so on, which did change the character of the nation. I don't know if economics lies at the heart of everything – sometimes I think it does – but as the working class became better paid, they became freer.

KUNZRU: Your work returns again and again to this middle-class social world and it seems to hover between a kind of wish to sweep away this ridiculous edifice and show what lies beneath it, all the libidinal desires and a sense that these social conventions are all that's holding back some sort of deluge of sex and death. Do you have a set moral position with regard to that? Is there something that you see that is valuable in these social conventions, or are you just in the business of tearing them down so something else can be put in their place?

BALLARD: I write about middle-class people because they're the people I know. I've no experience of working on a factory floor. I've no experience of living among really poor people. I've never lived on a sink estate. The last fifty years I've lived in a quiet suburb, Shepperton. Most of the characters in my fiction are middle-class.

KUNZRU: I suppose what I'm trying to get at is the fragility of those conventions. You're writing in the name of some sort of decency: there's a strong sense of disgust at things like inequality and exploitation running through your work, but at the same time there is always something rising up from underneath – you quite like opening the vent to let the psychopathology bubble up.

BALLARD: My thoughts about psychopathology are not specifically related to life in England. They're related to my feelings about human beings in general.

KUNZRU: Are they bound up with class?

BALLARD: I don't think so. I think it's the nature of the beast. Human beings do have huge reserves of psychopathology which are repressed

– thank God – by the forces of law and order. By social conventions – some of them self-seeking. I tend to pick middle-class characters in my novels because a) they're the people I know best and b) the middle classes have more discretionary spending power. It's no accident that so many of the post-war cultural trends – television ownership, video recorder ownership, the transformation of the home into a sort of film studio with all the latest gadgets – have taken place in the suburbs. The Beatles and the Rolling Stones came from the suburbs. People have more money to spend. They can indulge whims. They can play games.

I remember about thirty years ago some British mercenaries were at work for one of the local warlords in the Congo or somewhere, and they were put on trial and they were all dressed in sort of chinos and cotton jackets and this was all shown on television. I remember maybe a day later I was walking through Walton-on-Thames and I saw a whole load of young men with shaven heads wearing these chino outfits and big military boots and this was the mercenary look which became quite fashionable out in the suburbs, taken straight from the TV screen. I remember there was a little bit of a scandal in the local newspaper when some young men got hold of an American car and painted it to look like an LAPD squad car with shields on the black and white doors and flickering lights. They used to drive around Walton in this, and the police stopped them on the grounds that they were impersonating a police vehicle or something. Well, I don't think a big Chevrolet with 'LAPD' on the side is going to remind anyone of a little Ford Mondeo.

KUNZRU: Fantasy America in the suburbs; in the British suburbs there's always been an injection of Americana.

BALLARD: People have got more money there. They can indulge themselves. So that's why I've tended to set a lot of my fiction in the suburbs. I'm not that interested in class in the English sense of the term, in the sense that it intrigued Evelyn Waugh or Kingsley Amis.

KUNZRU: You're not interested in dissecting fine distinctions in class.

BALLARD: No. I'm much more interested in what lies inside the animal. I think human beings are rather dangerous and they do have reserves of psychopathic behaviour which they call on at certain times, but there we are.

KUNZRU: In *Miracles of Life*, you talk quite a lot about your discovery of psychoanalysis and surrealism and I wonder whether you could say a bit about how that mapped on to what had happened to you previously – it seemed to have the character of a recognition.

BALLARD: The thing about my wartime experiences, and indeed my whole experience of Shanghai which itself was a war zone really from 1937 onwards, was that it left me when I came to England with a lot of questions – 'who are we?', 'what's the nature of reality?'; also 'who am I?' I was well aware during the internment years that I was wrapped up in the war in ways that most other people weren't. Teenage boys are always looking for someone to hero-worship. I think I did admire the Japanese for reasons I wouldn't feel today.

KUNZRU: Because they were powerful?

BALLARD: They were brave. And that's very important to a twelve-year-old. The way they defeated the British army, an army three times the strength of theirs at Singapore, the way they sunk the *Repulse* and the *Prince of Wales*, which had been sent out without any air cover 'to teach those little Nips a lesson' – I can hear those voices to this day. I rather looked down on British valour and rather admired the Japanese, but of course as the war moved on I found new heroes to worship, in particular the US air force, but that was childhood. I was aware at the time that I was more involved with some of the more dubious aspects of the war. Your motives become tremendously confused. To some extent I wanted the war to continue, partly because I knew we were safe as long as the Japanese were guarding the camp, and partly because the war released certain feelings that aren't visible in peacetime. The war clearly touched my imagination in a way. I needed answers, so to go back to your question, some of those answers seemed to be provided by surrealism and psychoanalysis.

KUNZRU: Is there any particular surrealist work that was very important to you at that time?

BALLARD: I remember reading *Civilisation and Its Discontents*. This was when I was at school in England at the age of sixteen or seventeen. It has that wonderful last paragraph where Freud speculates whether, having come to terms with the sexual instinct, we would be able to cope with the death instinct. This seemed to me very profound. And the surrealists of course duplicated in their paintings so many of the scenes I'd seen in Shanghai during the war. War is rather surrealist. You see photos of the Blitz in London. Buses on the tops of blocks of flats. Incredible juxtapositions. Also they weren't conformist. They were revolutionary, really, in spirit, which is something I wanted to see.

KUNZRU: You wanted to see a revolution?

BALLARD: In England, in particular. Yes. In a way, it came in the sixties.

KUNZRU: It certainly seems you found kindred spirits in the avant-garde in the sixties. You talk about meeting Martin Bax and the *Ambit* people and you write very warmly about Michael Moorcock as well. Would you say you found an intellectual community that hadn't existed for you before?

BALLARD: Yes, I think I did. Bax, of course, was a doctor, whereas Moorcock was editing a science fiction magazine [*New Worlds*], but there was a commonality of interest. Because, after all, underpinning science fiction is science, and in many ways medical science – after astronautics – was the dominant science in SF. Ah, but all that seems so long ago. It *is* long ago.

KUNZRU: Talk to me about SF and the opposition you draw between outer space and inner space.

BALLARD: As I say in the autobiography, I was unusual amongst science fiction writers in not really having read any SF when I started writing it in my mid-twenties. I'd read Wells' novels and short stories, but not much else. I was very attracted to science fiction because it had huge vitality. Meeting British and American SF writers of the sixties, I felt a sort of ferment of ideas and possibilities which I never had meeting mainstream English novelists. All they induced was a kind of overpowering headache and a wish to leave for the South Seas.

KUNZRU: Do you still have the same passion for science fiction?

BALLARD: No, because I think it's changed. I think probably science fiction has come to an end. It's simply because the world that science fiction envisaged is already here in many respects. In general, we're not interested in the future any more. In the 1930s, I can remember the encyclopaedias and magazines, adult magazines that I read then – *Life, Time, Colliers, Picture Post* – all of them obsessed with the future because so much was changing: new antibiotics, new forms of mass travel, the jet engine, a whole new attitude towards leisure and the possibilities of life, and so on and so forth, enormous changes taking place, underpinned by scientific discoveries of one kind or another. That was all tremendously exciting, particularly as there was a new kind of psychology emerging, a new kind of people were being born from the airports and hospitals and the first giant supermarkets, and, of course, our roads because mass car ownership arrived in the sixties and really changed people's lives in a radical way.

I think science fiction's future is already our past and I think it's very difficult to recapture our excitement about change, because that's what science fiction thrives on – change – and whether science fiction can discover a new future, I don't know. Somehow I doubt it. It's rather like surrealism. A small number of science fiction writers, mostly British and American, created this new world and a new world-view, just as a very small number of surrealist painters, no more than half a dozen, created what we think of as modern surrealism. And in way you can almost compare it to Hollywood. Its greatest period was probably the forties and fifties, when entertainment cinema was discovering itself, and what it could do. Maybe these are all one-generation movements.

KUNZRU: It seems to me that you managed to produce something new in your work of the late sixties and early seventies by fusing pop art consumerism with this, I suppose, psychoanalytically derived, or surrealist, material, and this quasi-pornographic medical terminology for the body. You write about *The Atrocity Exhibition* as an attempt to find a new kind of emotional language that would incorporate personal feelings and things going on in the culture – do you see that as a key work in your career?

BALLARD: Yes, I think it was, without any doubt. I was terribly wounded by my wife's death, leaving me with these very young children, and I felt that a crime had been committed by nature against this young woman – and her children – and I was searching desperately for an explanation, something that would justify this awful event. To some extent, *The Atrocity Exhibition* is an attempt to explain all the terrible violence that I saw around me in the early sixties. It wasn't just the Kennedy assassination, which I think was a catalyst for the sixties – a young prince had been murdered, died on his wife's lap in full gaze of hundreds of millions of people; a terrible crime had been committed against Kennedy – but I think I was trying to look for a kind of new logic that would explain all these events. I think the appalling atrocities carried out during the Second World War, and the absolute waste of human life, and then the Vietnam War in particular – all these made me wonder what sort of human beings we are. Is it in our nature to be violent and cruel? Can one salvage anything from what we have? *The Atrocity Exhibition* was my small attempt to make sense.

KUNZRU: Can you draw out the elements of the logic that you applied, or discovered?

BALLARD: Difficult to do. I'm not sure Waterstones is the place.

KUNZRU: That's a good place to leave it. Thank you.

BALLARD: It's been a pleasure. Keep it low-brow, for Waterstones . . .

2008: James Naughtie. 'Up a kind of sociological Amazon': J.G. Ballard on *Miracles of Life*

Previously unpublished

James Naughtie is a BBC radio presenter, and the transcript below was originally broadcast on Radio 4 in 2008 after Ballard had completed *Miracles of Life*. The interview takes on the tone of an elegy, covering the whole fifty years of Ballard's writing career and indeed the entirety of his life, yet it's also a kind of dissection, in Ballard's own terms, of the entire body of his life's work. Naughtie persists with the metaphor throughout the interview, seeing Ballard's medical training at Cambridge as both setting an analytical pattern which would dominate his writing, and providing the hope of answers to the many deaths – from the deaths of wartime Shanghai, to the death of his wife Mary in 1964 – that Ballard had had to endure and survive.

What seems to intrigue Naughtie most is the way in which, given his childhood of such direct contact with brutality and violence and his adulthood of exposure to personal tragedy, Ballard could possibly retain a sense of human optimism. Ballard's answer is ambiguous at best, but nonetheless clear: that the job of the writer is to 'tell stories that make sense'; or, in other words, as Ballard put it in his introduction to *Crash*, 'The writer's task is to invent the reality'. [DOH]

NAUGHTIE: Why 'Miracles'?

BALLARD: I think everyone's children, particularly at the moment of birth – if the parents are lucky enough to be present – everyone's children seem absolutely miraculous. I watched two of my children being born, and I was absolutely overwhelmed by this sort of creation on the grandest scale. This tiny infant – as I say in the book, far from being very new, very young – seemed ancient, streamlined by time, like one of the sculptures of the pharaohs. I think I was so transformed as a parent by these young children, in a way. They construct the universe for themselves, their little habits and favourite fantasies and dreams and passions, and things they always get into an argument about, particularly if you've got more than one. I had three children, and I was, kind of, conscripted into becoming a fourth child in the family. It's such an overwhelmingly rich experience.

NAUGHTIE: So when you came back to look at your own life, you apply that description of a miraculous beginning to life to your own surroundings in Shanghai, which was a sort of magical setting for childhood, despite all the deprivations that you suffered.

BALLARD: It was an extraordinary city on any level, I think partly because it was an artificial city. I mean, it's one of the few artificial cities in the world – Las Vegas, I suppose, is another one. I think they're both actually created with the same end in view – that is, money and how to make as much as possible in the shortest possible time. Shanghai was an anything-goes place. There were no restrictions of any kind. You know, if you wanted to build a replica of Buckingham Palace or the *Queen Mary*, you know, twice life-size, you could do it. You didn't have to ask anybody's permission. The whole place was extraordinary in every respect.

NAUGHTIE: What about the illusions that you refer to there, because in many ways it was quite open about what it did as a city, by your description. It was rough and ready, it was a moneymaking machine. It was corrupt. It was full of bars and brothels and all the rest of it. In a sense it didn't have illusions. It said, well, 'this is just what we are'.

BALLARD: That's absolutely true. I mean, I've often said that if you fainted from hunger on the streets of Shanghai and fell to the pavement, you'd just lay there and die. These are the hardest pavements in the world. The kind of notions about Social Security, for example, that we take for granted were completely absent then. I mean, there was no

Social Security. If you were a starving peasant and you managed to get through the cordons of Shanghai police beating you back, there was nothing. I mean, there were no Red Cross workers to greet you.

NAUGHTIE: There's a very moving series of passages in the book, where you describe your reactions to this country on arriving back just after the war. This is where you observe life around you, and compare your idea of the old country to the reality.

BALLARD: Looking at the English people around me, it was it impossible to believe that they had won the war. They behaved like a defeated population. I wrote in *The Kindness of Women* that the English talked as if they had won the war, but acted as if they had lost it. They were clearly exhausted by the war and expected little of the future. Everything was rationed – food, clothing, petrol – or simply unobtainable. People moved in a herd-like way, queuing for everything. Ration books and clothing coupons were all-important, endlessly counted and fussed over, even though there was almost nothing in the shops to buy. Tracking down a few light bulbs could take all day. Everything was poorly designed – my grandparents' three-storey house was heated by one or two single-bar electric fires and an open coal fire. Most of the house was icy and we slept under huge eiderdowns like marooned Arctic travellers in their survival gear, a frozen air numbing our faces, the plumes of our breath visible in the darkness.

I think we, in a way, came out of the war the worst, I think, of all the major powers who took part in it. Much of France was untouched. It wasn't immediately obvious, as you stayed in your hotel in Paris or travelled south of Paris, that there had been a war at all, whereas Britain showed terrible devastation. Most of the major cities and ports from Southampton to London, Manchester – you name it – had been heavily bombed over an extended period and large sections of Birmingham were just heaps of rubble. It's really hard for people to understand what it was like, and given that nothing had been replaced during the war years – not a building had been painted, you know, not a window had been replaced – everything looked so dilapidated.

NAUGHTIE: It's interesting that your observations of that time when you arrived home were laced with an awareness of class which you thought couldn't be ignored. And yet when you came to write full-time, in the late fifties, early sixties, you weren't one of those English novelists or short-story writers who wrote about the peculiarities of class. Why do you think that was?

BALLARD: Partly because I'd had no experience of the English class system. Out in Shanghai, everyone really was sort of – what you would call it – managerial middle-class. I mean, the same sort of class that you would find if you went out to Dubai and lived among the British expats there or, you know, Calcutta, or Mexico City. It's a sort of professional class that emerges that has its own ways of doing things, that prefers to drive, you know, BMWs rather than Mercs and so on. I'd had no experience of the English class system, so when I came here, sustained by this mythical England of the *Just William* books and Christopher Robin, I thought, 'my God, the whole thing – it's a delusion', and the people taken in are the middle classes themselves. They believe that it's all cricket and 'spinsters cycling to evensong', in John Major's immortal phrase. I think England became a vast puzzle. I mean, I was up a kind of sociological Amazon. You needed to be an anthropologist . . .

NAUGHTIE: Ah, this is interesting, because you studied medicine at Cambridge. Now, you didn't stick with it. You abandoned it and took up literature at one point, but you also had an interest in psychoanalysis, for example. So you were always interested in the sort of nervous system underneath, how the body kept going. In a literary sense, was something like that the origin as well?

BALLARD: Yes, I think. I studied medicine for a couple of years, and most of it consisted of dissecting the human cadaver. It was a very, very important experience for me; I think it came only second to my experience of the camp during the Second World War. When I came to England, I was still carrying all these memories of the thousands of dead Chinese I'd seen, ever since the Japanese invasion in 1937 – the bodies that lay in the streets. I think I was carrying a huge cargo of death really and I couldn't understand why all this had happened. Why did human beings behave in such a bestial way towards each other? Because there is no doubt the Japanese behaved atrociously towards the Chinese.

The behaviour of the Japanese in China from 1937 onwards was very close to genocide; they looked down on Chinese as an inferior people. I mean, the things that went on in an educated officer class: the Japanese officer class took part in competitions to see how many Chinese they could behead with their swords. All that was just . . . it was impossible to understand it . . . and in a way the anatomy, the dissecting room, was a way of exploring death at very close quarters.

NAUGHTIE: Yet you confessed to a certain admiration for the courage of the Japanese.

BALLARD: As a boy, yes. I don't now, but as a twelve-year-old you couldn't help but admire the way the Japanese embodied all the manly and military virtues, fighting to the last man and so on.

NAUGHTIE: And the code of honour.

BALLARD: Yes, a tremendous code of honour – bushido. An impressionable twelve-year-old finds a lot to admire in that sort of military ethos. Just as English boys of twelve, over here, admire the Black Watch, admire commandos, but it's something that adults need to be a little more sceptical about.

NAUGHTIE: So you are cutting up cadavers, you were aware of the bestial urges that lurk in all of us, or in many of us, from your own experience, and then you began to write, and you discovered – slightly to your surprise, but also to your pleasure – that you could make a living out of writing. Then the terrible tragedy of your wife's death, with almost no warning – psychologically, was that personal tragedy another of the things that took you deeper into the kinds of analyses that mark out so many of your books?

BALLARD: Yes, I think there's no doubt about that. I think my wife's death was a reminder that you couldn't pretend that, you know, death had left the stage. Death was present in the world, it was liable to make an entrance on to the stage . . .

NAUGHTIE: . . . in the midst of life . . .

BALLARD: . . . in the midst of life, in a very unexpected moment. I felt at the time, and still do, that nature had committed an appalling crime against this young woman, and her three very young children, and how to explain this death was a huge imaginative and emotional challenge.

NAUGHTIE: Because you didn't have any religious template that you could place on it.

BALLARD: None, nothing. My parents were agnostic – so was I – but I had this inkling that perhaps the imagination was a door that I could open, and somewhere, on the other side of this doorway, I would find a realm where two and two made five. That sounds sort of *Alice in Wonderland*-ish . . .

NAUGHTIE: Well, of course, one of the realms you did end up in, without any background really, was science fiction, and here you were walking through a door into worlds that no one could imagine, let alone have experienced, and you did it, from a standing start. It looks extraordinary in a way, glancing back.

BALLARD: Yes, I mean, in some ways I was very fortunate that I stumbled across this form of fiction. which I never really read. I mean, I read the short stories and novels of H.G. Wells, but not much else. Most science fiction writers, American and British, started writing science fiction in their teens. I didn't really start reading it in any depth until I was about twenty-three, twenty-four, and then I found I had a kind of flair for it, and it also coincided with a period of great change in England. This is what I wanted to see happen here, there was so much that needed to be changed.

NAUGHTIE: We're talking about the sixties now?

BALLARD: Yes, and I felt the old traditional, class-bound England that I'd come across in 1946 when I arrived here needed to be laid out on the psychoanalyst's couch and thoroughly analysed. I wanted to dismantle it and see what this strange creature was made of.

NAUGHTIE: It was a sort of cadaver that you could get to work on.

BALLARD: It was, but I also felt I could see change was coming. I'd been to the United States and I'd seen that already, by the early sixties, we were getting the first supermarkets, the first motorways. We were getting consumer society, television and the like, and we were turning into a kind of . . . media landscape, and I thought, 'this is interesting, because we're all going to be Americanised, sooner or later, whether we like it or not'. And science fiction was, above all, American – it described an Americanised future.

NAUGHTIE: By the time you came to write *Kingdom Come*, many years later, you came to see this consumerism as, really, a dark force – something that was all-pervasive, and almost had evil intent, or worked in evil ways.

BALLARD: Yes. I've always been drawn to consumerism and Americanisation of daily life but I've always been aware that there's a sort of dark side to the sun. In the case of *Kingdom Come* – which describes, really, a high point reached by consumerism in this country a year or two ago – I suggest that consumerism could evolve into something very close to fascism. When you go into these vast shopping malls, you're being seduced into a semi-ritualised, mass affirmation.

NAUGHTIE: This kind of dissection of consumerism, or of the way people behave, I suppose was the same process that was going on in *Crash*, which became a cult book in many ways. It was filmed, and was still being read many years later when similar books had maybe passed away quite quickly, and it involved a narrator who became extraordinarily involved – erotically, emotionally, in violent ways, sometimes with corpses [sic], or with people being cut up on motorways. It's a terribly dark story, but it does seem to be quite close to the centre of your life as a writer.

BALLARD: That's probably true, and in some ways I regret it. I mean, now and again I open *Crash* and I think, 'My God, this is horrific. This man is clearly mad.' And then it takes me a while to realise there's a J.G. Ballard who brought up three very happy children . . . I find it a shocking book to read. I literally have to put it down and take a few breaths. In a way it's a sort of psychopathic hymn – there's almost a religious dimension to it, in a peculiar way.

NAUGHTIE: In some ways *Crash* is about your life as a writer, because it's about a narrator who is involved and who's also exposed. In the course of the book, his feelings are laid bare, which of course is what writing's all about.

BALLARD: Yes. I think it's a cry of anguish, in a way – a cry of outrage. It took me a long while to get over my wife's death and it's something I was reminded of every day: I was making sausage and mash for her three children. I think it was another attempt to make, you know, 'two and two equal five'. Once you've cracked that particular nut, if it's possible to do so, you know everything seems to be a bit easier, but I'm not sure it is.

NAUGHTIE: Many people who didn't follow you into science fiction, and don't know that book, came to know you through *Empire of the Sun*, which, of course, became an extraordinary success, and although it described horror it also celebrated human dignity.

BALLARD: In a way, it shows the lengths that human beings will go to survive. The instinct for survival is intensely strong, no doubt about that. People will give up everything: every shred of dignity, every dream, every illusion – their most cherished fantasies – just to live for another half-hour. It's a terrible thing to have to face but it's true – war is a corrupting experience, it's corrupting in the sense that violence is quite seductive. It has an appeal in that you can understand a world entirely given over to brutality and violence, whereas peace – civilised life in the everyday sense of the term – is much more ambiguous. In fact, we keep discovering there are things about ourselves that don't quite accord with this notion that we are civilised inheritors of the whole Enlightenment tradition, and that we live in welfare societies and, you know, care for each other. Something happens that reminds us that maybe it's not quite that straightforward – war is very corrupting because it is so clear cut – and people have a ruthlessness about the need to survive that is unmistakable.

NAUGHTIE: What are the important things that survive war?

BALLARD: I think memories of companionship, and comradeship of soldiers and servicemen and women who've been through combat together. I think that draws on very deep feelings of companionship.

NAUGHTIE: It's obvious that you value these feelings, and you know they're there because – despite your pessimism about the consumer society, about the capacity for violence that lurks in people – you're a jovial man. Despite all that, you appear in many ways to be an optimistic man. How do those two things sit together?

BALLARD: I am optimistic on the whole, but I'm rather suspicious of human beings, and I think this goes back to the war, when I'd visit a friend's apartment and there were empty suitcases lying across beds, and they'd just vanished . . . wind blowing through the curtains . . . 'What happened?' 'Oh, they've gone to some camp . . .'

NAUGHTIE: You tell the story of your father saying: 'the Japanese are coming, we're off, no more school, no more exams, it's over'.

BALLARD: Yes, absolutely – the sense that reality is a stage set that can be cleared at any moment. That came over very strongly, because children are very reliant on stability and convention. They take for granted that their parents are maintaining this friendly place called Home. I think the experience of war undermines all that. I've always been a little sceptical about what I'm told – there's nothing new about that nowadays – nobody trusts a politician, and I think I'm sceptical about consumerism because it's really all we've got left. The main pillars of British society have always been the monarchy, the Church of England, the class system, respect for the armed forces, and so on. And all these pillars have been knocked down. Politicians are distrusted, and we think of them, really, as – many of them, anyway – a collection of rogues. The Church of England has lost a lot of its authority, so has the monarchy. So what we have is consumerism. I'm not suspicious of consumerism, but the problem arises when it's all there is left. I mean, if you go out in the London suburbs, away from our great museums and Houses of Parliament and art galleries, theatres and the like, into a world where all you have are retail outlets, you suddenly think, 'my God, how can you live here?' In fact, I do live there. It's that sense that there's nothing other than a new range of digital cameras, or what have you, to sustain one's dreams . . .

NAUGHTIE: In the memoir, you use Shanghai as the endpapers of the book. It's quite a long way into the book before you leave, after the years in the camp, but then you go back, and it's striking to look at your reflections, having known it as a boy. In a strange way, it had changed utterly but not at all.

BALLARD: I think that's true. When I went back in 1991, I spent a week there with the BBC team. At first sight the city was totally transformed. There were hundreds of high-rise buildings, TV towers, vast new road complexes, and the former city had spread outwards for miles. Across what had once been the countryside was a vast urbanised area. But then, down at street level, I saw the old Shanghai, all the art deco mansions of the French concession built in the 1930s, the Provençal villas, those white Bauhaus boxes that the Germans built in the 1930s, all those half-timbered Tudor mansions, one of which we lived in, which was British. Any nationality sort of built a replica of its most cherished architectural myths, and a lot of this was still there – amazingly.

NAUGHTIE: You describe Shanghai somewhere in the book as being known – or coming to be known – as the wickedest city in the world. It's a kind of uproarious wickedness, though, isn't it?

BALLARD: I think if you weren't starving on the pavements in the 1930s and 1940s, Shanghai was a lot of fun, because everything was so cheap. If you weren't doing well, it was a different story altogether – but that's not a story we often hear.

NAUGHTIE: When you came to write the memoir, which is not hugely long, you were trying to distil ideas and experiences, and describe them as beautifully and simply as you could, despite all those years as a writer which involved a great deal of 'display' and a great deal of self-examination. Did you learn anything more about yourself, looking back, that had eluded you before?

BALLARD: Yes I did, I learned a lot about myself. I don't want to spell out my strengths and weaknesses – I'm not sure what my strengths are, although I've got a pretty shrewd idea what my weaknesses might be – because I don't think we should sit in too many moral judgements on ourselves. Life can be difficult, there's no doubt about it – even at the best of times – and we don't have, as human beings, enormous resources of kindness, goodwill and the like – what we think of as positive virtues. You know, we're a rather confused collection of highly intelligent mammals, but we're quite capable of stabbing each other in the back if no one's looking. I think I learned, writing the book, that in many ways I've been as much a victim of certain dreams and delusions as the English living in Britain were during the war.

NAUGHTIE: But the writer's life isn't a delusion – you've lived it.

BALLARD: Absolutely, that's what we're trying to do, we're trying to tell stories that make sense, and I hope the stories I've told, and this one – which I suppose is my last story – I hope that makes sense too.

Afterword:
Script-writing the Future

Dan O'Hara

There is a sweetly pathetic moment in a 2003 interview J.G. Ballard gave to the musician Graeme Revell. Revell tells Ballard of a chance social encounter with an acquaintance's girlfriend, who mentions casually and in passing that she has to wake up early the following morning, as she must have enemas for her work. Both Ballard and Revell realise that the girl must work in the porn industry, yet what is so characteristic about Ballard's reaction is his immediate assumption that the enemas are the true star of the films, and not merely the porn actors' necessary preparation before filming. 'Asian babe enema films?' he asks.

One could easily mistake Ballard's own misunderstanding for the naivety of an older generation, less well versed than our own in the sordid variety of recondite recreations the internet has made commonly available. Yet it's a typically Ballardian imaginative prolepsis, in which he invents a perverse conjunction of man and technology five minutes before it comes into being. If, over the last fifty years of his writing career, it has often seemed that Ballard was living five minutes into everyone else's future, it's also often seemed that his unconscious was somehow script-writing that same future. It is this strangely prophetic quality of Ballard's thought that has most frequently attracted new admirers; it is a degree of unsentimental cultural insight that seems at once mundane and uncanny.

This same prophetic quality has also alienated readers, especially those who would avoid any literature tainted with an association with science fiction. Many readers, sad to say, are as uninterested in real

485

futures as they are in imaginary ones. Ballard has on occasion suffered the traditional fate of the satirist, ostentatiously ignored by the targets of his satire; yet Ballard is not a satirist. Rather, in tandem with his prophetic gifts, it seems that Ballard has invented new ways of offending his potential readers. Partly this is to do with the solidly middle-class British characters who populate his novels. Ballard violates a new standard of decorum when he takes dramatic staples such as violence, murder and sexual idiosyncrasy, but then normalises them, placing their psychopathology within the middle classes, rather than depicting such perversions as the sole province of mad princes and degenerate aristocrats.

Though I also recognise Ballard's special relationship with the future, it is more often not the content but the shape and style of his thought, and especially his prose, that continues to compel my own admiration. I can still remember my first readings of Ballard's fictions, and the cold shock of sensationlessness created by his clinically precise prose. He seemed to me to wield words as though they were advanced surgical technologies, alluringly bright yet fatally dangerous, and the poetic cadences of his sentences had a kind of machine-like, metronomic authority. They still do, of course, and if I describe my initial reactions to Ballard's books as memories, it is not because the books have changed. Rather, the books have changed this reader.

In his introduction to this volume, Simon Sellars speaks of his own admiration for the force of Ballard's futurism, a logic which Ballard repeatedly exercises in each of these interviews. Yet it may seem perverse to edit a collection of interviews when one's own preference is founded on a deep respect for the writer as a stylist, as mine is. My view is that, just as writing is for the writer a form of thought, speech also presupposes writing, and Ballard's characteristic written cadences are in evidence even in these interviews. There is always a certain latent violence discernible in Ballard's use of language, whether it be written or spoken, which seems only appropriate to his ambiguous hymns to violent psychopathology.

Nietzsche, in his *Genealogy of Morals*, proposed that violence lay at the pre-origins of language. According to Nietzsche, cruelty is the mechanism with which man creates for himself the capacity to remember *words*, abstract symbols of meaning. The violent marking of the body, whether it be tattooing, scarifying, castrating or burning, is the event that, using pain as its impetus, gives man a sign which has a meaning for him; and so is it, in Nietzsche's view, that such writing on the body becomes the fount of both language and human memory. This lesson is one which Shylock in *The Merchant of Venice*, for example, understands all too well, and his bloody desire for the famous 'pound of flesh' exemplifies the point. Ballard too recognises this primordial appeal of language as a violent tool of division and signification, and while he most often posed as a cautionary novelist, warning his readers against reading his metaphors too literally, his use of language burns with the species' corporate memory of the illicit thrill of its originary violence. To read Ballard is, sensually, to undergo a kind of psychic autopsy under the gentle administration of the author's general anaesthetic – a discomfiting yet strangely compelling experience, with all the allure of the slow-motion car crashes on our TV screens from which we so often recoil, yet away from which we also cannot bear to tear our eyes.

What I find evidence of in these interviews and conversations is a quintessentially Ballardian habit of thought which inherits both its linguistic precision and its poetry from Ballard's previous lives as a teenage addict to *Popular Mechanics* magazine, as a student of anatomy at Cambridge, as an editor for the journal *Chemistry and Industry*. The traces of these various apprenticeships are still discernible in the way Ballard shapes his sentences and selects his vocabulary with a careful sense of the exact word at the right time. That these interviews are themselves so replete with quotable phrases and off-the-cuff epithets merely reinforces the impression that Ballard's speech originated in the same patterns of thought as did his writing, and indeed, Ballard is often so fluent in his expression that one wonders if there were really any difference between the two, in his own experience of his own thought. Yet these traces of his previous careers, while they betray his training in a scientific use of language, cannot explain the poetic menace and aura of inevitability that the least of his pronouncements carries.

I've observed elsewhere that Ballard's fictions can claim to be universal because his characteristic landscapes and motifs speak directly to an atavistic, Jungian collective unconscious. As Martin Amis put it, Ballard 'seems to address a different – a disused – part of the reader's brain'. It seems to me now that it is also Ballard's language, whether in speech or written prose, that addresses an older part of our brains; and, curiously, it is this more ancient component of linguistic imagination that we have to come to terms with if we wish, like Ballard, to recall the future.

Dan O'Hara, Rio de Janeiro, Brazil, March 2012

Index

Index

Index

Index

Index

Index

Index

disaster stories 50–1, 88–90, 202–4

female characters 203–5, 305–6, 312

fragmented/non-linear xii, 2–3, 7, 8, 52, 73–4, 74–5, 91, 92–3

horror imagery 158–60

isolation 69–71, 80, 89

landscape 5, 6, 16, 19, 20, 31, 51, 76–7, 79–80, 82

layers 4–5

linked 8

looking at a lake with bright metallic scum 56, 64

metaphors including diamond, sand, water 11–12, 39

personal and autobiographical material 27

real people and real names 372–3, 396–7

reality 12, 27, 37, 38, 45–6, 52, 62–3, 75–6, 94–5

repetition and recurring characters 3–5, 52–3, 69–70, 304–5, 369–70, 398, 459

retrospective 2–3

scientific language 104, 237–8

spinal column as memory of the past 11–12

time 6, 7–8, 11–12

violence-as-leisure 132

working forensically 315–17, 354–5

see also doomsday scenario; narrative techniques

Natali, Vincenzo 402, 439

National Gallery, London 393

National Physical Laboratory (Teddington) 47, 121, 196–7

Nature 17

Naughtie, James 473–83

neurology and psychology 244–5, 271

the new 43

New Arts Lab 22, 31, 40, 387

New Directions (publishers) 294

new European sensibility 192–3

The New S.F. 1

New Society 90

New Statesman 420

New Wave xi, 14, 17, 22, 53, 125, 126, 134, 136–9, 141, 366

New Worlds xii, 3, 14, 17, 18, 22, 36, 48, 136, 139, 217–18, 366, 370, 386

New York Review of Books 95, 342

Newman, Barnett 387

'News from the Sun' (1982) 207

Newsweek 194

Newton, Helmut 160, 161

Nicholls, Peter 72

Nicholson, Jack 150

Nietzsche, Friedrich, *Genealogy of Morals* 486–7

Niven, Larry 208

Nixon, Richard 269

Nordlund, Solveig 224–30

Norman, Barry 328

'Notes from Nowhere' (1966) 10

nuclear war and armament xv, 56, 57–8, 64, 135, 221–2, 293, 307

Obrist, Hans Ulrich 383–95

    The Conversation Series 383

Observer 209

obsession xix, 182, 183, 212–13, 215, 228, 235–6, 238, 250, 268, 270, 305, 370, 457–8

Oi! music 147

Oldenburg, Claes 318

Olympia 294

Olympia cat show 397

Olympia Press (publishers) 217, 350

Omni 136

Ono, Yoko 25

optimism 8, 15, 73, 123, 218, 298, 371, 410, 473, 480–1

Orphée (film, 1950) 157

Orr, Carol xv, 56–71

Orwell, George 209, 295, 349, 408

    Animal Farm 437

    Nineteen Eighty-Four 88, 103, 210, 233, 358, 437, 443

Oswald, Lee Harvey 149, 151

Out of the Past (film, 1947) 163

Index

Index

Index